# The Sony Alpha NEX-7

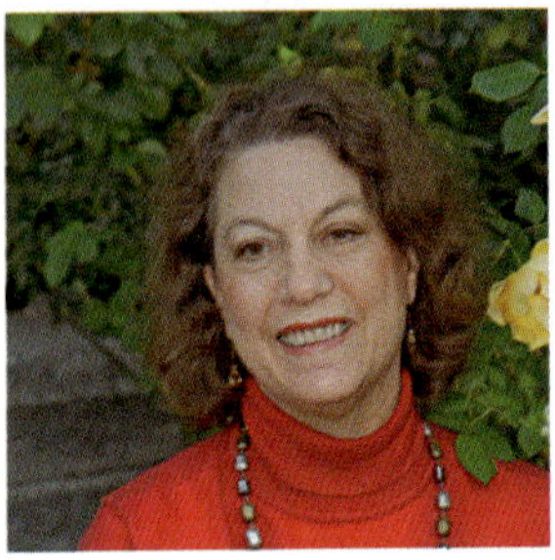

**Carol F. Roullard** has been an avid photographer since her high school years, where she first experimented with black-and-white artistic composition. Since then, she has continued photographing, mainly nature and architecture. Carol has used a variety of cameras covering a wide range of makes and models, from simple point-and-shoot cameras to complex professional-level cameras. Carol produces fine art photography and is utilizing her previous art business experience for her new online gallery.

As a former Project Management Quality and Compliance Engineer, Carol spent a number of years developing procedural and quality control methodology for IT projects. In addition, she has developed and conducted training sessions covering best practices for procedural and quality control, breaking down complex subjects into easy-to-use approaches to learning.

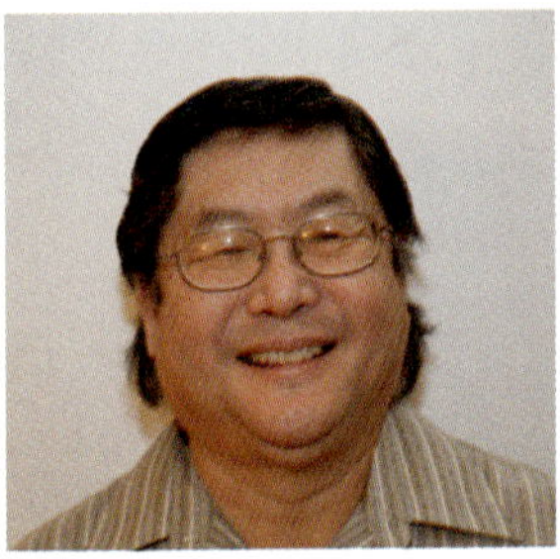

**Dr. Brian Matsumoto** is a retired research scientist who has worked for 30 years recording experiments with a wide range of film and digital cameras. He now spends his time photographing with a variety of cameras and lenses. He enjoys exploring how a camera's potential can be expanded by pairing it with specialized optics such as microscopes and telescopes. He carries a camera on all his hikes and enjoys photographing nature. In addition to the four books he has written for Rocky Nook, Dr. Matsumoto has published several articles and has had his photographs published in a number of periodicals. He is experienced in the technical aspects of photography and has taught courses on recording scientific experiments with digital cameras.

# The Sony Alpha NEX-7

## The Unofficial Quintessential Guide

Carol F. Roullard
Brian Matsumoto

rockynook

Carol F. Roullard
Brian Matsumoto

Publisher: Gerhard Rossbach
Editor: Joan Dixon
Copyeditor: Jeanne Hansen
Layout and type: Jan Martí, Command Z
Cover design: Helmut Kraus, www.exclam.de
Printer: Friesens Corporation
Printed in Canada

ISBN 978-1-937538-11-8

1st Edition 2012


Rocky Nook, Inc.
802 East Cota Street., 3rd Floor
Santa Barbara, CA 93103

www.rockynook.com

Distributed by O'Reilly Media
1005 Gravenstein Highway North
Sebastopol, CA 95472

Library of Congress Cataloging-in-Publication Data

Roullard, Carol F.
The Sony Alpha NEX-7 : the unofficial quintessential guide / by Carol F. Roullard and Brian Matsumoto. -- 1st edition.
pages cm
ISBN 978-1-937538-11-8 (pbk.)
1. Sony digital cameras--Handbooks, manuals, etc. 2. Photography--Digital techniques--Handbooks, manuals, etc. I. Matsumoto, Brian. II. Title.
TR263.S66R66 2012
771.3'1--dc23
2012027244

*To all our family and friends.*
*Without them, life would have little meaning.*

# Acknowledgements

Every camera book starts with a concept and a blank piece of paper. Writing it becomes a labor of love. One spends months of research, testing, discussing, writing, and rewriting. Nothing in this book was written without being tested, many times more than once.

As with our previous books, we relied on several friends and business associates to supply feedback, inspiration, and additional accessories. We would like to extend special thanks to Stuart Warter for his encouragement and lending us equipment to expand our testing of the Sony NEX-7. In addition, Matt Parnell of Sony Electronics Inc. and Scott Dordick of Acratech Inc. were very gracious in supplying product photos. A special thanks goes to Jim Solliday, president of the Microscopical Society of Southern California, for his continued support and evaluation of digital SLRs in microscope applications.

Last but not least, one of the benefits of publishing through Rocky Nook is being able to work with their team of experts. Not only do we appreciate our publisher for their help, kindness, and professionalism in support of our goal, but we have been fortunate to also build a strong friendship. As with our previous books, the Rocky Nook team has been invaluable in helping us complete this book. We have appreciated input and support from Gerhard Rossbach (Publisher, CEO), Joan Dixon (Managing Editor), and Matthias Rossmanith (Project Manager). A special thanks goes to Jeanne Hansen (Copyeditor) and Jan Marti (Layout). Everyone has been wonderful at fielding our questions and working diligently toward completing the project.

As with our other books, a special thanks goes out to our families and friends for being patient and understanding when our time with them was limited and our conversations were often single-minded about the Sony NEX-7.

Carol Roullard
Brian Matsumoto

www.VistaFocus.net

# Preface

At the time of writing this book, the Sony NEX-7 was still using firmware version 1.00. Although the camera was initially released near the end of 2011, the torrential rains and floods in Thailand interrupted its distribution, and shipment resumed in early 2012. This book went to print in October 2012, and it is testament to the quality of the NEX-7's firmware that there have been no new releases.

But life and camera development do go on. One day there will be a new firmware release, and it will not be represented in this book. The best way to handle this is to review the Sony firmware addendums when you download a new firmware version. If Sony releases a major firmware change, we will determine the feasibility of an updated book edition.

As you get to know the Sony NEX-7, you will develop uniquely personal methods of using the camera. We have included many of our own experiences and recommendations throughout the book. They work for us, but depending on the type of shots you want to take and your own personal needs, you will most likely develop some variations.

Hopefully, our experiences and recommendations will save you time and angst as you learn to use this complex camera. The NEX-7 is truly a remarkable and complicated camera packed into a compact size. It does so much, and does it well.

At first glance, the Sony NEX-7's menu can be intimidating. Many of the buttons and dials have dual purposes. The addition of many customization opportunities makes it a complex machine. But as you use the camera and become familiar with it, you will pare down what you use and how you use it. Your use of the camera functions will take on a rhythm and will become something you know by heart—enabling you to consistently obtain high-quality still pictures and movies. We have experimented with all of the shortcuts, such as Auto HDR, DRO, and Handheld Twilight. We encourage you to experiment with the creative aspects of this camera, such as the many Creative Style and Picture Effect options.

As we wrote this book, we continued to be thrilled with the camera's capabilities, sharpness, and ease of operation. We had seen this with the Sony A77 model and were very impressed that so much of what worked well in that camera was transferred to the NEX-7 model. This camera's size and operation has continued to transform some of our photography practices. As much as we love the Sony A77, it is very nice to carry around this much smaller, yet capable, camera that gives us high-quality results. We are sure you will feel the same way.

Enjoy your Sony NEX-7 camera.

# Table of Contents

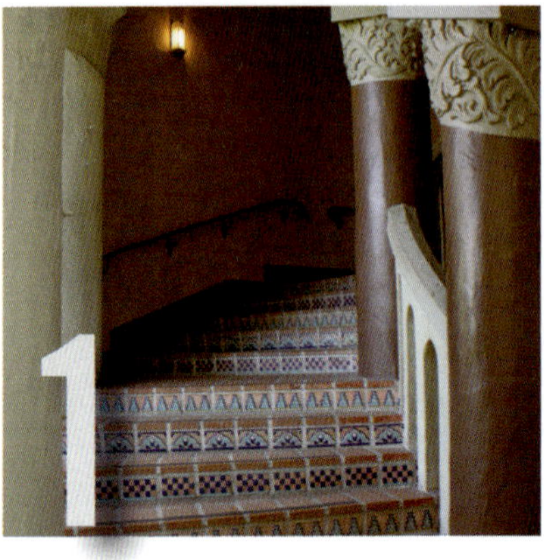


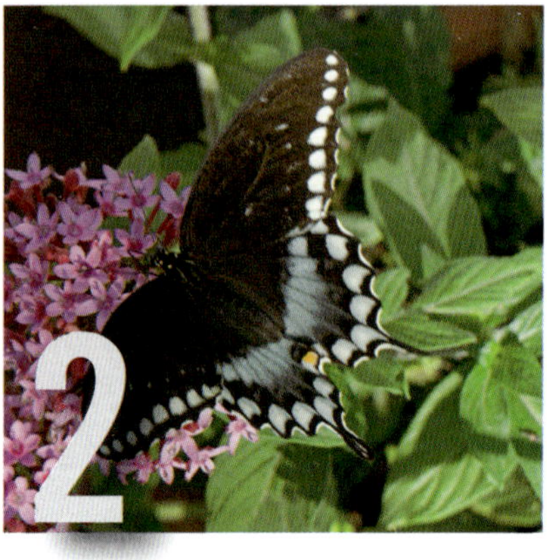

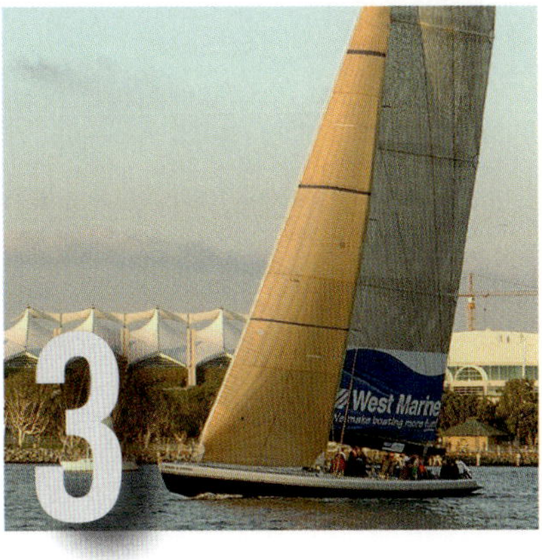

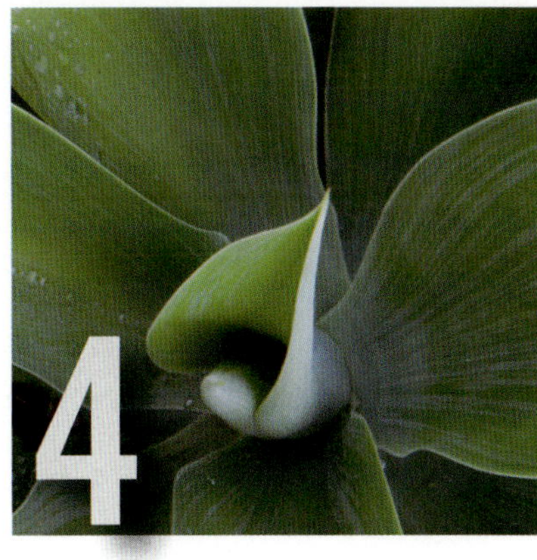

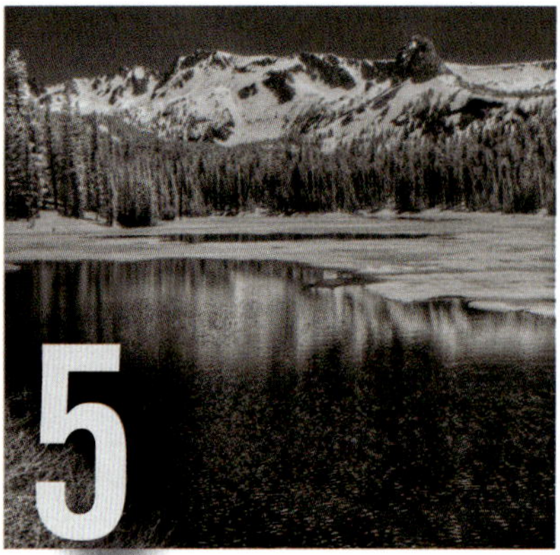

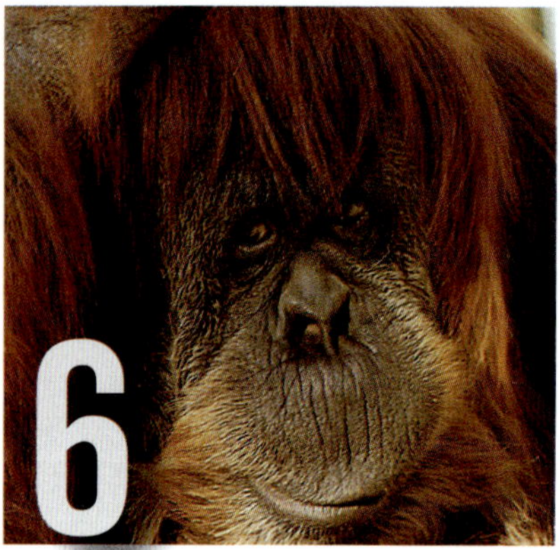

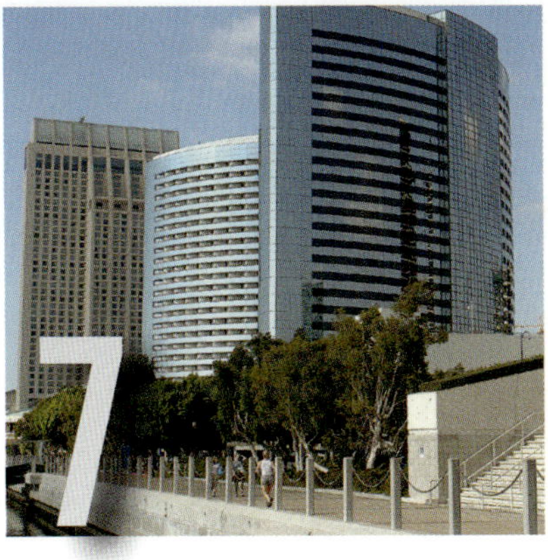
7



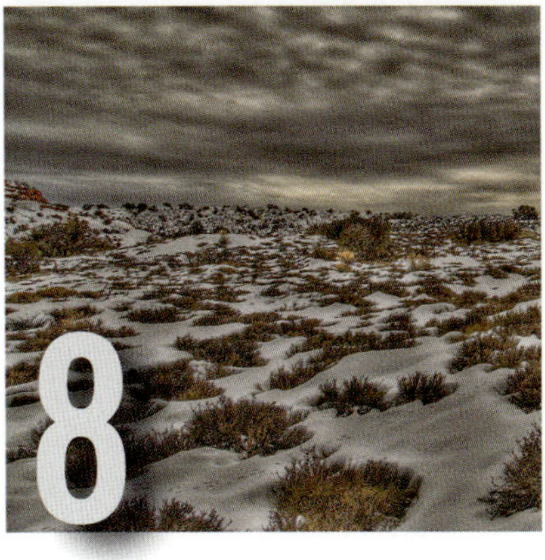
8

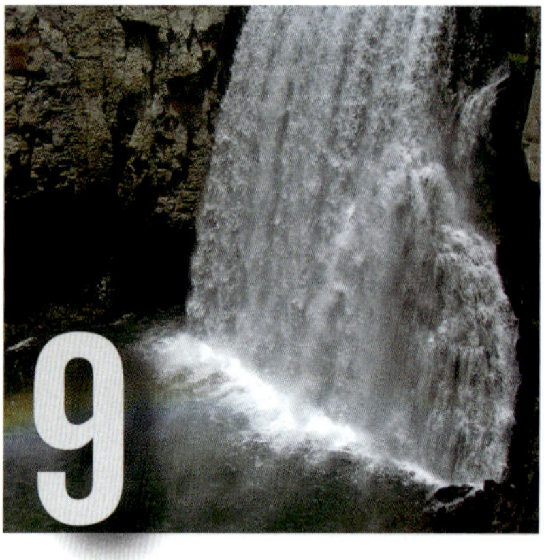
9



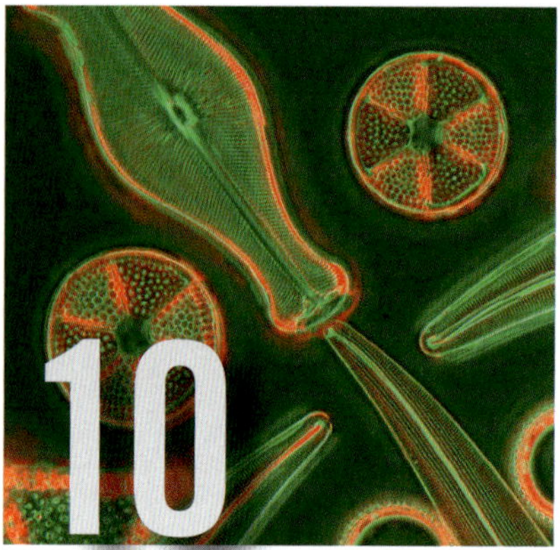
10

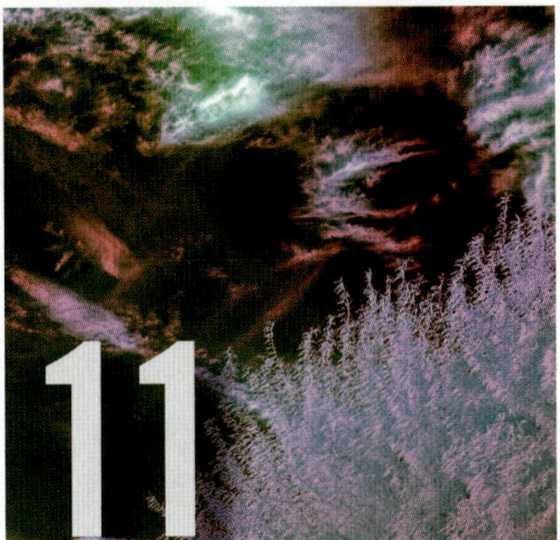
11



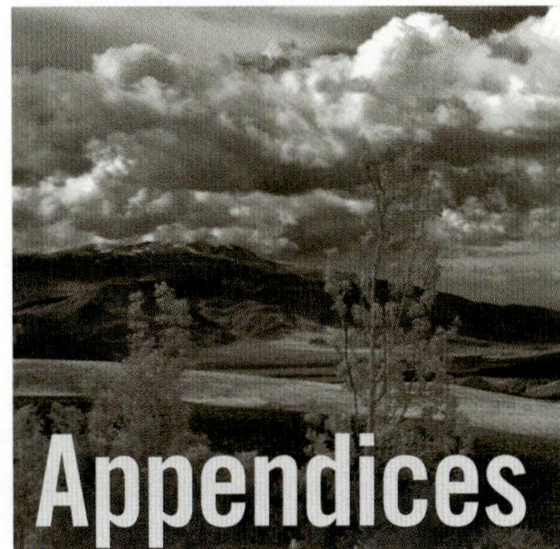
Appendices

# Camera Body Reference

(Product photos throughout the book courtesy of Sony)

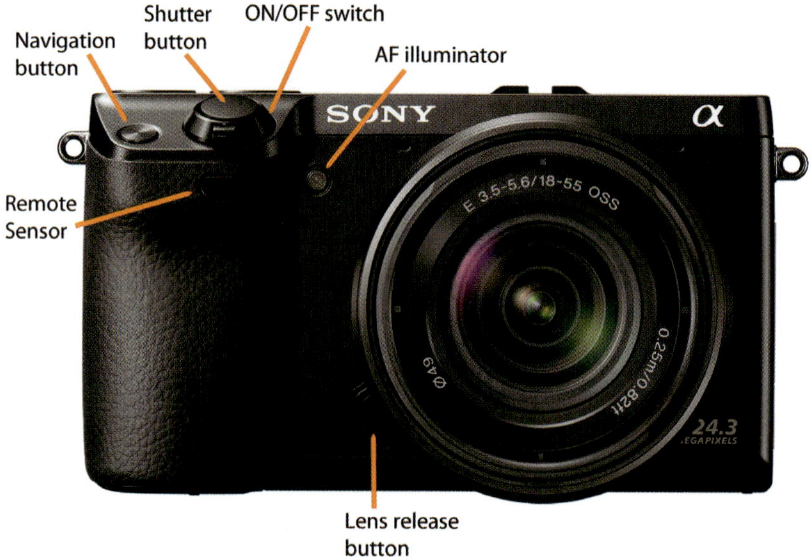


**Figure A**: Sony NEX-7 camera front

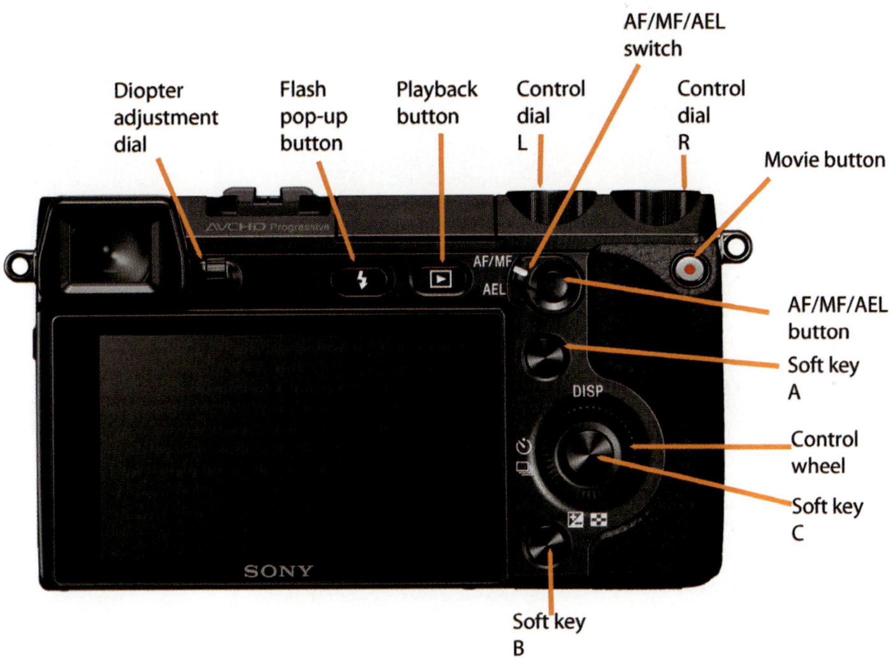


**Figure B**: Sony NEX-7 camera back

1

# Chapter 1: Getting Started

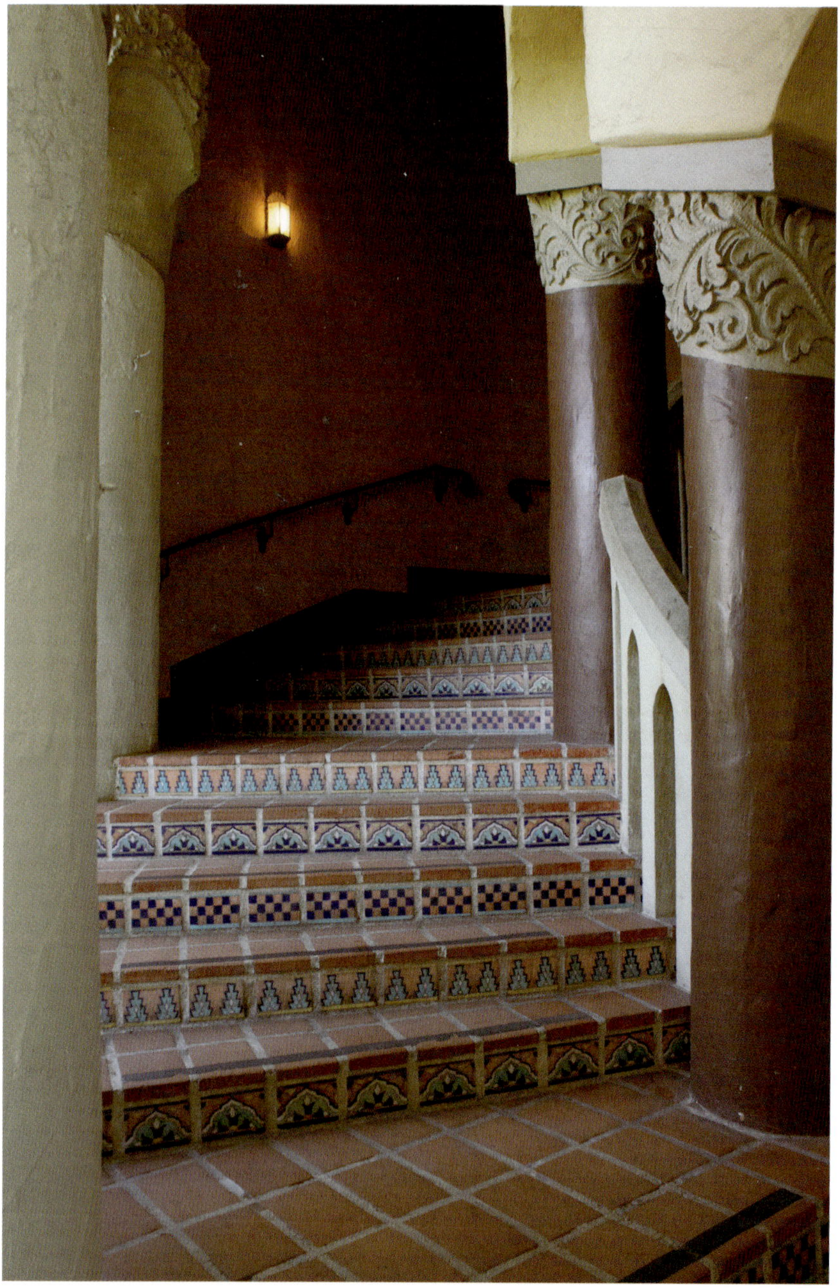

## Introduction

At the time of this writing, the Sony NEX-7 is the most advanced mirrorless camera in the Sony lineup. The camera uses the 24-megapixel sensor of the Sony A77 and A65, which makes it one of highest-resolution cameras in its class. In spite of this, the camera is remarkably small, weighing in at half the weight of the A77. Although the NEX-7 cannot be described as a pocket camera, its size and shape allows it to be easily carried everywhere. Plus, the camera's compact size and sleek lines make it look less intimidating to a camera-shy subject (figure 1-1).

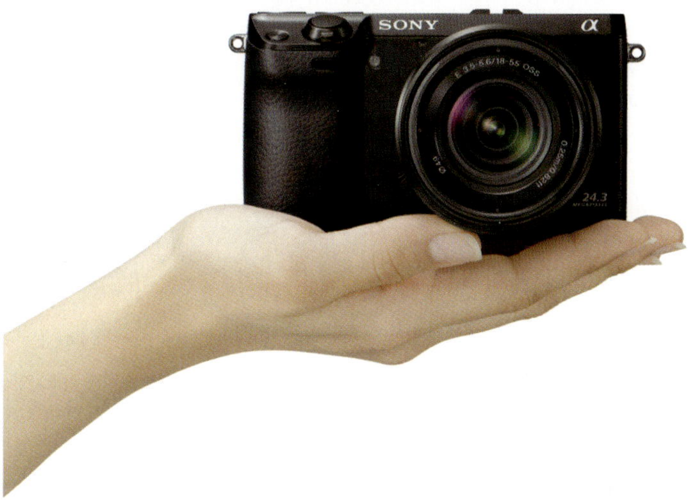


**Figure 1-1**: The Sony NEX-7 is a compact interchangeable lens camera

Unlike a digital single-lens reflex (DSLR) camera, which requires a mirror to direct light to an optical viewfinder, the Sony NEX-7 is mirrorless. Light goes directly to the sensor, which drives either an electronic viewfinder (EVF) or a rear LCD screen (figure 1-2). Both display the image and the effects of the camera settings before the photographer takes the picture, thereby ensuring that errors in white balance or exposure can be corrected before the shot is taken. In addition, the absence of a mirror makes the camera virtually vibration free when a picture is taken. In contrast, a DSLR with an optical viewfinder is prone to vibration when it rapidly lifts the mirror and slams it to a stop at the top of the mirror chamber so light can reach the sensor for exposure. The sudden impact of the mirror and the rapid movement of the mechanical shutter's first curtain vibrate the camera body during exposure. For high-magnification work, this movement blurs the recorded image.

On some Internet forums, a few people have complained about the inferior view through an EVF compared to that of an optical viewfinder. To some extent this is true. For example, the optical finder image has a greater dynamic range, so the photographer can study details in areas of bright highlights and dark shadows. In contrast, a photographer who views through an EVF can see the highlights, but the shadowy areas may appear as impenetrable masses of black. This disadvantage is counter balanced by the view through the Sony NEX-7's viewfinder being larger and brighter than most optical viewfinders. This is especially evident in cameras that use an APS-C sensor, which includes virtually all interchangeable lens cameras in the NEX-7 price bracket. Optical viewfinders whose apparent size matches that of the NEX-7 are found only in full-frame cameras, such as the Nikon D800 or Canon EOS 5D Mark III. Such cameras are significantly bulkier, heavier, and are more expensive than the NEX-7. An additional advantage of the EVF is evident in dim lighting where optical viewfinders become progressively dimmer as light levels drop. In contrast, an electronic viewfinder maintains its brightness, regardless of the light level. As compared to an optical viewfinder, the large, bright electronic viewfinder makes it easier to frame and compose the scene even in a dim setting.

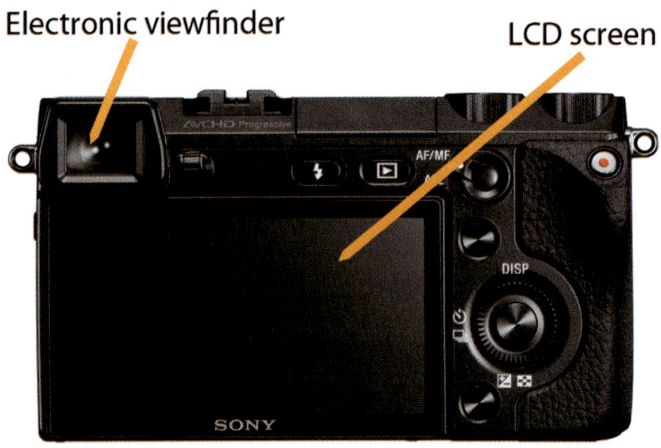


**Figure 1-2**: Back of Sony NEX-7 camera showing the two viewfinders

For us, the advantage of using an electronic display for composing our image (on both the EVF and LCD monitor) is that it increases our success rate in obtaining technically good photographs. Errors in white balance are immediately evident, and steps can be taken to correct this before the picture is recorded. The same applies to exposure. With a real-time histogram display and a view of how a given exposure records the subject, it is a simple matter to finely adjust the aperture or shutter speed for the best exposure. Finally, the electronic displays can provide a more precise metric for focusing. Because you can selectively enlarge portions of the image on both the EVF and LCD screens, the increased magnification ensures that you are precisely focused on your subject. This is especially critical for long telephoto work where there is little depth of field. Finally, the NEX-7 always provides an indication of depth of field. The camera displays the image at the working aperture of the lens, so you can estimate whether the background or foreground surrounding the subject is rendered sharply or blurred.

In spite of its small size, the Sony NEX-7 is one of the most capable cameras in its class and can generate professional results. For example, it has one of the highest pixel counts in a compact camera, 24.3 megapixels. This means the sensor can bring in enough data so you can enlarge your pictures and still have the detail hold up. We have printed sharp 20 x 30 inch prints without any detail degradation.

**Movies vs. Videos**

What is the difference? According to dictionary definitions, a movie is a captured series of pictures in the motion picture industry, and a video is recorded onto videotape or some other recording device for the television industry.

Both of these definitions ignore the camera's role in capturing the picture. Although we would rather call moving pictures recorded on a camera a "video," Sony has chosen to use the term "movie." To be consistent with their terminology, we will use "movie" in reference to the recording of moving pictures with the camera. There may be some cases where industry terminology is so predominate that we will use "video," but those will be the exceptions rather than the rule.

The absence of a hinged mirror provides several advantages. Perhaps the most obvious is automatic focusing when recording movies. Although DSLRs can record movies, you have to manually lock the mirror up and use the camera's sensor for focusing. Being mirrorless, Sony's automatic focus system does not have this requirement. Instead, the camera is always available for taking a movie, and all that is required is pressing the movie button.

Finally, an underappreciated aspect of this technology is the inclusion of an electronic first curtain shutter. When the sensor is exposed to light, the NEX-7 is virtually vibration free. Remember, the raising of its mirror and the movement of its mechanical shutter jars a DSLR. The absence of these two mechanisms ensures that the NEX-7 can remain stationary during use—an advantage for discriminating photographers who do not want to sacrifice sharpness because of camera movement.

## Dual Viewing System

The Sony NEX-7 has two electronic displays: an EVF with an eyepiece and the movable LCD screen on the back of the camera. Most digital camera users are familiar with the latter. Unlike some early EVFs, the viewfinder of the NEX-7 is extremely sharp with a good refresh rate. It replaces the optical viewfinder on DSLRs. There are tremendous advantages of having two electronic displays, which give the photographer lots of flexibility for framing and composing a photograph.

The rear LCD screen can be held at arm's distance and is convenient to use when the camera is mounted on a tripod. If you have to raise the camera above your head, you can tilt the LCD downward so you can aim and photograph over the heads of an intervening crowd of people. Or you can rest the camera on the ground and tilt the LCD screen upward to view and photograph a low-lying flower without having to lie down behind the camera.

The EVF, which has an eyepiece, is valuable for working in ambient sunlight when the intensity overwhelms the view on the rear LCD. It is also convenient when you can't disturb your surroundings with the light of the LCD screen, such as at a school play in a darkened auditorium. In addition, having the camera pressed up against your face helps steady the camera.

To conserve battery life, the EVF and the LCD screen are designed to work sequentially. When one is on, the other is off. The viewfinder is enabled when the camera senses that something, assuming your eye, is close to the eyepiece. When you move your eye away, the viewfinder turns off and the LCD screen turns on. You have a choice of how the switch occurs; it can be done either automatically (default) or you can set the camera so that just one of the display modes is in operation.

There are both advantages and drawbacks to each of the viewing displays. The Sony NEX-7 has a few differences in how the camera settings are displayed versus what you see in the viewfinder or on the LCD screen. As you use the camera and become familiar with its settings and buttons, you will develop personal choices as to which viewing system works best for you. In chapter 3 we will cover details about the LCD screen and the viewfinder and discuss how to display information on each of them.

## Diopter Adjustment Dial

There is one more thing you need to know about the viewfinder. It has a magnifier that needs to be focused on the screen. To the right of the eyepiece is a small wheel called the diopter adjustment dial (figure 1-3). Rotate the dial up or down until the objects in the viewfinder appear maximally sharp.

If you share your camera with others, they must make sure that the viewfinder is in focus for their eyes. If you are nearsighted (myopic) and your photographer partner is farsighted (hyperopic), you will have to adjust this dial whenever the two of you use the camera. This dial ensures that the photographer, whether nearsighted or farsighted, will have a tack-sharp image in the viewfinder.

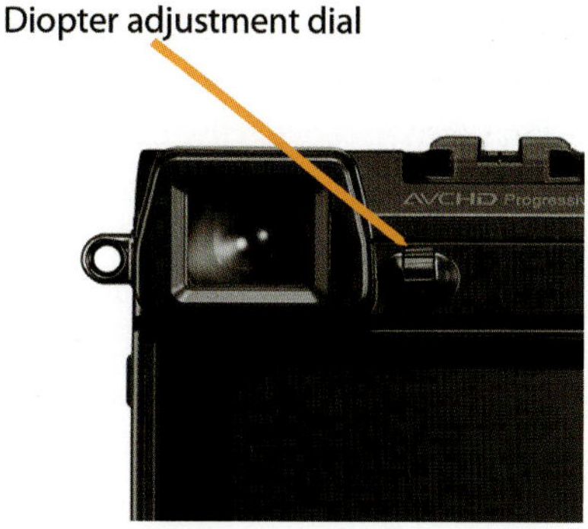


**Figure 1-3**: The diopter adjustment dial to the right of the viewfinder

## Setting Up Your New Sony NEX-7

When you take your camera out of the box, you will have the following components:

- Camera body: 24.3 effective megapixel Sony NEX-7
- E-mount 18–55mm zoom lens
- Front and rear lens caps
- Lens hood
- Rechargeable InfoLithium (NP-FW50) battery
- Battery charger (BC-VW1)
- Shoulder/neck strap
- USB cable
- Body cap
- Accessory shoe cap
- CD-ROM with Sony software
- Camera manual

Make sure you have everything before you assemble your new camera. First, fully charge your battery, attach the lens, and insert a memory card on which to store your pictures and movies. When you are done, you're ready to start.

## Battery

The supplied InfoLithium (NP-FW50) Lithium-ion battery should be fully charged before use. Insert the battery into the charger and plug the charger into an outlet. An LED light should begin to glow. This light provides several signals:

- Steady glow: The battery is charging.
- Rapid flashing (0.15 second intervals): The charging failed, and the battery may be defective. Remove the battery from the charger and reinsert it. If rapid flashing persists, replace the battery.
- Slow flashing of the amber light (1.5 second intervals): Charging is not occurring, probably because of too low or too high ambient temperatures (50°F to 86°F).
- Light turns off: The battery is fully charged.

Completely draining a battery of its charge can damage it. Make sure you fully charge the battery before using it. You will find that the battery may not last for a full day of shooting, and a spare will come in handy. For the active photographer it is not a question of whether you will need to buy a spare battery, but when. A battery does not last forever. As you continue to use the camera, the battery will progressively hold less charge. Most people make it a general practice to purchase a spare battery when they buy a camera. We recommend that you use Sony-certified batteries because noncertified batteries will void your warranty and may ruin your camera.

### Why Use a Certified Battery?

Buying third-party batteries is tempting because they can be less expensive. But using them is a risky proposition because Sony does not guarantee the quality of their construction. If the batteries damage your camera during its warranty period, Sony is not obligated to repair or replace your camera. Under the best conditions you may be happy with these batteries, so no harm is done. But you can also end up with a battery that may not hold as much of a charge or may drain too quickly. Or, in the worst-case scenario, the battery may damage your camera and the money saved by buying the inexpensive battery will be lost by having to repair or replace your camera.

## Memory Card

You need a memory card to use with this camera. Unlike some point-and-shoot consumer cameras, there is no internal memory for storing images, so the camera will not operate without a memory card! You may already have a compatible memory card from a previous camera. You can use another camera's memory card for your new Sony NEX-7 as long as it is an SD, SDHC, or SDXC card. If not, you will have to purchase one. But what should you buy?

The NEX-7 uses a Secure Digital (SD) memory card. These cards, about the size of a postage stamp, come in many varieties with various memory capacities and data transfer speeds. They are designated as SD, SDHC, or SDXC, which refer to the card's maximum memory capacity. Don't be too concerned about these designations because it is more important to know the memory capacity of the card (see the "Memory Cards" box) and its class rating.

You can use any manufacturer's SD, SDHC, or SDXC memory card of Class 10 or faster for both still pictures and movies. Sony currently sells an SDHC Class 10 card that holds 32 gigabytes (GB) of data for about $100. But you can opt for a 16 GB card (about $60) or an 8 GB card (about $40) instead. The SDXC cards are the most expensive and can have the highest memory rating. We find the 32 GB cards to be an economical choice and are perfect for a day of shooting or movie taking. A potential problem with high-capacity memory cards is that a failure in the card can result in a tremendous loss of data. For this reason, many photographers use several smaller-capacity memory cards so that if one goes bad, the loss of pictures is limited to that one card.

Memory cards are categorized into classes (2, 4, 6, 8, and 10); the higher the class, the faster the card can receive and record data. The size and class of the memory card you buy depends on how you will use the camera and how you plan to maintain the stored pictures and movies. If you plan to take a lot of movies, you will need a lot of memory with a fast speed rating. Generally, you should select a Class 10 card if you need to record movies in AVCHD format. We recommend using at least 8 GB to allow for enough storage space. If you are going to take mainly still photos, 4 GB should suffice.

Instead of using an SD card, you may decide to use a Sony memory stick card. They are not as common, and for a given memory capacity they tend to be a bit more expensive. Note that if you want to record both still pictures and movies on a Memory Stick PRO Duo, it must be the Mark 2 version. The Memory Stick PRO-HG Duo records still pictures and movies.

At the end of each shooting day, get in the habit of downloading the images from your camera to your computer. After the files are downloaded, erase the images on the card by using the camera's Format command. This allows you to start fresh the next day, minimizing the risk of running out of memory.

Although you can connect your camera to your computer with a cable and transfer the stored files directly, you can also download the files with a card reader. Remove the memory card from the camera and insert it into a card reader that is connected directly to your computer with a USB cable.

Many people keep several memory cards for those occasions when they will be doing a lot of recording and will not be able to download the contents to a computer. It's important to note that memory cards can fail, and having a backup will ensure that you can resume shooting if your primary card fails. For our own photography, we tend to use 32 GB Class 10 cards because they provide plenty of space and speed to accommodate a day's worth of shooting and movie recording.

### Memory Cards

The Sony NEX-7 user manual tells you approximately how many pictures or movies you can record on a memory card. The space used depends on the detail within the images and the file type.

Memory card criteria:

- SD memory card (8 MB to 2 GB)
- SDHC memory card (4 GB to 32 GB)
- SDXC memory card (32 GB to 2 TB)

Additional information:

- An SDHC memory card can be used with equipment that's compatible with the SDHC or SDXC memory cards.
- An SDXC memory card can be used only with equipment that's compatible with the SDXC memory card.

## Assembling the Camera

The battery and memory card sit next to each other and share a compartment on the base of the camera. When you invert the camera, you will see the cover with a sliding rectangular switch. Slide the switch to open the compartment, and slide the fully charged battery in the direction of the arrow painted on its side. The battery can be fully seated only one way; a set of ridges surrounding the contacts helps you orient the battery properly. You will hear a solid click when it is properly seated. You can now close the battery cover. To remove the battery, open the compartment to expose a small blue lever that blocks the removal of the battery. Push the lever to the side, and the battery will pop out.

The memory card compartment is next to the battery compartment and is revealed when you open the cover. When you insert the memory card, the end with the metallic reading bars goes in first. It will lock into position with a click. To remove it, push the top of the memory card to release the lock, and the card will pop out for easy removal. If the memory card is defective or if its contacts are dirty, a NO CARD message will be displayed in the top left on the LCD screen when you turn on the camera. If this occurs, remove the memory card and reinsert it. The message should go away. If it doesn't, the card may be defective and will have to be replaced.

Next, attach the lens to the camera body. Remove the rear lens and camera body caps. Store both caps in a safe place for future use. Inserting the lens is a two-step process. There is a white bump on the barrel of the lens and a white dot on the rim of the camera body's lens mount. Align these two indicators, insert the lens, and then rotate the lens clockwise until you feel and hear a click. The lens is now locked in position and ready to use (figure 1-4).

Last but not least, attach the camera strap. It should always be secured to the camera and placed either around your neck or over your shoulder when you're carrying or using the camera.

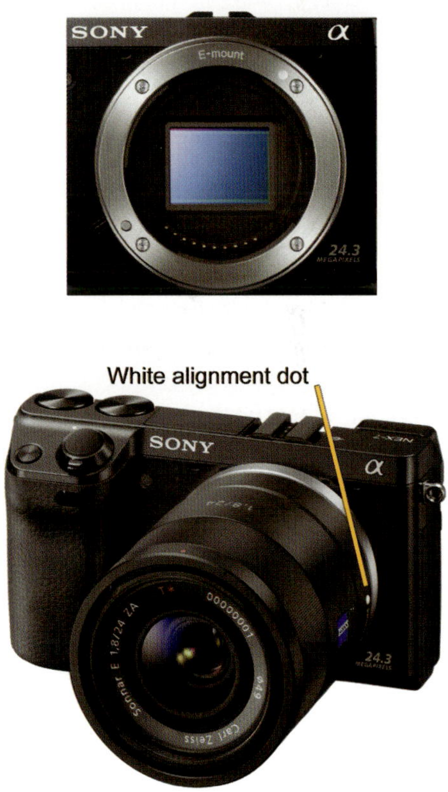


**Figure 1-4**: The camera body without and with the lens, showing the white alignment dots

## Protecting the Lens

There are several ways to protect your camera lens against damage. The first and most obvious is to keep the lens cap on when you are not using your camera.

The second is to use a lens hood when you are shooting to help keep errant objects from hitting the lens. Another benefit is that the hood increases image contrast by blocking light from the side of the lens, keeping it from entering the camera.

The third way to protect your camera lens is to use an ultraviolet (UV) filter. These threaded filters can be screwed onto the lens and serve as a clear optical lens cap. Sony sells these filters, but if you know the thread diameter of your lens, you can buy other brands.

The use of a UV filter is controversial. Some claim it's a good idea, and others claim the protection is minimal and the filter degrades image quality. There is an element of truth in both viewpoints. We find inexpensive, off-brand UV filters to be problematic. Sometimes the optical quality is so bad that it does degrade performance. To avoid this, we buy and use high-quality filters made by reputable manufacturers. Filters made by Tiffen, Hoya, and B+W are good and do not degrade lens performance. You may be surprised at their expense, but considering they are optically ground, polished, coated disks of glass, their prices are reasonable. We routinely mount high-quality UV filters on our lenses. Although there is a theoretical chance of losing some image sharpness, it's so slight that we don't notice it.

## Protecting the LCD Screen

Although the Sony NEX-7 LCD screen is made of a durable material, it can be scratched. This won't affect the camera's ability to take good pictures, but it can affect your ability to know when you have a great picture or when you need to improve the focus. We recommend that you purchase an LCD screen protector. Sony offers them for the NEX-7 at a nominal cost. We purchased their hard plastic model. It is sticky and is applied directly to the LCD. It comes off easily, so if it gets scratched you can replace it.

## Using This Book

The Sony NEX-7 is a perfect camera for photographers at all levels of expertise. If you are a beginner who doesn't know about EV, ISO, or shutter speed, you can just set the camera to Intelligent Auto mode and take pictures by simply pointing and shooting. After you learn some basic photographic concepts, you can improve your images by using the camera's SCN mode. By matching the SCN icon to the shooting situation, you are telling the camera how it should fine-tune the camera settings for shooting that specific type of subject. For instance, when you select the icon for sports action, the camera will use faster shutter speeds to freeze motion. When you select the macro icon, the camera uses slower shutter speeds and smaller apertures to achieve greater depth of field.

Eventually, you may decide to override some of the camera settings to take full advantage of the sensor's capabilities. This will empower you to more fully leverage digital post-processing on a computer. From there, you can take full control by setting the camera manually and using your judgment to set the aperture, ISO, and shutter speed. At this point you may decide that over- or underexposing an image will impart a mood to the scene. At this level an image is created rather than recorded. Further, the controls of the NEX-7 can be fully customized. This will enable you to change the settings without having to go into the camera's menu structure. After the camera is customized to your favorite settings, you will have most of what you need at your fingertips and will need to go into the menu structure only for special situations.

This book follows the natural progression of learning and using the NEX-7 camera, starting with the automatic modes, progressing through semiautomatic modes, and finally taking full control of the camera settings. We have covered additional functions along the way, such as how the camera settings are displayed, customizing the camera to your style, and utilizing additional camera features. Beginners can find helpful information in chapter 4, "Automatic Settings"; intermediate photographers can turn to chapter 5, "Taking Control of the Camera"; and expert photographers can refer to chapter 6, "Manual Operation of the Camera." Regardless of your skill or interest level, this is an exciting camera to use.

Learning how to use the NEX-7 is made difficult by the multitude of commands and features available to you. Rather than try to toss all the information at you at once, we will take a graded approach. First, we will introduce the most important features so you can start operating the camera with a minimum of effort. This will allow you to start taking pictures quickly. In this chapter, we also include a description of how to navigate through the menus. This will prepare you to use the camera to its fullest potential.

## Turning On the Camera

After you have inserted the battery and formatted the memory card, you are ready to turn on your camera. The ON /OFF power switch is on the top right side of the camera, around the shutter button (figure 1-5). Move the lever so the indicator matches up with the ON option.

The first time you turn on the camera, you will be asked if you want to set the camera's internal clock. This information is recorded with each picture and movie—a valuable detail if you wish to organize your photographs. Before we cover setting the camera's clock information, let's first examine how to navigate through and set values for the camera's extensive menu commands.

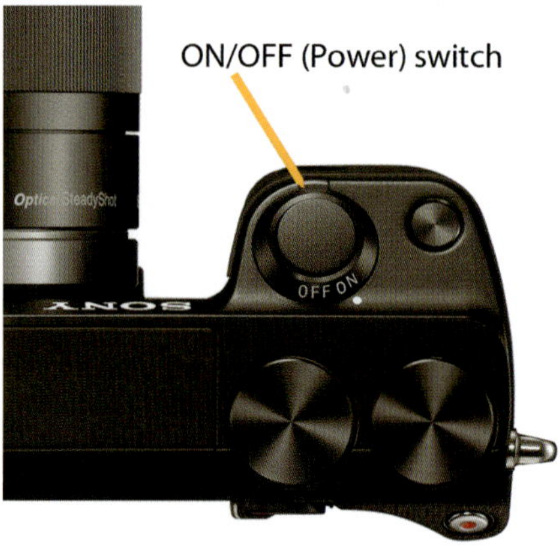


**Figure 1-5**: ON/OFF power switch on top of the camera

## Camera Navigation

Navigating through the camera's menu and using its buttons and dials can appear, at first, to be a daunting task, but it really can be quite simple. In fact, by learning them as you use the camera, you can reduce the frustration in deciding which one does what. This section starts with the rudimentary controls, and then as you read this book, you will be introduced to the buttons and commands as you need them.

## Control Wheel, Buttons, and Dials

The first step in controlling the NEX-7 is learning to use its external controls to explore the commands and menu. When you first turn the camera on, you will see a live view of your image on the rear LCD screen with text and icons for camera settings. Figure 1-6 shows the LCD screen in Live View. For the purpose of explaining the data, we left the lens cap on so the command settings are easy to see.

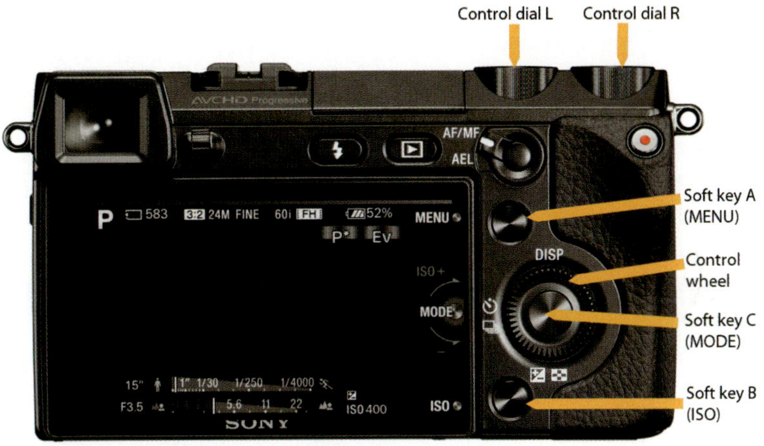


**Figure 1-6**: Camera controls (soft keys, control wheel, control dials) and associated icons on LCD screen

The control wheel, control dials, and soft keys are used to navigate through the menu structure with soft key C used to select and initiate command values.

In figure 1-6, note the ridged circle with the word "MODE" on the extreme right of the screen (to the left of the control wheel). It marks the function of the center button of the control wheel. In this case, when you press this button, you enter the shooting mode function. Sony refers to this button as soft key C. It does not have a defined name because its role can be changed. For example, the alternate function for this button is CUSTOM. But assuming you just turned on the camera or have not customized it yet, the button will be labeled MODE.

The control wheel is the main command center on the camera because it concentrates several operations. Its edge is rimmed so you can rotate it easily with the tip of your finger. This provides a rapid way to change settings. In addition, the wheel's rim functions as a set of four buttons. If you press the rim at the 12 o'clock, 3 o'clock, 6 o'clock, and 9 o'clock positions, you will see operations initiated. What is activated depends on whether you are reviewing a framed image, playing back a stored image, or navigating through a menu. For example, if you are navigating through the menus, these four points serve as cursor controls for moving your selection box up (12 o'clock), right (3 o'clock), down (6 o'clock), or left (9 o'clock). Soft key C (in the center of the control wheel) will process an operation, such as executing a command. Playing with these controls will make their operation intuitive. For example, you can navigate through menus by pressing the rim of the wheel, and then you can select and execute commands by pressing soft key C. In many cases, rotating the wheel will rapidly move through selections.

Notice the word "MENU" opposite a silver icon on the LCD screen. To the right of the icon is the physical button called soft key A. Press this button to enter the camera's extensive menu structure.

## Menu Structure

When you press the MENU button, you will see a screen showing six general divisions: Shoot Mode, Camera, Image Size, Brightness/Color, Playback, and Setup (figure 1-7). Each menu category name indicates what its content pertains to. As we saw, Shoot Mode contains the camera's different shooting modes. The other five categories contain a list of commands.

You can move through the icons by rotating the control wheel or either of the control dials (figure 1-6). You can also move through the icons by pressing the rim of the control wheel. Experiment to see which works best for you. When you get to the menu icon you want, press the center of the control wheel.

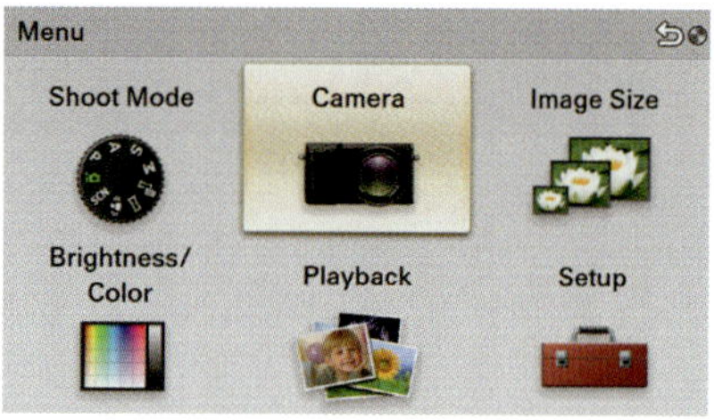


**Figure 1-7**: The camera's six menu icons: Shoot Mode, Camera, Image Size, Brightness /Color, Playback, and Setup

You will make extensive use of the soft key buttons and the control wheel when you navigate through the menu and individual command structure. As mentioned earlier, you can use the rim of the control wheel like a set of cursor keys to move the selection box (highlighted area surrounding the Camera icon, as in figure 1-7). When you find your topic of interest, press soft key C. Think of the control wheel's rim as a cursor control and soft key C as the enter command.

Now we'll look at one of the menu category structures. Move away from the Camera icon and navigate to the Image Size icon (figure 1-8), then press soft key C. The first group of Image Size commands will be displayed (figure 1-9).

If you want to return to the previous screen without selecting anything, press soft key A. Note that there is an icon with a curved arrow on the top right of the screen that indicates exit (figure 1-9) and when pressed, it takes you out of the menu sequence.

The command options are displayed as a sequence of rows (figure 1-9), or they may be displayed as a series of icons (figure 1-10). The display monitor usually can't show all the commands on one screen, so you will need to scroll through them with either the control wheel or the control dial L, or by pressing the control wheel rim. This will move the cursor up or down, one command line at a time. For rapidly moving through a long list of commands, the control dial R will move the cursor through five commands up or down with each click of the control.

We have two suggestions to speed up the process. First, use the control wheel and rotate it. Second, and perhaps better, use control dial R, which is on the top right corner of the camera. There are two dials side by side. The innermost dial is control dial L, and the outermost dial is control dial R. Control dial R is like a page up or page down command that shifts through five commands with each click. This can be a tremendous time saver when you have to find a command in a long list. Control dial L moves the selection box up or down, one command per click. When the command values display as a short rotating list of icons, both of the control dials work the same.

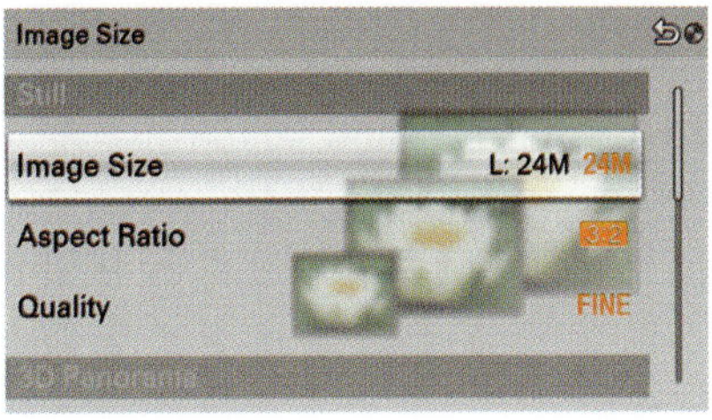


**Figure 1-8**: Menu structure with commands displayed in list format

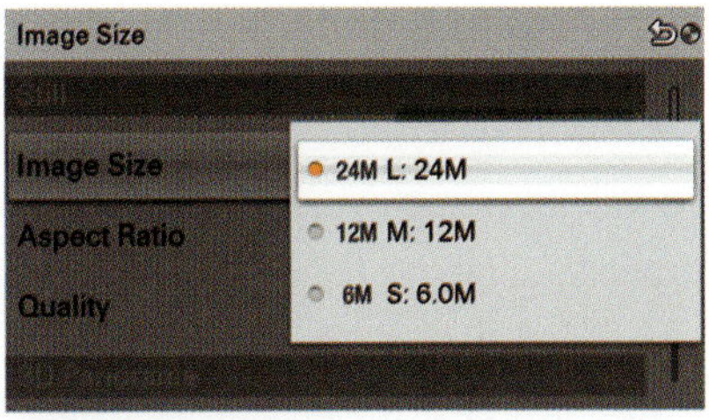


**Figure 1-9**: Menu structure with a command's options displayed in list format

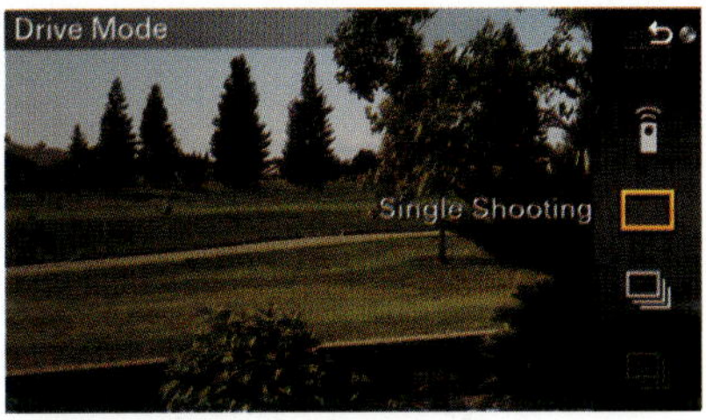


**Figure 1-10**: Menu structure with command options displayed as icons

Navigating through the extensive menu structure can be a confusing and time-consuming operation. Chapter 7 ("Customizing the Camera") will show how you can dedicate the programmable camera buttons so you don't have to use the menu when you're shooting.

All the active commands are displayed with black lettering. Commands that are inactive or disabled appear in gray letters. For example, the Panorama: Size command is enabled only when the camera is initialized to take a Sweep Panorama image. Otherwise, it is disabled and shows up in the menu with gray letters. Figure 1-11 shows the FINDER/LCD Setting command in gray letters, and the other commands are shown in black letters.

As you move through the menu structure, the scroll bar on the right side of the screen indicates how far the displayed commands are within the category's menu. This gives you an indication of whether you are at the beginning, middle, or end of the list of commands.

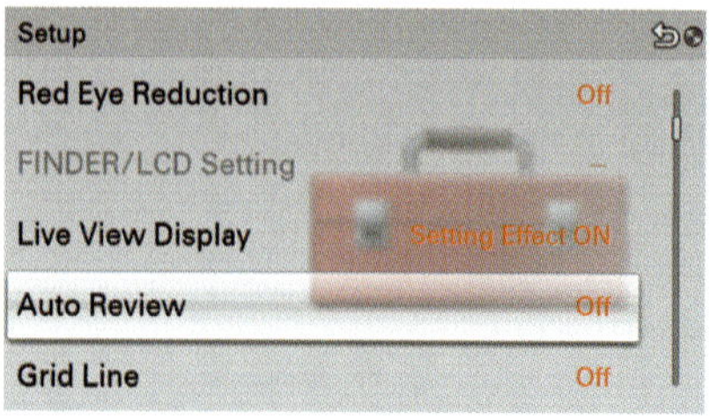


**Figure 1-11**: Enabled and disabled commands

The next step is to identify what Sony calls soft key B. When you are in Intelligent Auto mode, this icon will not be present, and the button is inactive. When you are in more advanced modes, the icon for this button appears. Looking back to figure 1-6, you can see the ISO icon, and soft key B is now active. Remember that the icons for the soft keys can change depending on how you customize the camera.

### What if You Don't See MODE, but You Do See CUSTOM?

Most likely, when you turn on your camera the LCD screen will show MODE for soft key C. But if you purchased your camera used, the previous owner might have customized it, and therefore you might see CUSTOM displayed on the LCD screen to the left of soft key C. If that is the case, you should restore the camera to its default values:

1. Press soft key A to the right of MENU (displayed on the LCD screen). A series of icons will be displayed.
2. Rotate the control wheel to highlight Setup (the icon with the toolbox).
3. Press soft key C, and the screen will change, showing a list of commands.
4. Scroll through these commands by rotating the control wheel until you see the command Reset Default.
5. Highlight the command and press soft key C. The screen changes and displays an x at the top right of the screen. This is opposite soft key A and will exit the command. At the bottom of the screen is the command OK, next to soft key B.
6. Press the button (soft key B) to execute the command and reset the camera's menus to the factory default values.

Knowing how to restore the camera to its default settings is important. When you explore the camera's more complex commands and operations, the operations may not be executed as expected. Sometimes this is operator error, and sometimes it is due to a software malfunction. If you suspect the latter, restoring the camera to its default settings may solve the problem. In the course of preparing this book, we found it necessary to perform this restoration several times.

### Menu Command Nomenclature

We refer to various Sony NEX-7 camera commands throughout this book. To help you quickly locate them within the menu structure, we use the following notation:

MENU>Main Category (Section name)>[value1], [value2]

The Main Category will always be one of the following six values: Shoot Mode, Camera, Image Size, Brightness/Color, Playback, or Setup.

Some of the Main Categories display a gray bar with the section name (figure 1-12). In those cases, they will be listed in parentheses next to the Main Category. If the menu command has subordinate commands, they are separated by > until the command being discussed is reached. We include command values in brackets when they pertain to the subject being covered.

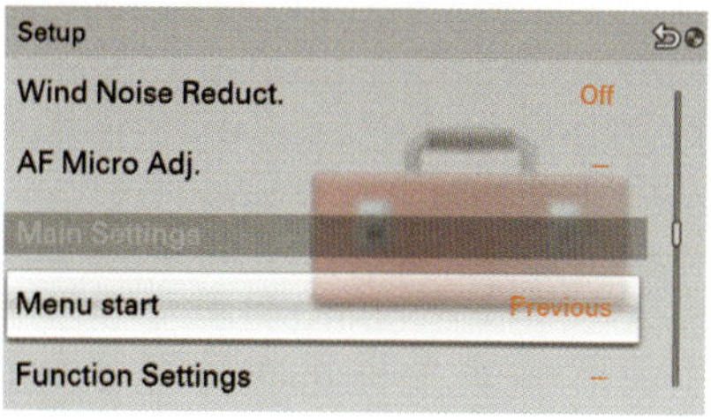


**Figure 1-12**: Setup category's Main Settings section

The following command line tells you the Menu start command has two options, Top and Previous, which can be found in the Main Settings section of the Setup menu.

MENU>Setup (Main Settings)>Menu start>[Top], [Previous]

## Triple-Dial-Control

When you are in many of the Intelligent Auto modes, you will note that many of the camera's controls are inoperable. Three of these controls— the control wheel, control dial L, and control dial R—are important for more advanced camera operation, but they are of limited use in Intelligent Auto mode. These controls are mentioned in menu navigation, but their role in changing the camera's functions will be discussed more fully later in the book. Suffice it to say, these controls are used when photographing in semiautomatic or fully manual modes. We mention these controls because Sony cleverly integrated them to help you rapidly control your camera. Sony refers to this new feature as the Triple-dial-control and introduces it in the front of the user manual. It is a tremendously convenient way of rapidly changing camera settings, but it will not do too much in the point-and-shoot modes.

## Setting the Camera Date, Time, and Area

Entering the date and time for your camera is a great way to learn about maneuvering the controls. It also illustrates how Sony provides plenty of prompts to help you execute a command.

Setting the area, date, and time is easy. Press soft key A (MENU) and then select the Setup icon. You will see that pressing the rim of the control wheel or rotating the wheel with the tip of your finger can move the selection box. When the Setup icon is highlighted, press the center of the control wheel (soft key C) and you will see a long list of commands. You can slowly scroll through these commands by pressing the 12 o'clock or the 6 o'clock position of the control wheel's rim. Or if you wish to move through the commands rapidly, you can rotate the wheel with the tip of your finger. Eventually you will find Date/Time Setup. Highlight the command and then press soft key C. A quick way of showing this sequence is as follows:

MENU>Setup (Main Settings)>[Date/Time Setup]

This is our shorthand for describing how to select the commands. Note that the words "Main Settings" are included because of Sony's design of the menus. When the list of commands becomes too long, Sony provides some order by grouping the commands into sections. So in the case of Setup, you will see that there are the following sections: Shooting Settings, Main Settings, and Memory Card Tool. These provide convenient breaks, and we make note if a command is within the group because it can be a time saver.

When you select [Date/Time Setup] you will be rewarded with an icon for daylight saving, date, and time (figure 1-13). The screen gives you plenty of prompts. The arrow heads show that pressing the rim of the control wheel left or right will move through the selections, while pressing the rim of the control wheel up or down will change their values. You will see, on the right of the screen, that "OK" overlays the symbol for soft key C. Pressing this will accept your settings for date, time, and daylight saving. If you do not want to make any changes, look for the soft key A icon which indicates you can go back. Pressing this key will exit you out of the command without changing the settings.

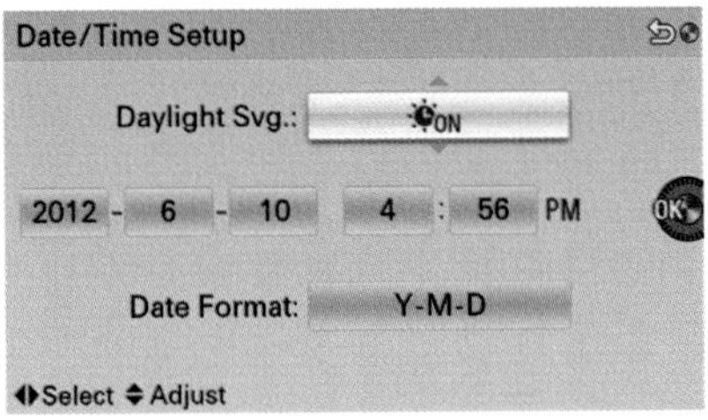


**Figure 1-13**: Date/Time Setup display screen with the clock's date and time set

You should also make sure that you have set your location for the clock with the following command:

MENU>Setup (Main Settings)>[Area Setting]

You will see a small world map with a white region indicating the time zone that is to be selected. As before, you have plenty of prompts so you can find the time zone that you want your camera to be set for. If you travel, you can establish the local time.

**Maintaining the Camera's Date and Time Information**

In addition to the replaceable battery pack needed to turn on and operate the camera, there is a small internal battery for maintaining the date and time settings. Inserting a fully charged battery pack recharges this internal battery. Even if the main battery is depleted, the internal battery has sufficient power for three months of operation.

Press the right or left rim of the control wheel to move across the world map's available time zones. Stop on your current time zone and press soft key C to accept it.

**Daylight Saving Time**

Most areas in the United States observe daylight saving time. In the spring and fall, the time is set forward or backward one hour, respectively. The Date/Time Setup command's [Daylight Svg.:] option allows you to specify if your current location is in daylight saving time. If so, the camera takes this into account when calculating the current time. Unfortunately, as you travel in and out of daylight saving time zones or switch from daylight saving to regular time, you need to reset the [Daylight Svg.:] indicator to reflect the current situation and location.

## Error Messages

The Sony NEX-7 has a large number of self-explanatory information and error messages to help guide you through setting up and using the camera. There are also many error messages that need additional explanation. See appendix B for a list of these error messages and resolutions in alphabetical order.

## Reinitializing Commands to Default Values

As you use the camera, you will set, change, and reset command options frequently. At times the camera may get confused, or you may need to start over with the camera's default values. Use the following command to restore all of the NEX-7 settings to their default values.

MENU>Setup>Initialize>[Reset Default]

When this command is executed, it will return the camera back to the original values. If you have customized the camera or changed any of the settings, you will have to restore your special features manually, but there are exceptions. The camera's date, time, and area, plus face registration information, are not deleted.

## Cleaning the Sensor

When you change the lens, dust particles can enter the camera body and land on the sensor. On the recorded image they can be seen as blurred shadows. You can help prevent this by removing and replacing the lens quickly. Avoid windy areas when you do this. You should also try to make the switch holding the camera body so the lens opening is facing downward to help prevent any dust from falling into the body cavity.

However, the entry of dust is inevitable. The Sony NEX-7 removes dirt from the sensor by shaking it off at high speed. Each time you turn the camera off, it automatically cleans the sensor with ultrasonic vibrations. There may be times when you think an extra cleaning is needed, and you can accomplish this using the following command:

MENU>Setup (Main Settings)>Cleaning Mode

Although these cleanings shake the dust and debris off the sensor, some foreign particles are resistant to being removed. You can take them off by doing a manual cleaning. First, take off the camera lens. Use a manual bulb blower to clean the sensor surface. It is best to hold the camera with the lens opening facing down so the dust particles can fall out of the camera.

Do not use a pressurized can of gas to blow out the camera's interior because any dirt in the nozzle can be blown with enough force to damage the sensor. Also, if propellant is expelled, it can be difficult to remove from the sensor's surface. Do not touch the image sensor with your fingers or the blower. If you have any problems or concerns, take your camera to a professional.

## Recommendations

If you want to take pictures immediately, set the Shoot Mode to Intelligent Auto. Use the control tools (such as the rim of the control wheel and soft key C) to activate the mode. As you use the camera and move into other shooting modes, you will need to become familiar with the other control tools. Although Sony introduces the Triple-dial-control early in the user manual, be advised that these controls are not used fully in the camera's automatic modes. For example, the control wheel is used, but control dials L and R are hardly used in Intelligent Auto or the SCN modes.

The exception to this is using the control dials to navigate through the menus. We found that control dial R is invaluable because it allows you to scroll through the menus, five command lines at a time. When you are searching for a specific command, it will allow you to rapidly move through a long command list. After you see the command displayed on your screen, you can select it by moving one command line at a time with either control dial L or the rim of the control wheel.

Because these control tools vary in their operation, we recommend that you watch the LCD screen. Here, the function of camera dials and buttons will be displayed, helping you to choose which physical control you should activate. If you decide to further customize the control tools, as described in chapter 7, you will find that you will hardly ever have to dive into the camera menus. You will be able to access the functions that are most important to you by using the external dials and keys.

We recommend that you use only Sony-certified batteries and appropriate memory cards to ensure quality and equipment functionality. We also recommend that you always have at least one fully charged spare battery and an additional memory card on hand.

2

# Chapter 2: Photography Basics and the NEX-7

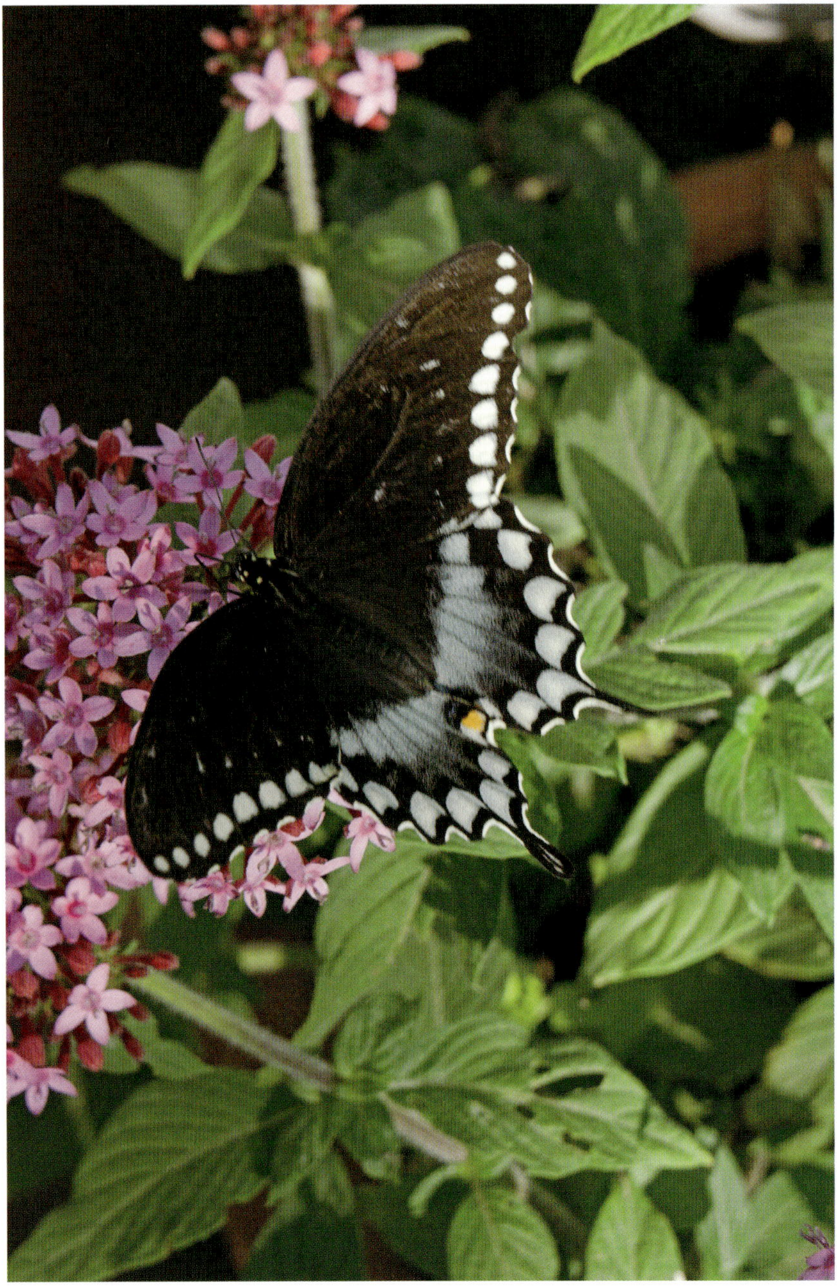

## Introduction

The Sony NEX-7 comes with a 200-plus page manual listing scores of menu commands and options. This can discourage the most experienced users, let alone a person attempting to move beyond a simple point-and-shoot camera. But don't be discouraged; these commands don't have to be mastered all at once. Indeed, you may decide that you wish to use the camera solely in point-and-shoot mode and not worry about camera settings. The NEX-7 can do this. But it also provides you with tools to override automatic settings and impart your artistic interpretation of a scene.

With its automatic settings, the camera tries to generate razor-sharp images. But you may want to blur portions of the image—for example, turning a background with fine detail into a dreamlike backdrop that concentrates the viewer's attention on your subject. When you know how camera settings affect an image, you can think outside the box. As you gain control, you will also learn commands that make the NEX-7 more responsive when you photograph fast-moving subjects and events.

This chapter describes the basics of exposure, depth of field, shutter speed, and sensor sensitivity and how camera settings affect these four items. In essence, our goal is to provide an intuitive rather than a scientific grasp of how the camera renders a sharp and detailed image. You will gain a sense of what the automatic settings are doing. By understanding them and taking pictures in automatic modes, you will learn how and why you may need to change the camera settings. The most important thing to realize is that there are several ways to get a sharp picture; for example, the combination of settings that are best for portraits are not the same as those for scenic shots.

In the Intelligent Auto and SCN modes, the camera does everything and you do virtually nothing. In Intelligent Auto, to get the best combination of settings your camera tries to identify the type of scene you are shooting. For example, if the camera focuses on a subject 10 inches away, it knows you are shooting a closeup or a macro shot. If the camera focuses at the horizon, hundreds of feet away, it knows you are photographing a distant subject and taking a scenic shot. The camera tries to adjust its shutter speed, lens opening, and sensitivity to best record that subject. You just have to accept the image the camera gives you.

Unfortunately, the camera's identification of the subject is not always accurate, and it can choose a combination of settings that are not optimal. This is not to say that the picture is unusable, but it has characteristics that may not bring out the best features of the subject. To get more control and improve accuracy, you can use the SCN mode to match your subject to a predefined scene category, such as sports activities, portraiture, or low-light conditions. Switching from Intelligent Auto to SCN mode will increase your percentage of good photographs. Eventually, you may want to take over the process entirely—looking at the scene, previsualizing the picture, and setting the controls to record your interpretation of the subject.

## Basic Photography Concepts



A photograph is a two-dimensional rendering of a three-dimensional object. The camera's light detector, called a sensor, is flat. A lens projects light from the subject onto the sensor. If the distance of the lens from the sensor is not adjusted precisely, the image will be blurred, causing a loss of definition. Furthermore, only one plane that is parallel to the sensor is rendered at maximum sharpness—in other words, the subject will be in focus only if it occupies this plane. Objects in front of or behind this plane become progressively blurred as their distance from the in-focus subject increases. Eventually the out-of-focus portions of the image appear as a complete blur.

By reducing the size of the lens aperture, you can create an image where both near and far objects appear sharp. So, we have a control, the lens aperture, for extending or limiting the range of sharpness. By opening the aperture, we create a shallow depth of field and can selectively pick which planes will be sharp, and the other planes will be blurred. This is shown in figure 2-1, where the balcony on the left is photographed with the aperture set to f/2.8. Only the balcony is sharp. By closing the aperture, we increase the depth of field to sharply record a larger area in front of and behind the balcony. Not only is the intended object sharp, but the background and foreground areas are sharp as well.

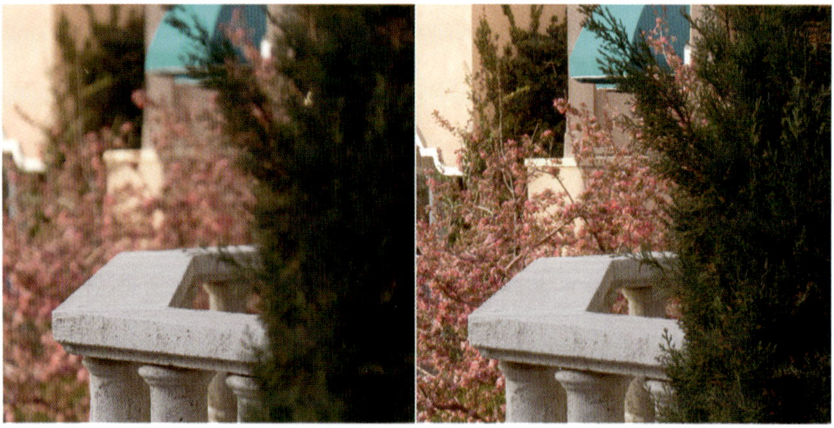

**Figure 2-1**: Shallow versus deep depth of field

### What Are Sensors and Images?

A digital camera uses a solid-state device with millions of individual photosites for converting light into an electrical signal. An individual photosite is the physical basis of a pixel, the smallest unit for sensing light. In the NEX-7, there are more than 24 million pixels in a 6000 x 4000 rectangular array. Signals from these sensors are transmitted to the camera's viewing screen. Together they make up the mosaic of intensities and colors that become an image. The viewed image is a numerical expression that can be manipulated mathematically. This enables the camera to alter the image's appearance. Then it can be stored on an internal memory card.

The sensor can record only a limited intensity of light. If there is too little light, you will record a black photograph with no detail; if there is too much light, your image will be brilliant white with no detail. If you provide the correct amount of light, your sensor will record a picture that is rich in details. Again, this differs from our visual perception of the world where we can view a much broader range of light intensities. To record these intensities, you have to adjust the amount of light that reaches the sensor to ensure proper exposure.

Three things control exposure. The first is lens aperture, which regulates how much light enters the camera body. The second is shutter speed, which regulates how long the sensor is receptive to light. A short shutter speed of 1/1000 second provides less light to the sensor than a long shutter speed of 1 second. The final control is ISO, which is essentially an electrical adjustment to increase the signal from the sensor. Think of it as a sensitivity control—the higher the ISO, the more sensitive the sensor is to light.

In summary, to record a technically sharp picture, you must properly focus the subject onto the sensor and ensure that the intensity of collected light lies within a prescribed range. You can define and describe how to set the camera's controls to get this result. This is what the camera does on its own when you set it to an automatic mode, which explains why point-and-shoot cameras work so well. Artistically, however, there is no universal setting that always renders a perfect image. An artistically satisfying image may require you to set the controls differently than the optimum settings for sharpness or exposure. For example, a running athlete can be photographed with a relatively long shutter speed to blur the arms and legs, creating the impression of movement.

## File Formats



Your digital camera records your images on a memory card. Most likely you will transfer these files to your computer at some point. From there you may want to prepare the pictures for printing or sending in emails. The same is true with the movies you record. You may download them to your computer for editing, or you may compress them to send as attachments. Either way, knowing how you are going to work with your recordings will determine your file format (type).

For still photography, the camera allows you to choose whether to record your images as RAW or JPEG files. RAW files are the equivalent of digital negatives. You cannot use them directly; you have to process them first. In other words, they require special software, and this means either buying or updating additional software, such as Photoshop. However, this is an advantage for those who like to process their images. RAW files are supposed to contain all the information collected by the sensor. This data gives you the greatest range of adjustments for post-processing your images. You can easily correct errors in white balance and effectively adjust the contrast, bringing out details in the shadows or bright areas. Because of the information content, these files are large—up to 24 MB in size.

On the other hand, working with JPEG files is very straightforward. Almost all imaging packages can open and work with them. The camera compresses the data from the sensor before storing it as a JPEG file. In essence, these files are already processed, and the degree of digital enhancement you can later make is limited. The Sony NEX-7 can and does manipulate the image. Before you capture the image, you can specify the degree of sharpness, contrast, or color rendition you want to apply and save to the file. Quality photographs can be achieved directly out of the camera, but the photographer has to take more care in correctly adjusting exposure and white balance at the time of picture taking. There is less flexibility in correcting mistakes in exposure or color balance when processing JPEG files on your computer.

### JPEG and RAW Defined

**JPEG:** A JPEG image file is compressed using a method developed by the Joint Photographic Experts Group. This compression produces a loss of information from the original image file that cannot be restored. The file has the extension JPG (commonly used on Windows computers) or JPEG (commonly used on Macintosh computers).

**RAW:** A RAW file is a digital camera file that is minimally processed. It retains all of the data originally captured by the imaging sensor. A Sony NEX-7 RAW file has the extension ARW.

When you start using your NEX-7, you will find that JPEG is the default file type. This is an easy-to-use file format that is readable and usable by almost any computing device. You can choose to make these files very small so that you can send them as e-mail attachments or view them on your cell phone.

So, which file type should you use? Well, the simplest answer is to use both. The NEX-7 allows you to simultaneously record an image in both RAW and JPEG formats. This gives you the best of both worlds—the full image processing potential of a large RAW file and the convenience of a generally accessible, small JPEG file. To record an image in both RAW and JPEG formats, press soft key A (MENU) and proceed to the following command and select the [RAW & JPEG] option:

MENU>Image Size (Still)>Quality>[RAW], [RAW & JPEG], [Fine], [Standard]

The option [RAW] only saves a RAW file while [Fine] and [Standard] save only JPEG files. The disadvantage of saving both RAW and JPEG formats is it consumes more memory on the SD card. However, memory is inexpensive, and the convenience of having both files is compelling. One problem with this strategy is that Sony has several unique exposure techniques that require you to record only in JPEG mode. Since these techniques are valuable for shooting in low-light conditions, you may find yourself changing your camera settings to save files only as JPEGs. When you do, you have the choice of recording in [Fine] or [Standard] qualities. Your choice will depend on how much detail you wish to retain in the image. To record the most detail, choose [Fine]. To take up less space on the memory card, record less detail by choosing [Standard]. The difference between these files types is that a greater degree of software compression is applied to [Standard]. We choose the [Fine] option since these JPEG files are small enough for our purposes, and we see little value in further compressing the files.

You can also shrink the file size by reducing the number of pixels in the file. The Sony sensor generates a 24 megapixel [24M] image; but you can reduce the pixel array to 12 megapixels [12M] or to 6 megapixels [6M].

MENU>Image Size (Still)>Image Size>[24M], [12M], or [6M]

We do not save the files with the smaller pixel count. Programs like Photoshop will allow you to specify a different pixel array for a file, so we prefer to downsize our pictures on the computer. RAW files are saved only as 24 megapixel files because they are not compressed by the camera. If you need to make the pixel array smaller to post your pictures on the web or send them as e-mail attachments, you can always do this later during post-processing. To give you an idea of how selecting the file format affects your shooting, refer to table 2-1, which shows how many images or how much movie time can be recorded on a 2 GB memory card. Be advised that the numbers in this table are approximate. You may get more or fewer pictures, or different movie recording times, depending on the details within the scene.

| File Format | Image Size | Compression | Image Capacity (2 GB SD card) | Comments |
|---|---|---|---|---|
| JPEG | 6000 x 4000, 24 Megapixels | Fine or Standard | 218 or 361 images | Easy to open on all computers. |
| | 4000 x 3000, 12 Megapixel | Fine or Standard | 391 or 539 images | Easy to open on all computers. |
| | 2000 x 3000, 6 Megapixels | Fine or Standard | 564 or 714 images | Easy to open on all computers. |
| RAW | 6000 x 4000, 24 Megapixels | None | 79 images | Needs special software to open. Sony provides Image Data Converter 4.0. |
| AVCHD | 1920 x 1080 | FX, FH, PS | 9–10 min | Needs special software to edit. Sony provides PMB for Windows. |
| MP4 | 1440 x 1080 | 12 MB | 20 min | Digital file for computers. |
| | 640 x 480 | 3 MB | 1 hr, 20 min | Digital file for computers. |

**Table 2-1**: File format overview

For taking movies, there are two different file formats: AVCHD and MP4. AVCHD stands for Advanced Video Coding High Definition. It provides the highest spatial and temporal resolution for recording your movies (1920 x 1080 pixels), and it is the default movie mode for the Sony NEX-7. There are two types of AVCHD: 60i/60p or 50i/50p. The former is the American standard, and the latter is the European standard. Where you buy your camera determines which of these two AVCHD formats are used. Files stored with these formats can be used to project your movie directly from your camera to your television. Or, with Sony's PMB software, they can be burned onto a disk for playback on your television.

The MP4 file format is simpler to work with on the computer, albeit at lower resolution. If you want to shoot in MP4 mode, you must select it to override the camera's default setting.

MENU>Image Size (Movie)>File Format>[AVCHD 60i/60p], [MP4]

AVCHD movies can be edited with your PMB software, but they have massive amounts of data. As a consequence there are recommendations to use AVCHD formats for movies you want to play back on your HD television. There are two ways to do this: you can attach your camera directly to a high-definition TV (HDTV), or you can use PMB to make DVDs or Blu-Ray Discs for playback to your HDTV.

Keep in mind that movie files can contain enormous amounts of data. To circumvent this issue, AVCHD files are highly compressed, and the degree of compression influences how easily they can be edited on your computer. Sony's PMB software will allow you to do this on Windows computers, but it is not compatible with Apple computers. For Apple users, iMovie can edit your AVCHD movie files.

Saving a movie in the MP4 format creates a file that computers can handle more easily. So, if you are working with the AVCHD format and find it is difficult to use with your computer, you can switch to recording your movies as MP4 files, which are easier to edit. These files can easily be attached to e-mails, placed on websites, or inserted into PowerPoint presentations.

Both the AVCHD and MP4 file formats have specific record settings. Table 2-2 contains AVCHD record setting values. The numbers 24M, 17M, and 28M indicate megabits per second (Mbps), the amount of data being streamed. Higher numbers, such as 28 Mbps, mean more data is being transmitted and there is less compression and less loss of image quality. Lower numbers mean less data is being transmitted and there is a higher compression being used, which reduces movie quality.

| Record Setting Option | Fields per Second | Average Bit Rate | Quality |
|---|---|---|---|
| 60i 24M(FX) | 60 | 24 Mbps | Medium |
| 60i 17M(FH) | 60 | 17 Mbps | Standard |
| 60p 28M(PS) | 60 | 28 Mbps | Highest |
| 24p 24M(FX) | 24 | 24 Mbps | Medium |
| 24p 17M(FH) | 24 | 17 Mbps | Standard |

**Table 2-2**: Record setting values for AVCHD files

When file format = [AVCHD 60i/60p]:

MENU>Image Size (Movie)>Record Setting>[60i 24M(FX)], [60i 17M(FH)], [60p 28M(PS)], [24p 24M(FX)], [24p 17M(FH)]

Table 2-3 contains MP4 record setting values. There are two recording options for MP4: 1440 x 1080 pixels and 640 x 480 pixels (VGA).

When file format = [MP4]:

MENU>Image Size (Movie)>Record Setting>[1440 x 1080 12M], [VGA 3M]

| Record Setting Option | Average Bit rate | Pixel Array |
|---|---|---|
| 1440 x 1080 12M | 12 Mbps | 1440 x 1080 |
| VGA 3M | 3 Mbps | 640 x 480 |

**Table 2-3**: Record setting values for MP4 files

These two record setting options for the MP4 format demonstrate the differences in data being sent. At 12 Mbps, each movie frame has 1440 x 1080 pixels. In contrast, when the bit rate is reduced to 3 Mbps, each movie frame is reduced in size (less data), and only 640 x 480 pixels are being processed. The effects of compression are seen in this case as a reduction in the overall pixels available for viewing, so a 3 Mbps movie provides a smaller size frame (640 x 480 pixels) than a 12 Mbps movie (1440 x 1080 pixels).

## Shutter Button

The shutter button is on the camera's top right panel. When you press it down halfway, you will feel an increase in resistance. Even though the camera has not fired, you can stop there and hold this position. It is a control point that initiates many of the camera's settings. For example, a half press of the shutter button starts automatic focusing. When focus is obtained, the lens is locked and a green circle lights up in the lower left corner of the screen (table 2-4). As long as you maintain pressure on the shutter button, you can aim the camera to another area without changing focus. To take the picture, press the shutter button down fully. This is a useful technique to master for situations where the camera does not focus on your chosen subject. This sometimes occurs when the subject has no fine details or when the scene is cluttered with material in front of or behind your desired subject. We describe how to solve this problem in the next section on focusing.

| Focus Indicator | Condition | Status |
|---|---|---|
| ● | Steady green light | Focus is locked and the camera is ready to shoot. |
| ((●)) | Green light | Continuous AF is in operation, and focus has been achieved. |
| (( )) | Green light | Camera is in Continuous AF and is attempting to find focus. Camera is not ready to shoot, and the shutter button is disabled. |
| ● | Flashing green light | Unable to find focus. |

**Table 2-4**: Display screen focus indicators

## Focusing

As mentioned earlier, the camera lens focuses the scene onto the sensor. You have to tell the NEX-7 whether you wish to focus automatically or manually. Normally the camera is set for automatic focus, and beginning photographers just accept that everything will be sharply recorded. But automatic focusing can be surprisingly difficult. The problem is that sometimes not all regions in the scene may be usable for focusing. For example, the camera will focus on near objects while blurring far objects, or vice versa.

In Intelligent Auto mode, the camera favors focusing objects in the center of the field of view. This is a logical strategy because it is the most likely place for your subject. However, the camera sensor covers such a large area that it may focus on the wrong region and blur your subject. Intelligent Auto tries to reduce this by using powerful image analysis software. Facial detection is one example. The camera identifies a face, locks onto it, and uses it for the focus point.

If you notice that the camera cannot find focus, you will have to take an active role. One strategy is to find a subject that is approximately the same distance from you as your subject. Aim and focus at this surrogate, pressing the shutter button halfway to obtain the focus confirmation signal. By maintaining pressure on the shutter button, you can keep the focus locked and move the camera to aim at the subject you wish to record. After you frame your image to your liking, press the shutter button fully to take the picture.

Working with automatic focus requires understanding the cues for judging what is in focus. For the NEX-7 it is contrast. When objects are out of focus, their edges are blurred and the transition between light and dark is gradual. When it is brought into focus, the object's edges are sharply defined, emphasizing the transitions from dark to light. Basically, a sharp in-focus object has a greater range and more intensity values than a fuzzy out-of-focus object. So to achieve accurate focus, you have to find a subject that has some variation in light and dark. Trying to find focus on a blank wall can be impossible.

The previous paragraphs describe the Single Shooting automatic focusing mode, where the camera attempts to find focus; after focus is found, the lens is locked.

MENU>Camera>Autofocus Mode>[Single-shot AF], [Continuous AF]

But the camera can be told to focus continuously. In Continuous AF. Shooting mode, if the object moves toward you or away from you, the camera will update its focus setting. The camera has green icons in the viewfinder and rear LCD screen to tell you how automatic focusing is doing (table 2-4). If you see green brackets, the camera is in continuous autofocus. If a green circle appears within the brackets, the camera has established focus. If there is no green circle, the camera has not yet established focus. In Intelligent Auto and most of the SCN modes, you will find that the camera determines the Autofocus Mode for you. For example, most of the time it is set to Single-shot AF; however, if you choose the SCN mode [Sports], the camera will use Continuous AF. This makes sense for a situation where you expect the subject to be actively moving about and you need the camera to maintain focus.

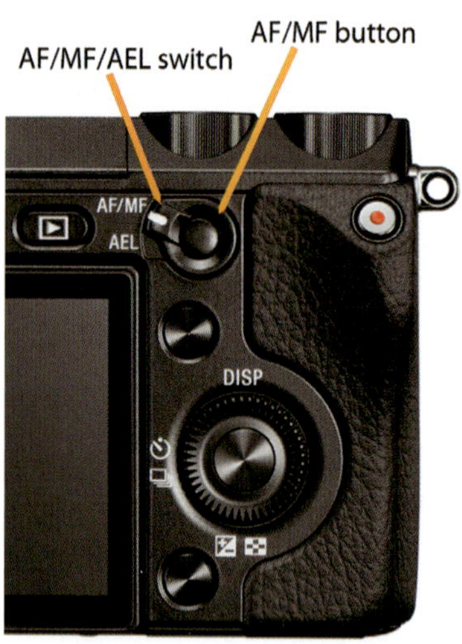


**Figure 2-2a**: AF/MF button and AF/MF/AEL switch set to AF/MF

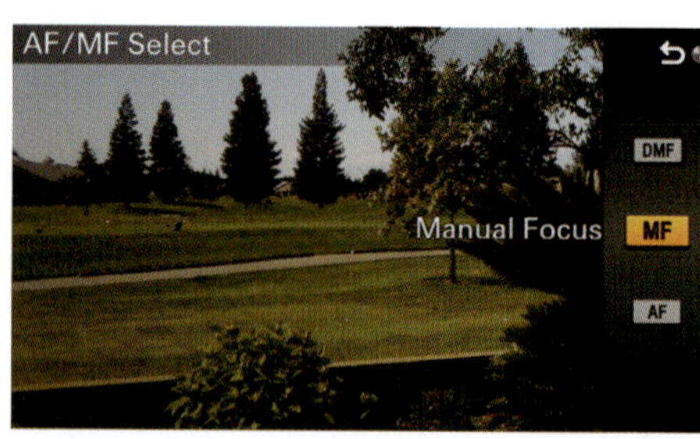


**Figure 2-2b**: AF/MF Select command with MF selected

As good as automatic focusing is, you may need to take over and focus manually (figure 2-2a). Turn the AF/MF/AEL switch lever to AF/MF. Then press the AF /MF button and turn the lens-focusing ring until the image is maximally sharp in the display screen. For most photography, you will not need to do this. However, it is comforting to know you have this capability even when you have the camera in Intelligent Auto mode.

Manual focus can also be set with the following menu command (figure 2-2b):

MENU>Camera>AF/MF Select>[Manual Focus]

Find and select the Manual Focus icon by using the control wheel and soft key C.

We will more fully discuss how to use manual focus in chapters 5 and 6. Fortunately, automatic focus is reliable, and when used with the kit lens and most subjects it will deliver pleasingly sharp pictures.

**Advanced Focusing Features: Face Detection and Object Tracking**

Although we will discuss them in more detail in chapter 4, this is a good place to mention that advanced focusing features exist so you can watch out for them as you experiment with your new camera.

Face Detection identifies a person's face then focuses on it. When you use either Intelligent Auto or certain SCN modes, the default is that Face Detection is set to [On (Regist. Faces)]. However, you can turn Face Detection off in these modes.

MENU>Camera>Face Detection>[Off], [On (Regist. Faces)], [On]

When you select [On] or [On (Regist. Faces)], you will see a frame or box surrounding each of the detected faces. The frame's color indicates the face detection status. A white frame indicates that the face has priority and the camera will focus on it. When you lock focus by pressing the shutter button halfway, the frame turns from white to green. When several faces are in the viewfinder, they may all be surrounded with a frame. The gray frames are detected as faces, but they will not be used for focusing.

The command [On (Regist. Faces)] is for faces you have taught the camera to recognize. When this command is used, the camera focuses on and exposes for these preferred people. Registering faces is discussed in chapter 4.

The other advanced focusing mode is Object Tracking. Here you tell the camera that you want a subject to be tracked or followed as it moves about within the display screen.

MENU>Camera>Object Tracking>[Off], [On]

When this command is activated, the camera attempts to follow an object for focusing. Theoretically, this would be a useful feature for photographing active children or pets. Object Tracking is initiated by setting the Object Tracking command to [On] and then pressing soft key B to set the target area. However, Object Tracking can lose the targeted subject, so you should experiment with it before relying on it for a critical shot. It works fairly well for a subject that is moving slowly and is in front of a simple, plain background.

Table 2-5 shows display screen icons indicating when both Face Detection and Object Tracking features are activated.

| Display Screen Icon | Description |
|---|---|
| 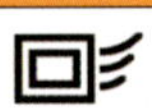 | Object Tracking activated |
|  | Face Detection activated |
| 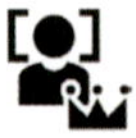 | Face Detection and Registration activated |

**Table 2-5**: Object Tracking and Face Detection features activated icons

### Exposure (Shutter Speed, Aperture, ISO)

Capturing an image that shows all of the subject's detail requires the sensor to collect all of the scene's light levels. This is done by properly setting the shutter speed and aperture opening to adjust the amount of light that falls on the sensor. If these adjustments don't provide enough light, the signal from the sensor will be insufficient and the recorded image will appear dark. This condition can be ameliorated by amplifying the output signal from the sensor, so the recorded image appears bright.

Aperture control means adjusting the f-stop, which regulates the amount of light passing through the lens. The f-stop is the ratio between the diameter of the lens and its focal length. The important thing to realize is that a lens set at f/5.6 transmits the same intensity of light whether it is a telephoto or a wide-angle lens.

Another way to regulate the amount of light falling on the sensor is by controlling the duration of exposure. This is the role of the shutter, where the shutter speed reflects the time the sensor is exposed to light. An exposure of 1/30 second allows twice as much light to be collected by the sensor as a shutter speed of 1/60 second. When the Sony NEX-7 is used in Intelligent Auto mode, shutter speeds can range from as long as 30 seconds to as short as 1/4000 second.

### What Are F-Stop Numbers?

F-stop numbers represent the ratio of the lens opening to its focal length. They provide a measure of consistency for using lenses of different focal lengths or magnifications. A telephoto lens with a focal length of 400mm and a wide-angle lens with a focal length of 14mm both pass the same intensity of light when they are set to f/16.

One thing to be aware of is that f-stops on many zoom lenses vary depending on where you set the zoom ring. Usually the lens is more open when it is used at wide-angle settings, and it becomes narrower when you use a telephoto setting. Fortunately, because your NEX-7 measures light at the sensor, these variations of light intensities resulting from zooming in or out are compensated for.

There are advantages to using both the aperture and shutter speed to control how much light reaches the sensor. First, you have control over a much broader range of light intensities. Closing the aperture and shortening the shutter speed are additive; doing both reduces the effect of the light more than doing just one or the other. So the intensities you can work with range from using the longest shutter speed with the widest aperture opening to the shortest shutter speed with the narrowest aperture opening. Aperture openings are expressed in numbers and the smaller numerical values indicate that the lens is transmitting more light. Shutter speeds are also expressed in numbers and it is assumed that they represent a fraction of a second. So a shutter speed of 1/125 is often seen in the viewfinder as simply 125.

In addition, multiple combinations of aperture and shutter speed settings can produce an equivalent exposure. For example, setting the aperture to f/2 and the shutter speed to 1/60 second is, in terms of exposure, the same as setting the aperture to f/16 and the shutter speed to 1 second. Equivalent exposures can be obtained by the judicious selection of aperture and shutter speed, allowing you to vary the appearance of a photograph. Being able to vary one or the other allows you to control the appearance of your image for artistic effect.

For example, with a fast shutter speed, flying birds can be rendered as tack-sharp objects suspended in space; or with a slower shutter speed, their flapping wings can appear blurred to give the impression of rapid movement. To obtain an equivalent exposure with these two shutter speeds, the faster one requires the lens aperture to be opened up to admit more light, and the slower one requires the aperture to be closed down to admit less light.

Another advantage of varying the aperture is increasing or decreasing the depth of field. Closing down the aperture increases the depth of field, while opening the aperture decreases it. When using a small aperture to achieve greater depth of field, you will need a slower shutter speed so enough light still reaches the sensor.

You can use depth of field to direct the viewer's attention to the subject. For example, when you take a portrait of a model standing in front of a window, you can focus on the model's face and blur the background by opening the aperture to provide a shallow depth of field. To offset the increase in aperture, you would use a shorter shutter speed to reduce the amount of light falling on the sensor. Again, the dual control of shutter speed and aperture comes into play.

Occasionally, when working in a dim environment you may need to raise the shutter speed or narrow the aperture, further limiting the amount of light that reaches the sensor. You can offset this by increasing the ISO. For digital cameras, raising the ISO increases the output from the sensor so that an image can still be recorded at low light intensities. The cost is some image degradation. Usually the range of light that the sensor can record (called the dynamic range) is reduced, and the image becomes granular—that is, areas that should be rendered as smooth tones become speckled with blotches of color, so that definition is reduced. This is referred to as image noise.

**What is ISO?**

ISO stands for International Organization for Standardization. Historically, this term referred to the sensitivity of film to light. Today, when it is associated with digital cameras, it refers to how much gain can be employed to generate a brighter image.

Technically, a sensor's sensitivity to light does not vary—it generates a signal that is proportional to the amount of light falling on it. However, the sensor has an amplifier that increases the strength of a weak signal when the ISO number is increased. By raising the ISO, you can capture images in dim light.

To obtain the highest image quality with the Sony NEX-7, we recommend using ISO 100. We don't hesitate to raise the ISO when working in dim light; however, we prefer not to use an ISO greater than 1600. For us, the compromise in image quality is too great.



Basically, you have three variables for controlling exposure: aperture, shutter speed, and ISO. These three variables allow you to impart an ambience to your pictures. Intelligent Auto tries to identify the subject and match the three variables to produce a final image, but its ability to identify the scene is limited. To improve the quality of your pictures, you can take advantage of the SCN mode and choose a setting that matches your subject. The necessary adjustments are discussed in chapter 4.

## White Balance and the Appearance of Colors

We live in a world of color, with our eyes and brain working together to help us identify hues correctly in all lighting conditions. Our vision works so well that we don't expect an object's appearance to vary based on its location—whether in direct sunlight, shade, or indoors under a desk lamp.

But when you're using a digital camera, the recorded image reflects the object's changing appearance under varying lighting scenarios. If nothing is adjusted within the camera, an object will be recorded with different color shades when it is recorded under different lighting conditions. For example, indoor light makes objects appear ruddy, and sunny outdoor light makes them look neutral. To match our visual impression of what the object should look like, digital cameras have an automatic white balance (AWB), which adjusts the balance of colors so that when an image is saved, the object's hues look the same no matter the lighting condition.

2

When the NEX-7 is used in Intelligent Auto or a SCN mode, the camera sets white balance (WB) to AWB to automatically compensate for variations in lighting. For the most part, it does a good job of ensuring that colors appear natural. But, as you gain experience, you may want to control WB by going outside the automatic modes and setting the camera shooting mode to P, A, S, or M. We describe this process in more detail in chapters 5 and 6.

For the most part, the Sony NEX-7 does an excellent job of rendering the object's colors, and you can always alter the WB later with image processing software. If you choose to do this, be sure to save your files in RAW as adjusting white balance by image processing is easier when working with this file format.

## Drive Mode Function

When you're taking pictures, the camera will fire either one shot for each press of the shutter button or a continuous set of shots for as long as you hold the shutter button down. To select which of these modes to use, press the Drive Mode button positioned at 9 o'clock on the rim of the control wheel (figure 2-3). When it is pressed, the Drive Mode options are displayed on the rear LCD screen (table 2-6). You can navigate through the options with the control wheel.

MENU>Camera>Drive Mode>[Single Shooting], [Cont. Shooting], [Spd Priority Cont.], [Self-timer], [Self-timer (Cont.)], [Bracket: Cont.], [Remote Cdr.]

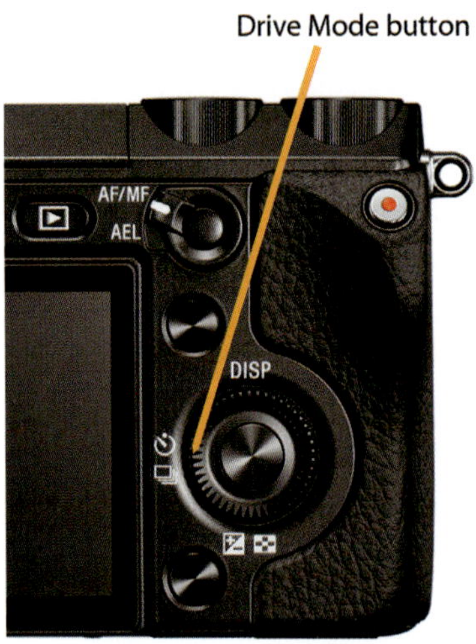


**Figure 2-3**: Drive Mode button

| Drive Mode Icon | Drive Mode Name | Option | Description |
|---|---|---|---|
| | Single Shooting | | Records one image per press of the shutter button. |
| | Cont. Shooting | | Records continuously while the shutter button is pressed (3 shots/second). |
| S | Spd Priority Cont. | | Records continuously while the shutter button is pressed (10 shots/second). |
| | Self-timer | | Delays firing the camera after the shutter button is pressed. |
| | Options | 10 | 10-second delay. Use this option when you don't have a remote release and need to get into a group shot. |
| | | 2 | 2-second delay. Use this option when you don't have a remote release and you want to eliminate camera shake resulting from pressing the shutter button. |
| | Self-timer(Cont.) | | Delays firing the camera after the shutter button is pressed and fires a continuous set of shots. |
| | Options | C3 | Delays firing for 10 seconds and then fires 3 shots. |
| | | C5 | Delays firing for 10 seconds and then fires 5 shots. |
| | Bracket: Cont. | | To use, press and hold down the shutter button. This function takes a series of 3 shots with the EV varied +/- by the selected amount. This command is not available in Intelligent Auto mode. |
| | Options | 0.3EV | Takes 3 shots, where first shot is recorded with the base exposure, then -0.3EV then +0.3EV exposure. |
| | | 0.7EV | Takes 3 shots, where first shot is recorded with the base exposure, then -0.7EV then +0.7EV exposure. |
| | Remote Cdr. | | When this option is selected, the camera fires in response to an infrared signal from a wireless remote control, available from Sony. This allows you to be away from the camera when initiating a shot. |

**Table 2-6**: Drive Mode options

### Single Shooting

With the Drive Mode's [Single Shooting] option, the camera fires once when the shutter button is depressed. Automatic focusing occurs in the instant just prior to taking the photograph.

You can select this function with one of two procedures. The first is to press the MENU button and navigate through the list of commands with the control wheel. Select Drive Mode and press soft key C to see your choices. Rotate the control wheel to move through the options, and select Single Shooting.

The other method is to press the Drive Mode button. This immediately puts you into the mode needed for selecting a specific command. This is the fastest way to change the drive mode, and it is the method we prefer to use.

### Continuous Shooting

You can set your camera to fire multiple shots per second (approximately three shots/second) (figure 2-4a), or you can set it to fire approximately10 shots/second (figure 2-4b). The Drive Mode option for the former is called [Cont. Shooting], and the latter is called [Spd Priority Cont.]. Aside from the firing speed, the predominant difference between these shooting modes is the control of automatic focus and exposure.

When it is set to the leisurely Cont. Shooting mode, the camera has time to focus and adjust the exposure between shots. In essence, both the focus and exposure can change as the scene changes. In contrast, the Spd Priority Cont. option, as the name implies, is mostly concerned with rapid firing, so the controls are set and locked prior to the first shot of the shooting sequence. If the lighting changes or your subject runs toward you, then the exposure and focus will not be able to compensate. Although you can select this mode by going into the menu, since the Drive Mode button is available by pressing the left rim of the control wheel, we see little need to access this function through the menu.

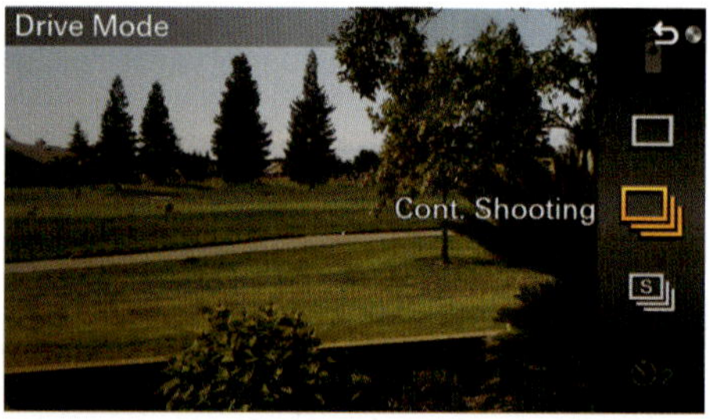


**Figure 2-4a**: Drive Mode with Cont. Shooting option selected

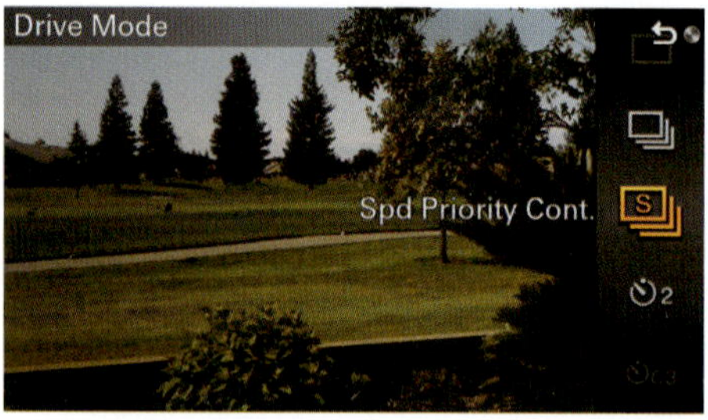


**Figure 2-4b**: Drive Mode with Spd Priority Cont. option selected

In a perfect world, one would expect that when you use continuous shooting, the camera would keep taking pictures until it fills the memory card. Unfortunately, this is not the case. The memory card is limited and does not have the speed to accept new pictures as fast as the Sony NEX-7 can generate them.

To circumvent this deficiency, Sony has engineered a fast memory buffer to rapidly accept and store your pictures. When this buffer is filled, which occurs when you rapidly fire a long continuous string of photographs, the camera slows down its shooting rate. It will not fire again until images are downloaded from the buffer to the SD card, which frees space in the buffer. In the Spd Priority Cont. setting, we observed that we can obtain about 11–14 pictures before the buffer fills. The variation in the number of pictures is due to the file sizes of the images; the lower number reflects RAW files, and the higher number is for small JPEG files.

### Delayed and Remote Firing of the Camera

To include yourself in a picture, you can use two other Drive Mode options. One is [Self-timer] and the other is [Remote Cdr.] (Remote Commander). The former is a method of delaying the picture taking. You press the shutter button, and 2 or 10 seconds later the camera fires automatically, without anyone being in contact with the camera. The 10-second delay option gives you enough time to press the shutter button and race out in front of the camera so you can take a picture of yourself. Another benefit of this option is that you can avoid the movement of the camera due to the pressure required when bearing down on the shutter button. This is particularly problematic when working with a microscope or telescope. To avoid this camera movement and ensure a sharp picture, you can use the 2-second self-timer delay, which automatically fires the camera 2 seconds after you depress the shutter.

Self-timer (Cont.) is an interesting modification of the 10-second delay self-timer command. It allows the camera to fire either three or five shots after 10 seconds. The rationale is that in a group shot, someone always seems to commit a faux pas that is captured by the camera. These momentary lapses can be failing to smile, looking away at the wrong time, or blinking just as the shutter fires. Working on the assumption that these problems occur randomly, Sony uses a statistical approach to get the perfect shot. It fires either three or five shots after 10 seconds. The assumption is that the more shots collected, the better the chance of getting a good one. You will find [Self-timer (Cont.)] in the Drive Mode command. Select the option and choose three or five images (3 Img, 5 Img). An optimist will use the three-shot option, and a pessimist will use the five-shot option.

2

The final way of firing the camera is to use the Drive Mode's [Remote Cdr.] option. This requires you purchase the Sony Remote Commander (RMT-DSLR1) accessory. It costs only $30 and is used to fire the camera with a beam of infrared light. Since the sensor for the beam is located on the front of the camera, you might expect that this device would be useful only if you are standing in front of the camera, aiming the remote directly at the camera. This is not the case. In a room we have been able to fire the camera while standing behind it. The beam has sufficient intensity that its reflection off the wall can fire the camera. This is good to know because the NEX-7 does not have any other remote firing device. When using this camera on a microscope, we routinely use the Remote Commander to avoid vibration.

### Bracket Cont.

The [Bracket: Cont.] option has limited availability. It is used for providing three images with different exposures, and it is available only in the semiautomatic (P, S, and A) modes or the manual (M) mode. Its application in these modes will be discussed in chapters 5 and 6.

## Recording Movies

### How to Take Movies

The NEX-7 is a hybrid that is adept at taking either movies or still pictures. To start taking movies, press the MOVIE button and then release it; you do not need to hold it down (figure 2-5). To stop recording, press the button again. The exposure (shutter speed, aperture, and ISO) is set automatically.

The NEX-7 also has a microphone on the front of the camera, just above the lens mount, to record sound.

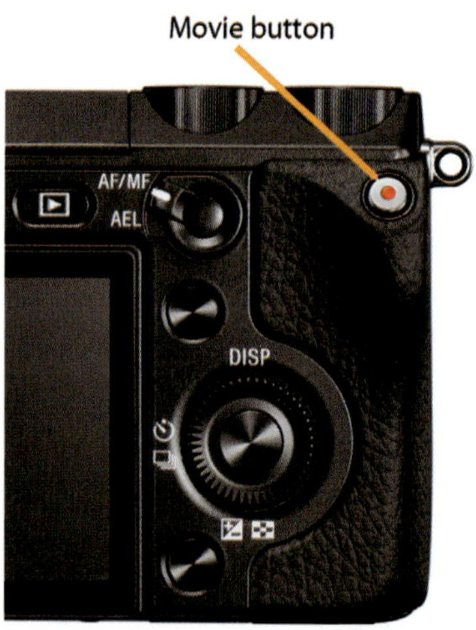


**Figure 2-5**: MOVIE button on back of NEX-7

## Movies and Your NEX-7

A new approach is needed for taking movies. It can be argued that it is more difficult to record a high-quality movie than a good still photograph. For one thing, stabilizing the camera motion is more important. A shift in the camera position is recorded by the subject's displacement in the recorded scene. In still photography, these movements can be ignored unless you jar the camera at the moment of exposure. So for professional-looking videos, mounting the camera on a tripod makes sense.

A second consideration in taking movies is the higher frame rate. Frequently, movies are taken at 24 frames (pictures) per second or faster. This limits how long of a shutter speed you can use. Obviously, if you are taking 24 individual shots per second, you cannot set the shutter speed to 1 second. You therefore do not have the range of exposures that you had for a still photograph. This limits your ability to take movies in low lighting.

File formats for movies and downloading the movies to a computer introduces some additional differences. First, movie files can be incredibly large. Also, if you record in the high-definition mode, you may be surprised by the number of subdirectories that are listed on the memory card to store the AVCHD files. Because of this complexity, it is important to keep the file format and file size in mind.

If you are new to taking movies, we recommend that you first install either Sony PMB software (Windows) or Apple iMovie software (Mac). Both of these programs can transcode high-definition AVCHD files. You'll need one of these programs to edit movies on your computer. They allow you to cut portions of the movie that are not germane and splice sections from other movies taken at other times.

If you don't have these or other similar programs, you can record your movies with the [MP4] option. You probably already have software on your computer that can view or work with MP4 files. One popular program is QuickTime 7 Pro, which works well with MP4 files on both Mac and Windows computers.

Before you start to record movies, think about how you will be using them. If you intend to display them on your HDTV directly from the camera or burn them to a DVD or Blu-ray Disc, by all means record the files in AVCHD. If you are an experienced videographer, this will be your preferred file format. If you are new to movies, we recommend you start with either the PMB or iMovie programs. If you connect your camera to your computer with a USB cable, these programs will prompt you to download your movies.

If you intend to send your movies to friends as e-mail attachments or upload them to a website, follow Sony's recommendation to save the files as [MP4]. These files are not as highly compressed as AVCHD files, and, after you transfer them to your computer, you can work on them easily.

# Chapter 3: Managing Your Images

3

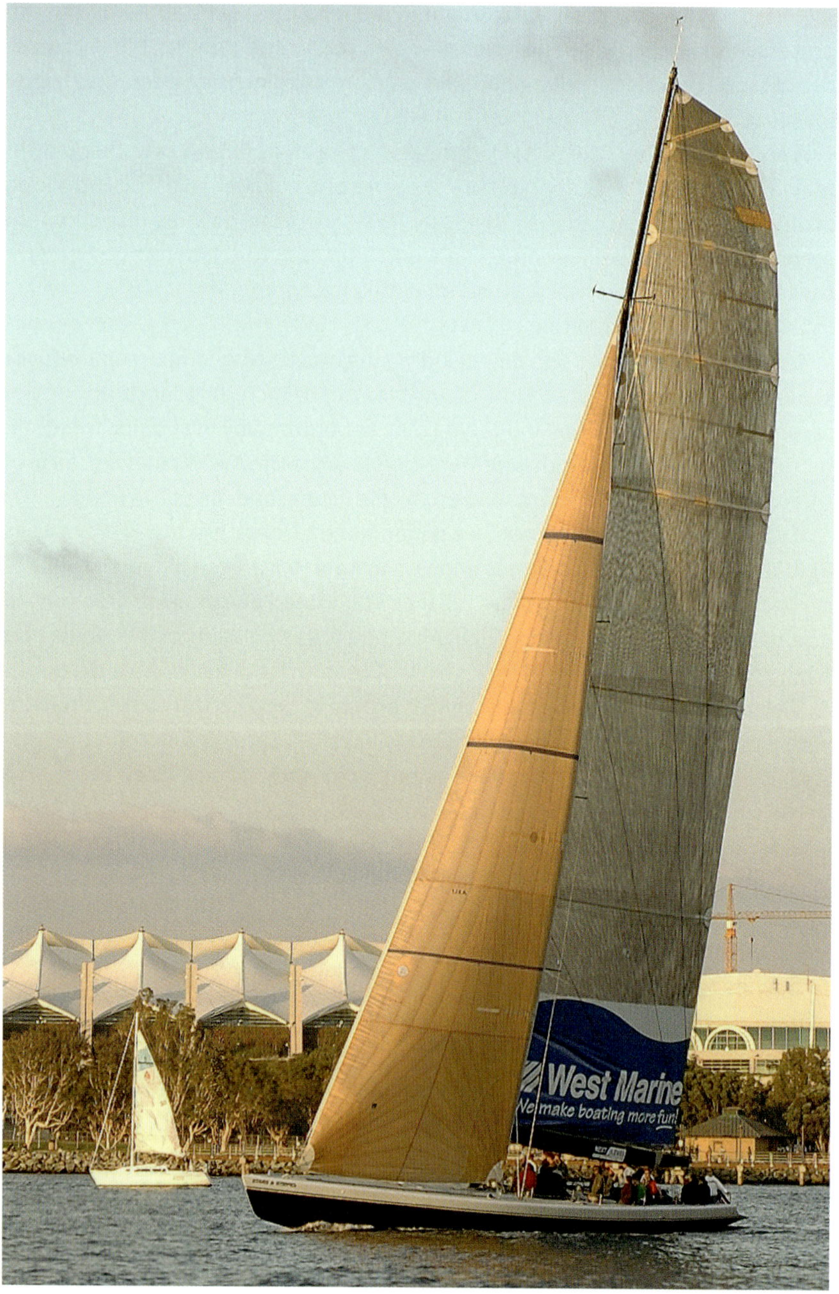

## Introduction

The electronic display screens (LCD screen and viewfinder) on the Sony NEX-7 serve two purposes. The first is to preview the subject, which helps you compose the image, check the focus, and ensure that the exposure and automatic modes are suitable for image capture. The second is to evaluate the recorded picture or movie after it has been captured. If needed, you can fine-tune the camera settings to ensure that subsequent images have the results you want.



Only one of the display screens work at any one time. The default is to have the viewfinder enabled when the camera senses the presence of something, presumably your eye, near its window. When this happens, the viewfinder turns on and the LCD screen turns off. You can view either screen with the assurance that the battery is not being drained unnecessarily.

Although they both serve the same purpose, each display has its advantages. The value of using the LCD screen is that it can be extended out from the body of the camera and tilted to face up or down so you can view from above or below the level of the camera. It also allows you to hold the camera while viewing both the subject and the back of the camera. This is an advantage when you are manipulating the camera's controls. The benefit of using the viewfinder is that it blocks the ambient light, enabling you to frame your subject when you are outdoors and the sunlight is too bright for you to view the subject on the LCD screen. A second advantage is the added steadiness gained when the camera's viewfinder is held against your eye. Be flexible and use whichever display provides the best results in a given situation.

This chapter covers how to preview and review your still pictures and movies, along with useful tools to evaluate your images and get the best results. As with everything on the NEX-7, there is often more than one way of accomplishing your goals. It is best to experiment. Over time, you will develop preferences that work well for you.

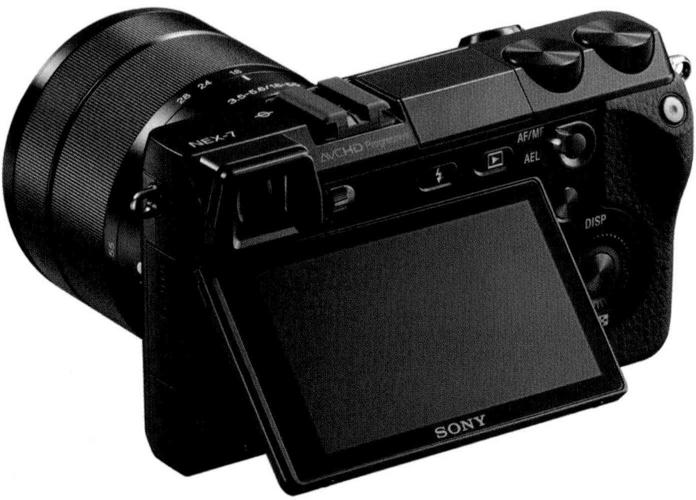


**Figure 3-1**: Tilting capability of the LCD screen

## The LCD Screen

The Sony NEX-7 uses a large, high-quality liquid crystal display (LCD), composed of 921,600 dots, located on the back of the camera (figure 3-1). It has a diagonal measurement of 3 in (7.5 cm) and is large enough to be viewed at arm's length. Unlike the viewfinder, you don't have to place the camera to your eye to see the LCD. Instead, you simply hold the camera, frame the picture, and press the shutter button.

The LCD screen's hinged display and ability to extend out from the camera body gives you more flexibility in how you hold the camera when working in cramped or awkward locations. For example, to frame a creative photograph from floor level looking up, it may be necessary to rest the camera base on the ground. With the viewfinder, or with a DSLR that does not have a tilting LCD screen, you would have to lie down behind the camera to frame and compose your subject. But the tilting LCD screen on the NEX-7 can be adjusted so the screen faces up, allowing you to look down on the framed subject from a kneeling position.

We already mentioned that a benefit of using the LCD screen is that you can see the camera commands and buttons simultaneously, making it much easier to navigate through the camera functions using either the menu or the buttons and dials. In addition, using the LCD screen makes it easier to view your framed image when the camera is mounted on a tripod.

You can adjust the brightness of the LCD monitor using the LCD Brightness command:

MENU>Setup (Main Settings)>LCD Brightness>[Auto], [Manual], [Sunny Weather]

Set the command to [Auto] to let the camera adjust the screen brightness based on the available ambient lighting. If you wish to control the screen brightness, set the command to [Manual] instead. Here you can adjust the brightness of the screen from –2 to +2 units of brightness.

If the manual control for increasing your LCD screen's brightness is inadequate, a condition that can occur on bright sunny days, you have another option. The NEX-7 has a [Sunny Weather] option on the LCD Brightness command. This brightens the screen beyond what is possible by setting the brightness to +2 on [Manual]. Of course, brightening the screen will deplete battery power, so reduce the brightness when it is no longer needed. Under conditions like this, consider using the Electronic Viewfinder as it shields the display from ambient lighting.

The camera senses which one of the electronic display screens is active at any given time, therefore the LCD Brightness command will work only if you are viewing the LCD monitor. If you attempt to set this command while looking through the viewfinder you will see an error message recommending that you use the LCD screen instead. The LCD Brightness command will not activate when you use the viewfinder.

## The Viewfinder

The Sony NEX-7's electronic viewfinder consists of a small half-inch screen of 2,359,296 dots with a magnifier. It provides a live view, with the camera settings displayed on the image prior to taking the picture. Its function corresponds to a DSLR optical viewfinder. In comparison, the Sony viewfinder provides an excellent, enlarged, and bright image, making composition easier. The viewfinder's magnifier allows you to view fine details conveniently. As described in chapter 1, you should focus the viewfinder to your eye by using the diopter adjustment dial. To do this, use the camera letter and number settings that are displayed in the viewfinder as your focus points. Using the diopter adjustment dial on the subject in Live View is less precise.

Unlike an optical viewfinder, you can display the camera's menu commands and options in the NEX-7 viewfinder, as well as graphical displays such as histograms. The control wheel, plus the left and right control dials, all function the same way as they do for the LCD screen. For example, when you review menu command settings, you can press the left or right rim, or rotate the control wheel. You can also move through the saved images by rotating the left or right control dial.

You can adjust the brightness of the viewfinder screen by using the Viewfinder Bright. command:

> MENU>Setup (Main Settings)>Viewfinder Bright.>[Auto], [Manual]



As with the LCD Brightness command, set the Viewfinder Bright. command to [Auto] to let the camera determine the screen's level of brightness. If you wish to control the screen brightness, set the command to [Manual] instead. Here you will be able to adjust the screen's brightness from -1 to +1 units of brightness.

The Viewfinder Bright. command works only when you are looking through the viewfinder. If you are setting this command while looking at the LCD screen, you will receive an error message to use the viewfinder to make the adjustments.

There may be times when the glare from ambient light is so bright that you cannot see the LCD screen clearly. In this case, use the viewfinder. Because of the juxtaposition of your eye to the viewfinder, its screen is in the shadow from your face, allowing you to see the screen in spite of bright outdoor lighting. Ironically, using the viewfinder can also be advantageous when shooting in very dimly lit conditions. For example, if you are photographing a stage production, a bright LCD screen can distract the performers and the audience. Another advantage of using the viewfinder is the stability gained by holding the camera against your face. This is invaluable when working with a long telephoto lens where the slightest tremor is magnified. Steadiness is even more critical when capturing movies, since all camera movement is recorded.

## LCD Screen versus Viewfinder

As mentioned before, you can have only the LCD screen or the viewfinder active at one time. Which one you prefer will depend on the types of pictures and movies you take, plus your personal style. When you have determined your preference, you can set the FINDER/LCD Setting command to conform to your style.

> MENU>Setup (Shooting Settings)>FINDER/LCD Setting>[Auto], [Viewfinder], [LCD Monitor]

The command's [Auto] option automatically switches between the LCD and the viewfinder. But some people find this to be annoying. For example, if your hand passes close to the viewfinder while you are using the LCD to set commands, it can turn off the LCD screen and hide the menus. Fortunately, you can turn off the automatic switching and have either the LCD or the viewfinder enabled exclusively. To do this, set the FINDER/LCD Setting command to [Viewfinder] or [LCD Monitor], depending on which screen you want active. Then only the selected screen will be active, and the other will remain dark.

## Data Display Formats

Reviewing the camera settings prior to and after recording gives you the opportunity to adjust the settings and ultimately record a better image. The following sections cover data display formats prior to and after recording a still picture or movie. Become familiar with each format. You may find that different data display formats work best with different scenarios.



### Previewing Data Display Formats

There are a maximum of nine data display formats available when you preview your images. All of them are available on the LCD screen, and only three of them are available when you use the viewfinder.

First, let's review all nine of the data display formats:

- Graphic Display (LCD only): Displays the full-size image with major shooting settings. There are two scales, one for shutter speed and the other for aperture, with the current setting indicated on the scales as a vertical bar.
- Display All Info. (LCD and viewfinder): Displays the full-size image with camera shooting settings superimposed around three of the image's borders.
- Disp. Basic Info. (viewfinder only): Displays the Shoot Mode, and exposure above and below the image.
- Big Font Size Disp. (LCD only): Displays full-size image with minimal shooting settings displayed in a large font superimposed on the top and bottom of the image.
- No Disp. Info. (LCD only): Displays the image with Shoot Mode and exposure settings.
- Live View Priority (LCD only): Displays a full-size image, Shoot Mode and the exposure settings in a vertical bar to the right of the image. Note that the navigation directions for soft key B, control wheel, and soft key C are not displayed.
- Level (LCD and viewfinder): Displays the full-size image, Shoot Mode, exposure settings, and the digital level gauge tool in the center of the screen. The gauge's indicator turns green when the camera is level horizontally and front to back.
- Histogram (LCD and viewfinder): Displays the full-size image, Shoot Mode, exposure settings, and the white live histogram in the lower right of the screen.
- For viewfinder (LCD only): Displays only camera settings without the image.

You can choose which of these nine formats will be displayed for the LCD screen. When you preview through the viewfinder, you have nothing to choose. The three viewfinder data display formats, Disp. Basic Info., Level, and Histogram, are always available. All three options display the same camera exposure data fields. Level and Histogram viewfinder data display formats have the level and histogram also displayed respectively.

How do you select which data display formats to have available when using the LCD screen to preview your images? The DISP Button(Monitor) command controls this decision.

MENU>Camera>DISP Button(Monitor)>[Graphic Display], [Display All Info.], [Big Font Size Disp.], [No Disp. Info.], [Live View Priority], [Level], [Histogram], [For viewfinder]

When you enter the DISP Button(Monitor) command, each of the data display format options are preceded by a check box. As you scroll through the options, a sample display screen shows in the lower right corner (figure 3-2). This will help you decide how the data display format will look when you preview your images on the LCD screen. Press soft key C to check or uncheck an option. You can check from one to all eight of the options. Press soft key B to save the option changes. Only the checked options will be available in preview mode.

After you select your data display formats, press the DISP button to cycle through the display formats. For example, say you select DISP Button(Monitor)>[Display All Info.], [Level], and [Histogram]. Each time you press the DISP button while previewing a framed image, you will cycle through these three display formats. If you also select [No Disp. Info.], your framed image will be displayed on the LCD screen with only the minimal data the next time you press the DISP button after viewing [Display All Info.].

There are two additional commands that can affect which data display format shows on the LCD screen or in the viewfinder.

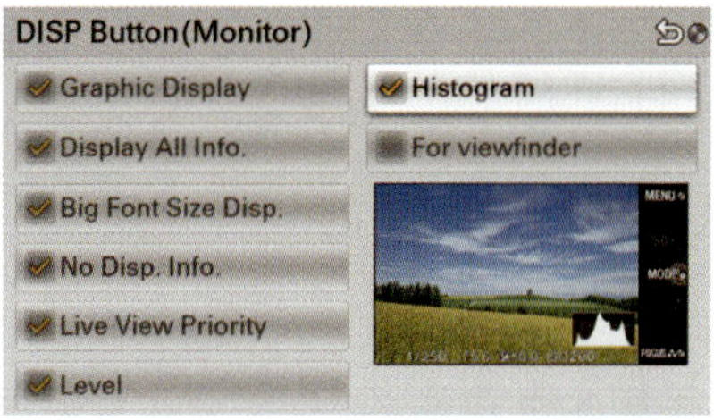


**Figure 3-2**: DISP Button(Monitor) command positioned on [Histogram]

MENU>Camera>Finder Display(DISP)>[Disp. Basic Info.], [Level], [Histogram]

MENU>Camera>LCD Display(DISP)>[Graphic Display], [Display All Info.], [Big Font Size Disp.], [No Disp. Info.], [Live View Priority], [Level], [Histogram], [For viewfinder]

So what is the purpose? In most cases you will use the DISP button to cycle through the available data display formats for both the viewfinder and the LCD screen. But sometimes you may wish to go directly to a specific display format, such as one with the histogram or the level, or maybe you want to see the name of the current data display format. You can execute the Finder Display(DISP) command or the LCD Display(DISP) command to view the name or change the data display format in the viewfinder or on the LCD screen, respectively.

Since the viewfinder has a fixed number of formats that are always available, the Finder Display(DISP) command has the same format options (figure 3-3). Since the DISP Button(Monitor) has eight options to choose from, the LCD Display(DISP) command will contain only the options that are checked in the DISP Button(Monitor) command. In other words, if the DISP Button(Monitor) command has only the [Histogram] option checked (figure 3-4a), the LCD Display(DISP) command will have only [Histogram] option listed (figure 3-4b). If you also check [Level] in DISP Button(Monitor), then [Level] will be added to the LCD Display(DISP) command's available options.

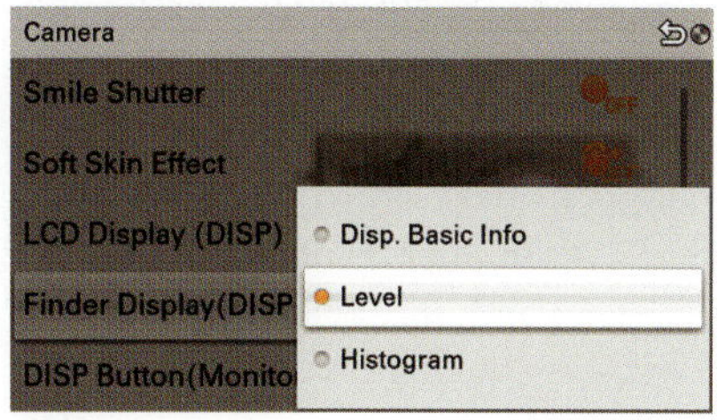


**Figure 3-3**: Finder Display(DISP) command positioned on [Level]

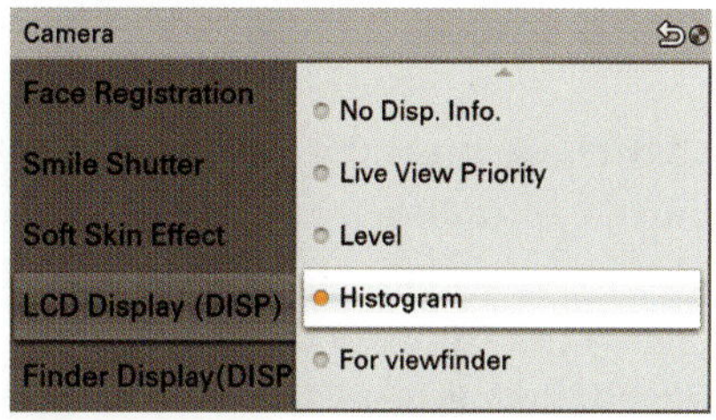


**Figure 3-4a**: LCD Display(DISP) command with only the [Histogram] option

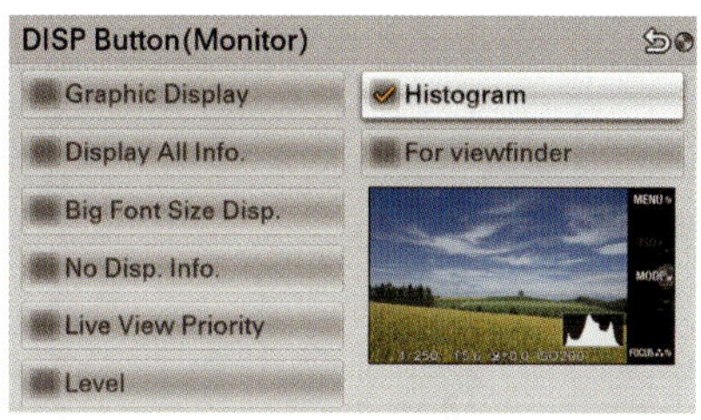


**Figure 3-4b**: DISP Button(Monitor) command with only [Histogram] checked

Important points:

- When you are previewing through the LCD screen, the DISP button cycles through all of the checked DISP Button(Monitor) options in order. When you are previewing through the viewfinder, the DISP button cycles through the [Disp. Basic Info.], [Level], and [Histogram] viewfinder display formats.
- The DISP button will cycle through however many data display formats have been checked. But not all of the display formats can be seen in some of the shooting modes. In some situations, the data display slot is filled with a different data display format:
  - The [Histogram] display format slot will be filled with the [No. Disp. Info.] format for the 3D Sweep Panorama and Sweep Panorama shooting modes.
  - The [Graphic Display] display format slot will be filled with the [No. Disp. Info.] format for the 3D Sweep Panorama and Sweep Panorama shooting modes.
  - The [For viewfinder] display format slot will be filled with the [Display All Info.] format for the 3D Sweep Panorama and Sweep Panorama shooting modes.

## Reviewing Still Picture Data Display Formats

When you review your still pictures, there are three data display formats available:

1. Image with recording data (figure 3-5a)
2. Image with histograms (figure 3-5b)
3. Image only, no data (figure 3-5c)

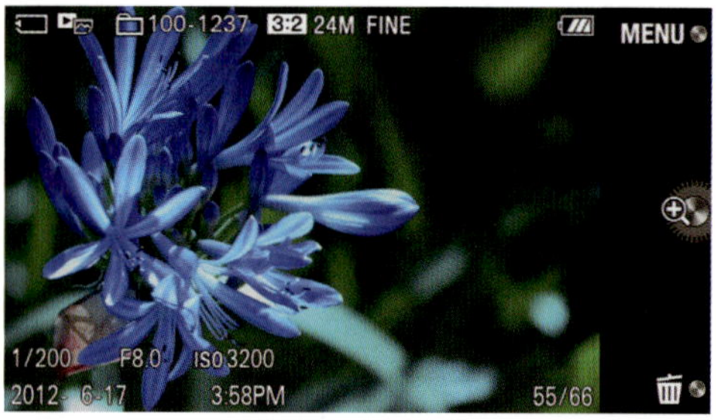


**Figure 3-5a**: Data display with recording data

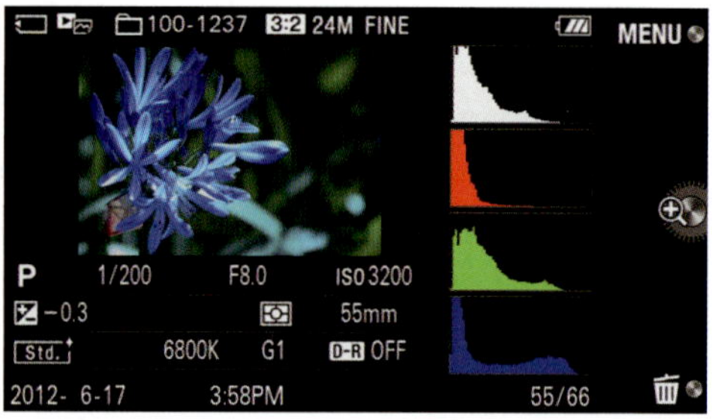


**Figure 3-5b**: Data display with histograms

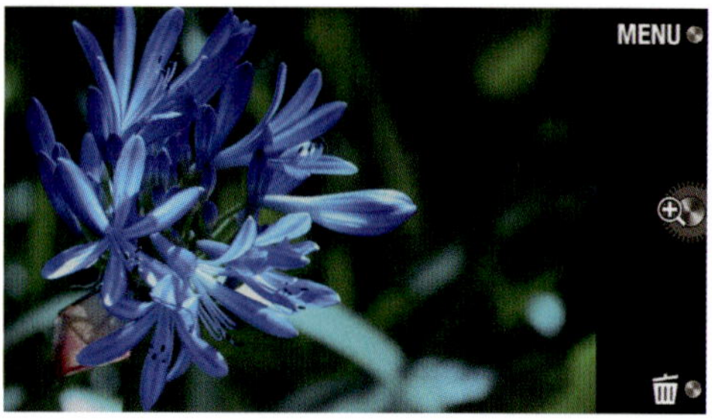


**Figure 3-5c**: Data display with saved image only

After you press the Playback button to review your saved pictures, cycle through the three display formats by pressing the DISP button.

Each display layout has its benefits. The recording data consists of the camera settings used to produce the image. This is invaluable when analyzing which camera settings work and which might need to be adjusted to improve the next shot.

The histogram view displays the intensity range of the luminosity and the three color channels (red, blue, and green) of the recorded picture. Thus, you can see if the sensor failed to capture all of the light and color intensities of the scene. This is important because if the full range of all colors were not captured, a color shift may be introduced if you change the brightness of the image during post-processing.

You will also see any overexposed, or blown-out, areas blinking from white to black, and any underexposed, dark areas blinking from black to white. This is an excellent way to determine which areas of the image were not recorded accurately by the sensor: highlights will be predominantly white with few intensity transitions, and underexposed areas will display noise and no detail.

## Reviewing Movie Data Display Formats

Unlike still pictures, only two data display formats are available when reviewing movies. After you press the Playback button, press the DISP button to cycle through the following formats:

- Movie with recording data
- Movie without recording data



The selected data display format is applied through the playing back of the movie. After the selected movie has completed, the camera will continue to play back each subsequent movie until all of them have been played back or you terminate the playback mode.

You do not have to play all the movies to find a specific movie. Remember, you start movie playback by pressing soft key C, and pause it by again pressing soft key C. You will see a prompt for this on the LCD screen. When you pause the image, you can jump to the first frame of a different movie by pressing either the left rim of the control wheel for the previous movie or by pressing its right rim for the following movie. Each press of the rim will jump to the next movie's first frame. At this point, you can see an overview of all the movies you've taken (thumbnail of their first frame) by pressing the bottom rim of the control wheel. This displays the image playback selection screen (figure 3-6). You can then select which movie you want by selecting the thumbnail of the first frame and by pressing soft key C (OK).

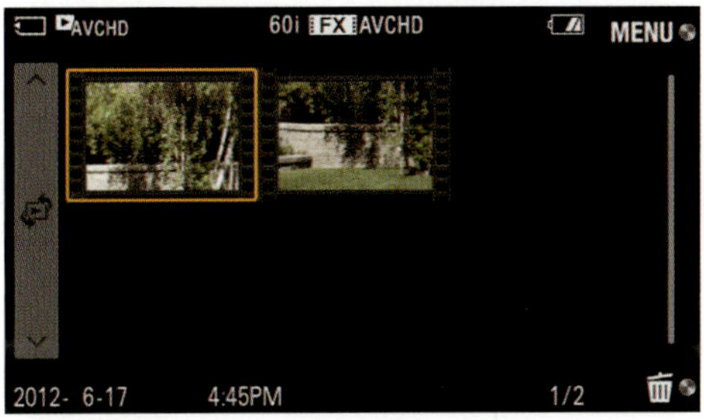

**Figure 3-6**: Image playback selection screen

# Preview Images

## Compositional Controls

In addition to data, the camera can project lines and grids onto the screen to aid you with composition. These overlays can help you align and frame your pictures and movies. They are not recorded or visible when the file is played back.

Use the following command to set these lines and grids:

MENU>Setup (Shooting Settings)>Grid Line>[Rule of 3rds Grid], [Square Grid], [Diag. + Square Grid], [Off]

The three grid line options each have specific patterns and benefits. The [Rule of 3rds Grid] pattern consists of a 3 x 3 array of rectangles (figure 3-7). This pattern allows you to position the main subject one-third or two-thirds of the way from any side of the screen. The [Square Grid] pattern divides the screen into an array of 6 x 4 squares to help you make sure the picture is well balanced and not tilted. The final pattern, [Diag. + Square Grid], divides the screen into an array of 4 x 4 rectangles with diagonal lines from the center to each corner, which helps you center the image in the frame. No grid lines are shown when the command is set to [Off].

All three patterns are useful in architectural photography and in scenic shots with a horizon. They help you avoid canting the subject by providing an alignment guide for buildings and the horizon. The pattern you use depends on where you wish to position the subject within your picture. Perhaps most importantly, all of the grid line display options correctly show the borders for your movies.

When you press the Movie button, you will see your screen change to accurately represent the borders of the movie you are recording. This will appear as a slight increase in magnification on your display screen, and a bit of your subject will be chopped off. To obviate this, use the grid mode. Prior to initiating a movie, the grid lines include a bracket mark (short horizontal line) just below and above each of the four corners (figure 3-8). These bracket marks demarcate the edges of your movie frame, and you use them to frame your subject for your movie.

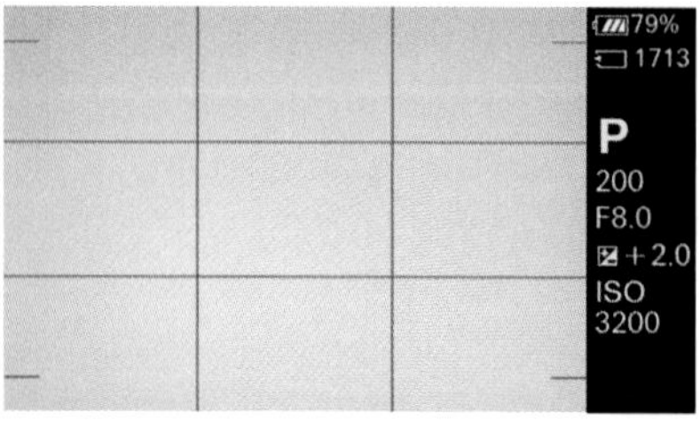


**Figure 3-7**: Rule of 3rds Grid

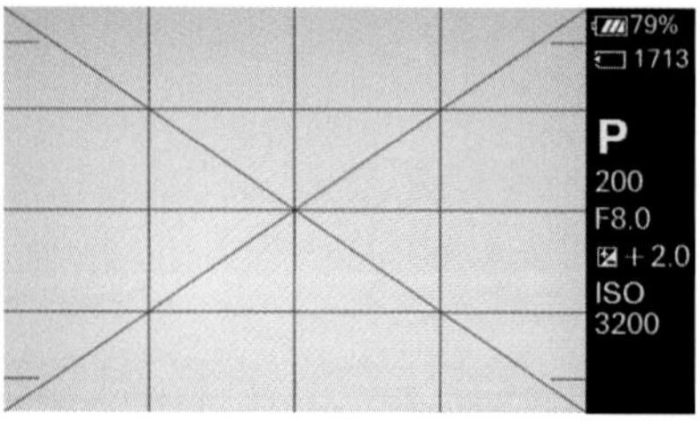


**Figure 3-8**: Grid line movie brackets with the Diag. + Square Grid

## Review Recorded Images

### Displaying Recorded Images

After you have recorded a still picture or a movie, you should review the results. This will give you the opportunity to replace the picture or movie with a better one. There are a couple of tools to help you do this. Keep in mind that when we refer to still pictures, we include both types of panorama shots.



### Auto Review or No Auto Review

The Auto Review command allows you to view a picture immediately after it has been taken and before you take the next picture. You can choose to display the picture for 2, 5, or 10 seconds, or you can eliminate the review by using the [Off] option.

MENU>Setup (Shooting Settings)>Auto Review>[10 Sec], [5 Sec], [2 Sec], [Off]

You will be automatically returned to Live View when the display time has elapsed or when the shutter button is pressed.

There are times when you will find it advantageous to turn this command to [Off] so the camera will return to Live View immediately after taking a picture. This eliminates any interruption to picture taking and enables you to continue viewing your object within the display screen. This is very important when shooting action or sports photographs where you need to follow a player. For example, you might be photographing a basketball player who just received a pass and needs to run toward the basket for a layup. An interruption to Live View could cause you to lose a perfect opportunity for your next picture.

### Reviewing Files with the Playback Button

You can review your still pictures using either the Slide Show command, discussed later in this chapter, or the Playback button, which puts the camera in playback mode. Movies and MP4 files can be reviewed only with the Playback button.

The type of file displayed—still pictures or movies—depends on two things. When you press the Playback button, the last type of image recorded dictates the images that will be displayed. If the last image recorded was a movie, only movies will display. If the last image recorded was a still picture, then only still pictures will display.

To select which type of image will be displayed the next time you press the Playback button, use the following menu command:

MENU>Playback>View Mode>[Folder View(Still)], [Folder View(MP4)], [AVCHD View]

Initially, each option displays the selected folder's saved images in groups of six. Rotate the control wheel to navigate through the images. The vertical bar on the right side of the screen changes as you move through the images, indicating the relative position of the displayed images within the total number of images saved in the viewed folder. The vertical View Mode bar on the left side controls the View Mode. For example, if you are displaying movie files and now want to review still pictures, navigate to the View Mode bar and press soft key C. When the View Mode menu displays, select either [Folder View(Still)], [Folder View(MP4)], or [AVCHD(View)] and press soft key C again.

Perhaps the easiest way to return to the right folder is the brute force strategy of snapping a quick image. If you snap a still picture, you will reset the folder type to playing back still pictures. Similarly, if you quickly start a movie and then stop it, you will have reset the Playback button's folder to movie files. Either way, keep in mind that saved files are reviewed based on file type.

### Playing Back Still Pictures

When you know you are positioned to display still images, press the Playback button. Either the last recorded or the last played back still picture will be displayed first. Rotate the control wheel to the right or left to display the next or previous saved picture, respectively. You can also press the right or left rim of the control wheel to advance to the next saved picture or to return to the previous saved picture. Note that the displayed images wrap around as you continue to rotate the wheel. Remember to use the DISP button to view the recorded data of the images through the different data display formats.

### Playing Back Panoramic Pictures

Both Sweep Panorama and 3D Sweep Panorama images play back differently than other still pictures. The image is displayed (figure 3-9a), but when you press the control wheel, the image is enlarged and in order to show its extent, the camera sweeps

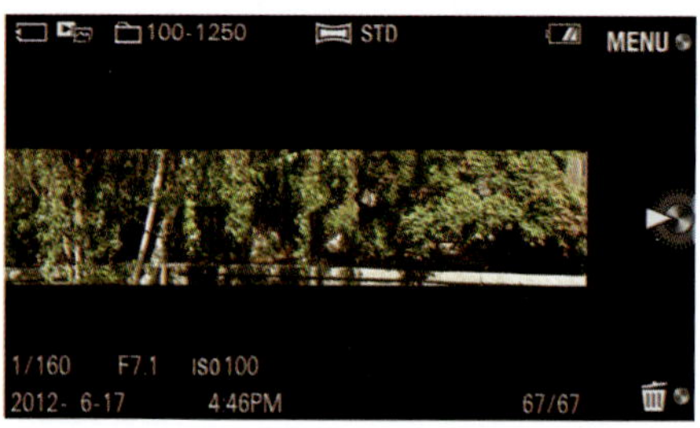


**Figure 3-9a**: Sweep Panorama playback; initial and final display

across the screen in the direction it was recorded (figure 3-9b). This gives you a closer view of the image and you can study its fine details. After the camera has played back the sweep the magnification is reduced so the full image is displayed again, as seen in figure 3-9a.

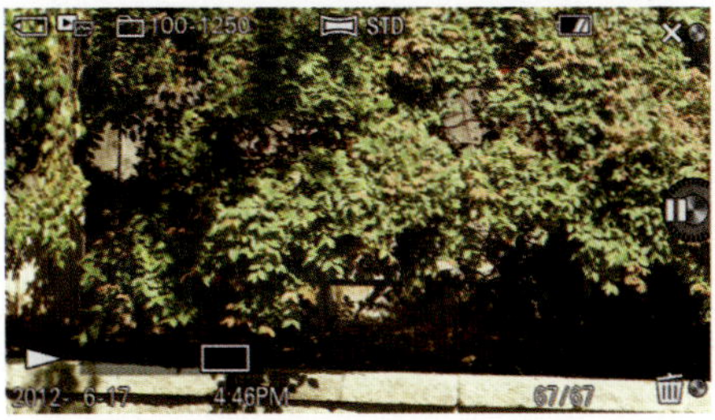

**Figure 3-9b**: During the playback sweep portion of a Sweep Panorama image

### Playing Back MP4 or AVCHD Movies

Only the first frame of a movie is seen as you cycle through the memory card files in playback mode. Press soft key C to start playing the movie. Pressing the DISP button toggles between just playing back the movie (figure 3-10a) and playing back the movie with operational information displayed, including the playback status, the playback bar (indicating the playback position), the number of seconds played, and icons representing rewind, pause, fast forward, etc. (figure 3-10b). You can also change the volume of the movie by pressing the bottom portion of the control wheel (figure 3-10c). Table 3-1 lists the operational steps to review your movies and change the volume.

Keep in mind that playing back a movie can mean automatically playing back multiple specific View Mode movies stored on the memory card. For example, if you have three saved AVCHD movies and the camera is positioned on the first one, initiating playback will play it and the two subsequent movies in succession.

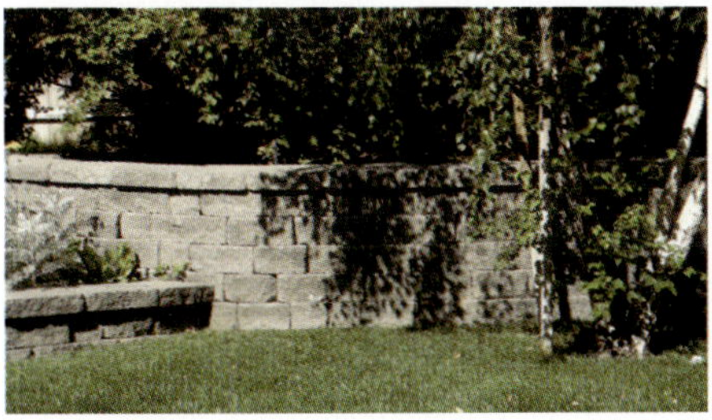
**Figure 3-10a**: Movie played back with no data displayed

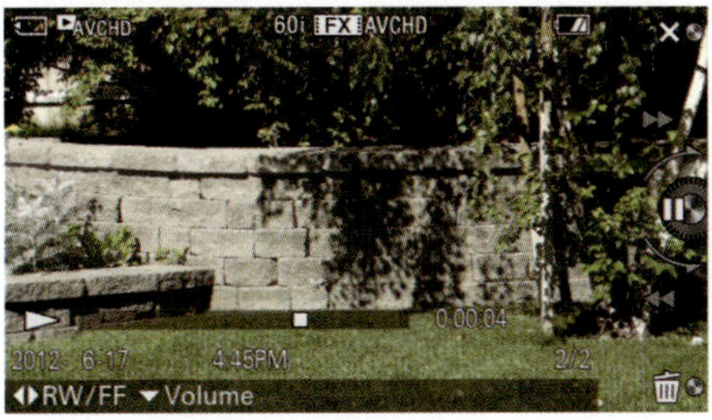

**Figure 3-10b**: Movie played back with operational data and controls displayed

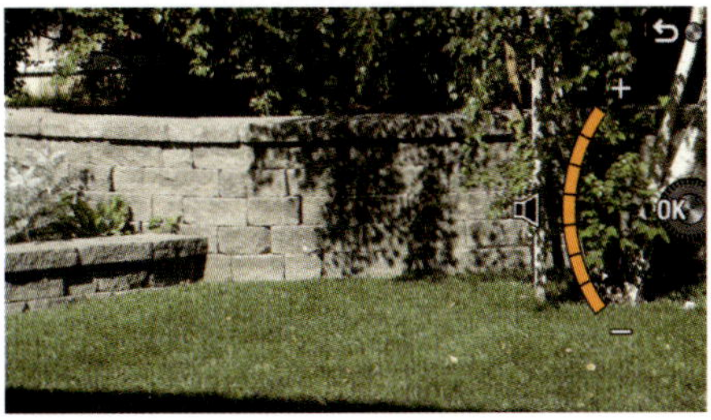

**Figure 3-10c**: Volume control vertical scale displayed

However, you do not have to completely play the first movie to see the subsequent recorded movies. While the first movie is playing, press Pause (soft key C). Press the right rim of the control wheel to advance to the next movie. Instead of the movie playing automatically, you will be positioned at the first frame. You can move to the first frames of each of your movies by sequentially pressing the right rim of the control wheel. If you wish to view a previous movie, press the left rim of the control wheel. When you are ready to play back the movie, press soft key C.

| MP4 and AVCHD Movie Playback Navigation | |
|---|---|
| **Function** | **Control Wheel and Control Dial Operations** |
| Play/pause | Press soft key C to initiate playback of the movie. While the movie is playing, press soft key C to pause it. Soft key C toggles between these two functions. |
| Stop | Press the shutter button to terminate movie playback and return to Live View. |
| Fast forward | While the movie is playing, press the right rim of the control wheel. The movie plays forward by skipping several frames at once and therefore has a jerky look. Playback will continue through all of the movies after the current movie. |
| Fast rewind | While the movie is playing, press the left rim of the control wheel. The movie plays back by skipping several frames at once and therefore has a jerky look. Playback will continue through all of the movies before the current movie at which time, the saved movies will start playing forward at normal speed. |
| Slow forward | While the movie is playing, press soft key C to pause it. Then rotate the control wheel clockwise by one click. The movie will start playing forward slowly. Playback will continue through all of the movies after the current movie. |
| Slow rewind | While the movie is playing, press soft key C to pause it. Then rotate the control wheel counterclockwise by one click. The movie plays backwards slowly several frames at a time and has a jerky look. Playback will continue through all of the movies before the current movie at which time, the saved movies will start playing forward at normal speed. |
| Reduce or increase volume level | Press the bottom rim of the control wheel to initiate volume change. When the volume control vertical scale displays on the right side of the screen, press the bottom rim of the control wheel to decrease the volume, or press the top rim of the control wheel to increase the volume. Volume setting is retained even if camera is turned off. |
| Display operational information | During playback, press the DISP button to toggle between displaying only the movie or the movie and the following information: playback status, playback bar, number of seconds played, date recorded, the number of the movie file that is currently playing (out of the total number of movie files), and available operational controls. Note that different operational controls display depending on whether the movie is playing or paused. |

**Table 3-1**: MP4 and AVCHD movie playback navigation

### Reviewing Multiple Pictures and Movies

You can view up to 6 or 12 images within a folder at one time. Which number you select is controlled by the Image Index command:

MENU>Playback>Image Index>[6 Images], [12 Images]

After you select an option, you can view the same number of images by pushing the Image Index button (bottom rim of the control wheel) while in playback mode (figure 3-11).

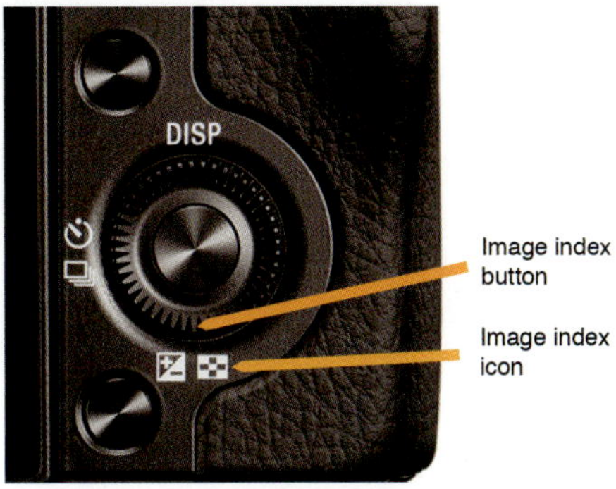

**Figure 3-11**: Image Index button

Regardless of how many images are displayed, you can rotate or press the rims of the control wheel to scroll and navigate through all the images. Press soft key C to view the highlighted image. You can continue to scroll through the images one by one or return to the multiple image view by pressing the Image Index button again.

Keep in mind that you will view images only from the last folder in which you have viewed or saved images, which is the View Mode command's current folder value. The Image Index screen is used to switch between folders. Navigate with the control wheel to the left View Mode vertical bar (figure 3-12). Press soft key C to activate the View Mode command. The current folder is highlighted. Select a different folder type and press soft key C. The Image Index screen will display the saved images within that folder type.

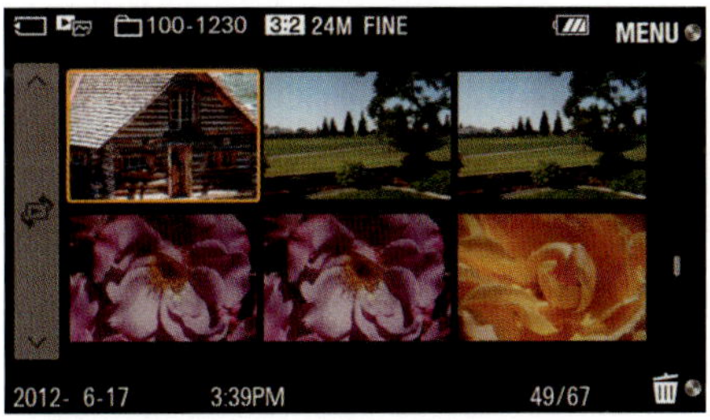

**Figure 3-12**: Image Index screen with View Mode vertical bar

You may see fewer than 6 or 12 images displayed when you first enter the Image Index screen. This is due to one of two things. Either there are fewer than 6 or 12 images saved within the folder, or you are at the end of the folder, seeing the last few saved images that can be displayed. You will be able to determine which scenario it is by looking at the bottom right corner of the screen where the highlighted image number, out of the total number of images, is displayed (figure 3-13).

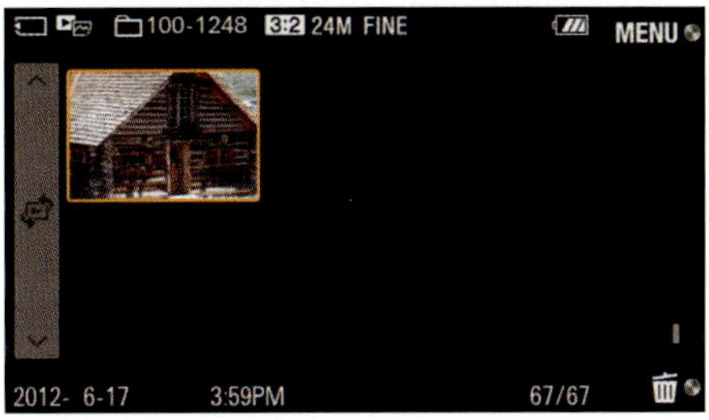

**Figure 3-13**: Image Index screen partially filled

## Reviewing Still Pictures with the Slide Show Command

The Slide Show command plays back all of the still pictures on the camera's memory card in sequence, starting with either the last played back or the last recorded image. The slide show can be played back on either your camera's display screen or on a compatible TV by joining it to your camera with an HDMI Type C (Mini) connector. You cannot include movies as part of a slide show, so this command is enabled only when the View Mode command is set to [Folder View(Still)].

To build and initiate a slide show, navigate to the following command:

MENU>Playback>Slide Show>[Repeat], [Interval], [Image Type]

After you enter the Slide Show command, you will see three submenus: the current settings for Repeat, Interval, and Image Type; the [OK] option; and the [Exit] option (figure 3-14).

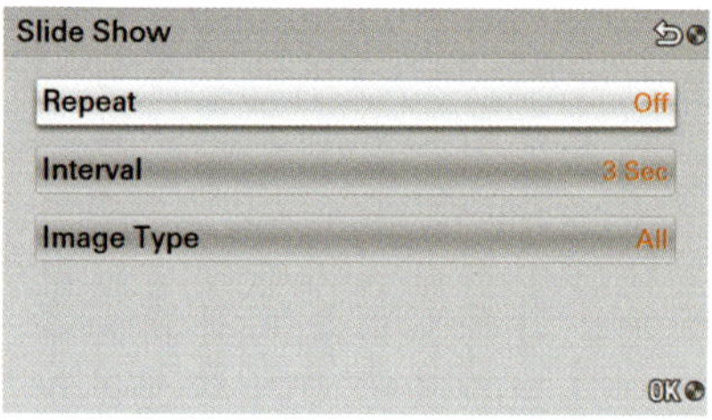


**Figure 3-14**: Slide Show command options

The Repeat [On] option enables the slide show to loop back through the pictures continuously. The [Off] value executes the slide show only once and then exits to Live View.

MENU>Playback>Slide Show>Repeat>[On], [Off]

The Interval option allows you to set the length of time each picture is displayed, ranging from as short as 1 to as long as 30 seconds.

MENU>Playback>Slide Show>Interval>[1 Sec], [3 Sec], [5 Sec], [10 Sec], [30 Sec]

Recording and viewing 3-D images is very popular. The Image Type option allows you to differentiate what the slide show contains. If you select [All] and you are viewing your images on your camera or on a TV that is incapable of 3-D, the images will be displayed in 2-D. When you attach the camera to a 3-D compatible HDTV and select [All], all of the saved still pictures display, including the 3-D images as 3-D. Or you can select the [Display 3D Only] option to present a slide show of only 3-D pictures. You will need to get 3-D glasses to see them.

MENU>Playback>Slide Show>Image Type>[All], [Display 3D Only]

Although the [Display 3D Only] option is displayed, it is enabled only when you have attached the camera to a 3-D compatible TV. To initiate the slide show, select the [OK] option (soft key B). Select the [Exit] option to exit the Slide Show command.

After a slide show begins, you have a couple of additional options. Press the right or left rim of the control wheel to navigate forward or backward through the slide show. You can also rotate the control wheel clockwise or counterclockwise to get the same results.



To terminate the slide show, either press the shutter button halfway to return to Live View or press soft key C to enter playback mode. At this point, the still picture data display formats are at your disposal when you press the DISP button. There is no way to pause the slide show.

### Create a Movie Show

Although the Slide Show command only plays back your still pictures, you can still see your movies played back on your camera or TV. Set the View Mode to [AVCHD View] and press the Playback button. Scroll through the movie files and highlight the movie file that you want to use as the first movie in the show. Press soft key C to start playing the movie. Since the playback continues to play each of the movie files, you will, in essence, have a movie show. You can do the same thing with your MP4 files by changing the View Mode to [Folder View(MP4)] and initiating playback.

Just like when you use the Slide Show command to view your still pictures, this method of viewing all your saved movies only is a quick way to determine their value when you are away from your computer. You will be able to do much more with your saved movies if you transfer them to your computer and create a show from there.

Creating a slide show with your camera is not for everyone. The command plays back all of the saved still pictures—the good and the bad. With that said, this is a quick way to view each one without having to manually scroll through them. A more satisfactory solution for presenting a slide show is to download your images to your computer and use software to create the shows. This way you can combine images from multiple memory cards, order the images to your liking, add image transitions, and maybe even add music, depending on the software you are using.

Keep in mind that the Slide Show command only includes still images saved on the inserted memory card. Therefore, if you need a permanent show, you must download your pictures to your computer and use third-party software to build a new slide show.

## Zooming In on Recorded Still Images

Just reviewing a recorded picture is not always enough to determine if it's a keeper. Sometimes you need to magnify the image to see if its fine details are recorded. Although you can't enlarge any movie files, you can enlarge all types of still pictures including panoramas. For non-panorama still pictures, press soft key C while in playback mode. Figure 3-15 shows the Magnifier icon superimposed on the control wheel.

Panorama pictures work a bit differently. When playing back the panorama, you must first pause the playback by pressing soft key C. At that point, the magnifying icon displayed is associated with soft key B.

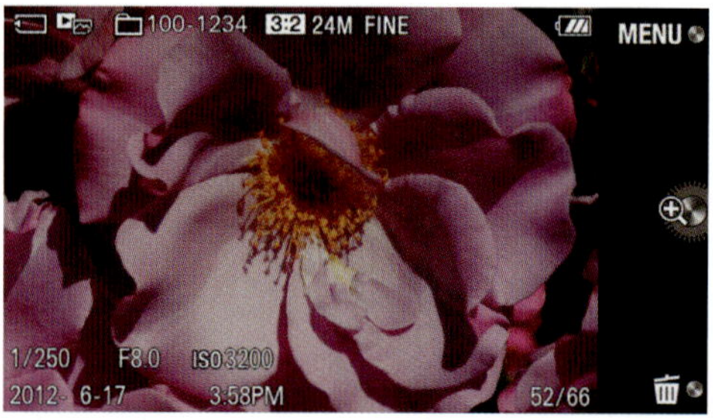


**Figure 3-15**: Magnifier icon superimposed on the control wheel

After the image is enlarged, a white box containing a picture of the original image is superimposed in the lower quadrant of the screen. Within this is a small orange box indicating the portion of the original image that is enlarged (figure 3-16). Each initial time you enlarge an image, the enlarged portion will be at the center of the picture.

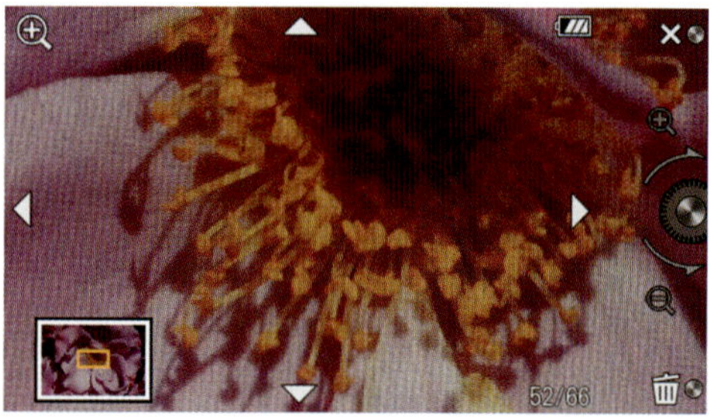


**Figure 3-16**: Magnified image with original image box superimposed

The amount the image is initially enlarged depends on the image size (table 3-2).

| Image Size | Magnification Scale |
|---|---|
| L | 1.0x to 16.7x |
| M | 1.0x to 11.8x |
| S | 1.0x to 8.3x |

**Table 3-2**: Played back image enlargement scale

Rotate either of the control dials or the control wheel to zoom in or zoom out of the picture. Four arrows surrounding the enlarged image indicate the directions in which you can move the displayed portion by pressing a corresponding rim of the control wheel.

You can also enlarge the image after you entered playback mode but before you have started playing back the picture by entering the Enlarge Image command:

MENU>Playback>Enlarge Image



This works the same way as entering playback mode and pressing soft key C to enlarge the image.

## Evaluating Exposure with Histograms

A histogram is a tool for evaluating exposure. It's a graphical representation of the range and distribution of light intensity values recorded by the sensor. Intensity values are represented on the horizontal axis (black to white), and the numbers of pixels are represented on the vertical axis.

Theoretically, a histogram has the shape of a classic bell curve, where the maximum is near the center, indicating that the brightness level of most pixels is in the middle—not too bright, not too dark. Practically, however, a histogram's shape may be distorted and not symmetrical. Figure 3-17 shows three histogram plots taken from the Sony NEX-7 LCD screen.

The left histogram indicates that the image is underexposed, meaning that not enough light is hitting the sensor; the middle histogram shows a properly exposed image; and the right histogram indicates that the image is overexposed, meaning that too much light is hitting the sensor.

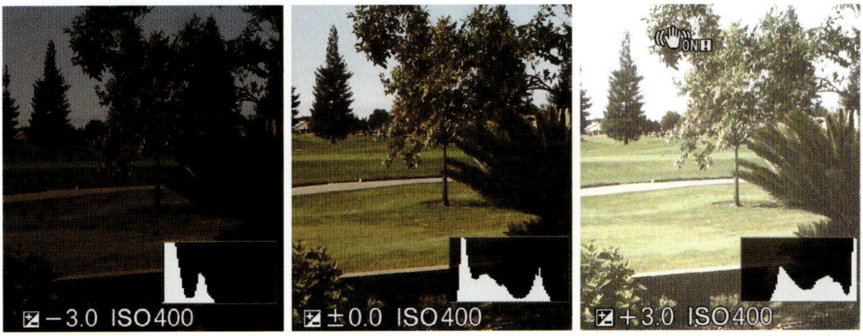


**Figure 3-17**: Histogram examples of an image that is underexposed, properly exposed, and overexposed

As you do more photography, you will notice that many histograms have multiple peaks, none of which are centered on the horizontal axis. This does not necessarily indicate poor exposure. Instead, you should watch for large numbers of pixels appearing at the extreme ends of the graph. If the histogram is skewed to the right, it indicates overexposure. If the curve piles up on the right side of the horizontal axis, then the number of pixels being fully saturated by light is increasing. These pixel outputs are at a maximum and they report the maximum white output. If the number of pixels is high, then it indicates they may be contiguous and this area of the sensor is fully saturated with light. Within this area, the bright areas are clipped. The photosites are fully saturated so there is no variation in brightness between photosites. They are recorded and saved as regions of absolute white. Conversely, if the histogram is skewed to the left and piles up against the left side of the horizontal axis, it indicates underexposure. The darkest regions of the scene are not being recorded, and they will exhibit increased noise. Either way, you will have problems—at the extreme right, the image will have burned-out highlights; at the extreme left, the image will have black shadows that lack detail.

The Sony NEX-7 displays a histogram when you preview your shot so you can adjust the camera settings prior to taking the picture. It displays a histogram again when you play back the picture so you can evaluate the results.

### Histograms in Preview Mode

To display the histogram during preview, make sure the Histogram data display format box (figure 3-18) is checked in the DISP Button(Monitor) command covered earlier in this chapter.

A histogram will not be displayed when you preview movies or panoramas.

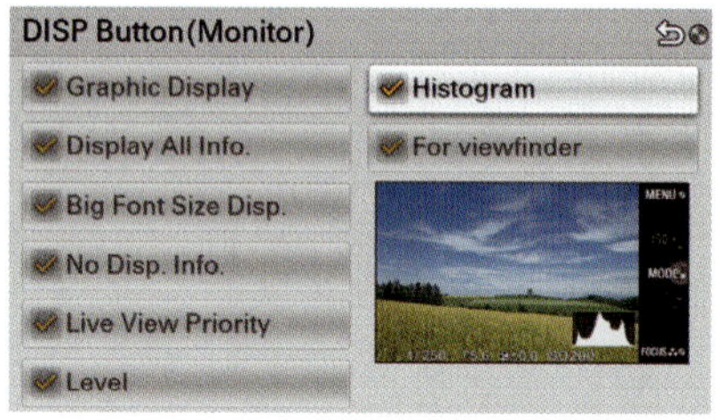


**Figure 3-18**: Histogram box checked in DISP Button(Monitor) command

Keep in mind that a histogram represents how the camera is measuring light at the current moment. It will change when the lighting changes or when you change the camera's settings or reframe the image. The live histogram is only an approximation. You can obtain more information by studying histograms during image review. For example, you can see how the color channels responded to your exposure. Also, the live histogram cannot show the results of a flash exposure. You will have to look at the histograms saved with the image files to determine the effects of using a flash.

### Histograms in Playback Mode

Histograms also allow you to evaluate an image exposure in playback mode after it has been recorded. Here, along with the overall white histogram, you will have additional color channel histograms (red, green, and blue) to help you further evaluate the image (figure 3-19). When you view individual color channel histograms, look for the curve shifted to the left or the right. This will let you know if a specific color is under- or overexposed, respectively.



Studying color channels is important because red, green, and blue channels have different sensitivities to light. If one channel is over- or underexposed, as evidenced by its histogram, your picture may take on a color cast. The luminosity (white) histogram may miss this detail. Luminosity is, at best, an average of light intensities, which is made up of intensities from the red, green, and blue photosites. For example, underexposed images show intensity values accumulating and spiking on the left border of the graph. This can be corrected by reshooting with an increased exposure. The reverse is true for overexposure.

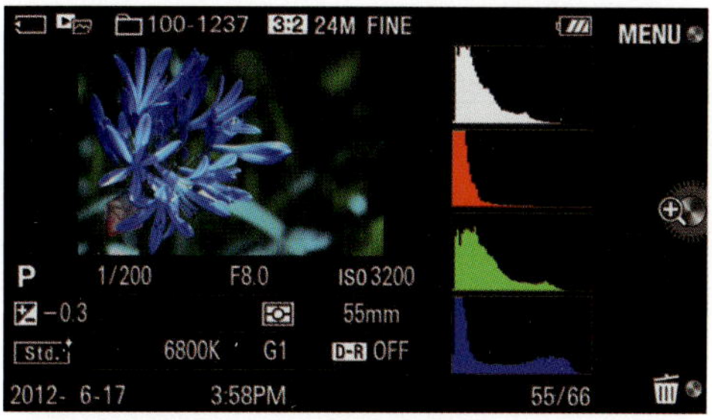


**Figure 3-19**: Histograms when reviewing a picture

## Protecting Saved Pictures and Movies

Have you ever intended to save a picture on your memory card and then inadvertently deleted it? It's frustrating when this occurs. The Protect command guarantees this won't happen when you tag the images you do not want to delete with the Delete command.

MENU>Playback>Protect>[Multiple Img.], [Cancel All Images], [Cancel All AVCHD view files], [Cancel All Movies(MP4)]

The [Multiple Img.] option always displays, but the cancel options depend on which View Mode folder is set:

- [Cancel All Images]: Displayed when View Mode is still pictures
- [Cancel All AVCHD view files]: Displayed when View Mode is AVCHD movies
- [Cancel All Movies(MP4)]: Displayed when View Mode is MP4

1. Use the [Multiple Img.] option to select images to protect. The saved images are displayed with a check box on the left side.
2. Scroll through the images with the control wheel. Press soft key C to indicate that the image should be protected. A check mark is entered in the box. To uncheck it, press soft key C again.
3. Press soft key A to exit the displayed images. Select [OK] to save the Protect indicators.

There are two ways to unprotect images:

1. Reenter the Protect command, select the [Multiple Img.] option, and uncheck the boxes one at a time.
2. Execute the available cancel option: [Cancel All Images], [Cancel All AVCHD view files], or [Cancel All Movies(MP4)].

Important points:

- The Protect command is enabled only if there is at least one image stored on the memory card.
- Protected images are not protected when a card is formatted. All image and movie files will be deleted when you reformat the memory card using the Format command.

## Deleting Saved Pictures and Movies

Not every picture or movie will be a keeper. As you view the saved images on the camera, you may want to delete one or more.

There are multiple ways to delete files. One way is to use the Delete button to delete one image at a time while in playback mode. The Delete function screen will be displayed with OK (soft key C) and Exit (soft key B) options. Press the OK button to delete the file, or press the Exit button to close the Delete function menu.

Another way to delete image files is to use the Delete command in the Playback menu. This method allows you to delete multiple images at the same time.

MENU>Playback>Delete>[Multiple Img.], [All in Folder]

The [Multiple Img.] option will display saved images one at a time with a check box on both the left and right side of the screen, if the file is unprotected. Use the control wheel or either of the control dials to scroll through the saved images. Press soft key C to check the box and mark the saved image for deletion. Press the OK button (soft key B) when you have selected all those images you want deleted. Press the OK button (soft key C) to complete the deletion process. Upon completion, you are returned to playback mode. Figure 3-20 shows the Delete screen with an image selected for deletion.

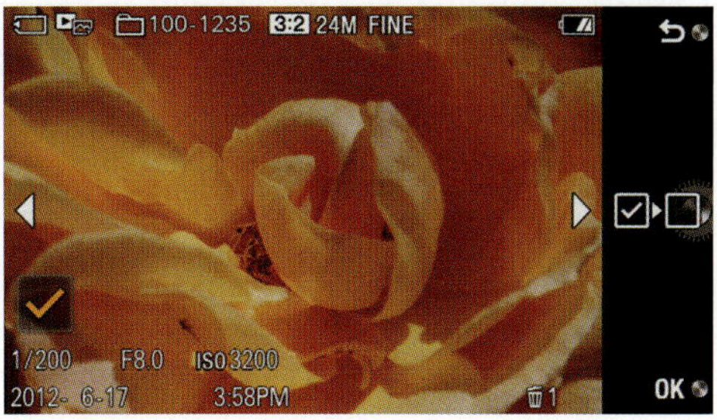


**Figure 3-20**: Image selected for deletion. Note the checked boxes on the left and right.

When the [All in Folder] option is selected, the follow message will be displayed along with the Exit (soft key A) and OK (soft key B) button icons: "Delete all images in this folder?" The folder name will also be shown.

The folder represents still pictures, AVCHD or MP4 movie files. Press the OK button to delete all of the images in the displayed folder. Press the Exit button to exit the Delete process. The Delete function does not erase files that are protected.

A third method is to reformat the memory card to delete all saved files regardless of file type:

MENU>Setup (Memory Card Tool)>Format>[OK], [Exit]

Executing this command will delete all stored files (even protected files) on the memory card.

Important points:

- The Delete command is enabled only if there is at least one image stored on the memory card.
- When you delete a saved file, it is permanently gone from the memory card.

## Working Outside the Camera

### Overview

There are many ways to view and manage your pictures and movies outside the camera. You can play them as slide shows on your computer or TV, print the pictures, e-mail them, and add them to your personal website. As technology evolves and new inventions are developed, you will most likely want to move your pictures and movies to these new arenas.

The technology you use depends on your equipment and software, as well as your level of knowledge. Rather than go into the details of how to use various technologies, we recommend that you consult your equipment and software manuals, along with their corresponding websites, for specific information on how to accomplish your goals.

### Downloading Pictures and Movies to Your Computer

Eventually you will want to download your pictures and movies from your camera's memory card to another device, most likely your computer, and then delete them from your memory card. Sony supplies Image Data Converter and PMB software to help you manage your files on your computer and create lasting files for you to share and view. Of course, you can use third-party software instead, such as Apple iPhoto (still photographs) or iMovie (movies), or Adobe Photoshop Elements.

There are two ways to download your picture and movie files to your computer. The first way is to use the supplied USB cable. Insert the cable into the mini-USB port on the camera and into the USB port of your computer. Typically, if you have installed Sony's Image Data Converter and PMB software on your computer, a prompt will pop up on your computer monitor with options to copy the camera files to your computer. This is a straightforward process, but it does consume camera battery power to move the files. If you deplete your battery during the download, your files may be corrupted and lost. If you use this download method, make sure you have a fully charged battery.

The second way is to download the files directly from the memory card. You can remove the card from your camera and insert it into a card reader that is connected to your computer's USB port. Card readers are devices that have a slot for one or more types of memory cards. Sometimes you don't even need a card reader; many laptop computers have an SD card reader built into the chassis. You simply insert the memory card into this slot and start your download.

This strategy works well with still photographs or MP4 files. However, it does not work as well for AVCHD files because they are stored on the memory card in a bewildering array of subdirectories, making it unclear what to download and where to save all the associated files. This is especially true if you intend to burn the movies onto a DVD so you can play them on your digital player. The PMB software knows how to deal with these subdirectories, so it is a logical choice for downloading your AVCHD movies to your computer. In this case, connect your camera to the computer with the supplied USB cable and let the software do the work for you.

If you want to process your files and use more advanced software than the programs supplied by Sony, you can use proprietary software. Apple Aperture ($80) and Adobe Lightroom ($149) are two programs that provide a way of organizing and manipulating images. More advanced users might want to try Adobe Photoshop ($699). Other options are Adobe Photoshop Elements ($99) and Apple iPhoto '11 ($15). There are even two free choices for either Windows or Macintosh computers: Picasa (www.picasa.google.com) and GIMP (www.gimp.org).

## Sony NEX-7 Software

Your Sony NEX-7 camera is delivered with a CD containing two software applications: Image Data Converter 4.0 and Picture Motion Browser (PMB). Both applications work with RAW and JPEG files, but to varying degrees. Image Data Converter works mainly with RAW files and allows some minor processing of JPEG images. PMB works most efficiently with JPEG files plus AVCHD and MP4 movies. Its controls for manipulating RAW files are not as extensive as Image Data Converter 4.0.

Image Data Converter works on either PCs or Macs, but PMB is only for PCs. To use either program, you will need to install the software onto your computer. If you are not already using third-party image processing programs, try these out and see if they suit your needs. We prefer using Aperture or Lightroom for working with our images, since these programs execute commands faster than Image Data Converter. However, if you're shooting in RAW format, Image Data Converter allows you to get the best-quality images from your Sony NEX-7 as soon as you receive the camera. With third-party software, you first need to make sure your software is current and capable of translating your Sony RAW files. The latest versions of Aperture and Lightroom will read and work with NEX-7 RAW files.

## Image Data Converter

Image Data Converter is image-processing software that works with Sony RAW files for adjusting brightness and WB and optimizing contrast. You can also apply Creative Style options and add shading compensation, sharpness, and noise reduction along with some other image-processing functions. Figure 3-21 shows a screen shot of an image opened in Image Data Converter with the Sharpness

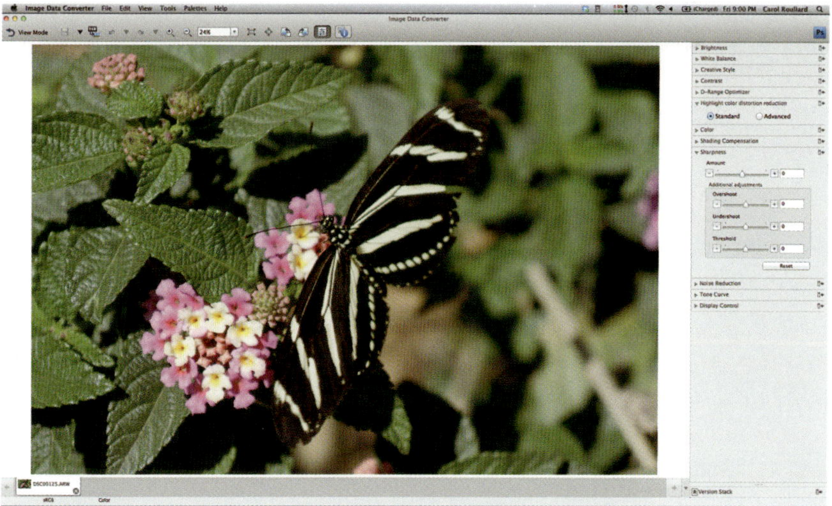


**Figure 3-21**: RAW image open in Image Data Converter

control open for modification. The software also lets you do some minor image processing to JPEG files, such as rotating an image and adjusting its tone curve.

If you do not have an image-processing program, Image Data Converter is definitely something to try out. We find it capable of producing excellent results, but, sadly, it takes time to process a RAW file and is not as easy to use as Photoshop or Aperture. However, remember Image Data Converter is free and it comes with your camera. We have worked with it on a Dell computer with a quad-core processor (i7) and a MacBook Pro with a dual-core processor. In both instances, the program was workable, but it took a second or two to execute a function or open a pull-down menu.

### Picture Motion Browser (PMB)

You can download your images (pictures and movies) onto your computer using PMB software. The program lets you organize and maintain files in folders (figure 3-22). Not only can you view your files by name or file type, or as thumbnails, but you can also add date information and organize them in a calendar structure.

PMB is intended mainly for image processing of JPEG and movie (AVCHD and MP4) files. You can crop your images and adjust brightness, color saturation, image sharpness, and tone curves. Plus you can remove red eye and rotate your JPEG pictures (figure 3-23). PMB also allows you to edit both AVCHD and MP4 movie files.

Although you can download your RAW files in PMB, it allows for only minor manipulations. Instead, PMB supplies a direct link to Image Data Converter so you can use this program to conduct more complex image processing tasks on your RAW files there.

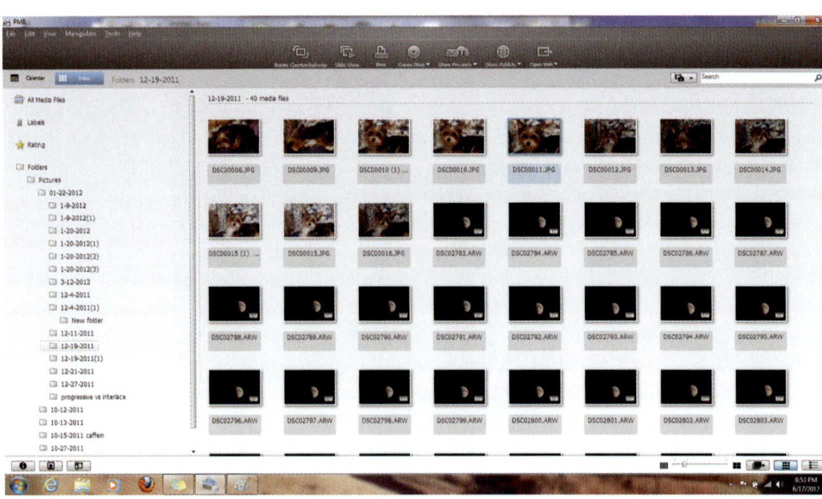

**Figure 3-22**: Organize and maintain files with PMB

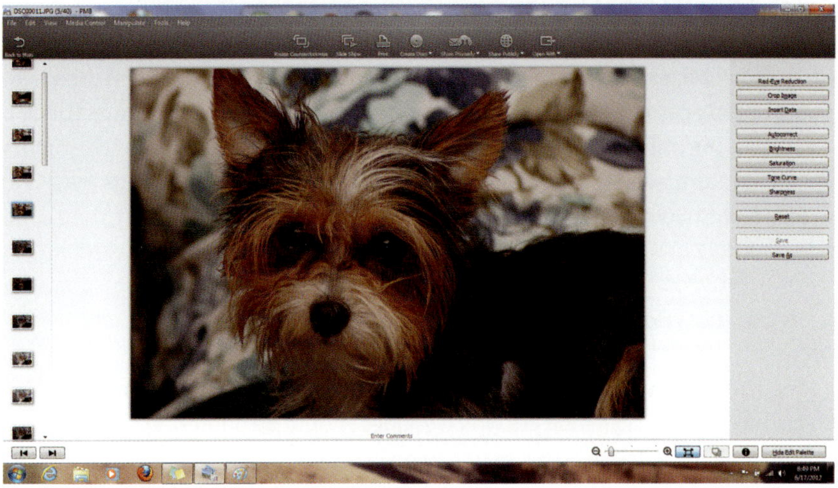

**Figure 3-23**: JPEG image open in PMB

## Playing Pictures and Movies on Your TV Screen

The Sony NEX-7 can be connected directly to your TV, but you will need to purchase an HDMI cable to hook them up. We recommend that you consult both the camera manual and the TV manual, as well as the manufacturers' websites, to get up-to-date information.

After the camera is connected, you can play your slide shows on your TV. One advantage of viewing your slide show on a wide-screen HDTV is its size. It is huge compared to the camera's LCD screen, making it possible to comfortably show your pictures and movies to several friends at once. You will be able to better appreciate the definition, color, and contrast of your pictures and movies when they are shown on a large screen.

To view 3D Sweep Panorama images, you must connect your camera to a TV that is capable of 3-D, and you need to have 3-D glasses. After the camera is connected, initiate 3-D playback with the following command:

MENU>Playback>[3D Viewing]

Initiate playback of your 3-D images by pressing the OK button, then press the right or left rim of the control wheel to advance to the next image or return to the previous image.

Important Points:

- 3D Viewing option is not enabled unless the camera is connected to a TV that is capable of 3-D.
- Only 3D Sweep Panorama images play back with this command.

## Printing Your Pictures

You can print your images with third-party software or the supplied PMB software, or you can utilize the Specify Printing command in the Sony NEX-7 and then take your memory card to a print shop that supports digital print order format (DPOF). Make sure the print shop can handle your images properly. Discuss any restraints the shop might have to make sure you can get the desired print results.

There are two controls within the Specify Printing command that should be addressed:

MENU>Playback>Specify Printing>[DPOF Setup], [Date Imprint]

The [DPOF Setup] control has two options: [Multiple Img.] displays the print check boxes so you can indicate which images should be printed, and [Cancel All] erases all of the existing check marks so no images are selected for print.

MENU>Playback>Specify Printing>DPOF Setup>[Multiple Img.], [Cancel All]

The [Date Imprint] control allows you to specify if you want to have the recorded date and time stamped on the printed copy.

MENU>Playback>Specify Printing>Date Imprint>[On], [Off]

Using DPOF is advantageous if you do not have a printer connected to your computer. You can take your memory card to a printing service, and they can use the information directly from the card to generate your selected prints. Some printers can use the DPOF data to generate your selected prints directly from the memory card. They usually have a card slot that does not need to be attached to a computer. Selecting images for printing is a straightforward process:

1. Select MENU>Playback>Specify Printing>DPOF Setup.
2. Select [Multiple Img.] to display the check boxes so you can select images for printing; select the OK button (soft key B).
3. Select MENU>Playback>Specify Printing>Date Imprint. Select [On] to indicate that the recorded date should be included on the print; select [Off] to prevent the date from being included on the print.
4. Press the OK button (soft key B) to activate the image selection process.
5. The first saved image on the memory card is displayed on the screen. Only DPOF-printable images have a check box displayed on the left side of the screen.

6. Scroll through the images. When you identify an image you wish to print, press soft key C. A check mark will appear within the box and in the print box in the lower left portion of the screen. Press the key again to uncheck the box if you change your mind.
7. After you identify all of the images you want to print, press the OK button (soft key B) to start to complete the Specify Printing process.
8. Press the OK button (soft key C) to finish the process or the Exit button (soft key A) to return the image selection process.



To unselect images for printing, either uncheck the box for a specific image or select the DPOF Setup [Cancel All] option and execute the following steps:

1. Select MENU>Playback>Specify Printing>DPOF Setup.
2. Select [Cancel All] to uncheck all of the boxes.
3. Press the OK button (soft key B) to activate the process.
4. Press the OK button (soft key C) to complete the deletion of the print indicators.

Important points:

- As with anything important, back up the contents of your memory card prior to handing it to a printer.
- The Specify Printing command is available only for JPEG still pictures. You cannot select RAW files. This is one good reason to save your files both in JPEG and RAW formats.
- The Specify Printing command is enabled only if the View Mode is set to Folder View(Still) and there is at least one image stored on the memory card.
- Although you can check the boxes for panoramic images, you may not be able to print them. It depends on the capabilities of the printer.
- Images shot in widescreen [16:9] format may have both of the sides cut off when they are printed.

## Recommendations

We leave the FINDER/LCD Setting to [Auto] so the automatic switching between the LCD screen and the viewfinder is operational. This way, we can quickly switch between the two display screens without making a change through the menu structure.

We usually set the Auto Review command to [Off]. We tend to shoot a series of pictures and then review them as a group. Some of the pictures take only a second to review; some take longer. Setting Auto Review to [Off] puts the review process in our hands. The advantage of using an electronic viewfinder is that most of your adjustments can be evaluated before you take the picture. Unlike an optical viewfinder in a DSLR, the more egregious errors of incorrect WB or exposure can be identified immediately and corrected before you take the picture. This makes picture taking very efficient and allows you to have a good success rate in the field.

It might seem like overkill, but we have concluded that it is best to select all of the data display formats for previewing the images. Although we have our preferences, we find that we use each of the display formats at least occasionally. Therefore, checking them all gives us the flexibility to use what we want at the time we need it without having to change any settings. If we decide we need the Level gauge, it's already available. We just have to press the DISP button to get the desired format.

We recommend that you review your histograms frequently. A histogram is an excellent tool for reviewing an exposure, both before and after recording. We use them often, especially in the camera's semiautomatic and manual modes.

We set the grid line command to the [Rule of 3rds Grid] option. This helps us balance the image composition with a minimal number of lines. The grid lines are prominent enough so you can see them when you want them, and they're faint enough to overlook when you don't.

Be aware that what may appear to be in focus on the LCD screen might not be in focus in the actual capture. We frequently use the enlarge functionality. It allows us to confirm that the image detail is in focus. Rather than spending money to print out the image only to find that important parts of it are not actually in focus, get in the habit of enlarging the image on the LCD screen. If it isn't in focus, you will most likely have time to make some adjustments and recapture the image.

Don't forget about the View Mode bar in the Image Index screen. Several camera functions work based on the current folder type. It is easy to get confused about why your movies aren't showing up on the Image Index screen. It may be that the camera's current folder type is not the one you think it is.

We are judicious about deleting files while photographing in the field. We occasionally weed out unacceptable images directly from the camera, but we find it much easier to do this cleanup process later when we view the images on our computer. To minimize the chance of being caught with not enough memory, we download the pictures to our computer after each photo shoot and then erase or reformat the memory card. This saves us time and battery power. On occasion, we will take time to protect our images. You may need to do the same, especially if you share your camera with someone else.

It is amazing how quickly you can fill up a memory card, especially if you shoot movies. Since the cost of memory cards keeps decreasing, we recommend you have a second or even a third memory card available. Without an extra card, you may end up having to spend your time reviewing and deleting saved images instead of taking pictures.

Most likely you will rely on your computer to manage your photos and movies. This may sound obvious, but get in the habit of downloading your pictures and movies to your computer soon after they are recorded, when your memory is still fresh.

Since we download the contents of our memory card to our computer, we don't use the DPOF print capabilities. We prefer to control our own printing. But this takes time, and you need to have your own equipment, so an easy solution is to utilize the Specify Printing command and send your files out to be printed by a third party.

Last, but not least, use your computer to build slide shows with Sony's PMB software or third-party software. Then store the results on a DVD so you can play back your saved memories on your computer or TV. An added benefit is that you can make copies of your DVDs to share with friends and family.

# Chapter 4: Automatic Settings

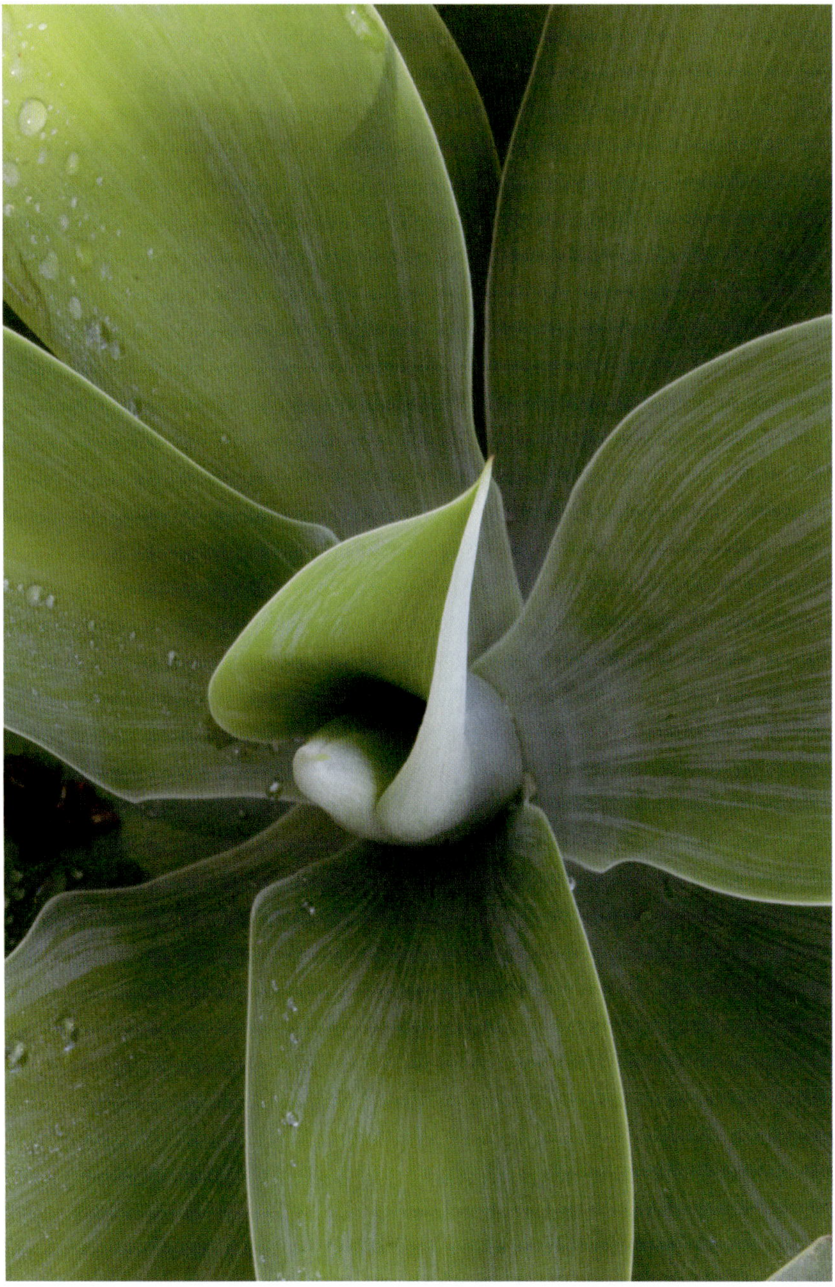

## Introduction

How you use the Sony NEX-7 depends on your expertise, your desire to control aspects of picture taking, and your creativity. Even if you do not know such photographic terms as f-stop, shutter speed, ISO, or EV, you can still take technically excellent pictures and movies using the Intelligent Auto mode. As mentioned in chapter 2, the automated camera settings can produce excellent pictures; however, the setting you use depends on the subject. The camera software tries to identify the subject and match it to the scene types, thereby ensuring the most efficient combination of aperture, shutter speed, ISO, and autofocus mode is used to take the picture.

Although Intelligent Auto mode is remarkably reliable, its scene recognition is not infallible. To increase the quality of your pictures you can use the camera's predefined scene modes. Set the Shoot Mode to SCN and select a scene type that best matches your subject so the camera settings will be optimized to record the subject.

This chapter covers the Intelligent Auto and SCN automatic modes. But first we must cover several functions that are available on the menu.

## Functions Available for Automatic Modes

Although many camera functions are available only when the Shoot Mode is set to P, A, S, or M, there are functions that can also be used when the camera is set to an automatic mode: Drive Mode, Flash Mode, Object Tracking, Face Detection, and Smile Shutter. In some cases, not all of the options within each function are available in the automatic modes. Although we cover them here for continuity, we refer to them again in chapters 5 and 6 when we discuss P, A, S, and M modes.

### Drive Mode Command

The Drive Mode command allows you to specify how the camera will act when you fully depress the shutter button. Select the command through the menu:

> MENU>Camera>Drive Mode>[Single Shooting], [Cont. Shooting], [Spd Priority Cont.], [Self-timer], [Self-timer(Cont.)], [Bracket: Cont.], [Remote Cdr.]

Each Drive Mode option has a specific use, and several options have submenus of their own. Table 4-1 lists each option along with a brief description.

<table>
<tr><th>Drive Mode Icon</th><th>Drive Mode Name</th><th colspan="2">Description</th></tr>
<tr><td></td><td>Single Shooting</td><td colspan="2">Camera fires one shot per press of the shutter button.</td></tr>
<tr><td></td><td>Cont. Shooting</td><td colspan="2">Camera shoots continuously as long as the shutter button is held down and the memory card has room to store the images. Camera maintains the selected firing rate at about 3 shots per second until the buffer is filled. After approximately 13 images, the rate of firing drops.<br>When the flash is activated, the continuous shooting slows down to allow for the flash to recharge before firing.</td></tr>
<tr><td>S</td><td>Spd Priority Cont.</td><td colspan="2">Camera shoots continuously at a higher speed than [Cont. Shooting] as long as the shutter button is held down and the memory card has room to store the images.<br>Camera maintains a firing rate of up to 10 images per second until the buffer is filled. After approximately 12 images, the rate of firing drops.<br>When using the flash, the continuous shooting is slowed to allow the flash to recharge before firing.</td></tr>
<tr><td rowspan="3"></td><td>Self-timer</td><td colspan="2">Delays firing the camera after the shutter button is pressed.</td></tr>
<tr><td rowspan="2">Options</td><td>10</td><td>10-second delay. Use this option when you don't have a remote release and need to get into a group shot.</td></tr>
<tr><td>2</td><td>2-second delay. Use this option when you don't have a remote release and you want to eliminate camera shake caused by pressing the shutter button.</td></tr>
<tr><td rowspan="3"></td><td>Self-timer(Cont.)</td><td colspan="2">Delays firing the camera after the shutter button is pressed and fires a continuous set of shots.</td></tr>
<tr><td rowspan="2">Options</td><td>C3</td><td>Delays firing for 10 seconds and then fires 3 shots.</td></tr>
<tr><td>C5</td><td>Delays firing for 10 seconds and then fires 5 shots.</td></tr>
</table>

| Drive Mode Icon | Drive Mode Name | Description | |
|---|---|---|---|
| BRK C | Bracket: Cont. | Takes a series of 3 shots with the EV varying +/- by the selected amount. The sequence of shots is as follows: base exposure, underexposed by selected EV, overexposed by selected EV.<br>Flash Mode is not active in this Drive Mode option. | |
| | Options | 0.3EV | Takes 3 shots in this sequence: base exposure, -0.3 EV, +0.3EV. |
| | | 0.7EV | Takes 3 shots in this sequence: base exposure, -0.7 EV, +0.7EV. |
| 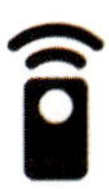 | Remote Cdr. | Camera expects the shutter button to be released with a wireless remote control, available from Sony. When the camera is attached to a TV, the remote can be used to control the camera playback. | |

**Table 4-1**: Drive Mode function options

The Drive Mode command is not available in Anti Motion Blur, Sweep Panorama, 3D Sweep Panorama, or in the SCN Hand-held Twilight modes.

### Why Does the Self-Timer Take More Than One Shot?

When you take a photograph of a group of people, it seems like one person is blinking or looking away just when the shutter is released. This can ruin the photograph, so Sony gives you the option of firing three or five shots after the self-timer has ticked off 10 seconds. Hopefully, at least one of the pictures will show everyone perfectly posed and you will have an excellent group shot of your family and friends.

In addition, some of the individual Drive Mode options have limited availability within Intelligent Auto and some of the individual SCN modes. Table 4-2 shows which Drive Mode options and suboptions are available in the Intelligent Auto and SCN modes. Keep in mind that the Drive Mode setting has no effect when you record a movie.

| Drive Mode Option Availability | | | | | | | |
|---|---|---|---|---|---|---|---|
| Automatic Modes | Drive Mode Options | | | | | | |
| | Single Shooting | Cont. Shooting | Spd Priority Cont. | Self-timer | Self-timer (Cont.) | Bracket: Cont. | Remote Cdr. |
| Intelligent Auto | E | E | E | E | E | D | E |
| SCN | | | | | | | |
| Portrait | E | D | D | E | E | D | E |
| Landscape | E | D | D | E | E | D | E |
| Macro | E | D | D | E | E | D | E |
| Sports Action | D | E | E | E | E | D | E |
| Sunset | E | D | D | E | E | D | E |
| Night Portrait | E | D | D | E | E | D | E |
| Night Scene | E | D | D | E | E | D | E |
| Hand-held Twilight | Drive Mode command is disabled | | | | | | |
| E = Option is enabled; D = Option is disabled | | | | | | | |

**Table 4-2**: Drive Mode options available in automatic modes

### Flash Mode Command

You can find the Flash Mode command in the menu as follows:

> MENU>Camera>Flash Mode>[Flash Off], [Autoflash], [Fill-flash], [Slow Sync.], [Rear Sync.], [Wireless]

The Flash Mode command allows you to specify how and when the flash will fire to give your subject the type of lighting you want. Table 4-3 lists each of the command's options along with a description and whether or not it is enabled. The Sony NEX-7 flash is covered in detail in chapter 10. Keep in mind that only [Flash Off], [Autoflash], and [Fill-flash] are enabled in Intelligent Auto and selected SCN modes (table 4-4).

| Flash Mode Icon | Flash Mode Name | Description |
|---|---|---|
| | Flash Off | Prevents the flash unit from firing.<br>This option is disabled in P, A, S, and M modes, and in the SCN predefined Night Scene, Hand-held Twilight, and Night Portrait modes. |
| AUTO | Autoflash | The camera decides when the flash is needed. You must first manually pop up the flash unit so the camera can fire in low light levels.<br>This option is enabled only in Intelligent Auto and the SCN predefined Portrait, and Macro, modes. |
| | Fill-flash | When this option is selected, the flash always fires and illuminates the subject. You must first manually pop up the flash unit before it will fire.<br>This option is available only in P, A, S, M, and in the SCN predefined Portrait, Sports Action, Macro, Landscape, and Sunset modes. |
| SLOW | Slow Sync. | Use this option with a slow shutter speed. The flash goes off and the camera's shutter is prolonged to properly expose the background that is not illuminated by the flash.<br>This option is available only in P, A, S, and M modes. |
| REAR | Rear Sync. | Use this option with a slow shutter speed. The flash goes off at the end of the exposure just before the second shutter curtain closes. If there is movement during the exposure, the resulting picture records the subject in its last position. If there is enough ambient light, the subject's movement during the exposure is captured as a blur.<br>This option is available only in P, A, S, and M modes. |
| WL | Wireless | This option requires a Sony external flash unit that is capable of wireless triggering. When such a flash is attached, it will send a pulse of light to trigger the firing of other external flash units when this command is enabled.<br>This option is available only in P, A, S, and M modes. |

**Table 4-3**: Flash command options

| Flash Mode Option Availability | | | | | | |
|---|---|---|---|---|---|---|
| | Flash Mode Options | | | | | |
| Automatic Modes | Flash Off | Autoflash | Fill-flash | Slow Sync. | Rear Sync. | Wireless |
| Intelligent Auto | E | E | D | D | D | D |
| SCN | | | | | | |
| Portrait | E | E | E | D | D | D |
| Landscape | E | D | E | D | D | D |
| Macro | E | E | E | D | D | D |
| Sports Action | E | D | E | D | D | D |
| Sunset | E | D | E | D | D | D |
| Night Portrait | Flash Mode command is disabled | | | | | |
| Night Scene | Flash Mode command is disabled | | | | | |
| Hand-held Twilight | Flash Mode command is disabled | | | | | |
| E = Option is enabled; D = Option is disabled | | | | | | |

**Table 4-4**: Flash Mode options available in automatic modes

## Object Tracking Command

The Object Tracking command (table 4-5) allows the camera to track and maintain focus on a subject as it moves throughout the framed image.

Select the command through the menu:

MENU>Camera>Object Tracking>[Off], [On]

| Object Tracking Icon | Description |
|---|---|
| 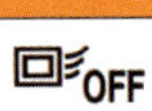 | Disables Object Tracking functionality |
| 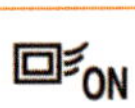 | Enables Object Tracking functionality |

**Table 4-5**: Object Tracking command options

When the Object Tracking command is set to [On], a small white box displays in the center of the display screen (figure 4-1a). Frame the image with the subject you wish to track in the center of the screen. Press soft key C to select the object. Now a white double box (a box within a box) will frame the selected object, and it will move as the camera or the object moves (figure 4-1b). Press the shutter button halfway to focus. If focus is obtained, the double box will turn green. The Object Tracking On icon next to soft key B will change to the Object Tracking Off icon after an object has been selected. To cancel tracking the selected object, press soft key B, at which time the Object Tracking On icon will again be displayed.

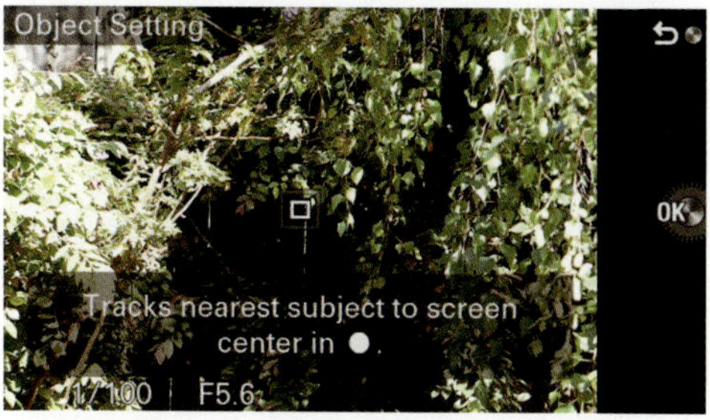

**Figure 4-1a**: Object Tracking selection screen

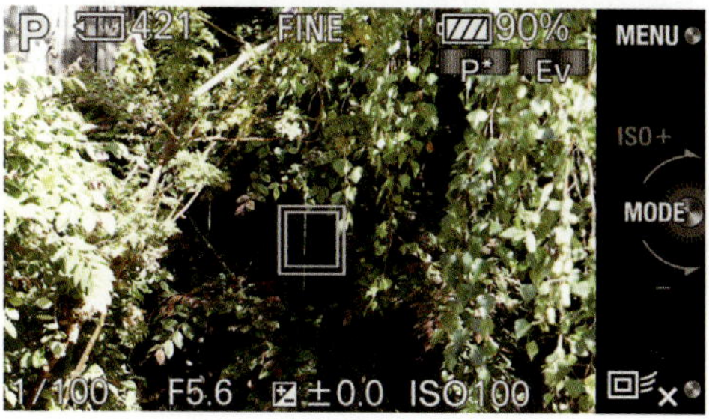

**Figure 4-1b**: Object selected for tracking

Object Tracking is based on recognizing the selected object's colors and details. You will most likely select only a portion of the subject you want to track. Make sure the part you select is detailed and colorful enough to differentiate it from other objects within the scene, otherwise the camera may have difficulty tracking the desired subject. You are now ready to take a picture. As long as the subject being tracked is still in the camera's view, the tracking function is retained when a picture is recorded.

Object Tracking is not available when recording a movie. Attempting to record a movie while an object is being tracked will terminate tracking, and the camera will revert back to the previous autofocus area. Once the movie has been recorded, the camera will revert back to Object Tracking mode.

The camera may have difficulty tracking under the following conditions:

- If the subject is not distinguishable from the rest of the framed image
- If the subject moves outside of the framed image
- If the subject moves too fast
- If the subject changes (for example, if a person turns around)

Object Tracking is not available in Anti Motion Blur, Sweep Panorama, 3D Sweep Panorama, or SCN Hand-held Twilight modes, and it is disabled if the AF/MF Select command is set to [Manual Focus] mode.

### Face Detection and Registration Functionality

Frequently, Face Detection is available in cameras with Live View sensors. Some cameras have elaborate face detection and registration commands; others, like the Sony NEX-7, keep it simple.

There are two parts to the Sony Face Detection process. The first part turns on Face Detection so the camera can determine if a face is in the framed image. The second part registers faces for the purpose of prioritizing focus. Basically, the camera registers a person's face, and when it is detected in an image, it will attempt to focus on each face in the order of its assigned priority. If you don't register the faces of your most important people and leave it to the camera's software to choose which face to focus on, you may end up with an unknown person as the focal point of your picture.

For example, suppose you are taking a picture of your children at the zoo while they are surrounded by strangers. You will want the camera to focus on your children's faces. This will occur if your children's faces are registered in the camera's memory and the camera can find them in the crowd. The camera will then focus on your children.

For a face to be recognized, the person must be facing the camera so that the facial features are clearly presented. The software bases its determination on detecting two eyes, a nose, and a mouth. Therefore, facial recognition will fail if the camera sees only the person's profile. Also, certain conditions, such as the face being too small in the frame or harsh shadows falling on the person's face, may interfere with face recognition.

The Face Registration process generates a library of portraits that you compile. You can register up to eight faces and order them by priority, which the camera will use to determine which recognized face acquires focus first, second, and all the way up to eighth. This way, if you have a group picture, the camera will determine whether any of the registered faces are detected in the image and establish focus based on the priority saved in the face registration command. You can register multiple images of the same person to help ensure they are found in a group shot.

Important points:

- Up to eight faces can be detected within one framed image.
- The Face Detection/Registration functionality is enabled for single still picture shooting modes. It is not available in Sweep Panorama, 3D Sweep Panorama, Anti Motion Blur, and the SCN Hand-held Twilight modes.
- Face Detection/Registration can be activated when taking movies.
- Nonhuman faces cannot be detected.
- Obscuring facial features with sunglasses, hats, or poor lighting, can prevent the successful registration and/or recognition of a face.

- Face Registration information is not deleted when you execute the Reset Default command.
- Face Detection/Registration is not available when the Autofocus Area [Center] or [Flexible Spot] options are selected. You can use it only when the [Multi] option is selected.

**Why Doesn't Face Detection Recognize My Cat?**

Even with two eyes, a nose, and a mouth, your cat's facial proportions are uniquely feline and are therefore not the same as a human face. Face detection and recognition software looks for facial structures and proportions that are characteristic of humans.



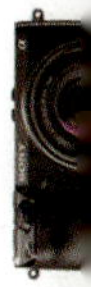

### Activating Face Detection

It's easy to activate face detection by selecting the following command:

MENU>Camera>Face Detection>[Off], [On (Regist. Faces)], [On]

The Face Detection command has three options (table 4-6). Select the [On] or [On (Regist. Faces)] option and press soft key C to activate it.

| Face Detection Icon | Face Detection Name | Description |
| --- | --- | --- |
|  | On (Regist. Faces) | Activates Face Detection and prioritizes focus for registered faces.<br>Face Detection is automatically set to this value when Smile Shutter is on. |
| ON | On | Activates Face Detection but does not use registered faces to establish focus prioritization. |
| OFF | Off | Deactivates Face Detection. The camera is oblivious to a face in the framed image unless you select it as an object for tracking.<br>Face Detection is not available in shooting modes that involve recording more than one image: Sweep Panorama, 3D Sweep Panorama, Anti Motion Blur, and the SCN Hand-held Twilight shooting modes. |

**Table 4-6**: Face Detection command options

## Registering Faces

The Face Registration command is accessed through the MENU button:

> MENU>Camera>Face Registration>[New Registration], [Order Exchanging], [Delete], [Delete All]

First, have your subject available in sufficient lighting. Then execute the following steps:

1. Enter the following command:

> MENU>Camera>Face Registration>[New Registration]

2. Frame the face of the person you wish to register (figure 4-2a). Make sure the person is facing the camera so you can capture the entire face. A white box will display in the center of the screen. Position the camera so the person's face is within the white box.
3. Press the shutter button halfway; green-cornered brackets will appear in the center of the white box. Adjust the framed face so it is centered within the green-cornered brackets (figure 4-2b).
4. Press the shutter button to register the image.
5. The camera will determine if there are sufficient facial characteristics to register the face. If there is, you will be asked if you want to register the face. Press the OK button (soft key C) to register it (figure 4-2c). If there is insufficient information, the camera will inform you that it cannot register the face and ask you to start again.

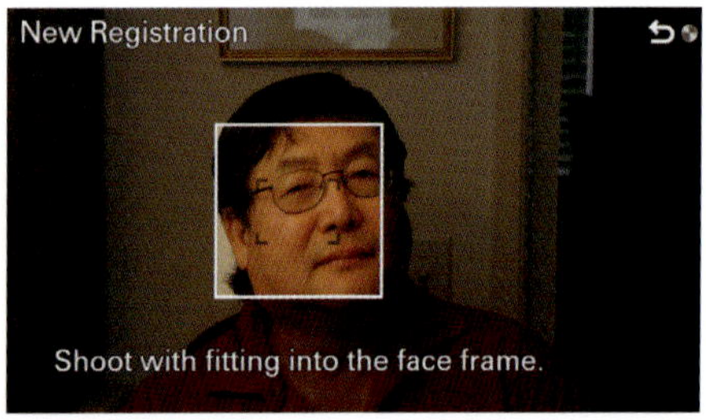


**Figure 4-2a**: Face framed for registration

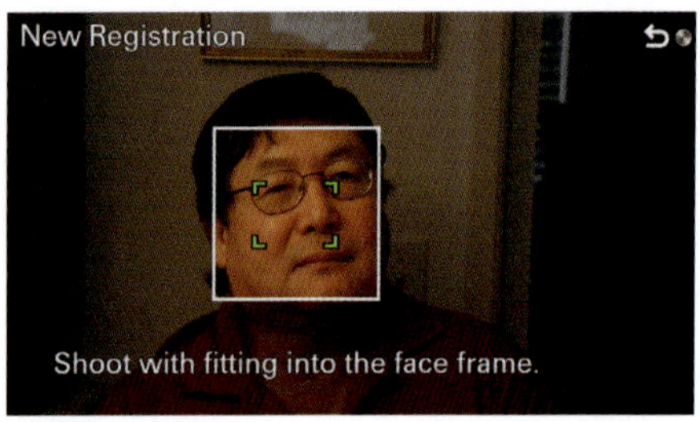


**Figure 4-2b**: Face framed in green-cornered brackets

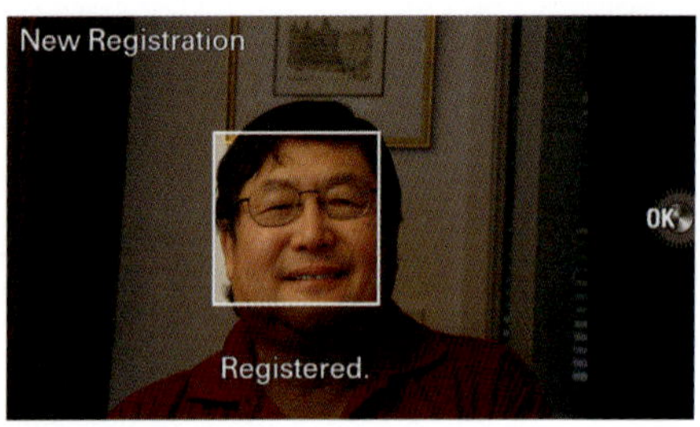


**Figure 4-2c**: Face registered

The [New Registration] option is enabled only if there are slots available to register a face. If all eight slots are filled, the option is disabled. In this case, the [Delete] option must be used to remove at least one registered face before another face can be registered. The [Order Exchanging] and [Delete] options are enabled after at least one face is registered.

### Assigning Priorities to Registered Faces

Each time you register a face, the image is stored in the next available slot. You can see the order when the [Order Exchanging] option is selected. The top left slot is assigned first priority, the slot to its immediate right is assigned second priority, and so on down to the bottom right slot, which is ranked eighth priority. To change the order, follow these steps:

1. Enter the following command:

   MENU>Camera>Face Registration>[Order Exchanging]

2. Highlight the face you wish to reorder (figure 4-3a). The face will be enclosed in an orange box. Press soft key C to select the face. The face will be underlined with an orange line. An orange double-arrow vertical bar displays to the left of the first slot, indicating where the selected image will be moved if you press soft key C again (figure 4-3b).
3. If you want to move the selected face to another location, rotate the control wheel to position the vertical bar to the left of the slot where you want the selected face to be moved to.
4. Press soft key C to accept the new location (figure 4-3c).

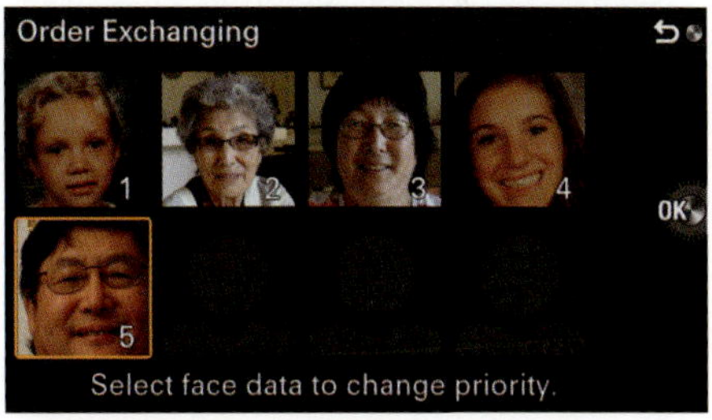


**Figure 4-3a**: Highlighted face

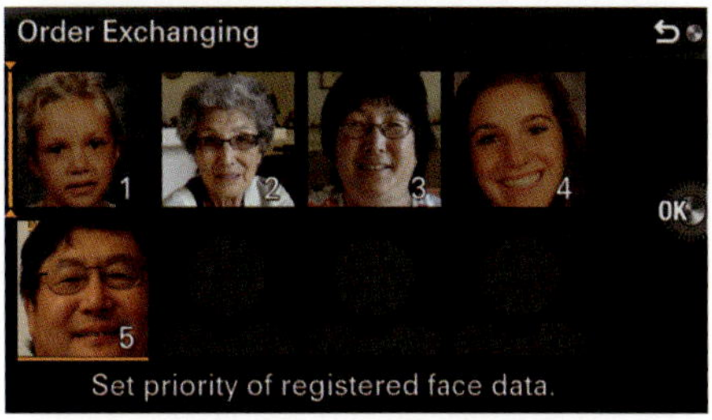


**Figure 4-3b**: Pending location for selected face

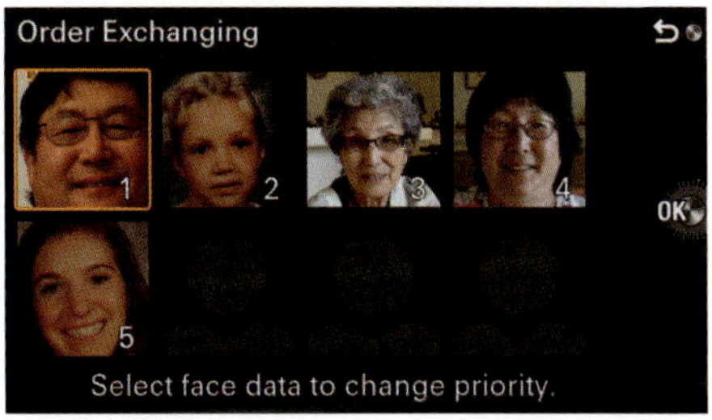


**Figure 4-3c**: New location for selected face

### Deleting Registered Faces

Keep in mind that you can always change the registered images. This is especially important with a growing child, whose face will mature and will need to be updated in the register. You can delete old images that no longer reflect how the person looks.

To delete a registered face, follow the steps below.

1. Enter the following command:

   MENU>Camera>Face Registration>[Delete]

2. Eight boxes are displayed on the screen, with the first box enclosed in an orange frame. Each box contains an image of a person you have registered, or the box is empty. Turn the control wheel right or left to select the image you wish to delete. The orange box moves to each selected slot. Press soft key C to select an image for deletion.
3. A confirmation menu displays.
4. Press soft key C again to delete the selected face. Press soft key A to cancel the deletion.

To delete all of the registered faces at one time, follow the steps below.

1. Enter the following command:

   MENU>Camera>Face Registration>[Delete All]

2. A confirmation menu displays.
3. Press soft key C to delete all of the registered faces. Press soft key A to cancel the deletion.

### Using Face Detection and Registration

When Face Detection is set to [On] or [On (Regist. Faces)] and the camera can detect or recognize several faces, it surrounds each face with either a white or a gray box. A white box indicates the face will be used to establish focus. If your camera is set to (On (Regist. Faces)), then focus will be established based on the focus priority in the registry. The following list shows the sequence of colored boxes:

- If the camera frames a single face, only a white box encases the face.
- When you press the shutter button halfway, and the camera locks focus on the face, the white box turns green.
- If several faces are within the frame, several boxes appear surrounding the faces and the following occurs:
  - Box is either gray or white. White indicates the faces that the camera intends to focus on. Generally, these will be the registered faces.
  - When you press the shutter button halfway, the faces that are used as the points for focus will each have a green box.

The Face Detection function is not available in Manual Focus mode, Sweep Panorama, or 3D Sweep Panorama shooting modes.

### Smile Shutter Functionality

How many times have you said, "Say cheese" and still found that the person did not smile when the picture was taken? The Sony NEX-7 can prevent this. After focus is obtained, the Smile Shutter command instructs the camera to automatically take a picture when it detects that a person is smiling. Furthermore, you can set the degree of smile sensitivity the camera uses to trigger the shutter. Table 4-7 contains the available options and values.

| Smile Shutter Icon | Smile Shutter Name | Description |
|---|---|---|
| OFF | Off | Does not trigger shutter when a detected face smiles. |
| | On: Slight Smile | Triggers shutter when a slight smile is detected. |
| | On: Normal Smile | Triggers shutter when a normal smile is detected. |
| | On: Big Smile | Triggers shutter when a big, full smile is detected. |

**Table 4-7**: Smile Shutter command options

Enter the following command to access the Smile Shutter options:

MENU>Camera>Smile Shutter>[Off], [On]

When the [On] value is selected, press the OPTION (soft key B) button. A submenu presents three levels of smile sensitivity:

MENU>Camera>Smile Shutter>On>[On: Slight Smile], [On: Normal Smile], [On: Big Smile]

Figure 4-4 shows the resulting display screen after [On: Normal Smile] is selected. Note the vertical smile meter on the left side, with the arrow indicating the level of smile sensitivity.

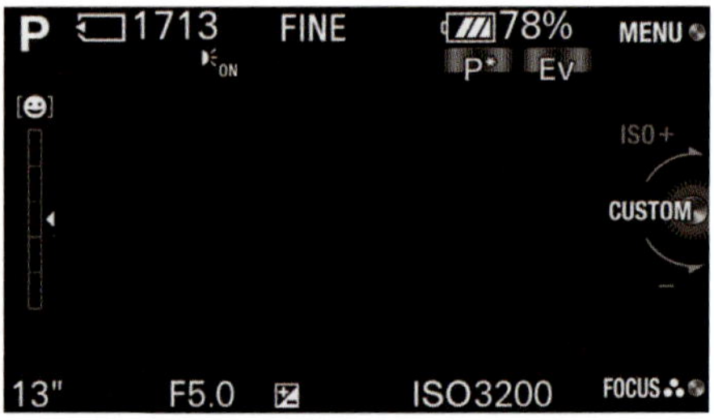

**Figure 4-4**: Smile Shutter display screen with Normal Smile selected

The next time the camera detects a face and obtains focus (the box around the face turns orange), it will try to interpret the person's level of smile, which is displayed on the smile meter. If the smile meets or exceeds the selected sensitivity level, the camera will automatically take the picture and will continue to take pictures until the person's smile no longer meets the selected level.

You can still manually take a picture even if the smile does not meet the sensitivity criteria. Maybe you have Smile Shutter turned on and your subject starts making funny nonsmiley faces. Just press the shutter button as usual to take a picture. The camera will resume taking pictures automatically when it detects a smiling face that meets or exceeds your chosen smile sensitivity level.

**How Does Smile Shutter Work with Multiple Faces?**

Say you have multiple people in your picture, and not all of them are smiling. You have Smile Shutter turned on along with Face Detection. Unfortunately, this function doesn't wait for everyone to smile. After the camera detects faces and obtains focus, all it takes is for one detected person to smile at or above the Smile Sensitivity level to trigger the shutter button.

Important points:

- Smile Shutter works in P, A, S, M (conditional), Intelligent Auto, and all SCN predefined scene modes, excluding Hand-held Twilight.
- You cannot use Smile Shutter in [Manual Focus] mode or Prec. Dig. Zoom.
- After it is turned on, the Smile Shutter command works only as long as you remain in the current shooting mode. When you change the shooting mode, the Smile Shutter command turns off automatically.
- Turning on Smile Shutter automatically turns on Face Detection. Turning Smile Shutter off will cause Face Detection to revert to its value prior to Smile Shutter being turned on.
- Smile Shutter does not always work as expected. What you might think is a big smile might be insufficient for the camera to trigger a shot.
- Only the Drive Mode [Single Shooting] and [Remote Cdr.] options are available when Smile Shutter is turned on. If Drive Mode is set to another value, it will automatically be changed to [Single Shooting]. It will be returned to its original value when Smile Shutter is turned off.
- If DRO/Auto HDR is set to HDR, Smile Shutter will take three shots and create an HDR image.



Although the Smile Shutter functionality works well when a person smiles, it is far from perfect. We find there are times when the camera takes a photo when the person frowns, has started to talk, or has moved their face.

## Shooting Modes

The Shoot Mode menu (figure 4-5) is the starting point for exerting control over how you shoot your pictures and movies. It provides you with a mixture of automatic and semiautomatic settings and additional artistic features.

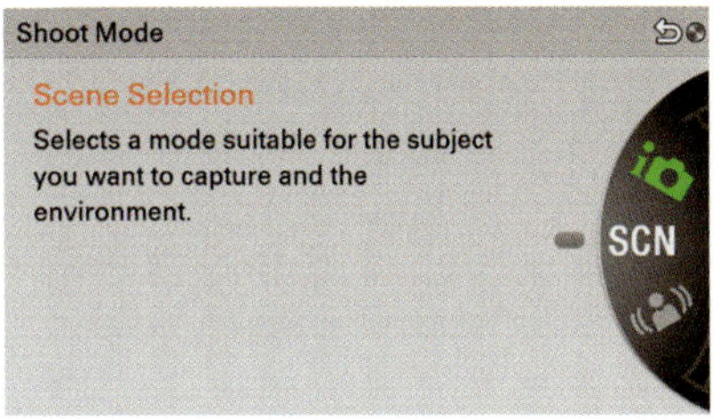


**Figure 4-5**: Shoot Mode set to SCN mode

There are nine Shoot Mode options. Table 4-8 lists each one along with a brief description. Press the MENU button. Navigate to the Shoot Mode icon and press soft key C. Rotate the control wheel to the desired mode. Press soft key C again to select the option.

| Shoot Mode Option | Description |
|---|---|
| Manual Exposure | The camera requires you to set both the shutter speed and aperture manually. |
| Shutter Priority | The camera automatically sets the aperture in response to your shutter speed setting. |
| Aperture Priority | The camera automatically sets the shutter speed in response to your aperture setting. |
| Program Auto | The camera automatically sets both the shutter speed and aperture and allows you change the two, in synchrony, so you can use either the aperture or the shutter speed you desire. |
| Intelligent Auto | The camera evaluates the framed image, attempts to identify the scene type, and sets the controls according to its evaluation. |
| SCN | The camera allows you to select a specific predefined scene mode. The camera adjusts its settings for the specific mode. |
| Anti Motion Blur | The camera fires six shots to provide noise reduction for low-light shooting. You can adjust the exposure by using the Exposure Compensation tool, which is not available in the [Hand-held Twilight] scene selection. |
| Sweep Panorama | The camera builds a horizontal or vertical composite panoramic image. |
| 3D Sweep Panorama | The camera builds a horizontal or vertical 3D composite panoramic image. |

**Table 4-8**: Shoot Mode menu options

We will cover the Intelligent Auto and SCN modes in this chapter. These options automatically control the ISO, WB, and exposure settings for each framed image. You cannot set ISO or WB in these modes.

The remaining Shoot Mode options require you to take more control and change the camera settings yourself. These semiautomatic and manual modes are covered in later chapters.

## Intelligent Auto Mode

In Intelligent Auto mode, the camera evaluates the framed image, assigns a scene type (table 4-9) and determines the proper exposure, ISO setting, WB, aperture, and focus for the image. The internal flash unit will not pop up on its own. If you want it to fire, you will have to manually pop it up before you press the shutter button.

When the scene type is determined, the camera displays the corresponding icon in the upper left corner of the display screen (figure 4-6). For example, say the camera determines that the framed image has a subject very close to the lens. It selects the Macro scene type and sets the camera controls to the best values for a closeup picture.

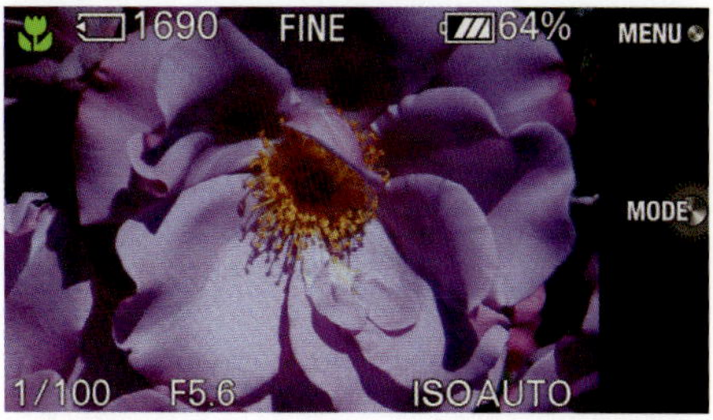


**Figure 4-6**: Intelligent Auto with Macro scene selected



| Auto+ Scene Icon | Scene Name | Description |
|---|---|---|
| | Night Scene | The camera determines that the image is a night scene with evening-type lighting. |
| | Tripod Night Scene | The camera determines that the subject is in a low-light situation that requires a tripod. SteadyShot is disabled. |
| | Night Portrait | The camera determines that the image is a night scene with evening-type lighting and contains a face. |
| | Backlight | The camera determines that the light is behind the focus area, causing a silhouette effect. The camera will adjust the ISO, aperture, and shutter speed to obtain a picture without using the flash unit. |
| | Backlight Portrait | The camera detects a face with the light coming from behind, causing the subject to look like a silhouette. The camera will adjust the ISO, aperture, and shutter speed to obtain a picture without using the flash unit. |
| | Portrait | The camera detects a face and attempts to establish focus and exposure for the face. |
| | Landscape | The camera determines that the subject is at a great distance and increases the depth of field. |
| | Macro | The camera determines that it is close to the subject. The aperture is narrowed to increase the depth of field. |
| | Spotlight | The camera determines the subject is illuminated by a spotlight and records the subject, leaving the background dim. |
| | Low Brightness | The camera determines that the environment has low lighting. The camera will adjust its ISO, aperture, and shutter speed to obtain a picture without using the flash unit. |
| | Baby | The camera detects a baby's face by interpreting its facial features and proportions. |
| | General (Default) | When the camera cannot identify the scene, it chooses generic settings based on lighting and focal point. |

**Table 4-9**: Intelligent Auto scenes, icons, and descriptions

Some of the parameters used for classifying a picture are based on what is lacking. The absence of a face means the scene is not a Portrait. The failure to focus on a close subject (i.e., within about 1 ft) means the scene is not a Macro. Frequently, the camera may identify a distant shot as a scenic shot, but as we mentioned earlier, this is not always the case.

There are times when the camera software is unable to determine a specific scene type. In this case, the Intelligent Auto icon is displayed on the screen and the camera chooses generic settings. You will get a good exposure, but the shutter speed, aperture, and ISO may not be optimal for the subject.

Therefore, several camera functions are not available in Intelligent Auto mode:

- None of the Brightness/Color menu commands are available, and they display error messages when pressed.
- Exposure-related menu commands are not available.
- The Bracket Drive Mode option is disabled.
- The Rear Sync. and WL (Wireless) Flash Mode options are disabled.

Scene identification in Intelligent Auto mode is imperfect. It should be considered a convenience. As you become more comfortable with using the camera, you can categorize the subject yourself and select the appropriate predefined scene mode using the SCN mode option.

## SCN Predefined Scene Modes

Intelligent Auto mode is a convenient way for new camera users to take pictures. But occasionally the modes fall short of taking the pictures you want. If this is the case, you can use the SCN mode to choose one of eight predefined scene modes (table 4-10).

| SCN Icon | SCN Name | Description |
|---|---|---|
| | Portrait | Use when you want to focus on people within the image.<br>This mode enables the Face Detection/Registration function. The detected face(s) acquire focus while the background is blurred. To increase blur, use a telephoto lens (focal length of 50mm to 70mm recommended) to reduce the depth of field. |
| | Landscape | Use when photographing distant objects outdoors. The camera closes down the lens aperture to increase the depth of field. |

| SCN Icon | SCN Name | Description |
|---|---|---|
| | Macro | Use when the subject is close to the camera. The definition of "close" depends on the lens you are using. For the DT18-55mm zoom lens, it is within 25 cm (about 10 in). You can use an accessory macro lens to shoot closer subjects. Because any camera movement will affect the picture this close to the subject, use a tripod for the best results. |
| | Sports Action | Use when taking pictures of a moving subject. Object Tracking is enabled (this is the only SCN mode that enables this function). The camera is set to a fast shutter speed and a higher ISO to freeze motion. The camera is in Cont. Shooting. When ready, press the shutter button fully and hold it down; the camera shoots continuously until you release the button. |
| | Sunset | Use when taking pictures of sunrises or sunsets. This mode enhances the red and orange tones in the image. You can try this mode even if you are not taking a picture of a sunrise or a sunset. |
| | Night Portrait | Use when shooting a portrait in a nighttime environment. Face Detection/Registration is enabled. The shutter speed is reduced to capture more light on the sensor. Use a tripod for the best results. |
| | Night Scene | Use when taking pictures in a nighttime environment. The shutter speed is reduced to capture more light on the sensor. Use a tripod for the best results |
| | Hand-held Twilight | Use this mode when shooting night scenes of a relatively stationary subject without a tripod. The camera utilizes internal image processing software to combine a number of shots into a single image to reduce image noise and blur (due to low light and camera shake, respectively). This option produces only JPEG files. If you have the Quality command set to RAW or RAW & JPEG, the camera automatically changes the file to JPEG Fine.<br>Your results can be unsatisfactory in the following situations: if the subject has too little contrast, which makes it difficult for the software to merge multiple images; if the subject moves significantly during the capture sequence; or if the image has repeating patterns that create a moiré effect, much like with flickering light sources such as TVs, computer screens, or fluorescent lighting. |

**Table 4-10**: SCN predefined scene modes

When you select SCN mode, the list of predefined scenes is displayed on the screen. Rotate the control wheel to move through the list. Each predefined scene mode includes a brief description to help you decide which one best suits your image (figure 4-7). Press the soft key C button to select a scene mode. The scene mode's icon displays in the upper left corner. The camera then applies settings based on the selected scene mode and the characteristics of the image.

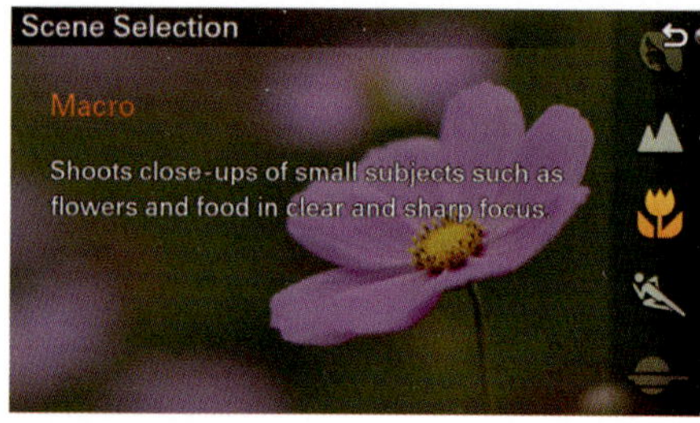


**Figure 4-7**: Description of Macro predefined scene mode

The SCN mode allows you to select the scene type rather than having the camera assign it for you. Although this is not always perfect, it helps improve the likelihood that the camera's settings will be in tune with the image and that you will improve the quality of your picture. Keep in mind that you cannot override exposure-related settings in predefined scene modes, though you can make some changes to Drive Mode, Face Detection, and Smile Shutter commands.

## Recommendations

If you want to use your camera quickly, we recommend that you try both the Intelligent Auto and the SCN predefined scene modes. Although it's likely that you'll want to take control of the camera settings yourself, both of these automatic modes are excellent for capturing a picture on the spur of the moment when you don't have time to evaluate the camera settings and lighting.

It's not always obvious how the camera software determines its automatic settings. As you take pictures, always evaluate them. Instead of just accepting the results, review your work and think about how the image could be changed and whether the changes improve or weaken the picture. For example, is it better to show action shots as frozen images, with all their details rendered sharply, or is it better to use a longer shutter speed and blur portions of the image to suggest speed? Check out the nuances of camera command settings for specific predefined scene modes. You can always view the settings for an image in the data display screen format described in chapter 3. Keep in mind that the camera software does its best guess and implements decisions based on what is considered a typical picture.

If you find that the results are satisfactory, you may remain an avid user of the automatic modes. However, the camera has many more capabilities that we believe you will want to explore. Chapters 5 and 6 cover using the semiautomatic and manual modes, respectively. These modes afford you more control over your photographic outcomes. Granted, there is a learning curve, but everything you are learning now provides the groundwork for those two chapters.

Although both the Face Registration and Smile Shutter clearly have value, and we recommend you try both features, you can get just as good results without it. The Smile Shutter function works well, but we have found some instances where the person was not smiling or was moving during the picture. We did not find that Face Registration consistently identified which face to focus on first, second, etc. Many times a nonregistered face gained focus first. This may have been due to the nonregistered face being closer to the camera. Regardless, we think we have more control using the camera controls that are described in chapters 5 and 6, where we can adjust how and where the camera establishes focus.

# Chapter 5: Taking Control of the Camera

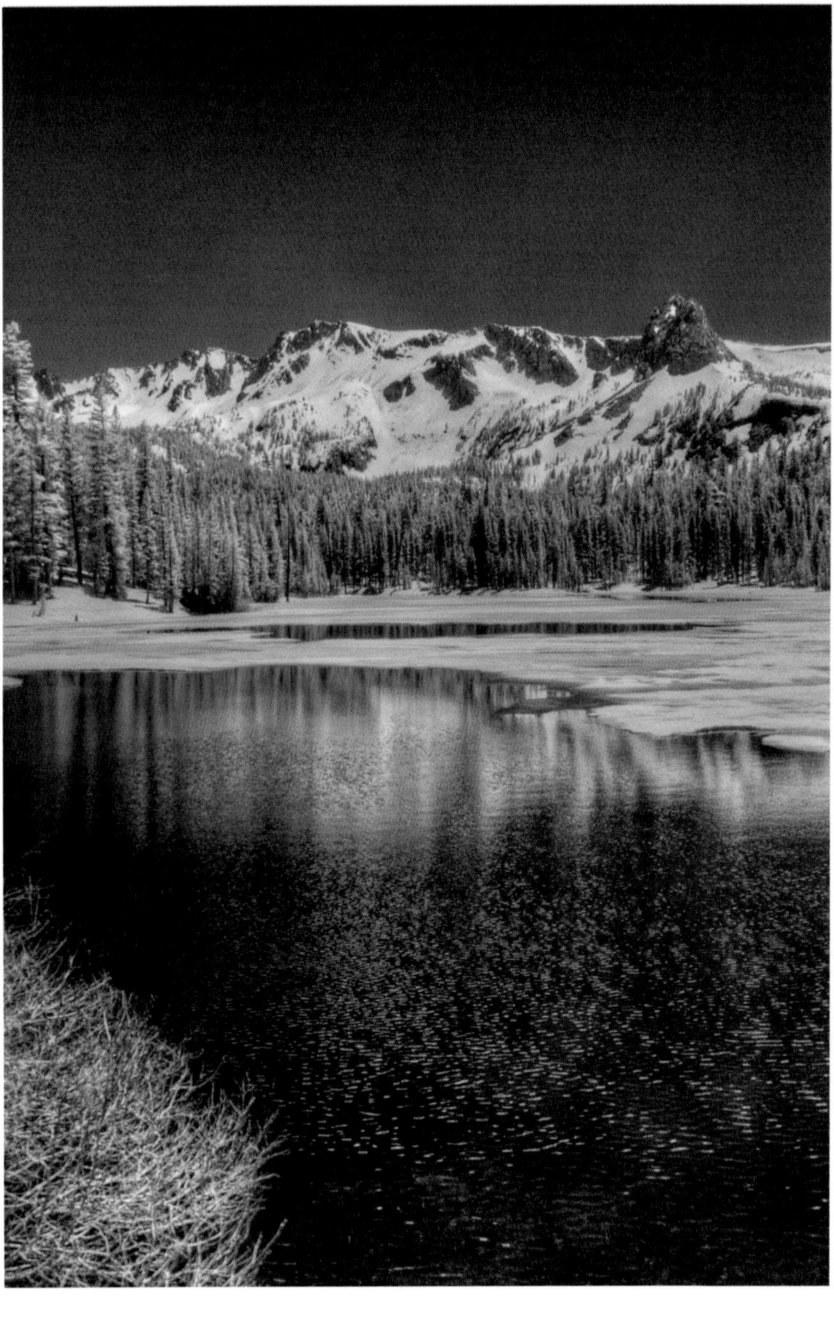

5

## Introduction

This chapter is about taking more control of your camera's operation. Intelligent Auto and SCN predefined scene modes automatically set the camera's focus mode, shutter speed, and aperture. Although this yields a sharp and properly exposed image, it prevents you from adjusting the camera settings and improving the image at a higher level.

You gain this improvement by using the Program Auto (P), Aperture Priority (A), and Shutter Priority (S) shooting modes. Essentially, the Program Auto (P) mode allows the camera to set both the aperture and the shutter speed for proper exposure. Unlike Intelligent Auto or SCN mode, you can now set the ISO and WB. Aperture Priority (A) requires the aperture to be set manually, and the camera adjusts the shutter speed for the recommended exposure. Finally, Shutter Priority (S) requires the shutter to be set manually, and the camera adjusts the aperture for the recommended exposure. By setting the shooting mode to one of these settings, you can override the camera's automatic recommendations and apply a bit more or less exposure. These adjustments allow you to adjust the image's color or to fine-tune the exposure to ensure you capture the entire intensity range of the scene.

The A and S modes allow you to control, respectively, the depth of field or the appearance of moving objects. Certain types of subjects require the aperture to be set at a constant value or the shutter speed to be locked on one value. These settings are not available in Intelligent Auto mode.

When you carefully evaluate your pictures and decide to exert greater control, you gain an awareness of what you should focus on. In automatic modes, the camera selects where to establish focus. It might use Face Detection or Object Tracking for focusing. But for difficult photographic conditions, these controls will be inadequate and you will want to set the focus precisely. This can occur only when you know what the camera is focusing on. In this chapter we will discuss how to target the automatic focus and how to override it so you can focus manually.

First we need to cover some of the general controls that become available when you quit using the automatic modes. Then we will discuss the P, A, and S modes. We'll save Manual (M) mode for chapter 6. Remember that these modes are selected through the menu structure. There is no physical mode dial like there is on most DSLRs.

Entering Shoot Mode is accomplished in one of two ways. The first will always work, but it requires two keystrokes. The second way requires one keystroke; however, it may not be available if the camera has been customized.

The two-keystroke method uses the MENU button:

MENU>Shoot Mode>[Manual], [Shutter Priority], [Aperture Priority], [Program Priority], [Intelligent Auto], [SCN], [Anti Motion Blur], [Sweep Panorama], [3D Sweep Panorama]

After you select the Shoot Mode icon, you can rotate the control wheel and highlight one of the modes, then press soft key C (figures 5-1 and 5-2).

The second way to enter Shoot Mode is to first see if soft key C is labeled "MODE" on the display screen. If it is, you can press the button, which will present you with the screen in figure 5-2. Rotate the control wheel to select the mode you want. Then press soft key C again, and you are ready to take a photograph in that mode.

A word of caution is in order here. If you do not see "MODE" on the screen, it is because your control wheel has been customized. In this case, either utilize the menu structure, or reset your camera by using the Reset Default command described in chapter 1. We will cover camera customization in chapter 7.

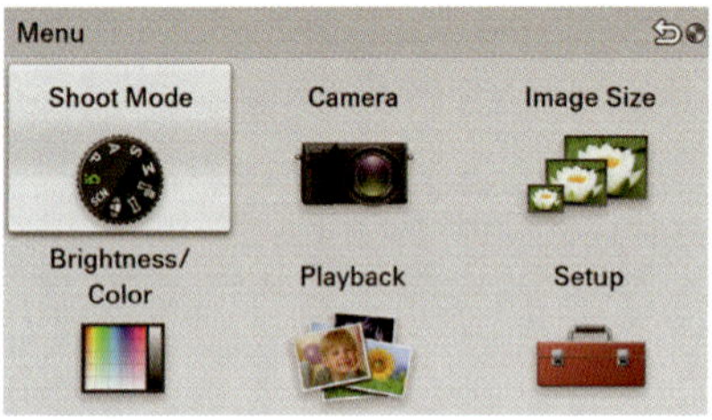


**Figure 5-1**: Pressing the MENU button displays Shoot Mode

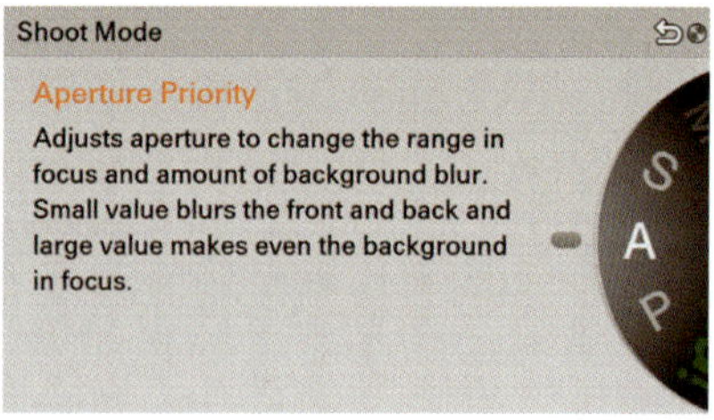


**Figure 5-2**: Entering Shoot Mode provides access to another screen

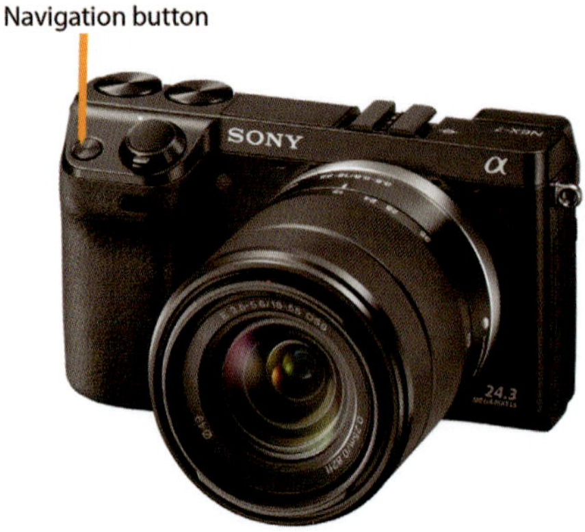


**Figure 5-3**: Front view of the camera showing the Navigation button

## Triple-Dial-Control Operation

Sony has coined the term Triple-dial-control to describe how the control wheel and control dials L and R work together to scroll through and select camera command settings (figures 5-3 and 5-4). When the camera displays a command, the control wheel and at least one of the control dials will work together to enable you to select a command value. This might seem complicated, but fortunately the NEX-7 displays helpful icons on the screen to let you know, albeit sometimes cryptically, what each control will do.

The Triple-dial-control process comes into play when you are within one of the commands and you want to scroll through its available options and select a new value. The easiest way to describe how the Triple-dial-control system works is to use the Navigation button.

By default, the Navigation button is set to display four different camera commands: Focus Settings (figure 5-5), White Balance Settings (figure 5-6), D-Range Settings, and Creative Style. When you press the Navigation button, any of these screens may appear. By default, the last one viewed is retained in the camera's memory and will be remembered even if you turn the camera off. Just remember that the selection choices are in a loop, so each press of the button moves to the next command on the Navigation button list until you return to Live View.

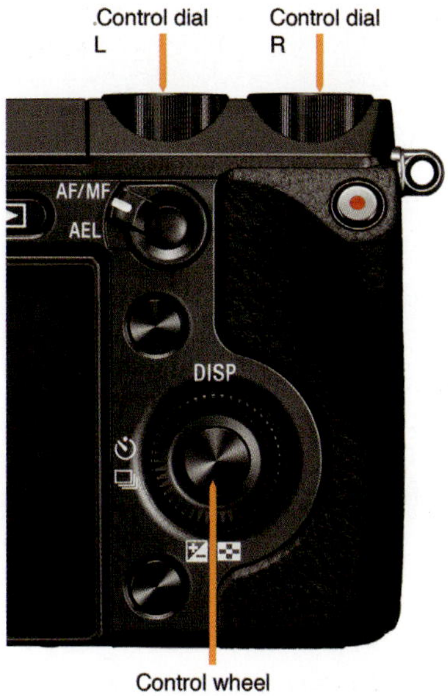


**Figure 5-4**: Rear view of the camera showing the control wheel and control dials L and R

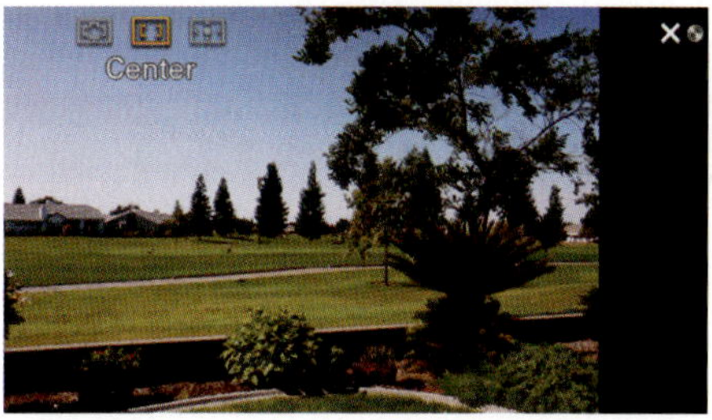


**Figure 5-5**: Navigation button screen showing focus settings

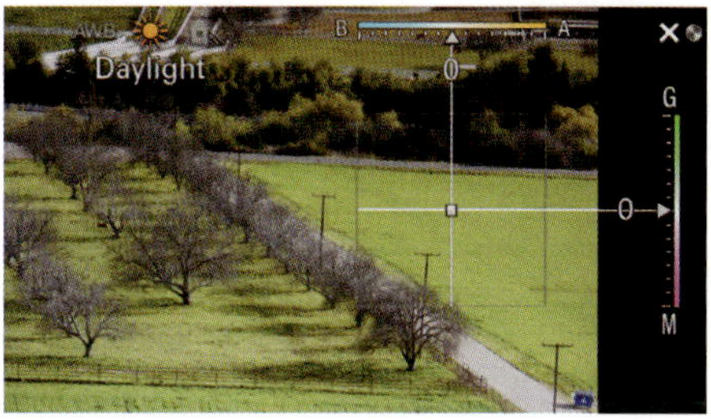


**Figure 5-6**: Navigation button screen showing WB settings

It is important to study the icons that display on the LCD with each press of the button. There are two on the upper right side, and a third one in the middle of the right side. The control dial icons are positioned on the upper right side to simulate the location of the dials. The control dial L icon is displayed to the left of the control dial R icon. The control wheel's active icon is displayed in the center of the right side of the screen, to the left of the wheel itself. Always view the display screen for the helpful icon information that tells you what each of the three controls will do if you use them.

A word of caution is in order here. If you have purchased a used NEX-7 or are borrowing one, the Navigation button and other control buttons may have been customized. Although the Navigation button cycles through the aforementioned commands, the list can be customized to include from zero to six commands, instead of the original four. In this case, you may not see the same commands as described here when you press the Navigation button. If you own the camera, go ahead and execute the Reset Default command to get the original settings back.

First, you will need to know how the semiautomatic commands operate. At the end of the chapter we will describe the semiautomatic modes themselves.

## Exposure Compensation

### Fine-Tuning Automatic Exposure

You can alter the exposure of your image when you enter P, A, or S mode. If you think the scene needs a little more or less light, you can press the bottom (6 o'clock position) rim of the control wheel. This activates the Exposure Compensation process.

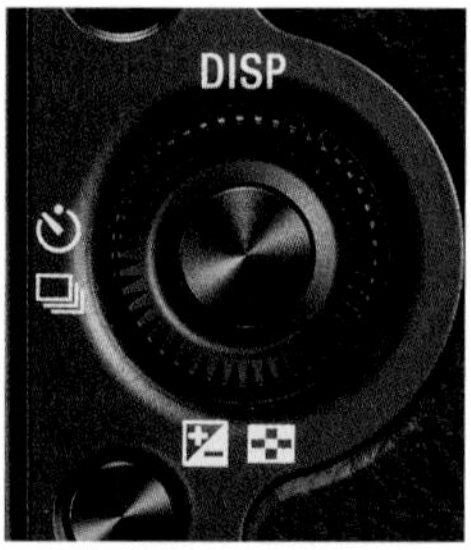


**Figure 5-7a**: Exposure Compensation button and icon

This is easy to remember, thanks to an icon below the control wheel that has a plus or minus symbol (figure 5-7a). After you press this key, the right side of the LCD screen changes and you will see a curved vertical scale with an orange dot (figure 5-7b). Its curvature is a reminder to vary the exposure by rotating the control wheel. When you do so, the orange dot moves within the scale's channel; a clockwise rotation raises it (increases the exposure), and a counterclockwise rotation lowers it (decreases the exposure). The scale provides a qualitative feel for the exposure changes, and a numeric display provides a quantitative measure of the change (figure 5-7c). Also, the brightness of the Live View screen varies, providing a visual cue of the exposure compensation effects. If you decide to accept your modified exposure, press soft key C. If you don't want to accept the changes, press soft key A to exit.

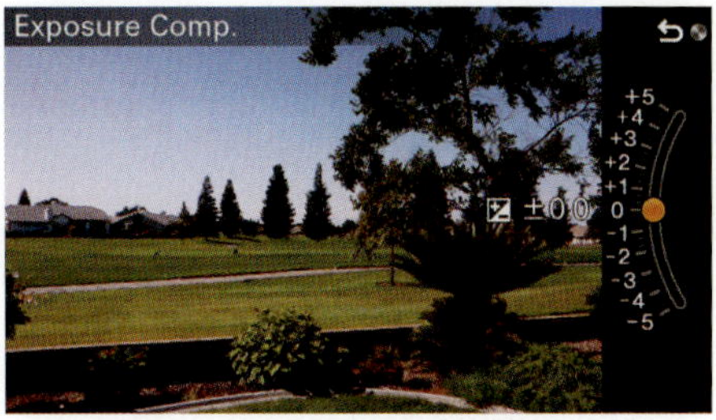


**Figure 5-7b**: No change from recommended exposure

Another way to alter the exposure, when the Shoot Mode is set to P, A, or S, is to simply rotate control dial R (figure 5-8a). This starts exposure compensation. Initially you will see at the bottom of the LCD screen ±0, indicating that no compensation has been applied. When you rotate control dial R, the 0 is replaced by numbers. Overexposure is indicated by +n, and underexposure is indicated by -n (where n is a numeric value that indicates the f-stop). In addition, a scale appears to provide a graphical representation of how far you departed from the camera's recommended exposure (figure 5-8b). Its center is 0 compensation, and it ranges from –5 EV (left) to +5 EV (right). You will also see a numeric readout of the exposure compensation.

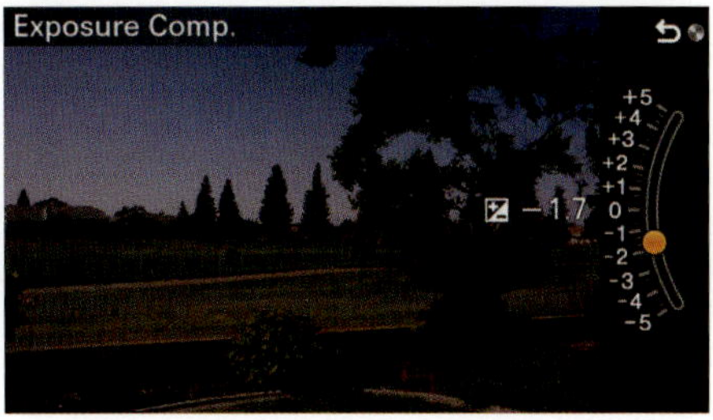


**Figure 5-7c**: Altered exposure providing 1.7 f-stop less exposure

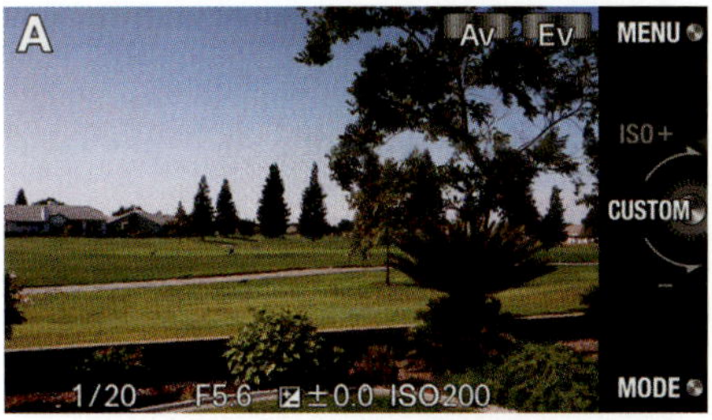


**Figure 5-8a**: EV indicated on control dial R icon

The two icons in the upper right corner of the LCD screen (figure 5-8a) represent control dials L and R. Variable information will display, depending on the selected Shoot Mode. Control dial L can display PV, TV, and AV (figure 5-8a). These letters stand for Program Shift, Time Value, or Aperture Value, and they indicate what is being changed when you turn the dial. In this case, control dial R always controls EV (Exposure Value), indicating it changes the exposure compensation. These icons will disappear in

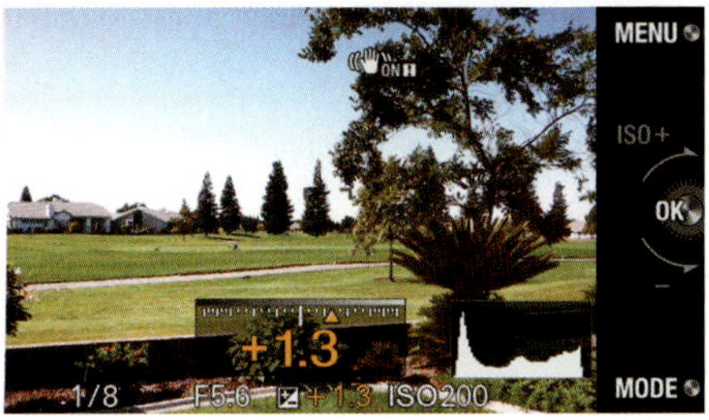


**Figure 5-8b**: Exposure Compensation scale

a few seconds and reappear when you press the DISP key, on the top rim of the control wheel at the 12 o'clock position.

You have two ways to alter exposure, so which should you choose? We prefer using control dial R because it provides minimal disruption of your view of the subject. For example, if you have a live histogram in your display, you can use control dial R to apply exposure compensation while you see its effect on the live histogram (figure 5-9a and figure 5-9b). In contrast, when you press the bottom rim of the control wheel to select Exposure Compensation, you get a new screen that replaces the previous view, so you cannot see the live histogram. Although it is visually attractive, the sacrifice of the live histogram display limits its value.

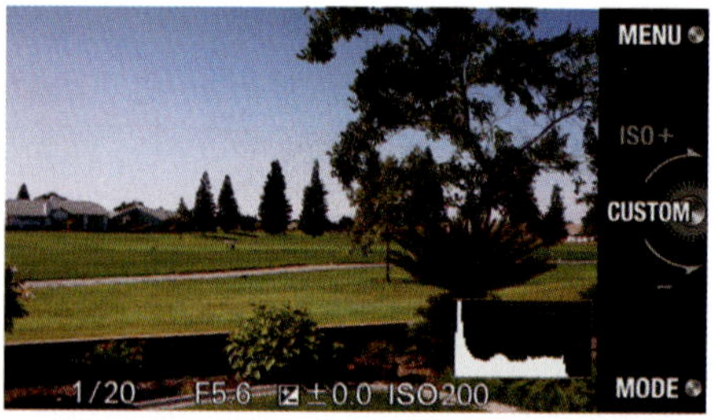

**Figure 5-9a**: Live histogram display with 0 EV

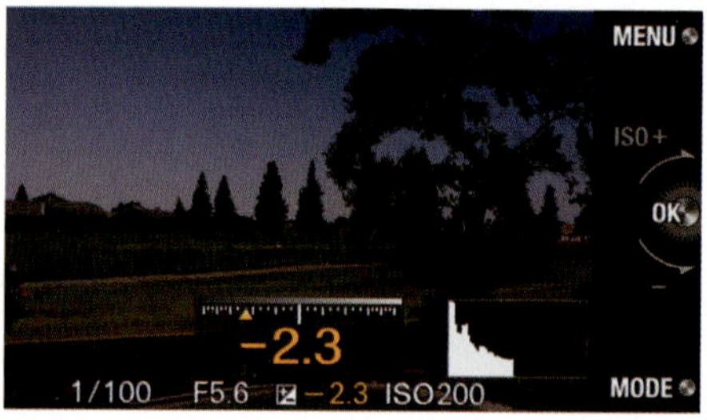

**Figure 5-9b**: Live histogram display with -2.3 EV

### What Are EV Values?

Even though the Sony NEX-7 has an accurate exposure system, you may wish to take over and either add to or subtract from the recommended exposure. This capability is always available to you with the Exposure Compensation scale. In this context, Exposure Value (EV) describes the difference between the recommended and the set exposure. The camera scale ranges from plus to minus 5 EVs; the midpoint, 0 EV, represents the recommended exposure. By rotating control dial R, you can choose up to five f-stops of over- or underexposure. The scale has finely inscribed increments that indicate a third of an f-stop. The camera conveniently provides a large numeric EV value as you rotate control dial R. This way you do not have to count or interpret the Exposure Compensation scale. Because the numeric display is shown as a decimal value, one-third of an f-stop is rounded to 0.3, and two-thirds of an f-stop is rounded to 0.7.

Your camera's recommendations are not always perfect. Its meter is basically a statistical sampling device, and the setting it suggests is a best guess. You can do better. One of the benefits of having an electronic viewfinder is its ability to preview your exposure settings before you take the picture. You may think that darkening or brightening the image provides a better mood for the scene. Or maybe the lighting situation is so extreme that you have to decide which areas—the bright highlights or the dark shadows—have to be sacrificed to capture the image. When you are in control, you can create an image that reflects the mood you are trying to convey to the viewer.

> **Tip: Histogram and Exposure Compensation**
>
> We like to view the histogram when overriding the camera's recommended exposure. Watching how the histogram graph changes position and shape helps us judge whether we are in danger of overexposing the highlights or underexposing the shadows. Unfortunately, when the camera is set to P, A, or S mode and you press the Exposure Compensation button, the Live View changes and you lose your histogram display. A better way of evaluating the exposure is to do it while watching the scene and the histogram. This is accomplished by displaying the histogram in the preview screen. Once seen, you can turn control dial R to provide exposure compensation, and then watch the changing appearance of the scene and histogram while altering exposure.



**Focus Mode: Identifying Where to Focus**

The Sony NEX-7 uses contrast to determine focus. By default, the camera uses 25 AF areas that are distributed across the entire screen for evaluating focus. This design ensures that anything in the field of view is available as a focusing target. As a focusing strategy, it has the advantage of speed. Anything within the frame of the display screen is available for focusing, and you do not have to aim the camera precisely. It is an excellent tool for action photography and quick snapshots because of its lack of discrimination. Set the autofocus area by using the following menu command:

MENU>Camera>Autofocus Area>[Multi], [Center], [Flexible Spot]

When setting this command you will see your options on the right side of the screen, and you can select one of them with the control wheel (figure 5-10a). Note that the default is [Multi] where the camera uses all 25 AF areas to determine focus. Face Detection works only with this setting.

When the shutter is pressed halfway, green brackets mark the area the camera has selected for focusing. If your subject does not have green brackets around it, it may be out of focus. One way to ensure that your subject is focused is to restrict the area within the frame that is used for focusing, then aim that area at your subject. You can do this by selecting either [Flexible Spot] or [Center] (table 5-1).

| Autofocus Area Icon | Autofocus Area Name | Description |
|---|---|---|
| 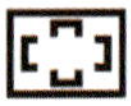 | Multi | The camera divides the framed image into multiple areas, measures the light in each, and determines which area to focus on. |
| 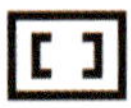 | Center | Only the center of the framed image is used to determine focus. |
| 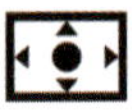 | Flexible Spot | You can select a specific spot for the camera to establish focus. |

**Table 5-1**: Three icons identify the focus areas



When you select [Flexible Spot] or [Center], focusing is restricted to a small region that is indicated by a small bracket.

A much faster way to access a screen for adjusting the camera's AF area is to press the Navigation button (figure 5-10b). This is normally available with the camera's default setting. The Autofocus Area screen is identified by the focusing area icons at the top of the screen, and the words "Focus Setting" will display for a couple of seconds on the bottom as a reminder of where you are in the Navigation cycle. The icons on the top of the screen show your choices for [Multi], [Center], or [Flexible Spot] (table 5-1). Rotating control dial L scrolls through the three icons.

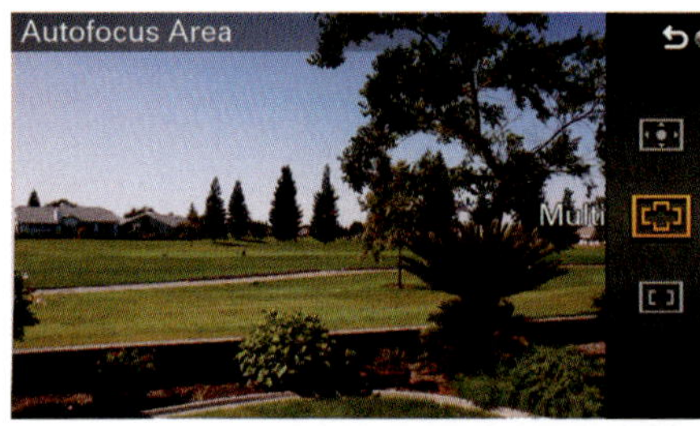


**Figure 5-10a**: Selecting [Multi] focusing area with menu command

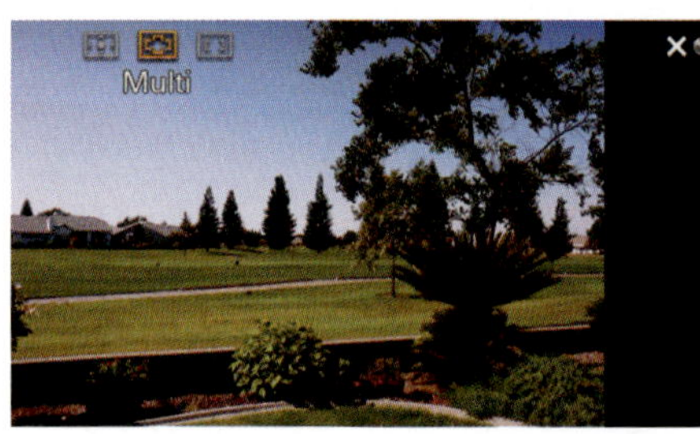


**Figure 5-10b**: Selecting [Multi] focusing area with Navigation button

## Isolating the Focus Point

When you select [Flexible Spot] with the Navigation button, you will see a gray bracket. At the sides of the screen you will see prompts that show how using control dial R or the control wheel will move the bracket (figure 5-11a). Using either of these controls will turn the bracket orange. You can position the bracket horizontally (with control dial R) and vertically (with the control wheel). After you position the orange focusing target to your satisfaction, you can press soft key A to set position and exit the screen to live preview. The orange bracket will change to a subtle gray and serve as a target for focusing. Menu commands can also be used to select [Flexible Spot] (figure 5-11b). This screen differs from figure 5-11a in that the control dial L positions the focusing spot vertically.

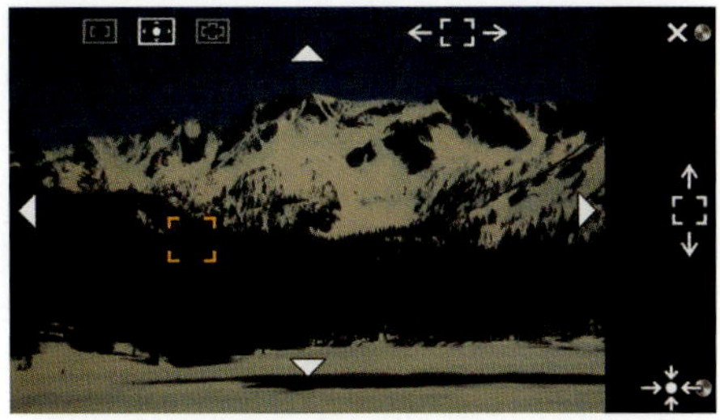

**Figure 5-11a**: Selecting a [Flexible Spot] area with the Navigation button

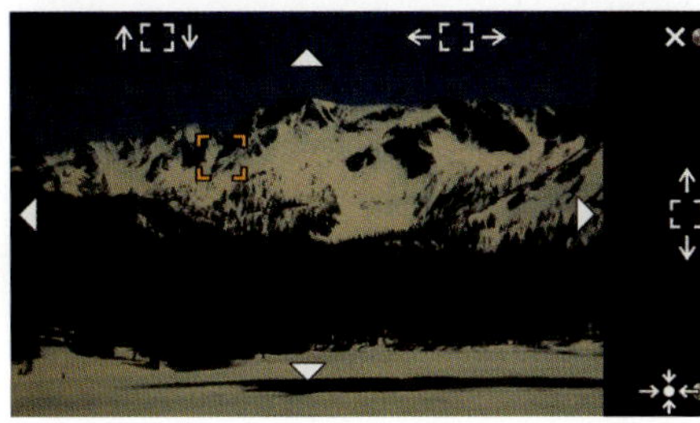

**Figure 5-11b**: Selecting [Flexible Spot] using the Menu

There is a handy shortcut to rapidly move through these points. If you want the focusing area to be restricted to the center of the screen, you have two choices. One is to use control dial R and the control wheel in the [Flexible Spot] setting, or you can simply press soft key B.

Another way to target just the center of the screen for focusing is to set Autofocus Area to [Center]. This places the focus bracket in the center of the screen, without the option of moving it.

### Choosing an Autofocus Area

Normally we set AF to the default option, [Multi], since it is reliable and rapidly acquires focus without the need to aim the camera precisely. Unfortunately, it does not always record the best picture. You may want only your subject to be in focus and the rest of the image to be somewhat blurred and deemphasized. This is when we use a single focus point by selecting either [Center] (the center focus point) or [Flexible Spot] (a focus point that lies outside the center of the screen).

For example, when photographing an animal from a distance, we like the animal's eyes to be recorded sharply with a reflective glint. We accomplish this by setting the Autofocus Mode to [Single-shot AF], described next, and select spot focusing. By aiming the focusing target at the eyes, we can lock focus with a half press on the shutter button. While holding the shutter button halfway, we can adjust our framing, knowing that the eyes will stay in focus. When we are satisfied with our composition, we capture the image by fully depressing the shutter button.

### Autofocus Mode

Automatic focus can be made to work once and then stop when it identifies focus using Single-shot AF, or it can be made to continually change focus using Continuous AF so that if the subject moves closer to or farther away from your position it is kept in focus. As mentioned in chapter 2, when you use Intelligent Auto or the SCN modes, this is set for you. For example, (Single-shot AF) is used virtually all the time, and (Continuous AF) is used only in the SCN Sports mode. When you start using the camera in P, A, S, and M modes, this is something you can set by using the following menu command:

MENU>Camera>Autofocus Mode>[Single-shot AF], [Continuous AF ]

Note: When viewing the live preview screen the abbreviation for [Single-shot AF] is AF-S while for [Continuous AF] it is AF-C.

### Autofocus in Dim Light

The camera needs light to operate the autofocus, so you may find that it cannot obtain focus in dimly lit environments. It solves this problem by projecting a red beam of light from the AF Illuminator, to illuminate the subject. At short distances, this provides enough light to achieve automatic focus. Although a red light is less obvious than a brilliant white beam, it can be annoying to audiences and performers—for example, if you are shooting a stage production in a dimly lit theater. To avoid this distraction, use the following command:

MENU>Setup (Shooting Settings)>AF Illuminator>[Auto], [Off]

The [Auto] value turns on the AF Illuminator light in low-light situations, whereas the [Off] value means the light does not turn on.

### Manual Focus: Overriding Automatic Focusing

Our discussion about using manual focus begins in this chapter and continues in the next. In this chapter we discuss overriding automatic focus and manually fine-tuning focus. In chapter 6, we describe using manual focus as the sole means of focusing.

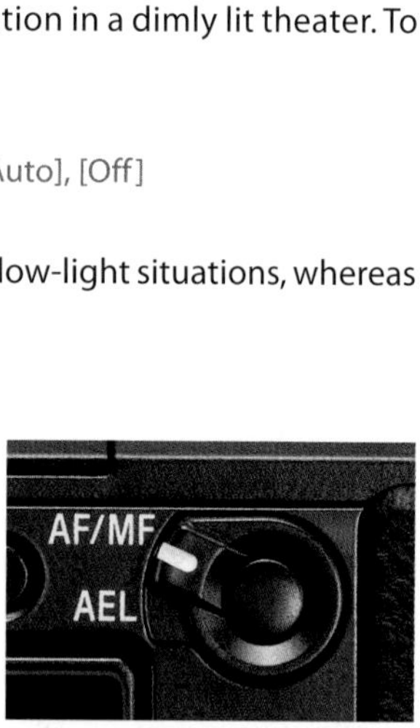


**Figure 5-12**: The AF/MF/AEL switch surrounds the button for executing these options

The AF/MF button (figure 5-12) on the back of the camera is convenient to use if you need to rapidly change the focus method from AF to MF. Just make sure that you set the AF/MF/AEL switch lever to AF/MF so you can switch from autofocus to manual focus by pressing the button. This is especially handy when working with macro lenses or long telephoto lenses. When you use autofocus, you might find that the shot is slightly out of focus because of an intervening object. Pressing the AF/MF button allows you to fine-tune the focus by turning the focusing ring on the lens. A useful adjunct to this command is to make the AF/MF button an On/Off switch—that is, when you press it once, the lens is in manual focus; when you press it a second time, it returns to autofocus. This is accomplished by reassigning the function of the AF/MF button. Use the following command and select [Toggle]:

MENU>Setup (Shooting Settings)>AF/MF control>[Hold], [Toggle]

The button's default is [Hold], which requires you keep the button depressed to maintain manual focus. Doing this briefly is not too cumbersome, but maintaining pressure on this button for several seconds is uncomfortable. For such occasions, we select the [Toggle] option.



The AF/MF Select command is a menu-driven command for selecting autofocus or manual focus:

MENU>Camera>AF/MF Select>[AF], [DMF], [MF]

This command seems redundant because you can use the AF/MF button, but it is surprisingly important. If you need to activate a focus-assisting feature called Peaking, you must set AF/MF Select to [MF]. Otherwise the Peaking feature is completely inactivated and there is no way to turn it on.

The roles of the [AF] and [MF] options are pretty clear; you simply set your camera to be used solely in autofocus or manual focus. The [DMF] option is a little more complicated. First, it works when the camera is in Single-shot AF mode, and it is activated when the camera locks focus. As soon as focus is established, it allows the NEX-7 lens-focusing ring to control focusing so you can adjust the focus to perfection. This mode does not work in Continuous AF mode.

## ISO

To get a feel for ISO, many film photographers use the Sunny f/16 rule: for a subject in open sunlight, set the shutter speed to the reciprocal of the ISO (1/ISO), and set the aperture to f/16.

The nominal sensitivity of the sensor in the NEX-7 is ISO 100, so on a sunny day, without clouds, you will get a properly exposed image by setting the shutter speed to 1/100 second and setting the aperture to f/16. For many photographers, increasing the ISO to ISO 800, will generate an image of acceptable quality. At this ISO the shutter speed is set to 1/800 second while retaining an aperture of f/16.

This makes the camera more suitable for action photography because the fast shutter speed will freeze the motion. In this way, ISO adjustment makes your camera a more versatile recording tool.

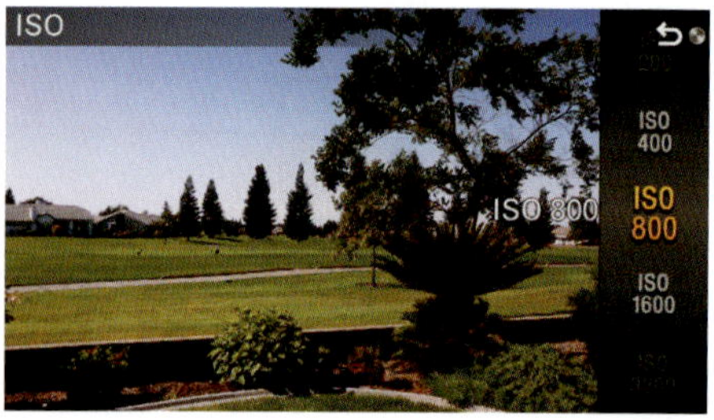


**Figure 5-13a**: Changing ISO with menu commands

When the camera is in Intelligent Auto or SCN mode it uses an Auto ISO setting, which varies the ISO for the subject and the lighting. Eventually you will find this limiting because you will want to set the camera for maximum picture quality, even if it means using a tripod. Experienced photographers usually prefer to set the ISO manually, so it's necessary to set the Shoot Mode to P, A, S, or M. We will discuss this more later; for now we will show you how to change the ISO setting.

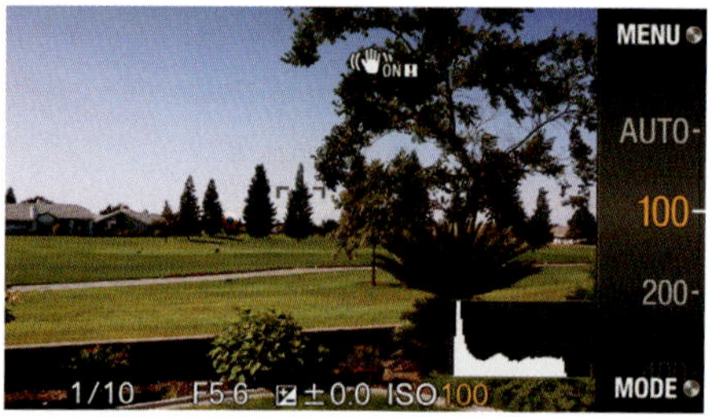


**Figure 5-13b**: Changing ISO with the control wheel

There are two ways to control ISO. Although it is the slower of the two methods, you can press the MENU button on the back of the camera (figure 5-13a) and use the following command:

MENU>Brightness/Color>[ISO]>[ISO *n*], [AUTO]
(Where [*n*] represents an ISO number from 100 to 16000.)

A customized key may be used to select ISO, and if done you will see a display as shown in figure 5-13b. We feel this is redundant because when you set P, A, S, or M modes, the LCD screen shows the curved arrows on the right side of the screen for changing ISO with the control wheel dial. In other words, changing ISO is a feature that is always available when using these modes, therefore dedicating a button for this function seems unnecessary. Simply rotating the control wheel dial is a faster and more convenient way of changing the ISO (figure 5-14).

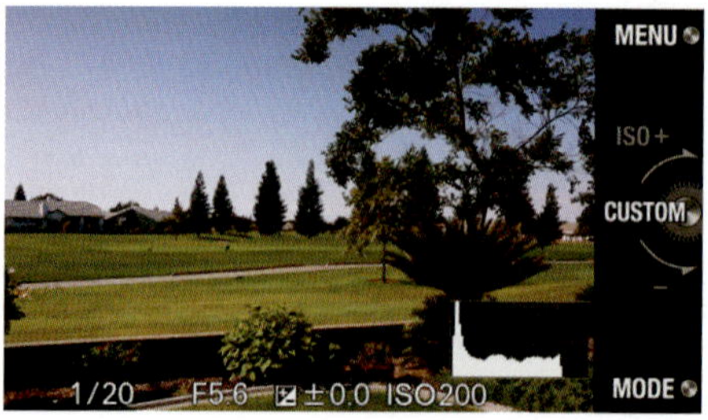


**Figure 5-14**: The control wheel with prompts for adjusting ISO

When you set your own ISO, you need to keep an eye on the shutter speed. If your shutter speed is too slow (becomes too long), it is more likely that your camera will move during the exposure and blur the image. These movements are due to hand tremors or wind. They can be reduced by bracing yourself against a solid support, or they can be avoided by mounting the camera on a tripod.

Another handy rule of thumb when shooting 35mm film is to use a shutter speed that is the reciprocal of the lens's focal length. If you set the lens to 100mm, then you should set a minimum exposure of 1/100 second. For digital photography, this guideline may be too conservative; some photographers find that because the sensor crops the image, the shutter speed should be 1/150 second. Other photographers may find that when the Sony SteadyShot stabilization feature is active, they can photograph handheld 1/50 or 1/25 second. We use the reciprocal of the focal length as our guide for setting the longest shutter speed to be used for telephoto work. This is a very conservative decision; however, we prefer erring on the side of safety.

Obviously, there are many variables that affect how slow a shutter speed you can use before the image is blurred. Remember, the way you hold the camera determines how steady it is. Using the viewfinder and bracing the camera against your face provides more stability than holding the camera at arm's length and composing with the rear LCD monitor. When possible, we brace the camera against a solid support, such as a nearby tree or pole. However, nothing beats a sturdy tripod, and arguably the finest details can be obtained only by using this accessory with a remote release.

### ISO and Noise: Image Degradation

The most obvious defect introduced by raising the ISO is noise—the granular appearance of color blotches in regions that should have smooth tones.

The Sony NEX-7 is not immune to these defects, and it exhibits greater noise at ISO 1600 and higher. However, this should not prevent you from shooting at high ISOs. Depending on how you use the resulting pictures, the noise effects may be inconsequential.

If your goal is to make images strictly for web use, you might be pleasantly surprised to find that the quality of your Sony NEX-7 at ISO 3200 is acceptable.

If our goal is to make large 24 x 36 inch prints, we have an upper limit of ISO 1600 and have been pleased with the results. For critical work, we make sure we shoot in RAW mode and use third-party software (e.g., Noise Ninja) to help reduce noise effects.

### White Balance

The Sony NEX-7 has to be calibrated so it can record colors accurately. In effect, the camera must be told what type of light is illuminating the subject. This task used to be performed manually; however, the method was inconvenient and would result in an image with horrible colors if the wrong light source was selected. This was especially true with DSLRs that relied on optical viewfinders.

To get around this problem, camera designers developed automatic white balance (AWB), which enables the camera to calibrate itself to the light source. In essence, AWB takes a statistical sampling of the image and makes a best guess about the type of light that is illuminating the scene. For the most part, it does a good job, and many photographers always use AWB. But, like all statistical sampling techniques, it can be fooled. This is most evident when working with indoor lighting. Fortunately, you can compensate for this in the Sony NEX-7 by selecting preset WB values.

To better control the appearance of your photograph, we recommend that you become accustomed to setting your own WB. Your results will be more consistent and more reproducible if you get into this habit. To do so, use the command below (see table 5-2 for a list of WB values).

MENU>Brightness/Color>White Balance>[value]

| WB Icon | WB Name | Description |
|---|---|---|
| AWB | AWB | WB is set by the camera automatically. |
|  | Daylight | WB is set for a subject in direct sunlight. |
|  | Shade | WB is set for a subject in the shade and not illuminated by direct sunlight. |
|  | Cloudy | WB is set for the subject on a cloudy, overcast day when the sun is hidden by cloud cover. |
|  | Incandescent | WB is set for the subject illuminated by indoor light (assumes the light is tungsten filament). |
| -1 | Fluor.:Warm White | WB is set for the subject illuminated by warm fluorescent light (3000 K). |
| 0 | Fluor.:Cool White | WB is set for the subject illuminated by cool fluorescent light (4100 K). |
| +1 | Fluor.:Day White | WB is set for the subject illuminated by day white fluorescent light (5000 K). |
| +2 | Fluor.:Daylight | WB is set for the subject illuminated by daylight fluorescent light (6500 K). |
| WB | Flash | WB is set for an electronic flash unit. Some yellow tints are added to enrich and warm up the picture. |

| WB Icon | WB Name | Description |
|---|---|---|
| | C.Temp./Filter | You can set the WB based on a specific color temperature value represented in kelvin units (K).<br>Light bulb packages should specify a kelvin rating. Set the WB to that specific value with the following steps:<br>1. Go to the White Balance command using the Navigation button.<br>2. Scroll through the option list by rotating control dial L. Select [C. Temp./Filter].<br>3. Press soft key B. The LCD screen will show the letter K opposite this button.<br>4. Scroll through the color temperature values by rotating control dial L.<br>5. Select the value that matches the kelvin rating on the package. Press soft key C to select the value. Press the shutter halfway to save the value and return to Live View.<br>6. Exit out of the White Balance command. |
| | Custom | Use this option to store a custom WB setting. |
| SET | Custom Setup | Use this option to set up a custom WB to be stored in the [Custom] option. |

**Table 5-2**: WB icons and light sources



The WB icons are displayed on the right side of the screen. Rotate the control wheel, control dial R, or control dial L to scroll through the WB options. When you find the WB preset you want to select, press soft key C (figure 5-15a). As you can see, the list of WB preset options is long.

Another way of accessing the WB function is by pressing the Navigation button. Press the button until you see the WB commands displayed on the screen (figure 5-15b). Using this method of selecting WB is a little more difficult because the icons are smaller. If WB is not assigned to the Navigation button, you can assign it by using the customization method described in chapter 7.

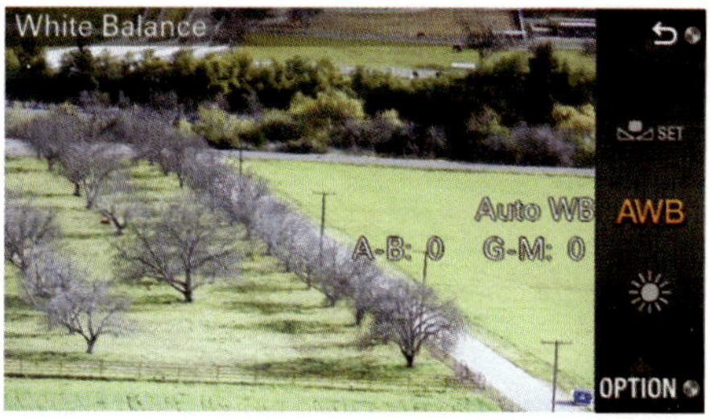


**Figure 5-15a**: AWB selected from menu commands

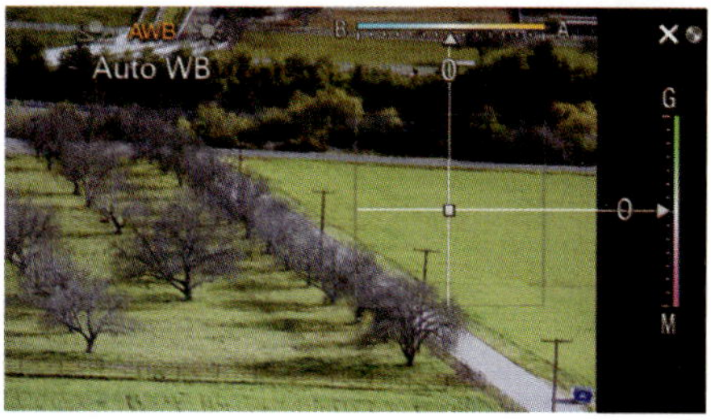


**Figure 5-15b**: AWB selected with the Navigation button

The icons in table 5-2 represent light sources and serve as mnemonics to help you select the appropriate WB preset. Two WB settings, [Custom Setup] and [C.Temp./Filter], require a value to be manually input. These more complex options will be described in chapter 6 when we discuss manual controls.

Remember that the icons for WB are only an approximation of the illuminant's color characteristics. For example, the [Incandescent] option assumes an idealized bulb emitting a specific color of light. In fact, indoor general use bulbs can have a wide range of color values, and only specialized technical bulbs are rated for a specific color. For example, in many homes, the brightness of an incandescent light can be dimmed, which shifts the color from a brilliant white to a ruddy red.

You select the WB preset by using a variety of controls; which controls you use depends on how you access the command. It is easiest to use when you select it as a menu command because all of the rotating controls (control dials L and R, and the control wheel) will scroll through the list of WB icons. In contrast, if you use the Navigation button, you have to be more careful which controls you use. When you enter the WB screen, only control dial L will scroll through the WB preset options, and control dial R and the control wheel are dedicated to finely adjusting WB. We will describe this control operation in chapter 6. For the time being, just use control dial L.

To illustrate the benefit of using a preset WB instead of AWB, compare the options when you use the camera indoors with incandescent lighting. In most situations the AWB image will have a warm tone, and the incandescent WB preset will provide a more neutral image. Which should you use? Artistically, you may prefer the AWB setting because it produces a warm mood, and most viewers assume that you are dealing with either indoor or candle lighting. For more technical work, such as scientific applications, you will probably use the incandescent preset and record a more neutral image.

Inaccurate WB occurs frequently under fluorescent bulbs. They vary so widely in their color output that the NEX-7 has four presets for them . All you can do is cycle through the four settings and see which one provides the most neutral color. Although Sony characterizes these presets as warm white, cool white, day white, and daylight color, you will find that these settings are not too helpful. Oftentimes they do not match the manufacturer's description of the bulb. To deal with such conditions, we will give you some techniques for manually adjusting the WB in chapter 6.

## Three Semiautomatic Modes: Shutter Priority (S), Aperture Priority (A), and Program Auto (P)

As mentioned earlier, using the P, A, or S shooting modes gives you greater control over the camera. You select these modes through the Shoot Mode menu. Unlike Intelligent Auto and the SCN modes, here you can select the shutter speed, aperture, WB, and ISO. This gives you greater artistic control in creating the image; however, there is the increased risk of selecting a setting that detracts from image quality.

### Shutter Priority (S)

To select Shutter Priority (S), set the Shoot Mode to S. You can then choose the camera's shutter speed, and the camera selects the aperture for proper exposure. This is advantageous for action shots. A fast shutter speed can keep a moving subject from being recorded as a fuzzy blur. Conversely, if you want to show a moving subject as an extreme blur (a streak across the frame), you can use this mode with a slow shutter speed.

When this mode is selected (figure 5-16a), the letter S appears in the upper left corner of the LCD screen (figure 5-16b), and control dial L is labeled with the letters TV (Time Value). This controls the shutter speed. The icon for control dial R is labeled EV (Exposure Value). Along the bottom of the screen you will see that the numbers for the shutter speed and aperture are glowing white. If you rotate control dial L, the shutter speed number turns orange and the value changes. The value for the aperture will change to keep the exposure constant. If you want to override the recommended exposure, rotate control dial R (EV) to physically change the aperture. When you reach the maximum or minimum aperture for the lens, the aperture value will start to flash. You will see the degree of exposure compensation at the bottom center of the screen.

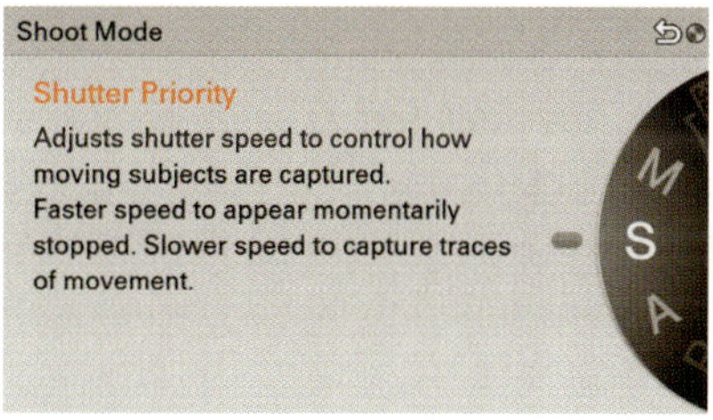


**Figure 5-16a**: Select the S mode with the Shoot Mode control

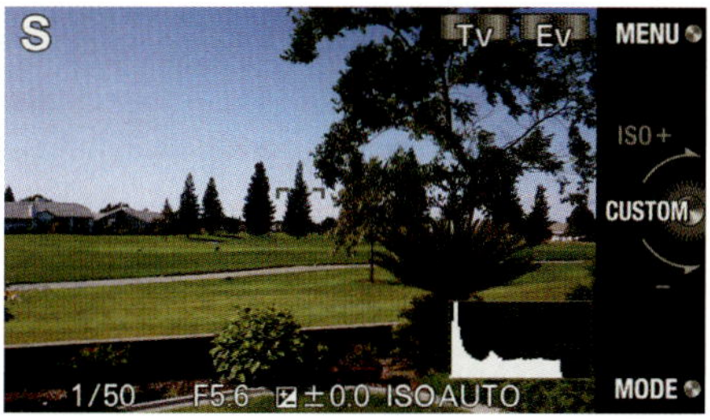


**Figure 5-16b**: When S mode is selected, control dials L and R are labeled TV and EV

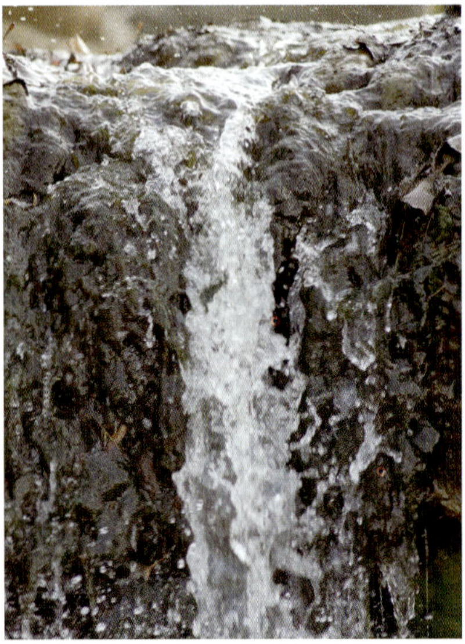

**Figure 5-17a**: A fast (or short) shutter speed freezes the appearance of moving water

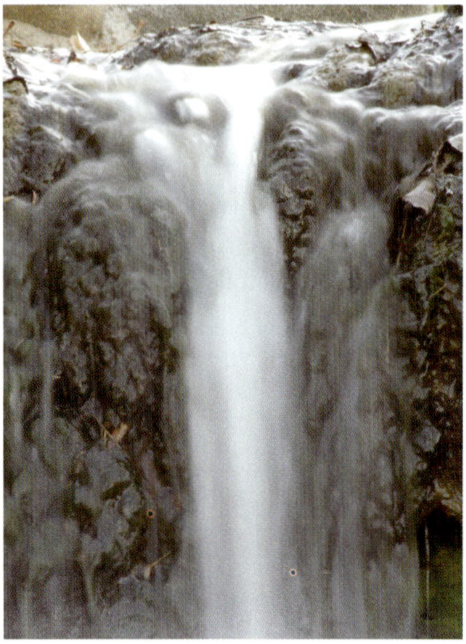

**Figure 5-17b**: A slow (or long) shutter speed gives moving water a flowing appearance

Controlling the shutter speed gives you artistic control of a moving subject. You may wish to use a fast shutter speed to freeze the motion (figure 5-17a), or you may wish to use a slow shutter speed to blur anything that is moving (figure 5-17b).

Another reason to use a fast shutter speed is to prevent the blurring effects of camera movement during handheld exposures. Obviously the chance of the camera moving is reduced if you use a shutter speed of 1/1000 second instead of 1/20 second.

When you use a shutter speed of 1/15 second or longer, camera movement can blur the image. It would be better to use a faster shutter speed to ensure that you capture a sharp image. You can accomplish this by increasing the amount of light on the subject with a flash, by opening the aperture, or by increasing the ISO. In all of these cases you can increase the shutter speed and reduce the likelihood of slight movements blurring your picture while the shutter is open. If none of these options are possible, you should mount your camera on a tripod and turn off SteadyShot by using the following menu command:

MENU>Setup (Shooting Settings)>SteadyShot>[On], [Off]

## Aperture Priority (A)

Aperture Priority (A) mode is the converse of S mode. Here you select the aperture, and the camera selects the shutter speed. This allows you to control the depth of field, which is critical for closeup photography where the depth of field tends to be shallow. If the aperture is opened, the shallow depth of field blurs the foreground and background surrounding the subject. This can be advantageous in portraiture where you focus on the model's face and force the viewer's attention to the area of interest.

In the A shooting mode, you see both the aperture value and the shutter speed at the bottom of the screen (figure 5-18). When you first enter this screen, you will see an A in the upper left corner, and you'll see labels on the control dials. The control dial L icon has the letters AV (Aperture Value), and control dial R has the letters EV. When you turn control dial L, the aperture number turns orange, and the shutter speed number remains white. The shutter speed will vary in proportion to the aperture. You can vary the exposure as described for S mode, except you change the shutter speed rather than the aperture when you rotate control dial R.

The NEX-7 has an unusual feature in the A mode. The lens opening changes immediately when you turn control dial L. As a consequence the display screen provides an immediate depth of field preview. Most DSLRs, and Sony Single-Lens Translucent (SLT) cameras, have a depth of field preview button that, when pressed, closes down the aperture so you can see the preview. With the NEX-7, you always have depth of field preview in the A mode.

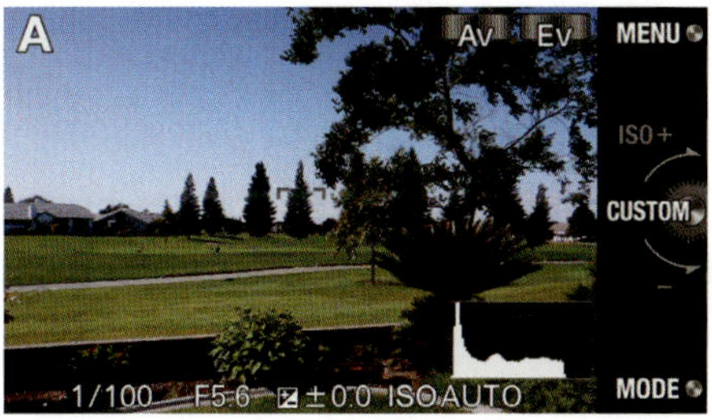


**Figure 5-18**: The A mode with aperture f/5.6 and shutter speed 1/100 second displayed in white

### Program Auto (P)

Program Auto (P) mode is similar to Intelligent Auto mode in that it sets both the shutter speed and the aperture, but it has an important difference: you are in complete control of both. You decide if the shutter speed should be fast or slow and whether the aperture should be wider or narrower. When you select P mode, the camera selects an aperture and shutter speed combination, and you will see a P in the upper left corner of the screen (figure 5-19a). If either the aperture or the shutter speed is inappropriate, you can change them with the Program Shift function. Simply rotate control dial L, which is labeled with the letters PV, and the values will change in synch so you maintain a constant exposure (figure 5-19b).

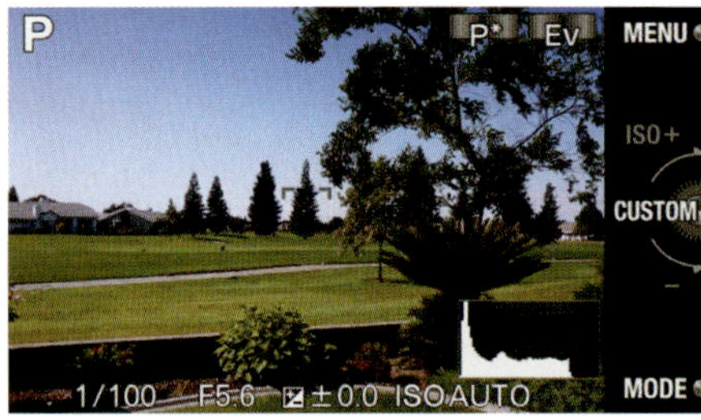


**Figure 5-19a**: Program Auto (P) with an aperture of f/5.6 and a shutter speed of 1/100 second

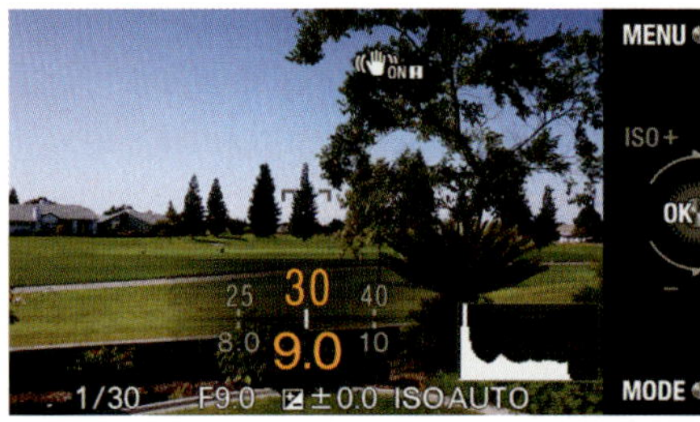


**Figure 5-19b**: Rotating control dial L changes the aperture to f/9.0 and the shutter speed to 1/30 second

You can also change the exposure with control dial R, which is labeled with the letters EV. You will see either the aperture or the shutter speed change as you apply exposure compensation.

## Recommendations

When you use the P, A, or S modes on your NEX-7 camera, you can start taking greater control of your camera. Many controls that were not available in the automatic modes are now accessible, and you can develop your own working style. You can now adjust the exposure, select the ISO, and lock in the WB.

For example, when we want to use the camera for point-and-shoot work we set the Shoot Mode to [P] and the ISO to [AUTO]. The camera sets the aperture, shutter speed, and ISO. If we do not care for the shutter speed, we can rotate control dial L to select a new combination of shutter speeds and apertures. If the exposure is not to our liking, we use control dial R to override the recommended exposure. We can also lock in our WB and adjust it to fit the scene. This will take some thought. For example, if you photograph a sunset and set the WB preset to daylight, the red hues will be recorded with greater saturation. In this situation if you leave the camera on Auto WB, it will attempt to neutralize the predominant red scene and capture a neutral shade.

When we are concerned about depth of field, we use the A mode because we can select the aperture, and the camera adjusts the shutter speed to provide the proper exposure. A narrow aperture increases the depth of field. A wide aperture reduces the depth of field. A little-known benefit of the NEX-7 design is that it provides a real-time depth of field preview. As you close or open the aperture, the display screen shows the depth of field that is seen by the lens. Rotating control dial L immediately sets the aperture so the sensor views the scene stopped down. Most DSLRs, and Sony SLT cameras, require the lens to be stopped down manually by pressing a depth of field preview button. This is not necessary with the NEX-7; what you see is what will be recorded.

When we deal with moving subjects or a long telephoto lens, we set the camera to S mode and set the shutter speed ourselves. As expected, the camera adjusts the aperture to set the recommended exposure.



In regard to ISO, we like to adjust the sensitivity of the sensor. For the highest quality work on a tripod or in the laboratory, we use ISO 100. For rapidly moving subjects in daylight, we use ISO 400–800. For dim light work, we use ISO 1600, and occasionally we use ISO 3200. At this high of an ISO, we will save the files in RAW and use third-party noise reduction software, such as Noise Ninja.

The majority of our photographs are taken with AWB. The camera does a satisfactory job of recording pleasing colors in subjects that are illuminated with various lighting sources. However, we have noticed that indoor lighting with incandescent lamps can throw off AWB. Under these conditions, our images have an orange-red hue. To obtain more neutral colors, we use the WB setting for incandescent lighting. However, there are situations when we choose a WB preset. For example, when shooting a sunrise or sunset with orange-colored clouds, we do not use AWB because the camera will attempt to neutralize the red hues. A deeper and, to our eyes, a more realistic rendering of a sunset is recorded when we use the [Daylight] preset.

Again, we recommend saving files in RAW format. Virtually all programs that read RAW files have a straightforward command for adjusting WB when it is set incorrectly in the camera.

# Chapter 6: Manual Operation of the Camera

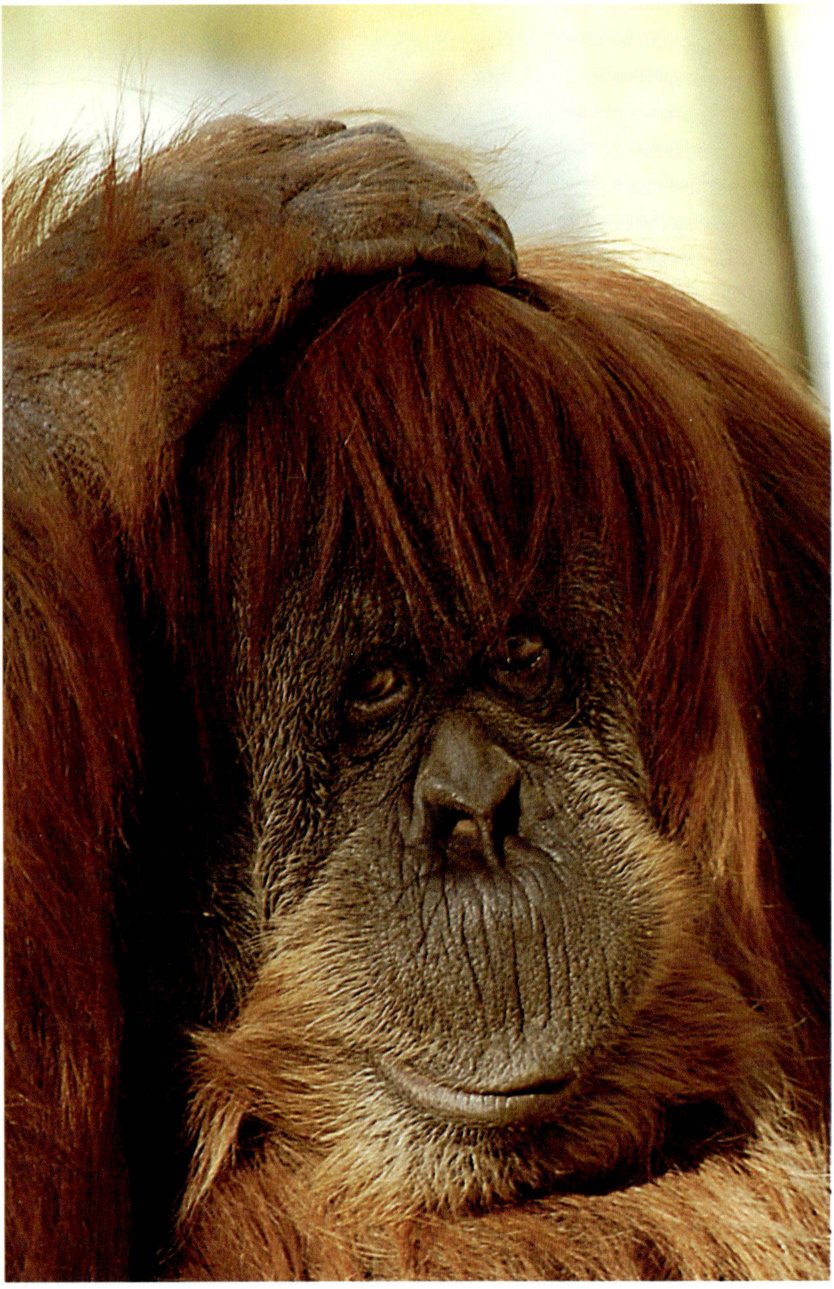

6

## Introduction

Where chapter 5 dealt with taking over partial control of camera settings, this chapter is about taking complete control of the camera and manually fine-tuning its settings.

There are times when you want the exposure and focus to be fixed to a constant value. For example, suppose you want to take a panoramic shot the old-fashioned way without using the NEX-7's Sweep Panorama feature (see chapter 8). To do this, mount the camera on a tripod, set the exposure to manual, and take a series of overlapping pictures by panning with the tripod head. The focus and aperture is fixed and is not allowed to change as you pan. After you take all the pictures, download them to your computer and merge them with third-party software to create your panoramic image.

The advantage of doing a panoramic image this way, which is more inconvenient than the automated Sweep Panorama mode, is the increased image resolution. By working with the full area of the sensor, you can collect a series of images that have a vertical height of 4000 pixels rather than the 2000 pixels generated with Sweep Panorama. A knowledgeable photographer can go further and create an even larger panorama by doing multiple sweeps and building one on top of the other.

Knowing how to set the camera to manual exposure and manual focus enables you to pursue strategies like this for improving your images.

In addition, we will cover some advanced features that you can use in P, A, and S modes. We didn't discuss them in chapter 5 because they involve camera settings that require you to take greater direct control of the camera. For example, rather than use incandescent or daylight preset WB settings, you will learn how to set the WB for any light source. This requires your active input by setting an illuminant's color temperature value or by calibrating your camera directly to the light source. Another useful technique is exposure bracketing, which creates a set of images (or bracket) in which each is slightly different so you can select the best image. For example, you can set a command to take a series of pictures where the exposure varies between each shot. Simplistically, this provides a shotgun approach for finding the proper exposure. It may be the basis for generating an image under difficult lighting conditions or for creating a surrealistic color rendition by using HDR and tone mapping post-processing techniques.

Taking control of your camera is full of experimentation with exciting results. The more you test the camera's capabilities, the better equipped you will be to extend your photographic abilities and create artistic, one-of-a-kind shots.

## Manual Exposure Mode Controls

Setting the Shoot Mode to Manual Exposure (M) displays an M on the display screen (figure 6-1a), with the shutter speed and aperture values displayed at the bottom of the screen as white numbers. You can change them by rotating either control dial L (TV) or control dial R (AV), respectively.

When you start rotating a dial, the numbers controlled by it turn orange and change in value. If you do not turn the control dial after 2 seconds, the orange numbers will change back to white. As you set the aperture or shutter speed, you will see a set of numbers changing at the bottom center of the screen, to the left of the letters M.M. The letters stand for Metered Manual. The changing number is the EV value showing how far off the settings are from the camera's recommended exposure. In figure 6-1b, the camera is set to −1.7 EV, a lower exposure than the camera recommends.

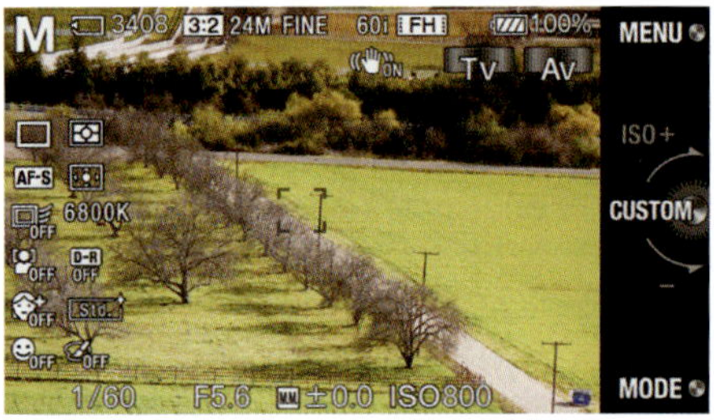


**Figure 6-1a**: Live View in M mode with the aperture and shutter speed set to the meter's recommendation

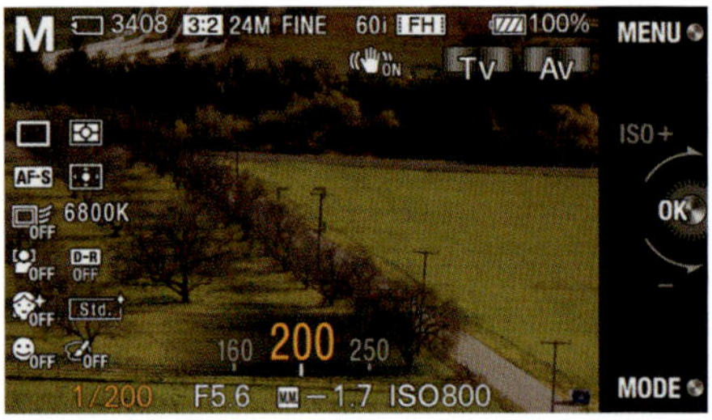


**Figure 6-1b**: Exposure set to -1.7 EV from the meter's recommended exposure

When the camera settings are at the recommended exposure, M.M. will show ±0. As you deviate from the recommendation, you will see the EV change in increments of one-third of an f-stop until it reaches either +2 EV or −2 EV. The M.M. value provides a way of applying a known offset to the recommended exposure. For example, you may set the camera so the reading is +1 EV. We do this when we record a snow scene and a large portion of the scene should be recorded as a brilliant white. If you simply follow the camera's recommendation, its exposure estimate is based on the assumption that the overall scene consists of mid-tone values. If, however, the scene is predominantly consisting of light tones, as in a snow scene, the camera will recommend an exposure that will record snow as being gray. We have determined that applying a +1 EV offset renders the recorded image so snow appears white. You can check the effects of offsetting the exposure by studying the LCD screen. The beauty of having a Live View camera is that you have a preview of the subject before you actually take the picture.

In M mode, the brightness of the NEX-7 display screen is an indicator for the appearance of the recorded image. If the sensor is receiving too little light to record an image, you will see a black screen. If the sensor is receiving too much light, you will see a brilliant white screen. Use control dials L and R to adjust the aperture and shutter speed until the image looks acceptable on the display screen.

### Extremely Long Exposure "B" Shutter Speed

M mode allows you to set exposures of up to two minutes. Turn control dial L (TV) to the left, which increases the value of the shutter speed numbers until you reach B (Bulb). This occurs just beyond a 30 second exposure. At this setting, the shutter opens when you depress the shutter button and remains open as long as it is depressed. Releasing the shutter button terminates the exposure. The B shutter speed is available only in M mode, while the longest shutter speed for P, A, and S modes is only 30 seconds.

For such long exposures, the camera should be mounted on a tripod. Any camera movement will blur the image, and it is difficult to hold the shutter button down for such a long period without jarring the camera. To accomplish this task easily, we recommend getting the Sony infrared shutter trigger (RMT-DSLR1 Wireless Remote Commander). When you set the shutter speed to B and set the Drive Mode to [Remote Cdr.], a single press of the remote's shutter button will open the NEX-7 shutter and keep it open. A second press closes the shutter.



**How Shutter Speed Numbers Work**

Normally the Sony NEX-7 shutter speed is measured in fractions of a second. When you see the number 4 by itself, it actually means 1/4 of a second. When you reach a shutter speed longer than 1/3 second, the display switches from fractions to decimals, so the next longest shutter speed is 0.4. From 1 second on, the ″ symbol follows the shutter speed number, so 1″ indicates one second, and 30″ indicates 30 seconds.

## Noise Reduction with Long Exposure

Images taken with long exposures may suffer from noise. This type of noise is evidenced by "hot" pixels that stand out. The Long Exposure NR command reduces this effect by using a procedure known as dark frame subtraction whenever the shutter speed exceeds one second. The Long Exposure NR command is as follows:

MENU>Setup (Shooting Settings)>Long Exposure NR>[On], [Off]

This process requires taking two images to create a single image, and will operate only in shooting and drive modes where only a single image is being recorded. It will not work if the camera is recording a continuous series of images, such as when using Anti Motion Blur, SCN Hand-held Twilight, or in either of the Panorama modes. Also, this command is not available in any of the Continuous and Bracket Drive Mode options. It works on both RAW and JPEG files.

When the Long Exposure NR command is turned [On] and the exposure is set to one second or longer, the following steps occur:

1. When the shutter button is pressed, the camera records the image, including the noise generated by the sensor.
2. The camera takes another exposure but does not record an image. This is the so-called dark frame, which creates a reference map for the previous image's noise pattern.
3. The camera subtracts the dark frame image from the first image to reduce the appearance of noise in the final image.

The Long Exposure NR command doubles the time it takes to record an image. For example, if you take a photograph with a 10 second exposure, the camera will automatically take a subsequent exposure of 10 seconds to create the dark frame. Then the camera processes the subtraction to remove the noise from the first image. For exposures that run more than several seconds, this can create a tedious wait, so some people turn this command off.

Most of our exposures are less than one second in duration, so having this command on makes no difference under these conditions. For the few pictures we have taken with exposures of several seconds, we have been pleased with this command's results, and therefore we leave it on. Again, with long exposures make sure you mount the camera on a tripod and turn off the SteadyShot option.

> **B Stands for Bulb**
>
> "Bulb" is a historical reference to a time when cameras had pneumatically driven shutters. To open the shutter, the photographer squeezed an air bulb, and to close the shutter, the photographer released the bulb. In modern cameras, the analogous operation is to press the shutter button to open the shutter and maintain pressure on the button to keep the shutter open. Releasing the shutter button closes the shutter.
>
> If you intend to use long exposures, we recommend that you get a remote shutter release. When you have the shutter speed set to B, pressing the remote shutter button once will open the shutter, and a second press will close it.

### Noise Reduction at High ISO

We previously mentioned that using higher ISOs results in increased noise and that we tend to photograph at ISOs lower than 1600. If you are forced to work at ISO 1600 or higher, you might want to try this in-camera noise reduction option. It works only on JPEG files and is used with ISO 1600 and higher. The High ISO NR command does not require a second exposure to capture a dark frame; instead, it works on just one image. You can set noise reduction to High, Normal, or Low. Use the following menu command to adjust the level of noise reduction:



MENU>Setup (Shooting Settings)>High ISO NR>[High], [Normal], [Low]

Noise reduction is essentially a blurring function that smooths out the appearance of noise, but it does so at the expense of image sharpness. When you apply higher levels of noise reduction, you get a smoother-looking image but an increased loss of definition.

This command can be used when you fire continuously at 3 or 10 frames per second. Be aware that the command can take some time to execute, so for a moment your camera may not be ready for the next shot. Therefore, applying the noise reduction feature may slow down the frame rate when you use continuous firing.

We set the High ISO NR command to [Low]. When shooting in low-light conditions, we prefer saving the picture as a RAW file and removing the noise later with third-party software. We use Noise Ninja, which seems to reduce noise with less detail loss than the NEX-7 High ISO NR option.

## Metering Modes

When controlling your exposure is critical, it is important to know where and how your camera's light meter measures intensity. The NEX-7's built-in light meter uses three metering modes (table 6-1). You can access the settings with the following command:

MENU>Brightness/Color>Metering Mode>[Multi], [Center], [Spot]

| Metering Mode Icon | Metering Mode Name | Description |
|---|---|---|
| 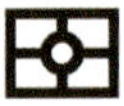 | Multi | The camera divides the framed image into multiple areas, measures the lighting in each, and determines an overall exposure. |
|  | Center | The camera biases its exposure on the central area and provides less emphasis on the periphery. |
|  | Spot | The camera uses only the center of the framed image to determine exposure. A faint circle on the screen indicates the area the camera will use. |

**Table 6-1**: Metering Mode command icons

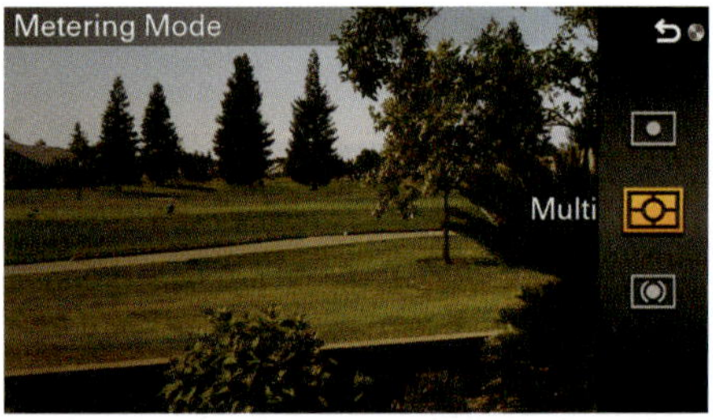


**Figure 6-2**: Metering Mode's three options with [Multi] selected

The default and most commonly used method is [Multi], where light over the entire area of the framed image is used to calculate the exposure (figure 6-2). This is more than a simple average—it is a complex computation that ensures a good exposure for a wide variety of subjects. Historically, many camera manufacturers developed these calculations for film cameras, and later they were refined for digital cameras. Although early versions of this option were unreliable, this has changed and has practically turned the NEX-7 into a point-and-shoot camera. The results are quite good, and you can refine them by studying the live histogram to adjust the exposure slightly. Again, the advantage of having a Live View camera is the ability to ascertain if you need to modify the exposure before you take the photograph. At the very least, [Multi] does a good job of putting your exposure in the right ballpark.

The second metering method is [Center], which uses an easily understood algorithm for evaluating exposure. It is based on the assumption that the most important part of the picture is in the center; therefore, the meter biases the exposure so the center of the display screen is well exposed. The peripheral areas are also measured and contribute to the overall exposure, but they are given less priority. Historically, this was a popular way to measure light in an SLR camera. Although this older technology has the virtue of simplicity, it is not as reliable as [Multi] area metering. We rarely use this type of metering since it results in a higher percentage of unacceptable exposures.

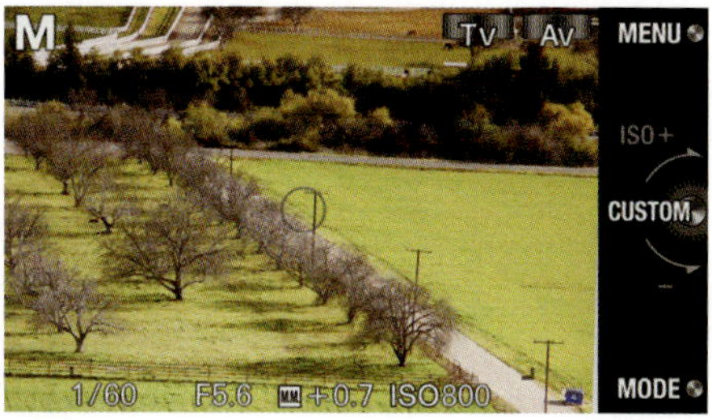


**Figure 6-3**: Display screen showing the spot meter's target circle for measuring light

The third and most direct way to meter is [Spot]. It is a natural for M mode. When it is selected, you see a small circle in the center of the screen that marks the area being measured for light (figure 6-3). By placing this circle over an area, you get a measure of the intensity from that restricted area; by aiming your camera so this circle covers the region you wish to expose, you can easily set your exposure. It requires finesse and thought to interpret the reading, but it is natural to combine this metering method with manual exposure. For example, we will use spot metering when photographing a stage play where the actor is lit with a spotlight and the remainder of the stage is black. Under these conditions, you determine the exposure for the person by using [Spot] to measure the light reflected off the actor's face. We find that giving the facial tones about +0.7 EV (for a fair complexion) records bright, clean skin tones. If we do not apply this correction, the skin tones appear overly dark. The black background behind the spotlight does not influence our exposure reading.

For technical work, we take advantage of spot metering when we copy manuscripts. We find that putting the spot meter on the white page and overexposing by 1.7 f-stop records an image with black text against a white background. If we do not apply exposure compensation, the white paper will appear dingy and will be a darker shade than it should be.

## Manual Focusing: Overriding Automatic Focusing

In chapter 5 we described how to use the AF/MF button for quickly resetting focus by switching temporarily to MF. These are important skills, and now we will introduce how to improve focus accuracy even more. You may find that the view of the subject does not provide enough magnification to see its finest details for accurate focusing. There are two methods for amplifying your view to ensure your focus is tack sharp.

First, let's briefly review how to set the camera to manual focus with a menu command:

Menu>Camera>AF/MF Select>[MF]

After this is set, you may want some focusing aids to help ensure that you record a critically sharp image.

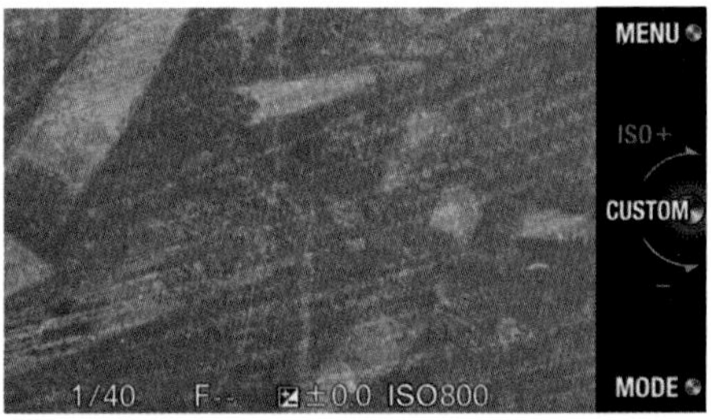


**Figure 6-4a**: Screen at 1x magnification, MF Assist [Off]

### MF Assist

Sometimes, to find perfect focus you need to magnify the image (figures 6-4a, 6-4b, 6-4c). For example, when we photograph the Moon with a telescope we find that an increased magnification of the display screen makes finding focus much easier. This can be accomplished by activating the MF Assist command:

MENU>Setup (Shooting Settings)>MF Assist>[On], [Off]

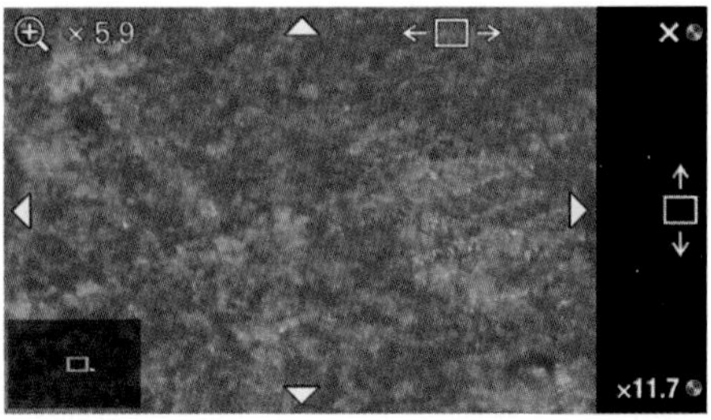


**Figure 6-4b**: Screen at 5.9x magnification, MF Assist [On]

A nifty command to supplement MF Assist is MF Assist Time:

MENU>Setup (Shooting Settings)>MF Assist Time>[No Limit], [5 Sec], [2 Sec]

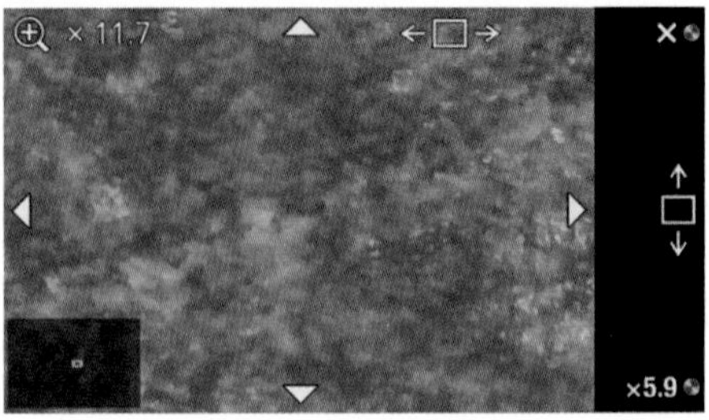


**Figure 6-4c**: Screen at 11.7x magnification, MF Assist [On]

Basically, when you stop focusing, the magnified view can persist for two or five seconds. If you have not moved the focusing ring for that amount of time, the magnification drops to 1x. The view can also stay at the high magnification indefinitely. If you use this option, you can return to your regular nonmagnified view by pressing soft key A or the shutter button halfway.

The major disadvantage of increasing magnification is losing the overall view of your subject. This gets worse if you raise the magnification to 11.7x, and to make matters worse, the image can become noisy. Admittedly, you can quickly return to full view when you press the shutter button, but the delay can be disconcerting. Because of this, we take advantage of the Peaking function.

## Peaking Function

The Peaking function is a colorization strategy that highlights the borders of in-focus areas with a fringe of color. You can determine the size and color of the fringes. They are not recorded with your picture or movie, and they appear only when you use manual focus. To set this command, you first have to go into the menu and set your lens to manual focus:

Menu>Camera>AF/MF Select>[MF]

After manual focus is set, the first of two Peaking commands, Peaking Level, becomes enabled. The Peaking Level command allows you to set the level of color the camera will display when the edges of the image are in focus (figures 6-5a and 6-5b):

MENU>Setup (Shooting Settings)>Peaking Level>[High], [Mid], [Low], [Off]

After you set Peaking Level to a value other than [Off], the Peaking Color command becomes activated, and you can select the color you want displayed:

MENU> Setup (Shooting Settings)>Peaking Color>[Red], [Yellow], [White]

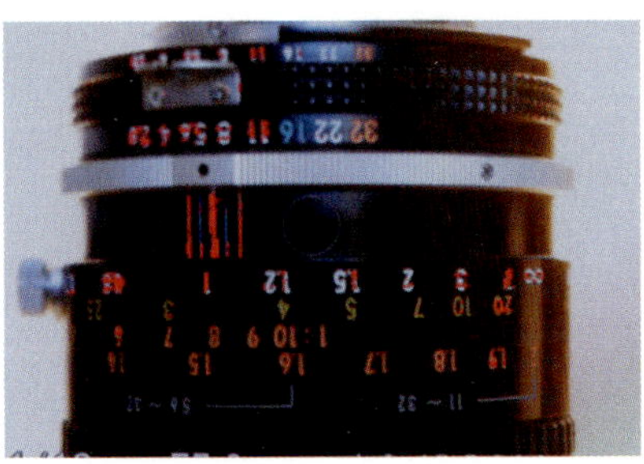

**Figure 6-5a**: Peaking activated at low setting

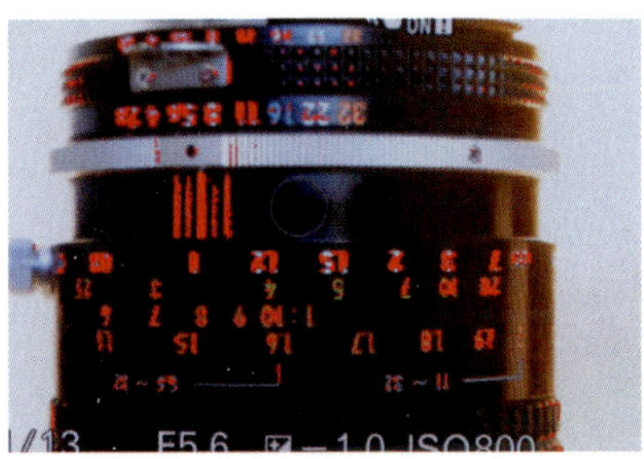

**Figure 6-5b**: Peaking activated at high setting

We use Peaking at the [Mid] setting with [Yellow] when we take pictures through a microscope or telescope. When we take pictures outside, we switch to [Red], which stands out much better in sunlight. For evening pictures, we usually switch to [White].

Peaking is seen only when you use manual focus by setting the AF/MF switch command to [AF/MF] and pressing the AF/MF button or selecting manual focus through the menus. An aggravating aspect of the NEX-7 menu system is that you have to use the menus to set the camera to manual focus before the Peaking command can be turned on. In our opinion, this is a small bug in the camera's software that we hope will be corrected in a firmware upgrade.

## Manual Adjustments for Color Temperature

In chapter 5 we described how you can use preset WB values by matching a light source to an icon. However, there are other ways to set WB but they will require more effort on your part.

First, you can always get to the WB screen through the menu:

MENU>Brightness/Color>White Balance

If the camera is still in its default configuration, you can also find a WB screen by pressing the Navigation button. If the screen does not appear on the first press, keep pressing the Navigation button until you see a screen with the words White Balance Settings displayed at the bottom of the screen.

Which method you use to find the WB screen determines how the control dials operate. If you access the WB screen through the menu, all three of the control dials change the WB preset. Rotating the dials will eventually lead you to an icon with C. Temp/Filter. Highlight the option and press soft key B (figure 6-6a). You will see a new screen (figure 6-6b), and then rotating the control wheel changes the color temperature value

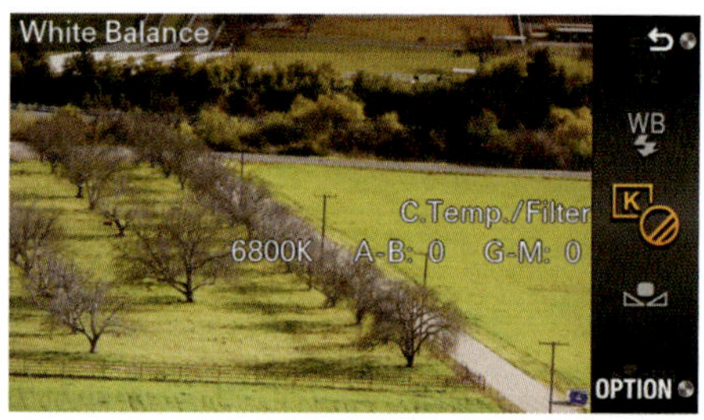


**Figure 6-6a**: WB screen from menu commands, C. TEMP./FILTER is highlighted

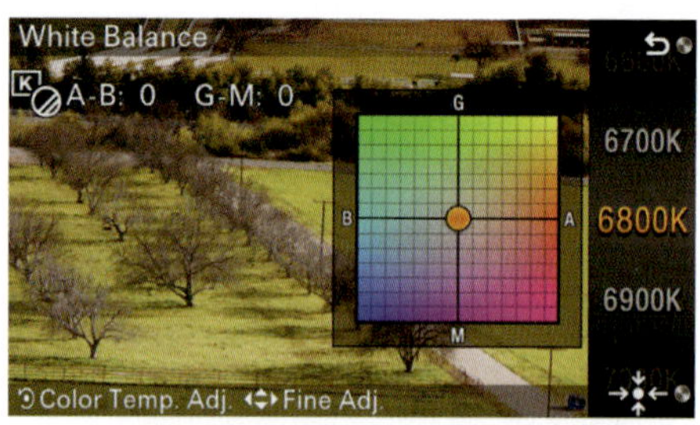


**Figure 6-6b**: New screen showing color temperature scale when soft key B (OPTION) is pressed in WB screen

from 2500 K to 9900 K. Select the K value by pressing soft key C.

If you use the Navigation button to enter the WB screen, things get more complicated since you can only use control dial L to change your WB presets. Do not use control dial R or the control wheel. They are used only for finely adjusting color balance.

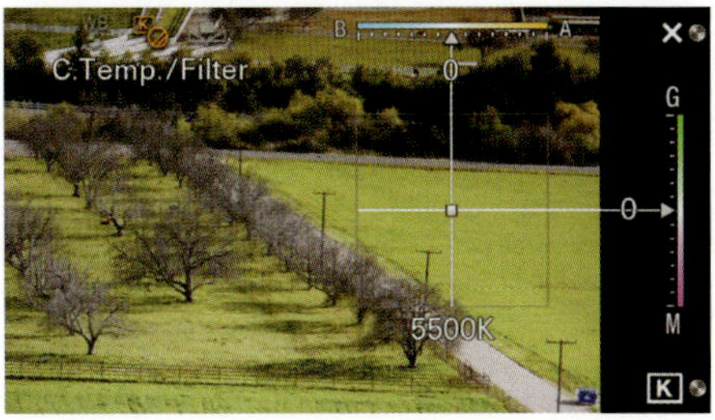


**Figure 6-7a**: Selecting C.Temp./Filter with the Navigation button

After you find the C. Temp/Filter icon, you will see that the soft key B icon displays the letter K (figure 6-7a). Press soft key B , and a series of numbers will display on the top left of your screen (figure 6-7b). Scroll through these numbers with control dial L. Again, do not use control dial R or the control wheel. We will discuss these adjustments later. When you find the K value you wish to use and you are ready to return to Live View, press soft key A.

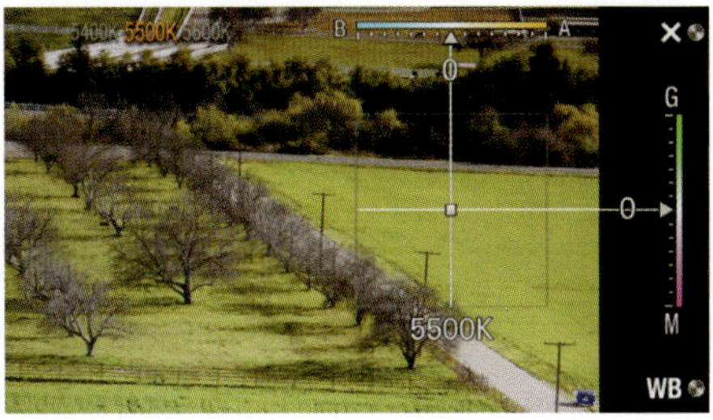


**Figure 6-7b**: After pressing soft key B, actual temperature scale is seen on top left corner. 5500K is selected.

The letter K is an abbreviation for Kelvin, a scale for specifying color temperature. Rather than discuss the scientific and physical basis of the scale, it is sufficient to say that you can dial in the correct numeric value to get an accurate color balance. To change the current number, rotate control dial L. You will see the effects of changing the WB color temperature by studying the screen. However, most photographers simply pull the temperature value included by the manufacturer with their photographic lights and enter the number into the [C.Temp./Filter] option field:

1. Press the Navigation button on top of the camera until you reach the WB function.
2. Scroll through the option list by rotating control dial L. Select [C.Temp./Filter].
3. Press soft key B. The LCD screen will show the letter K opposite this button.
4. Select the color temperature value by rotating control dial L. You can set this to an accuracy of 100 degrees between 2500 K and 9900 K.
5. When the number reaches the value you want, press the shutter button halfway to select the value and return to Live View.

To use these steps, you need to know the color temperature of the light source. An expensive color temperature light meter is the most accurate way to determine this value. Although, less accurate, check to see if the manufacturer of the light provides a K value. For example, the tungsten bulb on our microscope is rated at 3200 K, a value provided by the lamp manufacturer, Osram. So for microscope work, we use the control dial L to select this number.

As mentioned earlier, this is not as precise as using an independent color temperature meter. Many light sources are not rated. Worse, sometimes bulbs that are rated fail to maintain their ratings over the life of the bulb. This is especially true with tungsten filaments. As the bulb ages, its glass envelope becomes coated with tungsten, which colors the light from the filament. The older the bulb is, the cooler its color temperature becomes. Also, the color temperature depends on the operating current, where the bulbs emit a warmer color with a drop in voltage. In the case of fluorescent bulbs, there is a wide variation among manufacturers.

| WB Icon | WB Name | Description |
| --- | --- | --- |
| 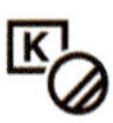 | C.Temp./Filter | This option allows you to set the WB based on a specific color temperature value represented in K units (kelvin). |
| 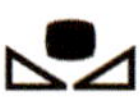 | Custom | Use this option to use a custom WB setting that has been saved by using Custom Setup. |
| 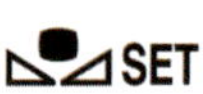 | Custom Setup | Use this option to set up a custom WB that is to be stored. WB value is retained even when the camera is turned off. |

**Table 6-2**: A listing of color temperature icons

### Custom White Balance

We have introduced a WB setting that does not use preset values, but rather requires the photographer to input values. A similar, and more automated version of this tactic is Custom WB. The icons for these two techniques are shown in table 6-2. Custom WB sets the WB manually by calibrating it to the light source, where it is then stored in the camera's memory. To do this, all you need is a blank sheet of white paper, then follow these steps:

1. There are two ways to execute this command. If you use your Navigation button, go to the Custom icon and press soft key B (Set). If you use the menu, get to Custom Setup (figure 6-8a) by using the following commands:

   MENU>Color Brightness>White Balance>[Custom Setup]

2. After you execute this function, you will see a screen with a finely inscribed circle with the message "Press shutter button to capture data of central area of screen."
3. Aim the inscribed circle so it is filled with the piece of white paper, and then press the shutter button (figure 6-8b). The white paper serves as a reflector and provides a screen for displaying the illuminant's color.

4. The screen shows the measured color temperature. You will also see the letters A-B (amber to blue) and G-M (green to magenta). These indicate the camera's tint adjustment.
5. These values will be stored in the register and will replace the previous Custom WB setting.
6. The camera is now calibrated and ready for use.
7. Once the value is saved it will be retained even if the camera is turned off. So you can always use the saved values by going to the Custom icon with the Navigation button or by using the menu commands. Activate and use this setting by pressing soft key C.

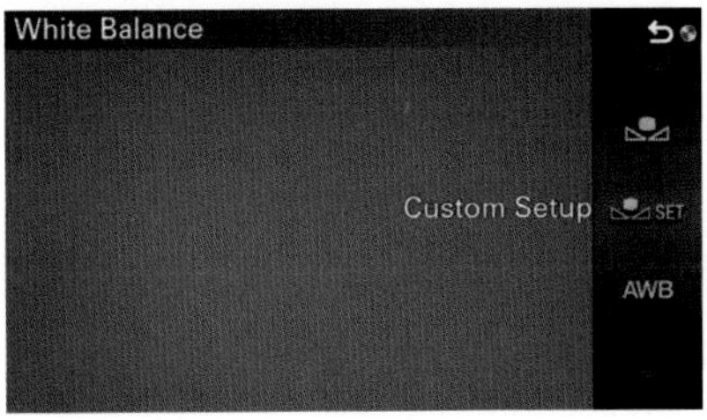


**Figure 6-8a**: WB set for Custom WB

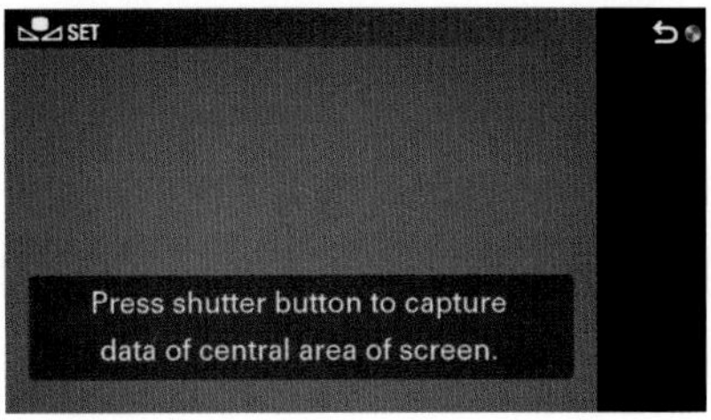


**Figure 6-8b**: Gray circle indicating where to place a piece of white paper in the frame

The camera stores the calibration value so it can be reused when required. It becomes a color preset that can be selected along with other preset values, and it is retained even when the camera is turned off. It is easy to use. In fact, we use it routinely for our technical photography. For example, when working with a microscope, we remove the specimen from the field of view and calibrate the WB setting against an unobstructed region. The camera is then calibrated to the light, which has the additional benefit that any color cast introduced by the lens is also removed. We noticed that the color temperature of incandescent bulbs changes with age. Using Custom WB just before a photo session compensates for this. Now when we photograph through the microscope we no longer use either the preset temperature for [Incandescent] or set the color temperature with degrees K.

Here is another suggestion for customizing your WB: instead of using a sheet of white paper, substitute an 18% gray card. This, as the name implies, reflects only 18% of the light and provides a handy reference for neutral colors under varying light conditions.

A gray card has other advantages. First, you can use it for Custom WB instead of a piece of white paper. Second, you can position it within your picture, in an unobtrusive location that can be cropped out of the final image. You can then use this point for the Specify Gray Point command when you process your picture with Image Data Converter. Although you can use a sheet of white paper, the danger is that one of the color channels may be clipped, improperly biasing your WB. By using the 18% gray card, you are assured that all of the color channels will be properly exposed.

### Fine-Tuning WB: Fine Adjustment of Blue-Amber and Green-Magenta

Undesirable color casts can still be present, and they are usually a result of unusual lighting conditions, such as when several different light sources illuminate the subject. For example, an interior scene might be lit by daylight streaming through the window, an incandescent light sitting on the table, and fluorescent lights hanging from the ceiling. These extreme conditions can be corrected by adding a slight tint to the image. The slight addition of a hue will be recorded in both JPEG and RAW files. Basically, you introduce an amber-to-blue or green-to-magenta hue.

When you select a WB preset with the Navigation button, you will see a square with lines on the display screen (figure 6-9a). A slight turn of either control dial R or the control wheel will display a multicolor square on the screen (figure 6-9b). This enables you to apply an additional color tint to your WB preset. You have a different set of controls when you select the WB with menu commands. When you select a preset, the icon for soft key B displays the word "OPTIONS" (you can see it in the lower corner of figure 6-6a). When you press soft key B you will see the color fine adjustment screen with an orange circle positioned in the center. The screen prompts you to press the rim of the control wheel to move the orange circle toward a color tint (figure 6-9c). Figure 6-9d shows the results of moving the orange circle and setting both A (amber) and M (magenta) to 7.

Similarly, if you use the Navigation button, you will see prompts for moving a small orange square horizontally by turning control dial R and moving it vertically with the control wheel (figures 6-9a and 6-9b). Control dial R shifts the color from B (blue) to A (amber), depending on which direction you go. The control wheel shifts the color from G (green) to M (magenta). Initially the crosshairs are in the center of the color fine adjustment square, but when you start fine-tuning the colors you will see the crosshairs move off center. Apply these controls until you neutralize any color cast on the viewing screen. A slight press of the shutter button returns you to Live View, and these values are now retained and are associated with your preset color setting.

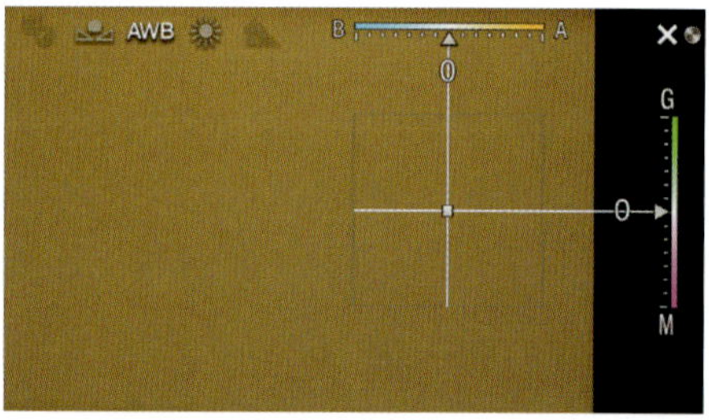


**Figure 6-9a**: WB color fine adjustment screen selected with Navigation button

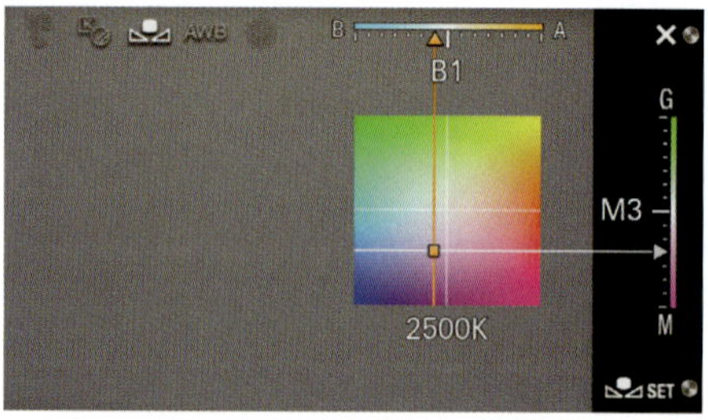


**Figure 6-9b**: WB fine adjustment being applied after selecting fine adjustment with Navigation button

These fine adjustment techniques are to be used for the color balance fine adjustment. When fluorescent or LED light sources are used, which emit a discontinuous spectrum of light, you may find that your images have color casts that cannot be removed by selecting a preset WB value. You can use fine adjustments to deal with this coloration within the camera. Now, we will describe how these color casts can be adjusted in your computer.

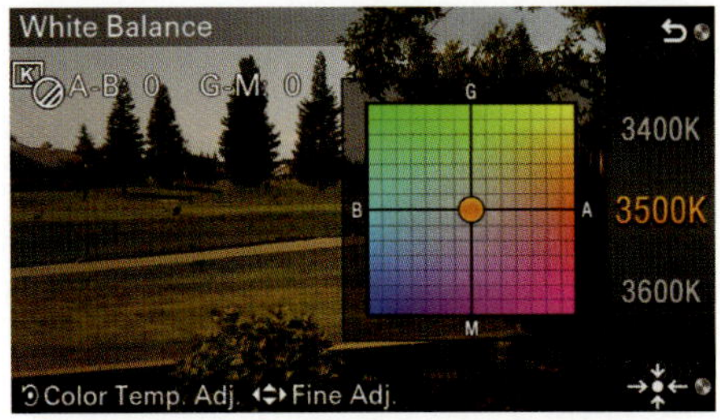


**Figure 6-9c**: WB fine adjustment selected with menu command

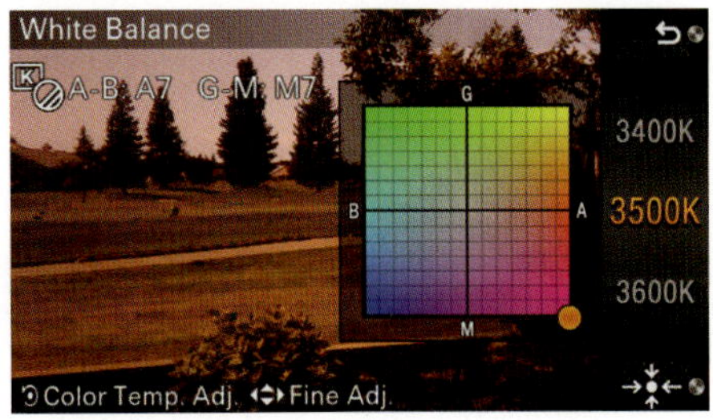


**Figure 6-9d**: Applying amber and magenta to WB selected with menu command

We prefer to use the computer and post-process the image to correct color casts. Although the NEX-7 provides extensive controls, it is easier to do these corrections on a large screen. We use either Sony's Image Data Converter software or third-party software, such as Photoshop or Aperture, for touching up RAW images (figure 6-10).

Earlier, we recommended that you save your images as both RAW and JPEG files. Each file format has its advantages. A major benefit of saving in RAW format is the ease of correcting WB errors outside the camera.

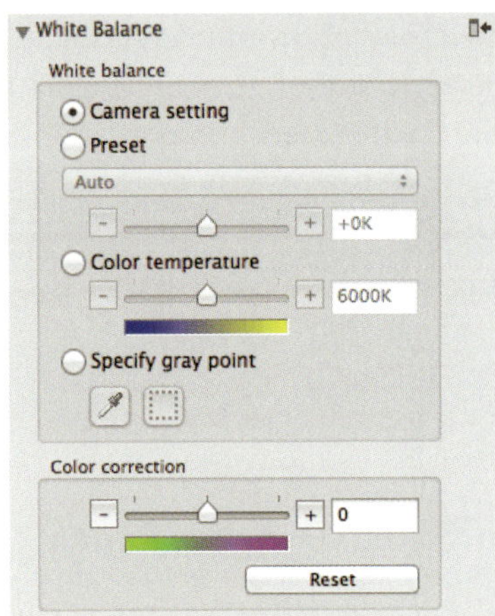


**Figure 6-10**: Image Data Converter controls for adjusting a RAW file's color temperature

Figure 6-10 shows a slider and a color temperature scale and fine-tuning WB in the Sony supplied software Image Data Converter. The slider allows you to rapidly evaluate different color temperature settings. Additionally, the option marked Preset displays a variety of light sources, enabling you to find your illumination type.

In the previous section, we mentioned including an 18% gray card within a picture. This technique can be used with the Specify Gray Point command to provide a neutral reference for adjusting WB. In addition, Image Data Converter has another slider called Color correction (figure 6-10) that you can use to adjust the tint from green to magenta. Together with the Image Data Converter's Color temperature control, you should be able to obtain an image with a neutral WB.

## Lens Compensation

To obtain the ultimate picture quality, the NEX-7 has software that corrects imperfections introduced by the lens. These imperfections include vignetting (peripheral shading), distortion (geometric distortion), and chromatic aberration (color fringing). Vignetting is uneven illumination in which the periphery of the image is darker than the center. Distortion indicates that straight lines bow in (pincushion distortion) or bow out (barrel distortion). Finally, chromatic aberration is when the subject's borders have red or blue fringes due to the inability of the lens to bring all wavelengths of light to the same focus.

Correcting these problems with software requires an in-camera database to catalog the lens defects and a processing algorithm to correct the image. Sony periodically provides updates to the camera's firmware, expanding the database as new lenses are introduced to its lineup. Remember, this correction is a software alteration of the image that provides a modified image file. For scientists who require unaltered images, these corrections should be turned off so the recorded image is shown with all of the lens defects.

The chromatic aberration and shading correction default setting is [Auto], so if the attached lens is in the database, its optical faults will be corrected in JPEG files. RAW files are not corrected, so they will show the image defects. Curiously, at the time of writing, the distortion default setting is [Off]. If you want to activate it, change it to [Auto].

Here are the three lens compensation commands:

MENU>Setup (Shooting Settings)>Lens Comp.:Shading>[Auto], [Off]

MENU>Setup (Shooting Settings)>Lens Comp.:Distortion>[Auto], [Off]

MENU>Setup (Shooting Settings)>Lens Comp.:Chro. Aber.>[Auto], [Off]

## Bracketing and Dynamic Range

The NEX-7 has a special feature for dealing with unusual lighting conditions. If it is difficult to judge exposure, the camera can capture several images, each recorded with a slightly different exposure. This shotgun approach helps you find the best exposure. This function is available by pressing the control wheel's rim next to the Drive Mode icon. When you have accessed the Drive Mode command, scroll through the options. You will see an icon with the letters BRK within a rectangle, followed by a capital C. At the bottom of the LCD display you will see that soft key B is labeled with OPTIONS. Press the button, and you will see Bracket: Cont.: 0.3 EV (figure 6-11a) or Bracket: Cont.: 0.7 EV (figure 6-11b) where the EV amount is used to vary the exposure plus or minus from optimum amount.

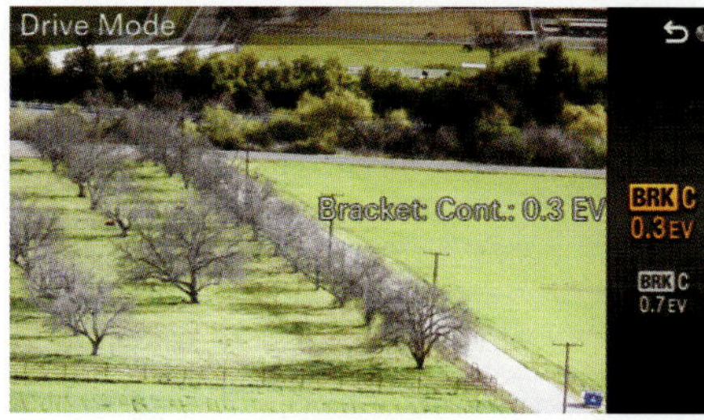


**Figure 6-11a**: Bracket: Cont.: 0.3 EV setting

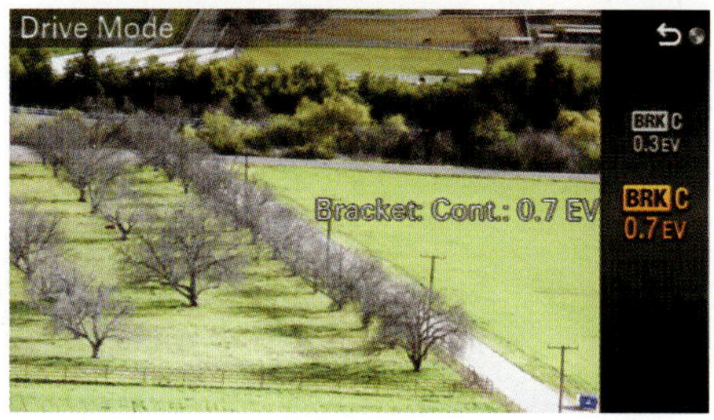


**Figure 6-11b**: Bracket: Cont.: 0.7 EV setting

Although the saved shots can be used to fine-tune exposure, we prefer using them for HDR photography. To do this, we download the three bracketed exposures to our computer and use HDR software to combine them into a composite image. With tone mapping software, we can alter the color and contrast to produce surreal images. This differs from the camera's Auto HDR function, which renders a more realistic image without extreme coloration.

The bracket shooting technique overcomes the sensor's limitations through image processing. For example, a single exposure concentrates on the midtones in a scene; therefore, a bright sky may be overexposed and deep shadows may be underexposed. When you bracket exposures, the first shot records the camera's optimum exposure (figure 6-12a); the second shot records detail in the highlights (figure 6-12b); and the third shot records detail in the shadows (figure 6-12c). The final composite HDR image shows detail in both the highlights and the shadows (figure 6-12d).

Individually, figures 6-12a, 6-12b, and 6-12c would be unsatisfactory, but with the right tone mapping software, you can merge them into a single image that has optimal information in the highlights, midtones, and shadows (figure 6-12d).

The only problem with how the Sony NEX-7 does this is that the range for HDR is too limited. You need to use the Bracket: Cont.: 0.7 EV option twice to cover -1.7 f-stops through +1.7 f-stops. To do this we set up our camera and shoot one bracketed series at +1 EV overexposure, with Bracket: Cont.: 0.7 EV. We then reset the EV to -1.0 for underexposure and execute Bracket: Cont.: 0.7 EV again to take another three shots.

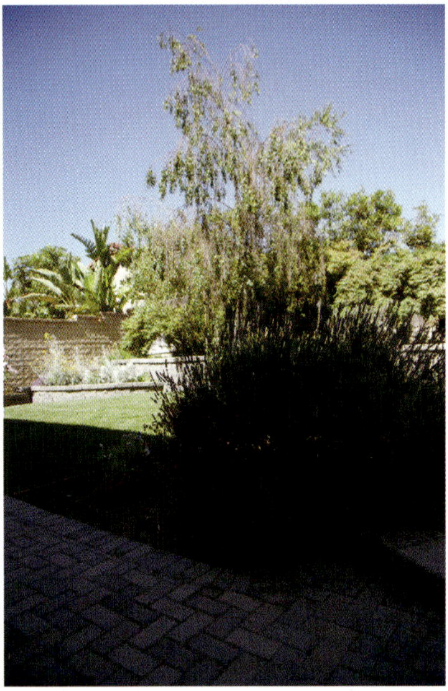

**Figure 6-12a**: Optimum exposure

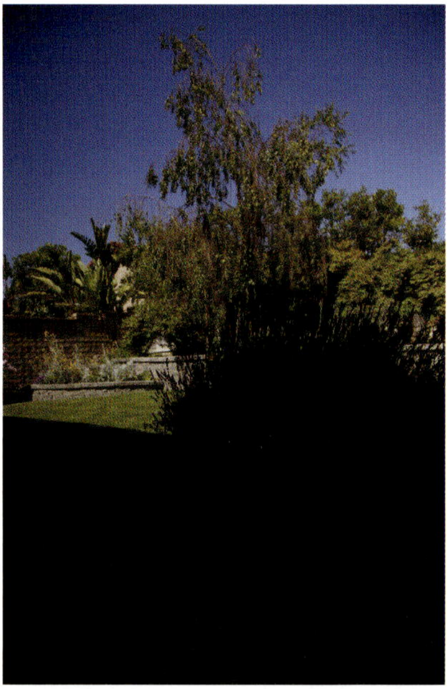

**Figure 6-12b**: Underexposed by 1.7 f-stops

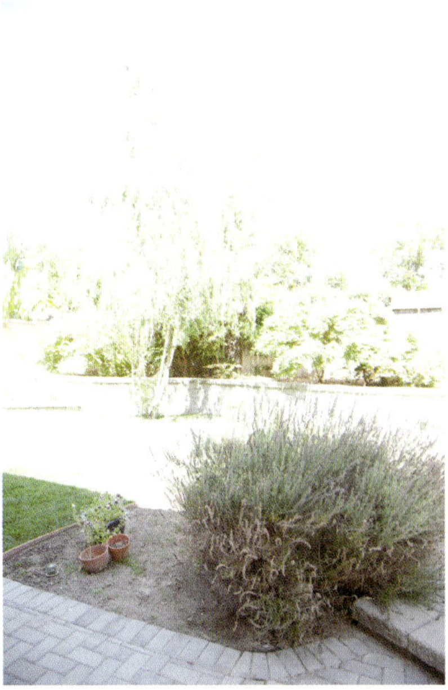

**Figure 6-12c**: Overexposed by 1.7 f-stops

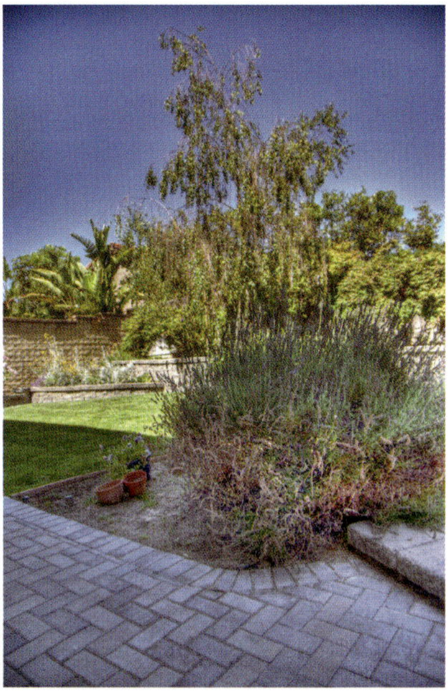

**Figure 6-12d**: Combined image using HDR software

## Recommendations

Manual operation of the camera is for perfectionists who want to obtain the best possible exposure and focus. Though it can be done by handholding the camera, the better strategy is to mount the camera on a tripod.

You might think that tripods are only for static landscapes, but this is not so. If you are a nature photographer working with extreme telephotos or macros, you will find a tripod invaluable. Its stability helps you judge focus critically and frame your pictures precisely. You can obtain high-quality images with lower ISOs and longer shutter speeds, and you can also work with f-stops that exhibit the sharpest part of the lens.

For our work with telephoto and closeup lenses, we use f/8 or f/11 and rely on MF. We may use AF at first, but for some subjects—especially animals in the field—we have to override AF and use MF. To ensure the most accurate focus, we use MF Assist.

We also find the Peaking function to be invaluable. It ensures that our subject is in focus, thus we acquire a higher percentage of sharp photographs. This reduces the need to delete out-of-focus images and to do reshoots. Set the Peaking Level to the [Mid] option first. From there, you can determine whether you need more or less color intensity. When you choose a color, consider one that will show up the best with the type of pictures you take.



When shooting outdoor scenes, we turn off AWB and set WB to one of the preset values. When working indoors with incandescent lighting, we use Custom WB. We do not use the fine adjustment of colors on the camera; instead we work with the saved file on our computer.

When photographing for HDR, we use bracket shooting instead of Auto HDR. We load the images in third-party software, such as Photomatix. After the photographs are merged, we use this software for tone rendering. If you decide to do this, first mount the camera on a tripod. Any shift in the camera position will blur the resulting picture when the images are merged. Then use the A mode to force the camera to maintain a constant aperture, and vary the exposure by automatically changing the shutter speed. Maintaining a constant depth of field is essential for merging the images; otherwise, you will lose definition in areas that are blurred as the depth of field becomes shallower.

# Chapter 7: Customizing the Camera

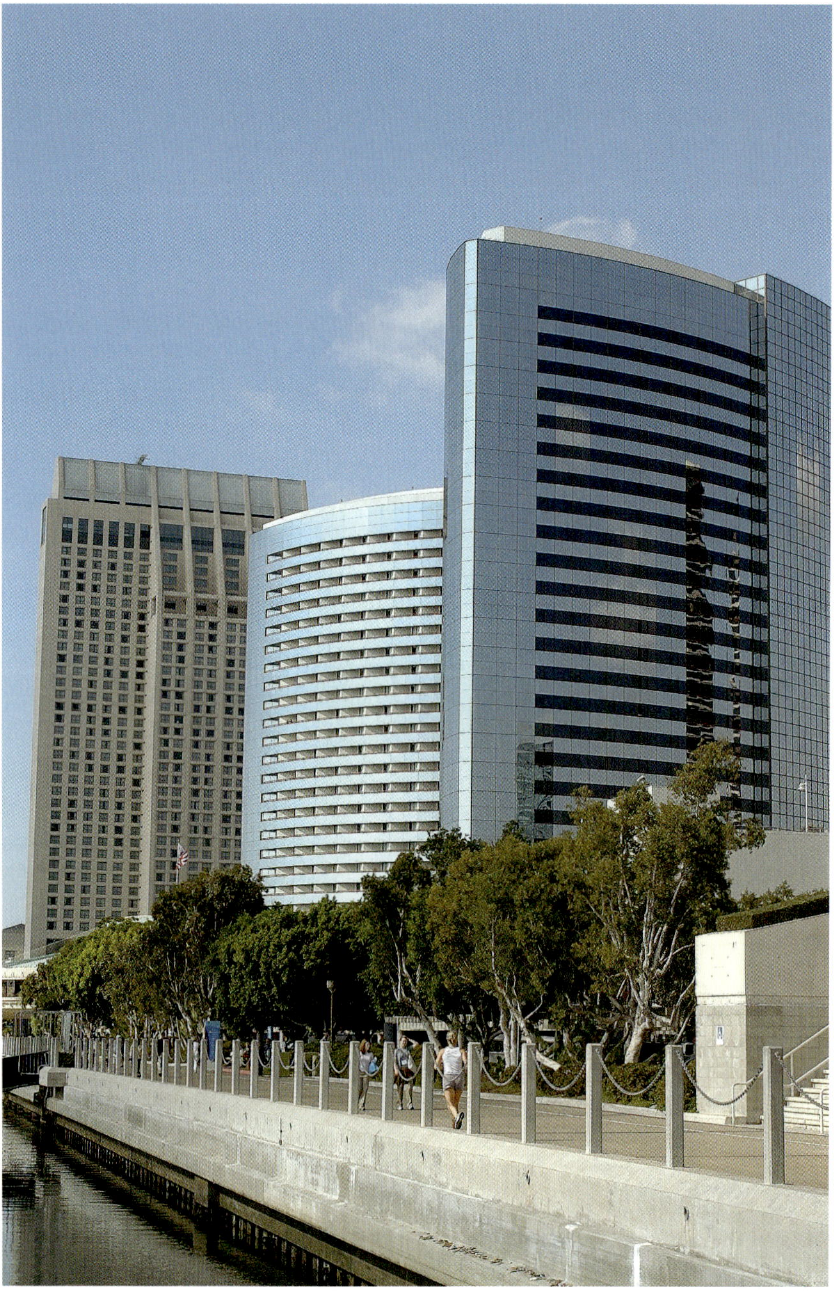

7

## Introduction

The easier it is for you to find the settings you need to record your picture or movie, the more likely it is that you will enjoy using your camera and get the results you desire. There are several NEX-7 commands that allow you to customize your camera's operations to better suit your photographing needs.

You have control over how the menu is displayed and whether help information is displayed as you navigate through the structure. Better yet, instead of searching through the menu structure to set a specific command, you can assign the command to one of the buttons. You can also apply a style or effect to your resulting images to save post-processing time.

All of these features will allow you to tailor your camera's operations to better suit your needs and save you time. How you customize your camera will depend on how you typically use the camera's features and your tolerance for using shortcuts verses navigating through the menu structure. If you have typically been a point-and-shoot camera user, we recommend that you limit how much customization you do at the beginning. Modify the camera gradually as you become more familiar with its capabilities and as you develop a style and preference. If you are already familiar with setting up camera options, most likely it won't be long before you start customizing your camera's operations to suit your shooting style.

## Customizing Buttons



The Sony NEX-7 has five buttons that can be customized—Navigation button, soft key B, soft key C, right key, and AF/MF button—to execute menu commands while previewing your images in P, S, A, or M modes only. How they are customized is controlled by two commands in the Setup menu: Function Settings and Custom Key Settings.

Combined, these two commands control 14 customization opportunities for you to assign a menu command to one of the buttons so you can access the command more quickly than through the menu structure (table 7-1). Without some customizing, you will find yourself constantly returning to the menu and navigating through its structure to find a specific command so that you can set it to a new value.

| Customization Main Commands | Customization Options | Condition |
|---|---|---|
| Function Settings | Function Settings 1 | Enabled |
| | Function Settings 2 | |
| | Function Settings 3 | |
| | Function Settings 4 | |
| | Custom Settings 1 | Enabled when one of the Function Settings 1 through 4 is set to the [Custom Settings] option |
| | Custom Settings 2 | |
| | Custom Settings 3 | |
| Custom Key Settings | AF/MF button | Enabled |
| | Right Key Setting | |
| | Soft key B Setting | |
| | Soft key C Setting | |
| | Custom 1 | Enabled when Soft key C Setting is set to the [Custom] option |
| | Custom 2 | |
| | Custom 3 | |
| | Custom 4 | |
| | Custom 5 | |

**Table 7-1**: Customization commands

Sony's use of the word "Custom" for commands and their values can lead to some confusion. Simply put, the Function Settings command controls the Navigation button, while the Custom Key Settings command controls the other four buttons.

Both the Function Settings and the Custom Key Settings commands have two tiers of commands: the main command and a set of subcommand options. To expand the number of customization opportunities, both main commands have lower-level options that, when selected, enable another set of subcommands with their own possible values.

The Function Settings command has four subcommands that are always enabled. Each of these subcommands can be assigned a value, one of which is called [Custom Settings]. Any one of the Function Settings 1 through 4 subcommands can be assigned this value, but logically it is best to set it to Function Settings 4. When it is assigned, three additional customization commands are enabled: Custom Settings 1, 2, and 3.

Just as the Function Settings command has a way to expand the number of customization fields, so does the Custom Key Settings command. One of the Custom Key Settings options, Soft key C Setting, has two options: [Shoot Mode] and [Custom]. When the [Custom] option is assigned to the Soft key C Setting, five more customization slots are enabled: Custom 1 through 5.

Confused? You are not alone. Review table 7-1 again. The two customized main commands, highlighted in green, contain a total of 16 options, which control a total of 14 customization opportunities. The blue highlighted subcommands are always enabled and ready to be assigned values. Setting one of the blue subcommands to [Custom Settings] or [Custom] will enable the respective subcommands highlighted in yellow.

## Navigation Button

The Navigation button (figure 7-1) is on the top right side of the camera. Its functionality is controlled by the Function Settings command. Each time you press the button while in Live View, the camera will cycle to the next assigned function.

Keep in mind that each time the camera is reset (Reset Default command), the Navigation button's operation will return to its default. We recommend that you write down your custom settings in case you need to reestablish them.

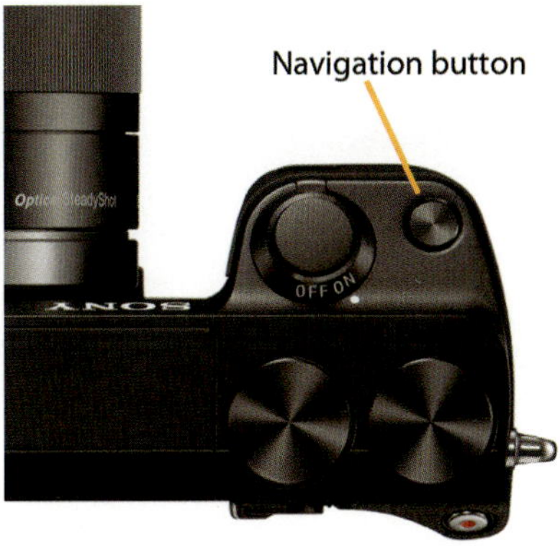


**Figure 7-1**: Navigation button

### Navigation Button Start Position

The camera's default has four functions assigned to the Navigation button. While in Live View mode, each press of the Navigation button will cycle through the four functions:

Focus Settings ⇨ White Balance Settings ⇨ D-Range Settings ⇨ Creative Style Settings

When you press the Navigation button enough times, you will be cycled back to Live View. But once you go past the initial press, the Navigation button's starting point depends on the Function Settings Start command:

MENU>Setup (Main Settings)>Function Settings>Function Settings Start>[Top], [Previous]

The [Top] option causes the Function Settings 1 option to be displayed first when you initially press the Navigation button, and then it continues to cycle through the Function Settings as you continue to press the Navigation button.

The [Previous] option will start the cycle of the Function Settings at the previous setting that was displayed the last time the Navigation button was pressed.

## Setting the Navigation Button

The Navigation button cycles through initially four function slots with the option to expand to six. You can add or delete functions or change their order. To change the Navigation button values, use the following command (figure 7-2a):

MENU>Setup (Main Settings)>Function Settings>[Function Settings 1], [Function Settings 2], [Function Settings 3], [Function Settings 4]

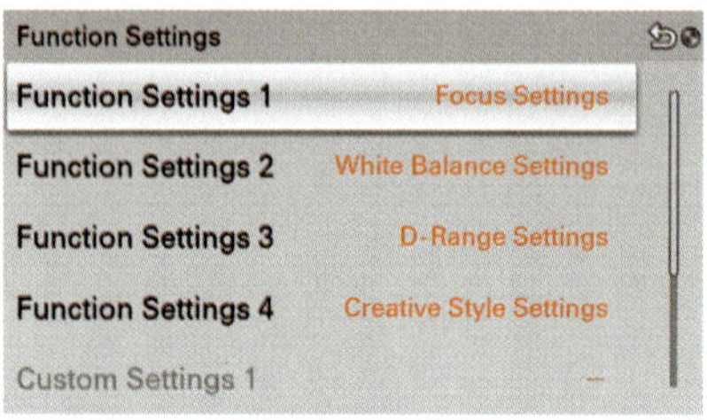


**Figure 7-2a**: Function Settings commands; none set to [Custom Settings]

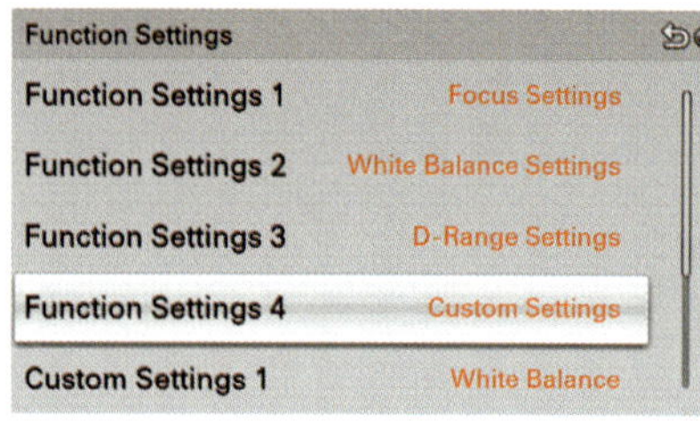


**Figure 7-2b**: Function Settings commands; one set to [Custom Settings]

Each of the Function Settings 1 through 4 commands have the same available options:

- Focus Settings (Function Settings 1 default)
- White Balance Settings (Function Settings 2 default)
- D-Range Settings (Function Settings 3 default)
- Creative Style Settings (Function Settings 4 default)
- Picture Effect Settings
- Custom Settings
- Not set

Setting one of the Function Settings commands to the [Not set] value voids the slot, so when you cycle the Navigation button through the assigned commands, the slot is bypassed.

If you set one of the four Function Settings commands to [Custom Settings], three additional Function Settings options that each represent a Navigation button slot become enabled (figure 7-2b):

MENU>Setup (Main Settings)>Function Settings>[Custom Settings 1], [Custom Settings 2], [Custom Settings 3]

Each of the Custom Settings 1 through 3 commands have the same available options:

- Exposure Comp.
- Autofocus Mode
- ISO
- Metering Mode
- White Balance (Custom Settings 1 default)
- DRO/Auto HDR (Custom Settings 2 default)
- Creative Style (Custom Settings 3 default)
- Picture Effect
- Quality
- Not set

Here too, setting an option to [Not set] voids the slot and it is bypassed, although a bit differently.

### Displaying Customized Button Settings

Each of the assigned Function Settings are shown singularly when you press the Navigation button, but the three Custom Settings will be shown at the same time with their assigned [Custom Settings 1] and [Custom Settings 2] function options displayed in a row along the top of the display screen, and the [Custom Settings 3] options displayed along the right side of the screen. They are strategically placed so control dial L will scroll through the [Custom Settings 1] options, control dial R will scroll through the [Custom Settings 2] options, and the control wheel will scroll through the [Custom Settings 3] options. To select an option, press soft key C. This illustrates the rationale of Sony's Triple-dial-control feature.

Figure 7-3a shows the Custom Settings 1 through 3 commands' values while figure 7-3b shows the corresponding LCD screen when the Navigation button displays the Custom Settings 1 through 3 values. Note the command names along with the command icons. The command names will disappear within about a second, leaving the command icons. This figure shows Custom Settings 1 through 3 as [Autofocus Mode], [Metering Mode], and [Picture Effect].

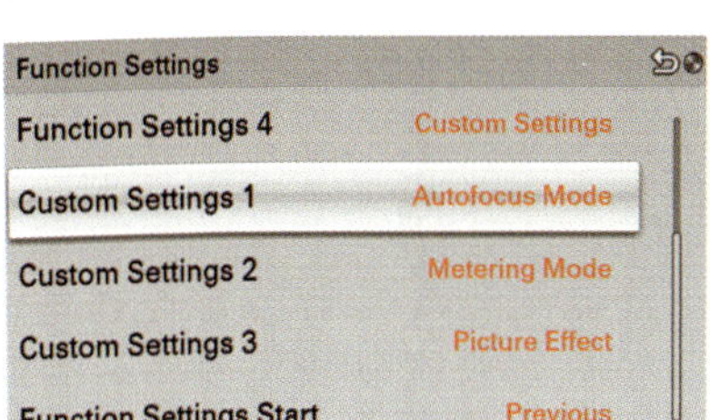


**Figure 7-3a**: Display screen showing the Custom Settings1-3 commands

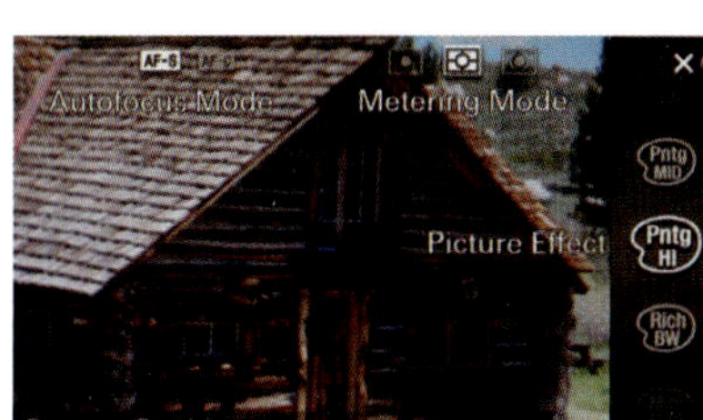


**Figure 7-3b**: Custom Settings 1-3 displayed on the LCD screen

If you set one of the four Function Settings to [Picture Effect Settings], be aware that the Picture Effect options will display when you press the Navigation button only when the Quality command is set to one of the JPEG-only formats. If Quality is set to [RAW] or [RAW&JPEG], the Navigation button will bypass it and display the next function.

## Customization of Other Buttons

In addition to expanding the role of the Navigation button, you can further modify your camera by assigning functions to four other buttons: AF/MF, right key, soft key B, and soft key C (figure 7-4).

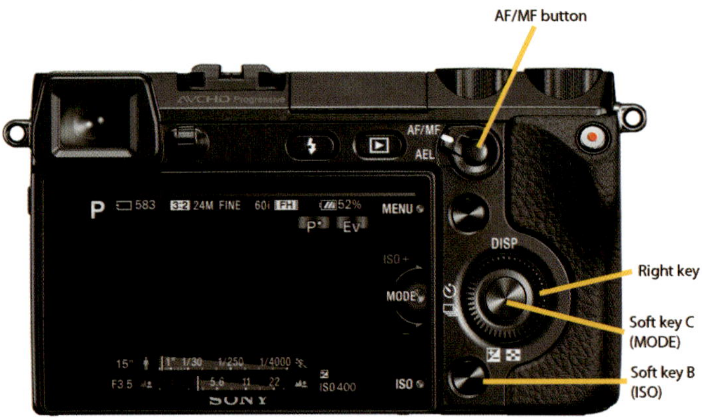


**Figure 7-4**: Camera body with customizable buttons

To customize the buttons, use the Setup menu's Custom Key Settings command (figure 7-5):

MENU>Setup (Main Settings)>Custom Key Settings>[AF/MF button], [Right Key Setting], [Soft key B Setting], [Soft key C Setting]

Just like the Function Settings command, you can expand the Custom Key Settings command's customization capability from four to a total of eight options when you assign [Custom] to the Soft key C Setting command.

Remember, just like the Function Settings commands, the Custom Key Settings are functional only in the P, S, A, and M shooting modes. You will see an error message if you try to execute the buttons outside of these shooting modes.

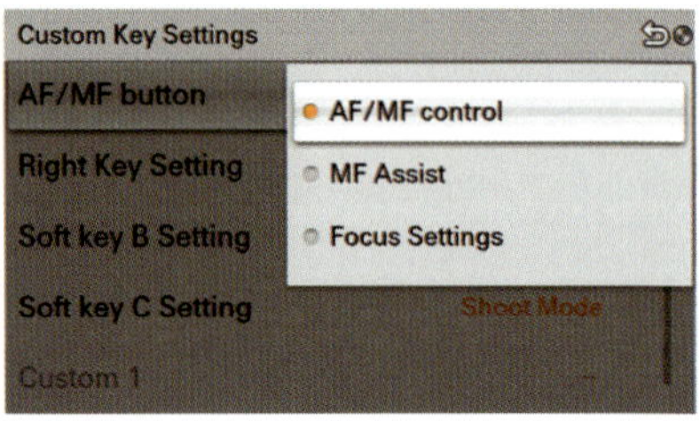


**Figure 7-5**: Custom Key Settings

### AF/MF Button Command

The AF/MF button controls the switching between autofocus and manual focus. Sometimes you will rely on having the camera automatically focus, but as your experience grows you will probably want to switch to manual focus so you can get the right picture.

You can use the menu to find the AF/MF related command and make the appropriate settings, or you can set the AF/MF button to display the related command for you, saving you the time and frustration of navigating the menu. Customize the AF/MF button with the following command:

> MENU>Setup (Main Settings)>Custom Key Settings>AF/MF button>[AF/MF control], [MF Assist], [Focus Settings]

Table 7-2 shows the relationship between the AF/MF button's value, within the Custom Key Settings command, and the executed command and possible values when the AF/MF button is pressed.

| MENU>Setup (Main Settings)>Custom Key Settings>AF/MF button | | |
|---|---|---|
| **AF/MF button Option** | **Executes Command's Value** | **Available Values** |
| AF/MF control | MENU>Setup (Shooting Settings)>AF/MF control | Hold |
| | | Toggle |
| | | Manual Focus |
| MF Assist | MENU>Camera>AF/MF Select | Autofocus |
| | | DMF |
| | | Manual Focus |
| Focus Settings | MENU>Camera>Autofocus Area | Center |
| | | Flexible Spot |
| | | Multi |

**Table 7-2**: Relationship between AF/MF button's customization value and executed command

When you customize the AF/MF button, use control dial L to navigate through the options, and use soft key C to select a value. Otherwise, the command's default value, [AF/MF control], will stay in effect.

## Right Key Setting Command

The control wheel has labels on the top, bottom, and left sides, but not on the right side (figure 7-6). The Right Key Setting command assigns what will be executed when the right key button (the rim on the right side of the control wheel) is pressed.

MENU>Setup (Main Settings)>Custom Key Settings>Right Key Setting

This command has an extensive list of 20 available options; the default value is [Not set]:

| | | |
|---|---|---|
| Shoot Mode | Soft Skin Effect | Creative Style |
| AF/MF Series | Quality | Flash Mode |
| Autofocus Mode | ISO | Flash Comp |
| Autofocus Area | White Balance | MF Assist |
| Prec. Dig Zoom | Metering mode | Focus Settings |
| Face Detection | DRO/Auto HDR | Not set |
| Smile Shutter | Picture Effect | |

Except for [Not set], each of the options will display its associated command when the right key is pressed in Live View. When the Right Key Setting command is set to [Not set], nothing will happen when the right key is pressed.

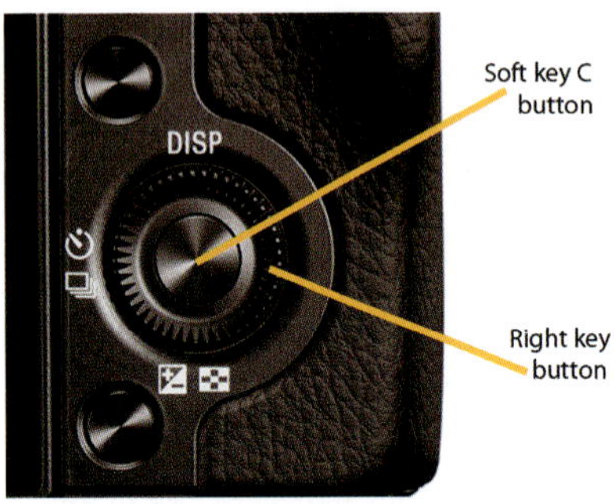


**Figure 7-6**: Customizable portions of the control wheel

## Soft Key B Setting Command

The Soft key B Setting command controls what occurs when soft key B is pressed in Live View. The default operation of this button is [Focus Settings].

MENU>Setup (Main Settings)>Custom Key Settings>Soft key B Setting

The 20 available options are the same as those for the Right Key Setting command are listed below:

| | | |
|---|---|---|
| Shoot Mode | Soft Skin Effect | Creative Style |
| AF/MF Series | Quality | Flash Mode |
| Autofocus Mode | ISO | Flash Comp |
| Autofocus Area | White Balance | MF Assist |
| Prec. Dig Zoom | Metering mode | Focus Settings |
| Face Detection | DRO/Auto HDR | Not set |
| Smile Shutter | Picture Effect | |

Here too, the [Not set] option will prevent any command from being displayed when soft key B is pressed during Live View.

Since the Object Tracking command utilizes soft key B to assign an object to be tracked, if Object Tracking is [On], the Soft key B Setting value will be inactive until Object Tracking is set to [Off].



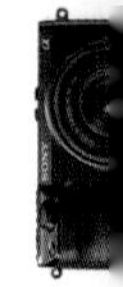

## Soft Key C Setting Command

The Soft key C Setting command controls what occurs when soft key C (figure 7-6) is pressed while in Live View.

MENU>Setup (Main Settings)>Custom Key Settings>Soft key C Setting>[Shoot Mode], [Custom]

Selecting the [Shoot Mode] option is straightforward and causes the Shoot Mode menu to display when soft key C is pressed. When the Soft key C Setting command is set to [Custom], five additional commands become available and allow you to further customize how soft key C works when it is pressed.

MENU>Setup (Main Settings)>Custom Key Settings>Soft key C Setting>Custom>[Custom 1], [Custom 2], [Custom 3], [Custom 4], [Custom 5]

### Custom 1 through Custom 5 Commands

When they are enabled, the Custom 1 through Custom 5 commands allow you to further customize your camera. The five additional commands will display in order within a horizontal bar across the bottom of the display screen when you press soft key C (figure 7-7). Press the right or left rim of the control wheel to navigate through the commands.

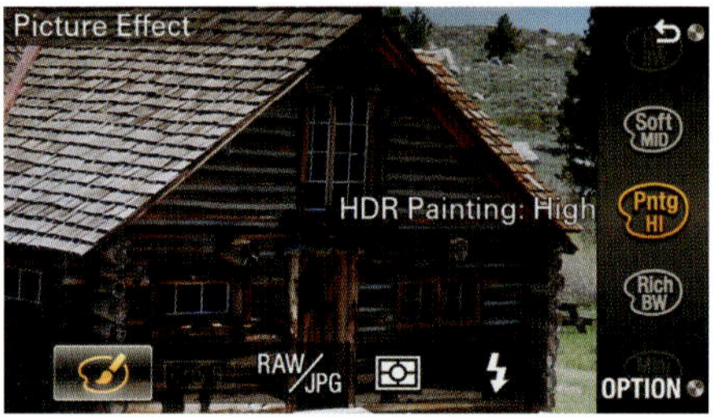


**Figure 7-7**: Custom settings display when soft key C is pressed

Each of the five Custom commands has the same list of available options:

| | | |
|---|---|---|
| AF/MF Series | Soft Skin Effect | DRO/Auto HDR |
| Autofocus Mode | Quality | Picture Effect |
| Autofocus Area | ISO | Creative Style |
| Face Detection | White Balance | Flash Mode |
| Smile Shutter | Metering mode | Not set |



Of course, you can set one or more commands to [Not set], and its corresponding slot on the display bar will be blank.

### Custom Key Setting Command Summary

Rather than fully customizing your camera, you may want to start with a few custom settings and see if you like to use them. Most likely it will take several changes to their arrangement before you settle on a workable location for the selected commands. We recommend that you first become more familiar with the camera and learn which commands you use frequently before you do any extensive customization. You can always change, add, or subtract your settings later. The camera will give you lots of hints, but you still need to remember how your camera's buttons and dials function. Once you have customized it, the camera will be a more responsive tool, capable of being quickly adapted to a variety of photographic requirements.

Important points:

- Although selecting [Custom] for the Soft key C Setting command enables the Custom 1 through Custom 5 options, you do not have to assign a function to each one. You can assign [Not set] to void any of the commands.
- When the MENU>Camera>Object Tracking command is set to [On], the custom setting of soft key B becomes invalid.
- The MENU>Setup (Main Settings)>Custom Key Settings>AF/MF button>[MF Assist] option is enabled only when the MENU>Camera>AF/MF Select command is set to [Manual Focus].
- When the MENU>Setup (Main Settings)>Reset Default command is executed, the camera is restored to the defaults shown in table 7-3. Make sure you have written down your customization settings in case you need to reassign them.

| Custom Key Settings | |
|---|---|
| **Customization Command** | **Camera Default** |
| AF/MF button | AF/MF control |
| Right Key Setting | Not set |
| Soft key B Setting | Focus Settings |
| Soft key C Setting | Shoot Mode |
| Custom 1 | ISO |
| Custom 2 | White Balance |
| Custom 3 | DRO/Auto HDR |
| Custom 4 | Not set |
| Custom 5 | Not set |

**Table 7-3**: Defaults for Custom Key Settings

## Customizing Buttons Summary

There are two ways to access the camera's functions: customize the buttons and control wheel; or navigate through the menu to find and change the individual commands. Searching and navigating through the menu structure is feasible but tedious. For example, you might want to turn on the Autofocus Area function. Press the MENU button, navigate to the Camera icon, and press soft key C. Then scroll down the list of commands until you get to Autofocus Area. Press soft key C to select it and display the command's options. Select the option you want, and press soft key C to apply it.

Doing this once is fine, but if this is a feature you are going to turn on and off regularly, you should consider setting Autofocus Area command as one of the Custom Key Settings, for example Right Key Setting. Then you can press right key once to display the Autofocus Area options. This is the same as if you went through the menu, but using a custom key to get here is much easier and a real time saver.

If you are creative, you can have your cake and eat it, too. If you reassign soft key C from [Shoot Mode] to [Custom], you still can have a one-step way to enter the Shoot Mode menu. For example, if you customize soft key B to [Shoot Mode], you will see MODE opposite that soft key B button. This way, a single button press will allow you to select any of the shooting modes. Rotate the control wheel to the shooting mode you want, for example P, and then select it by pressing soft key C. If you did not customize to have easy access to the shooting modes, you would have to press the MENU button and scroll to the Shoot Mode icon. Press soft key C and navigate to the P mode option. Then press soft key C again to select the shooting mode option. Since we seldom use the Object Tracking feature, we set the Right Key Setting to [Shoot Mode] so it is easily available.

These assignment commands will allow you to press a button and give you easy access to the camera's features. Keep in mind that you are not setting an actual value to a specific command, you are only obtaining access to the command options for the purpose of setting a value.

Note that your customization values will be lost if you need to reset your camera back to the default values. We recommend that you keep notes on your customization settings so if you need to execute the Reset Default command, you can easily go through the steps to reenter your customization settings.

## Utilizing Predefined Color Schemes

Although you can post-process your images, the Sony NEX-7 gives you the option to apply a predefined color scheme to your images when you capture the picture or movie. This is especially advantageous in that you can see how the altered color scheme can enhance your movie while recording. This can be done with either the Creative Style or Picture Effect options. Both of these functions are controlled by the menu commands.

### Creative Style Function

The Creative Style command has 13 options to choose from (table 7-4). Each option applies a different mood or style to your image.

| Creative Style Icon | Creative Style Name | Description |
|---|---|---|
| Std.+ | Standard | Default; captures image with natural coloration |
| Vivid+ | Vivid | Accentuates colors, making them stand out more |
| Ntrl+ | Neutral | Tones down colors, making them more muted |
| Clear+ | Clear | Captures images in clear tones with fluid colors in highlighted areas; good choice for radiant light |
| Deep+ | Deep | Enables intense coloration to stand out while maintaining color differentiation |
| Light+ | Light | Enables light color tones to brighten the scene, and increases contrast for better viewing |
| Port.+ | Portrait | Softens skin tones for a more pleasing effect |
| Land.+ | Landscape | Heightens saturation, contrast, and sharpness to produce more vivid and crisp results |
| Sunset+ | Sunset | Accentuates existing tones and adds warm sunset /sunrise tones |
| Night+ | Night Scene | Accentuates contrast to capture an image closer to the actual night scene |
| Autm+ | Autumn leaves | Accentuates existing tones and adds warm red, orange, and yellow tones |
| B/W+ | Black & White | Transforms the image into black-and-white with gradations of gray |
| Sepia+ | Sepia | Transforms the image into old-fashioned sepia coloration |

**Table 7-4**: Creative Style options and descriptions

When you select the Creative Style command, the displayed list of options is positioned at the command's current setting (figure 7-8). Rotate or press the top or bottom rim of the control wheel to navigate through the command's available options. You can also use control dial L.

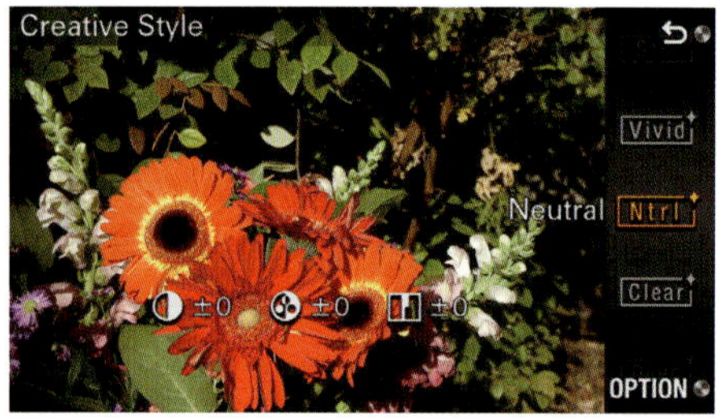


**Figure 7-8**: Creative Style menu

Although each style's name gives a hint on how the image will be affected, the only way to be sure is to preview its appearance on the display screen. As you scroll through each option, the camera applies the color scheme in Live View so you can evaluate the potential results. This will help you decide which style to choose. For example, applying [Vivid] to a multicolored floral image will have a much different effect than applying it to an image with one or two colors. In the latter case, you may find a different Creative Style to be more appealing.

The command goes a step further and allows you to fine-tune the contrast, saturation, and sharpness (figure 7-9) for all the Creative Style options except [Black & White] and [Sepia], where only the contrast and sharpness can be adjusted.

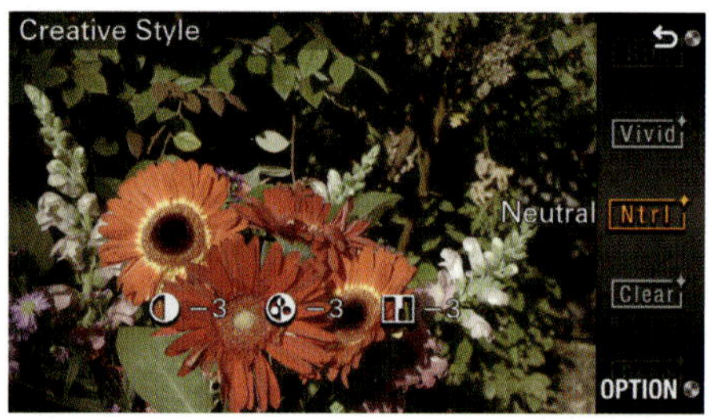


**Figure 7-9**: Creative Style fine adjustment options. Note the difference in coloration between this image and figure 7-8.

Each fine adjustment has a range from -3 to +3 that changes in increments of 1, which means you can increase or decrease the option by a factor of 1, 2, or 3. Your fine-tune adjustments are retained until you change them or execute the Reset Default command to return the camera to its default settings.

The effects of your selected color scheme and fine adjustments are best evaluated on the LCD display screen. Table 7-5 describes each of the available adjustments and their effects on the image.

| Fine Adjustment Icon | Condition | Status |
|---|---|---|
|  | Contrast | Controls the intensity of highlights and shadows. A +3 value increases highlight and shadow intensity, reduces white and black color variations, and gives the image a bolder, stronger look. A –3 value reduces highlight and shadow intensity, increases white and black color variations, and gives the image a smoother overall look. |
|  | Saturation | Controls the richness of the colors. A +3 value makes the colors bolder and accentuates them, giving the image more color contrast. A –3 value mutes and softens the colors, giving the image a more homogenous look. This fine adjustment option is not available for Black & White and Sepia Creative Styles. |
| 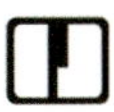 | Sharpness | Controls the appearance of edges. A +3 value heightens the edges, creating an edge that appears sharper. A –3 value softens the edges, creating a more blended look. Useful for hiding facial wrinkles and image noise. |

**Table 7-5**: Creative Style fine adjustment options

Important points:

- The Creative Style command is not available in Intelligent Auto and the SCN modes.
- You can set a Creative Style when Quality is set to RAW, and you will be able to see the results applied in the Image Data Converter program, but since the Creative Style is only saved with JPEG files, you will not see its effects on saved RAW files in many third-party software applications outside the camera, such as Photoshop and Aperture. In this case, the images will appear as though no Creative Style had been applied.
- Creative Styles are available for MP4 and AVCHD movie files.
- Creative Style is set to [Standard] when the Picture Effect function is selected.
- Saturation adjustment is not available for the [Black & White] and [Sepia] options.
- The selected Creative Style and its adjustments are retained even if you switch to another shooting mode or if the camera is turned off and back on.
- Creative Style is set to [Standard] and reset all adjustments to zero with the MENU>Setup (Menu Settings)>Reset Default command.
- You can apply a Creative Style within the Sony-supplied Image Data Converter software.

Selecting a Creative Style is easy. Just execute the following steps:

1. Select MENU>Brightness/Color>Creative Style, or press a customized button or wheel.
2. Rotate or press the top or bottom rim of the control wheel to navigate through the available options.
3. When you are positioned at an option you wish to apply, press soft key B to enter the Creative Style submenu to access the Contrast, Saturation, and Sharpness options.
4. Scroll through the selected adjustment options by pressing the right or left rim of the control wheel.
5. Rotate or press the top or bottom rim of the control wheel to navigate within the highlighted style's adjustment option if you wish to adjust it. Press soft key C to apply the style's adjustment.
6. Press soft key C to apply the style and its adjustments and exit back to Live View.

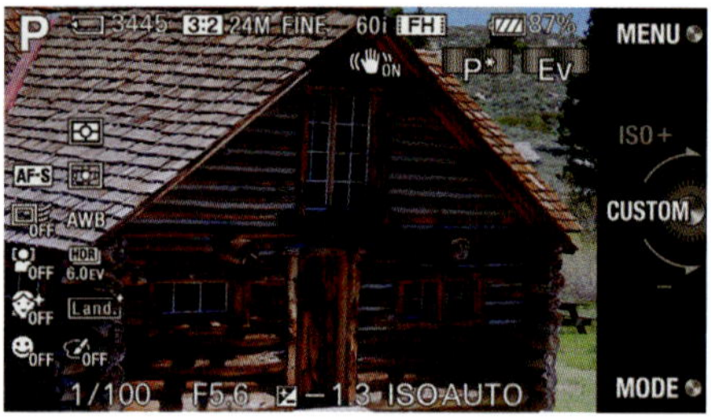


Figure 7-10: Creative Style icon displayed in the [Display All Info] data display format



Even if you made a fine adjustment, only the Creative Style icon will appear on the [Display All Info.] or [For viewfinder] data display format screen, without any indication of the fine adjustments you selected (figure 7-10). To view the fine adjustment values, you will have to revisit the Creative Style command structure.

### Picture Effect Function

The Picture Effect function lets you quickly apply a predefined effect filter while recording movies and JPEG picture files so you don't have to make the change during post-processing. This command will be disabled when Quality is set to a RAW setting. There are 12 Picture Effect options (table 7-6).

Several of the Picture Effect options have suboptions so you can further identify a focus area or specify how the colorization should be applied. For example, the Toy Camera option has the suboptions [Normal], [Cool], [Warm], [Green], and [Magenta], so you can apply a color tint to the Toy Camera effect.

| Picture Effect Icon | Picture Effect Name | Description | Suboptions |
|---|---|---|---|
| OFF | Off | Turns off Picture Effect. | |
| Toy | Toy Camera | Creates an image that looks as if it was taken with a toy camera. Colors and shadowing are more pronounced with less smoothness and gradation. | Set the color tone: [Normal], [Cool], [Warm], [Green], [Magenta] |
| Pop | Pop Color | Emphasizes color tones and makes them more vivid. | |
| Pos | Posterization | Emphasizes primary colors or, in the case of a black-and-white image, makes the black-and-white more pronounced. Creates a more contrasting, abstract look. | Select primary colors or black-and-white: [Color], [B&W] |
| Rtro | Retro Photo | Creates the image in an old-fashioned photo style using sepia and faded contrasts. | |
| Sfth key | Soft High-key | Creates a softer and more ethereal image. | |
| Part | Partial Color | Creates an image that retains one color and converts the rest of the image to black-and-white. | Select retained color: [Red], [Green], [Blue], [Yellow] |
| HC BW | High Contrast Mono. | Creates a high-contrast black-and-white image. | |
| Soft | Soft Focus | Creates a soft lighting effect. | Set effect intensity: [Low], [Mid], [High] |
| Pntg | HDR Painting | Takes three images and merges them to create a high dynamic range (HDR) image. The colors and details are heightened. | Set effect intensity: [Low], [Mid], [High] |
| Rich BW | Rich-tone Mono. | Takes three images and merges them to create a high dynamic range (HDR) image in black-and-white. | |
| Mini | Miniature | Creates an image with the main subject in focus and the background out of focus. Often used for miniature model images where the model is in focus and the background is not. | Set focus area: [Auto], [Top], [Middle(Horizontal)], [Bottom], [Right], [Middle(Vertical)], [Left] |

**Table 7-6**: Picture Effect options

Important points:

- Picture Effects can be applied only when Quality is set to JPEG files. If Quality is set to a RAW setting, the Picture Effect command is disabled.
- Picture Effect is automatically set to [Off] when the shooting mode is set to Intelligent Auto, SCN, Sweep Panorama, 3D Sweep Panorama, and Anti Motion Blur, and when a Creative Style option other than [Standard] is selected.
- The selected Picture Effect and its suboptions are retained if you switch to another supported shooting mode (P, S, A, or M) or if the camera is turned off and back on.
- Picture Effect is reset to [Off] when the MENU>Setup (Menu Settings)>Reset Default command is executed.
- While using a Picture Effect, you can adjust the exposure (shutter speed and aperture) with the exposure button.
- You can further adjust a Picture Effect in an image by using Sony-supplied Image Data Converter software.

Selecting a Picture Effect is easy. Just execute the following steps:

1. Select MENU>Brightness /Color>Picture Effect, or press a customized button or wheel.
2. Rotate or press the top or bottom rim of the control wheel to navigate through the available Picture Effect options.
3. When you want to apply a suboption, press soft key B to enter into the Picture Effects suboptions menu (figure 7-11). Rotate or press the top or bottom rim of the control wheel to navigate through the available Picture Effect suboptions. Press soft key C to apply the effect's adjustment.
4. Press soft key C to apply the effect and its adjustments and exit back to Live View.

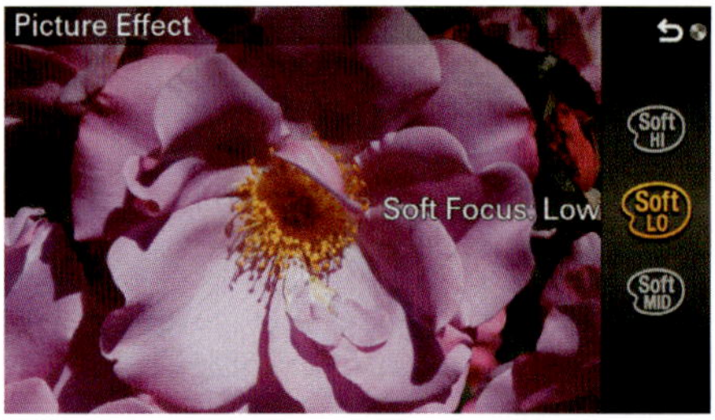

**Figure 7-11**: Picture Effect function's Soft Focus and suboption

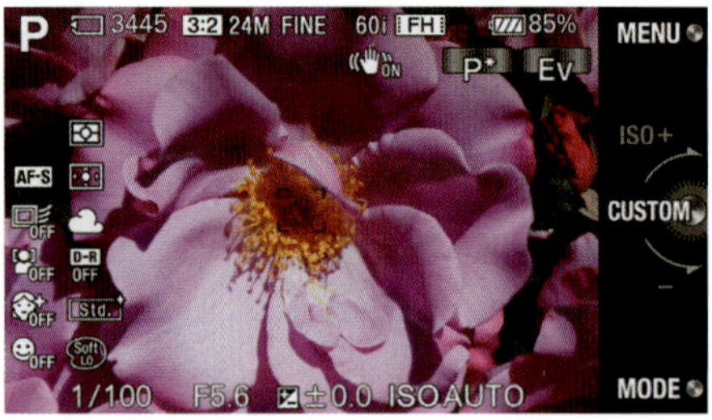

**Figure 7-12**: Live View with Soft Focus Picture Effect icon and Low suboption

An icon is displayed on the Display All Info and For viewfinder data display formats in Live View (figure 7-12) indicating the selected Picture Effect and suboption.

### Creative Styles and Picture Effects Differences

At first, applying a Picture Effect option might seem like a duplication of Creative Style, but it's not. The Picture Effect function's color repertoire is different, and you can pinpoint a focus area in several Picture Effect suboptions. You can use Creative Style options with all Quality settings, but you cannot use Picture Effect options when the Quality is set to capture RAW files. Creative Style and Picture Effect options are not available in automatic modes (Intelligent Auto and SCN); however, unlike Picture Effect options, you can use Creative Style options in Sweep Panorama, 3D Sweep Panorama, and Anti Motion Blur modes.

Both the Creative Style and Picture Effect functions colorize images, but both commands cannot be operational at the same time. The Picture Effect command automatically turns off when Creative Style is set to a value other than Standard. Creative Style automatically switches to Standard when a Picture Effect option is selected. In other words, each function defaults to a noncompeting value when you set the other to a nonstandard option.

### Creative Styles and Picture Effects Recommendation

Creative Style and Picture Effect options provide interesting color effects, with some limitations. Although you can modify a Creative Style's contrast, saturation, and sharpness via the camera, the allowable range may not be everything you want. Creative Style allows you to capture the image in both RAW and JPEG formats while still giving you the option of processing your pictures outside the camera. Picture Effect allows you to apply expressive filters to your pictures, but only to JPEG files.

We recommend that you play with both functions and see if any of the special styles and effects gives you results you like. If so, use them. One note of caution: many Creative Style options are subtle. The Picture Effect command has an [Off] option, but the nearest equivalent option for Creative Style is [Standard]; however, be aware that the [Standard] option has adjustments for contrast, saturation, and sharpness. If you don't want a Creative Style to affect your images, make sure these adjustments are set to zero.

## Help Guide Display

If you're new to the Sony camera line, you might want to use the help information displayed when you select a mode or a command. This is controlled by the Help Guide Display command:

MENU>Setup (Main Settings)>Help Guide Display>[On], [Off]

This command defaults to [On]. When the help guide is active, an informational screen tells you about the selected mode or command at the time it is selected (figure 7-13). This is great while you are learning the camera, but it won't take long before you know more about the camera's modes and commands than the informational screen gives you. We turned this feature off very quickly. Be aware that if you reset the camera's settings back to their default, the help guide screens will reappear.

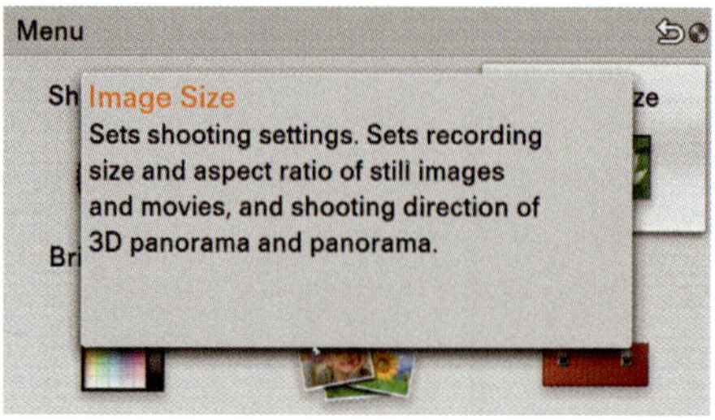

**Figure 7-13**: Help Guide Display

We noticed that the informational screen displays only when you move to a menu command, but not when you exit to the menu command from one of its options. We also noticed that the informational screen does not always display when you enter into a menu command's submenu. If the informational screen is not automatically displayed, scroll to another command and then back to the first command.

## Recommendations

Whether you use any of these customization features comes down to your own personal preference. We were very quick to change the Help Guide Display command to [Off].

With regard to customizing the camera's buttons, it again depends on how you use the camera. If you use this shortcut, be careful not to be confused by the camera's labels for each button. You can always set a button to a new function for a specific photo shoot and then change it back afterwards. If you find that you want to permanently set one of the buttons to another function and you tend to be forgetful, consider using some tape to relabel the button.

We recommend that you wait to customize the button functions until you are very familiar with the types of pictures and movies you will be taking. After we became more familiar with the camera and what settings we liked, we came up with a set of customizations that we tend to use often and therefore want to access easily. Table 7-7 contains our settings for each of the customization commands. We realize this may not be how you will want to set things up, and we might change our minds six months from now. But for us, with the types of shots we are currently taking, these settings are working well.

| Customization Main Commands | Customization Options | Condition |
|---|---|---|
| Function Settings | Function Settings 1 | Focus Settings |
| | Function Settings 2 | White Balance Settings |
| | Function Settings 3 | D-Range Settings |
| | Function Settings 4 | Custom Settings |
| | Custom Settings 1 | Metering Mode |
| | Custom Settings 2 | Autofocus Mode |
| | Custom Settings 3 | Quality |
| Custom Key Settings | AF/MF button | AF/MF Control |
| | Right Key Setting | Flash Comp. |
| | Soft key B Setting | Shoot Mode |
| | Soft key C Setting | Custom |
| | Custom 1 | ISO |
| | Custom 2 | Autofocus Area |
| | Custom 3 | Quality |
| | Custom 4 | Flash Mode |
| | Custom 5 | DRO/Auto HDR |

**Table 7-7**: Our current customization settings

If you want to add some ambiance to your pictures and movies, investigate the available options in the Creative Style and Picture Effect functions. We have enjoyed using both functions and have been surprised by how easy it is to capture an artistic image with little effort. We have even taken the results and done additional image processing on our computer using third-party software.

As mentioned earlier, the settings for Creative Style and Picture Effect are retained and automatically applied to your movies and pictures in most of the camera's modes. Therefore, when you don't want to apply any specific styles or effects, make sure that Creative Style is set to [Standard], with all of its adjustments at zero, and that Picture Effect is set to [Off]. There have been times we did not realize we had a subtle Creative Style being applied to our images.

# Chapter 8: Additional Features

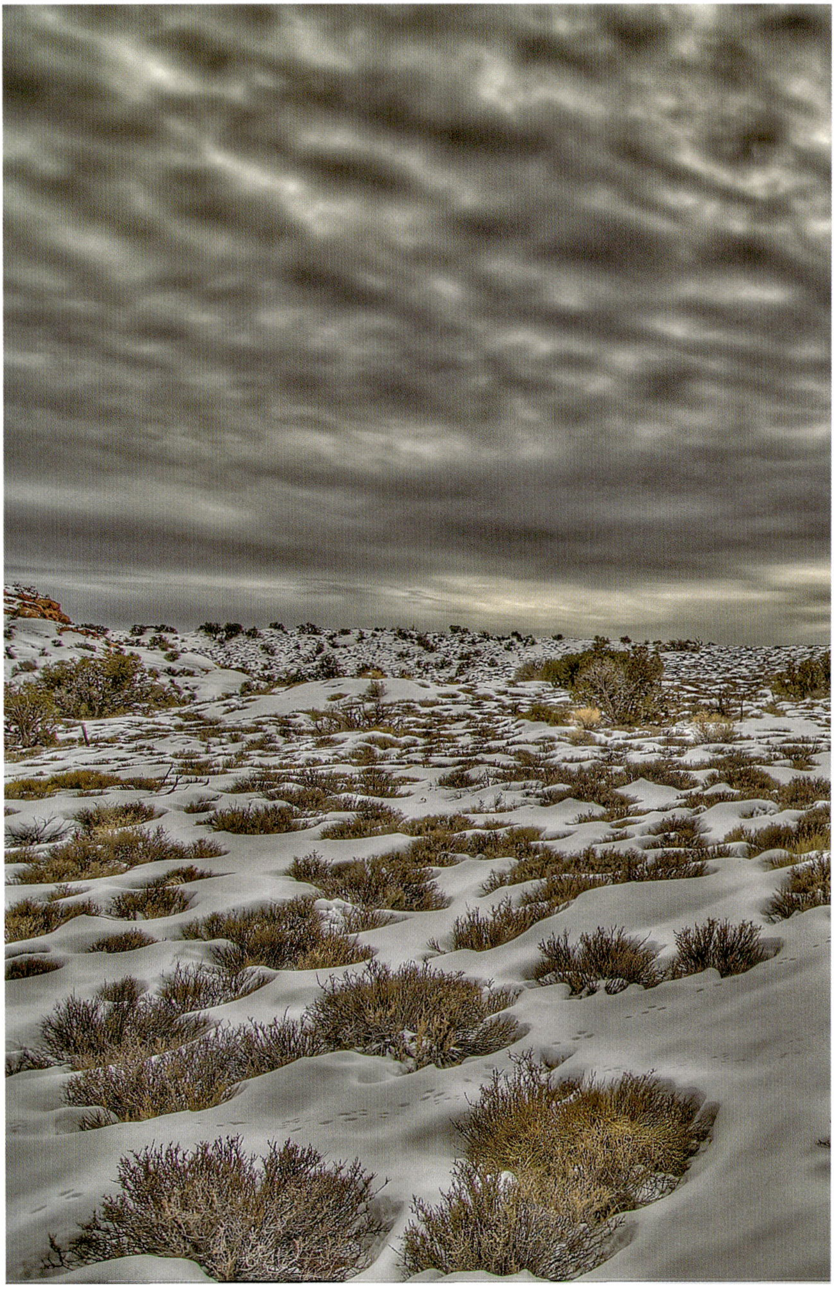

8

## Introduction

The Sony NEX-7 has many exciting features that give you the opportunity to capture unique pictures. Normally, applying these techniques requires downloading the images to a computer and then post-processing the image, but you can carry out many of these techniques automatically within the Sony NEX-7.

In this chapter, we cover the three remaining modes on the Shoot Mode menu: Sweep Panorama, 3D Sweep Panorama, and Anti Motion Blur. Each of these modes offers you an opportunity to capture a special image that would have been difficult and time consuming with more conventional photographic methods.

We will also cover the NEX-7's DRO/Auto HDR function, which allows you to record an image under lighting conditions when it is difficult to record enough detail in both the highlights and the shadows. If you expose for the highlights, then the shadow areas can end up being impenetrable black masses. If you expose for the shadows, the highlighted areas can be blinding white with little or no detail. When you use DRO/Auto HDR you can have an image that shows details in the shadows without burning out the highlights.

But first let's cover an often overlooked command, Dial/Wheel Lock, that can help prevent you from inadvertently changing your camera settings.

## Locking the Dials and the Control Wheel

At first glance you might wonder why you would want to prevent yourself from using all of your camera's controls. Well, if you ever ask a passerby to take a picture so you can get into the shot, you want to make sure that person doesn't mistakenly change your camera settings. Or if you have taken great pains to make sure your camera is set up correctly to record the perfect picture, but you need to go back and forth to stage the subject, you want to be sure you don't inadvertently brush one of the control dials and change a setting. It would be nice to easily lock the control wheel and dials so they can't accidently be turned as you handle the camera or pass it to someone else.

The Dial/Wheel Lock command allows you to disengage the control wheel and the two control dials, or just the control wheel, so rotating them will not affect the settings. This means you are limited to using the buttons and the rim of the control wheel to change any last-minute settings, but you can be assured that a simple brush of your hand won't cause you to re-create the shot.

MENU>Setup (Shooting Settings)>Dial/Wheel Lock>[All], [Control Wheel], [Off]

The default, [All], will disable all actions when the control wheel and the two control dials are rotated. You will still be able to press the control wheel rim and initiate its assigned action.

Set the command to [Control Wheel] to disable action only when the control wheel is rotated. You can still use the control dials to change settings. The [Off] option disables locking for all of the controls.

This command has a trick to activate the locking mechanism. You must first press and hold down the Navigation button for a couple of seconds. A Locked message will be displayed to indicate the camera is locked. Press and hold down the button again for a few seconds to deactivate the locking function. You can also deactivate the locking function if you change the command's value, but turning the camera off and back on will not deactivate it.

## Panoramic Modes

The Sony NEX-7 uses two modes to build a wide view of a scene: Sweep Panorama (figure 8-1) and 3D Sweep Panorama. Just as the names indicate, both of these modes create panoramic pictures—one as regular 2-D images and the other as 3-D images, which can be played back on 3-D compatible HDTVs. In both cases, the recorded images are created in JPEG format. The 3-D image has an additional Multi Picture Object (MPO) file, with the JPEG file, to create the 3-D effect on your HDTV.

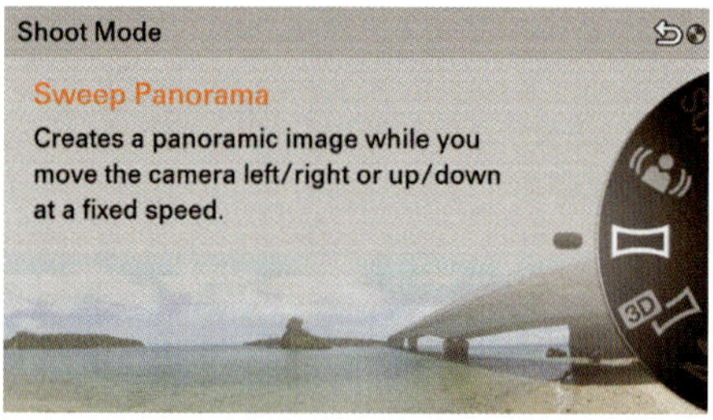


**Figure 8-1**: Menu set to Sweep Panorama

In both modes, a panoramic picture is created by slowly and smoothly sweeping (or panning) a large area horizontally or vertically. The camera rapidly takes a series of shots as you sweep. After this is completed, the camera stitches them together to form a panoramic image. But there are some conditions. The camera needs to be moved at a fairly constant rate—neither too fast nor too slow. You must also sweep on a level horizontal or vertical plane. This is an excellent opportunity to utilize the Level data display format discussed in chapter 3. If there is any substantial variation in the speed or level, the camera will stop shooting and display an error message.

During the sweep, the shutter speed, ISO, and aperture is set on the basis of the available lighting. The camera will not use a shutter speed longer than 1/60 second. The camera applies the exposure settings at the beginning of the sweep and does not change them during recording, so in extreme lighting conditions, the panorama may have areas that are under- or overexposed.

The camera does an excellent job of recording the individual shots and stitching them together. The software is very tolerant of small variations in the sweep rate and the level. Sometimes you can get some very interesting results. You may notice that if you take a Sweep Panorama with moving objects, such as cars speeding along a road, you can capture the moving objects several times so they appear cloned in the final picture. It's certainly worth experimenting with this mode.

The camera also automatically determines the ISO and the exposure. However, you can apply a selected WB, metering mode, and Creative Style option. You might find it easier to change some of these settings before entering Sweep Panorama or 3D Sweep Panorama modes. That way you won't have the panorama controls in the way when you view the effects of a creative style or a change to the WB. Keep in mind that the Navigation button, along with other button customizations, are disabled in both panorama modes. If you have customized your camera to access any of these commands, you will be out of luck and will have to access them through the MENU button.

You can't use the following commands in the Sweep Panorama and 3D Sweep Panorama modes: Flash Mode, any of the Drive Mode options other than Single Shooting, Picture Effect, Object Tracking, Face Detection, Smile Shutter, and DRO/Auto HDR.

When you play back the panorama images, there are two ways to enlarge the picture. With the first method, you must first pause the playback, then the magnifying icon is displayed and is associated with soft key B. In the second method, you enlarge the image after you enter playback mode, but before you start playing back the picture, by entering the Enlarge Image command:

MENU>Playback>Enlarge Image



Each panorama mode has two menu commands, Image Size and Panorama Direction. They are enabled after the Shoot Mode is set to the specific panorama mode. These commands control the size of the panorama and the direction in which you are required to sweep the camera.

## Sweep Panorama Mode Commands

To execute the mode commands from the displayed menu, navigate to the Shoot Mode and press enter. Turn the control wheel to the Sweep Panorama icon. The following commands control how the Sweep Panorama function works (figure 8-2):

MENU>Image Size (Panorama)>Image Size>[Standard], [Wide]

MENU>Image Size (Panorama)>Panorama Direction>[Right], [Left], [Up], [Down]

Sweep Panorama has two sizes: [Standard] and [Wide]. The picture's pixel count depends on the selected size and direction (table 8-1). With [Wide], you can pan farther and get much wider coverage in the resulting picture. You can sweep the camera in four directions: [Right], [Left], [Up], and [Down].

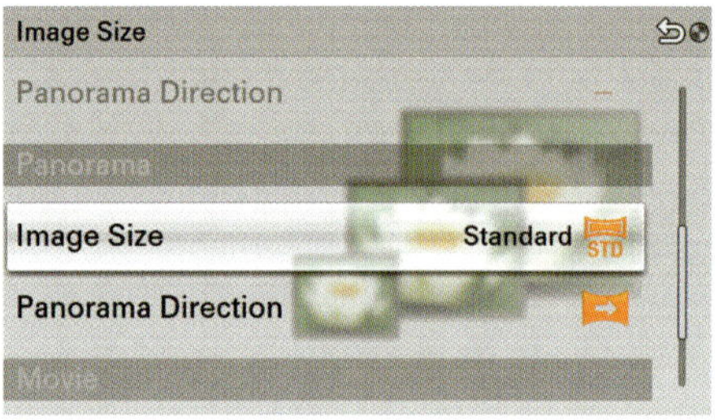


**Figure 8-2**: Sweep Panorama commands

Note that the [Standard] and [Wide] options produce pictures at the same height. Although the [Wide] version might appear shorter, it isn't. Instead, the whole picture is displayed smaller so you can see more of it on the display screen.

| Sweep Panorama Size | | |
|---|---|---|
| Panorama Direction | Standard<br>Equivalent Pixels | Wide<br>Equivalent Pixels |
| [Right]/[Left] | 8192 x 1856 | 12416 x 1856 |
| [Up]/[Down] | 3872 x 2160 | 5536 x 2160 |

**Table 8-1**: Sweep Panorama size

Figures 8-3a through 8-3d show Sweep Panorama results for several different combinations of sizes and directions.

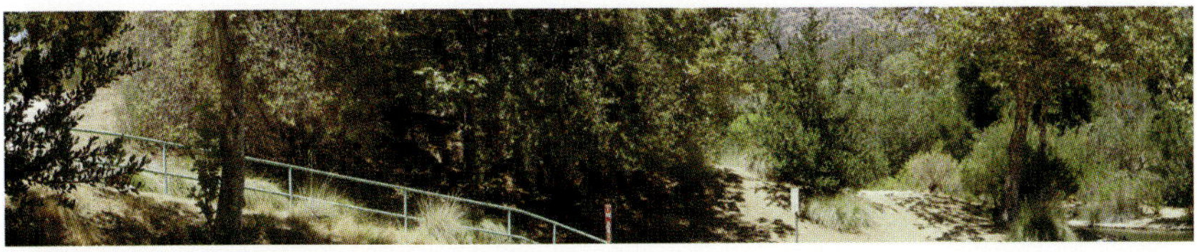

**Figure 8-3a**: Size/Direction = Standard/Right

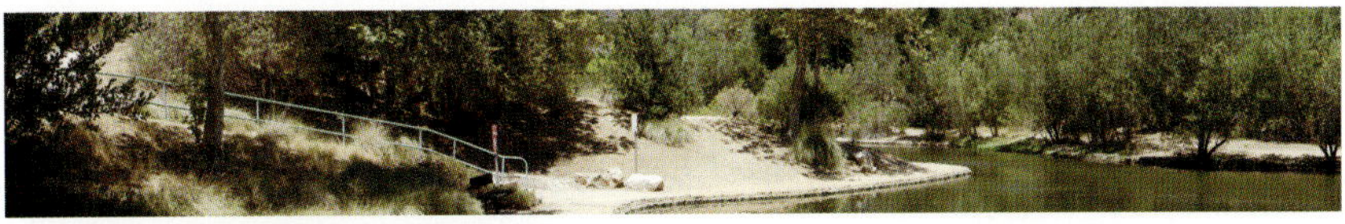

**Figure 8-3b**: Size/Direction = Wide/Right

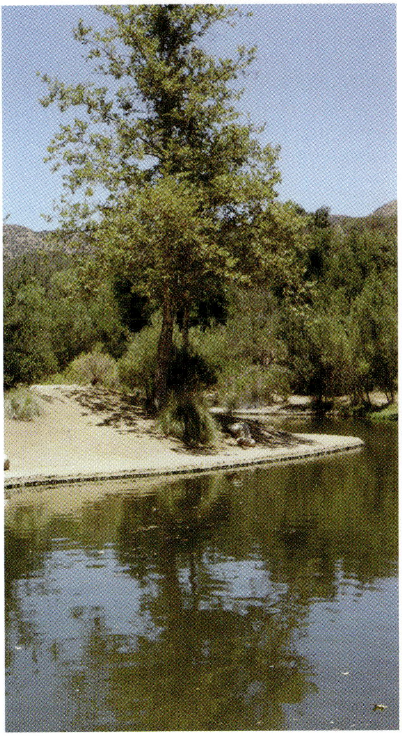

**Figure 8-3c**: Size/Direction = Standard/Up

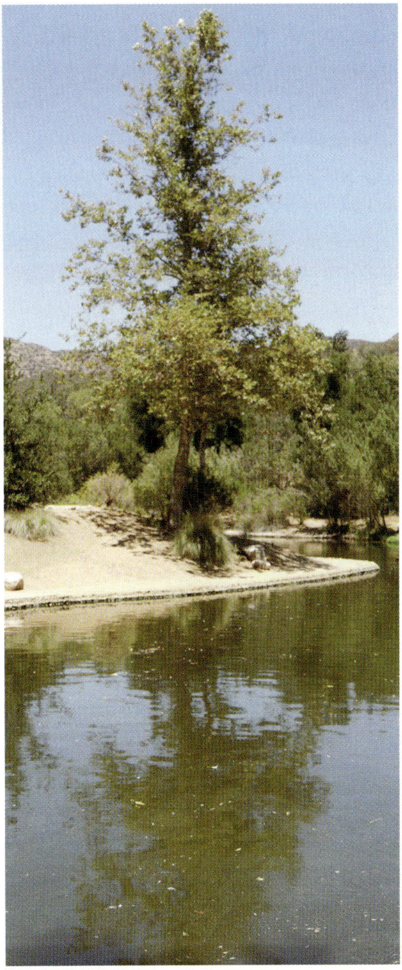

**Figure 8-3d**: Size/Direction = Wide/Up

### 3D Sweep Panorama Mode Commands

When you switch the Shoot Mode to 3D Sweep Panorama, the following commands are enabled (figure 8-4):

MENU>Image Size (3D Panorama)>Image Size>[16:9], [Standard], [Wide]

MENU>Image Size (3D Panorama)>Panorama Direction>[Right], [Left]

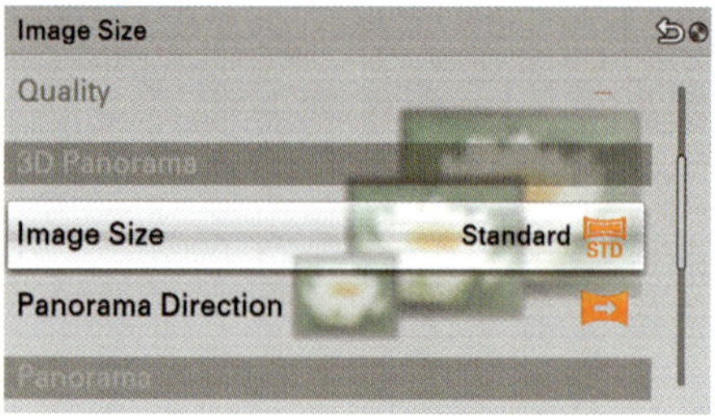


**Figure 8-4**: 3D Sweep Panorama commands

3D Sweep Panorama has three sizes: [16:9], [Standard], and [Wide]. As with Sweep Panorama, [Wide] allows you to pan farther and gives the resulting picture much wider coverage, but again it appears shorter than the [Standard] 3-D image when it is viewed on the LCD screen. The [16:9] size results in a 3-D picture with the least amount of panoramic width coverage. It has the same ratio as a movie, but it creates a 3-D still image. All of the panoramas in each of the three sizes store two files on the memory card: JPEG and MPO.

The 3-D mode has only two directions to choose from: [Right] or [Left]. This may seem limiting, but it actually isn't. Read the box on "Recording a Vertical 3-D Panorama" to learn more.

As with Sweep Panorama images, the pixel counts of 3D Sweep Panorama images depend on the selected size and direction (table 8-2).

| 3D Sweep Panorama Size (Equivalent Pixels) | | | |
|---|---|---|---|
| **Direction** | **16:9** | **Standard** | **Wide** |
| [Right]/[Left] | 1920 x 1080 | 4912 x 1080 | 7152 x 1080 |

**Table 8-2**: 3D Sweep Panorama size

Figures 8-5a through 8-5c show several combinations of size and direction.

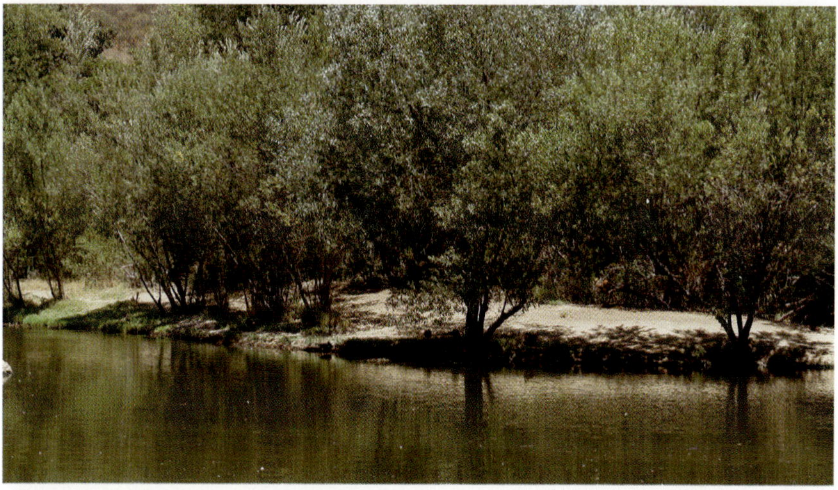

**Figure 8-5a**: Size/Direction = 16:9/Right

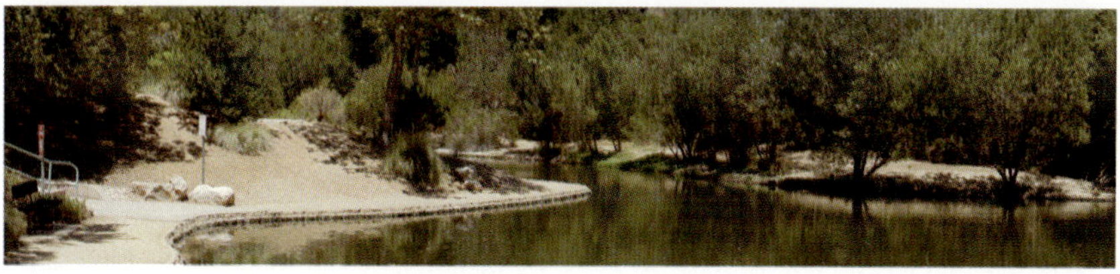

**Figure 8-5b**: Size/Direction = Standard/Right

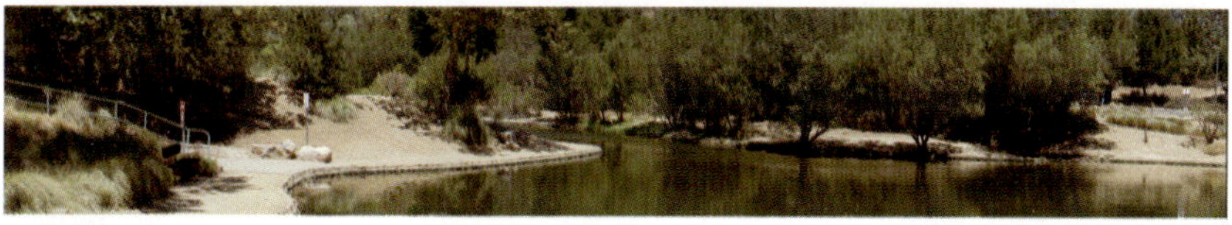

**Figure 8-5c**: Size/Direction = Wide/Right

### Recording a Vertical 3-D Panorama

Just because you have set the camera to sweep right (or left) doesn't mean you can't sweep up (or down) instead. The camera expects you to sweep at a constant speed, keep the camera relatively level, and move the camera in the direction of the arrow displayed in the viewfinder. As long as you do that (and the camera can obtain focus), you will get a panoramic image.

Let's say you want a 3-D panorama of a tall tree. You can select any of the three sizes. Set the direction to [Right] and hold the camera at 90 degrees with the arrow pointing upward. Position the camera to frame the bottom of the tree. Press the shutter button and shoot the panorama like you would normally, moving the camera in the direction of the arrow. The camera will handle the change in orientation just fine.

You can do the same thing for any of the Sweep Panorama sizes and directions. Just make sure you pan in the direction of the arrow seen in the Live View.

## Shooting a Panoramic Picture

After you select a panorama type, set its size, and choose the direction to sweep, the camera will display three things in the Live View:

- An arrow will correspond with the selected direction.
- A message will tell you to sweep according to the arrow.
- A two-tone screen will appear, in which one side is dull gray over the Live View and the other side is unaffected (figure 8-6). The line where the two sides meet is the point where the panorama will start.

Frame the image so the point where you wish to start the sweep is positioned just inside the nongrayed side of the display screen. Note that which side is grayed depends on the direction you select. If you select [Right], the grayed side is on the left of the display screen. If you select [Up], the grayed side is on the bottom of the screen.

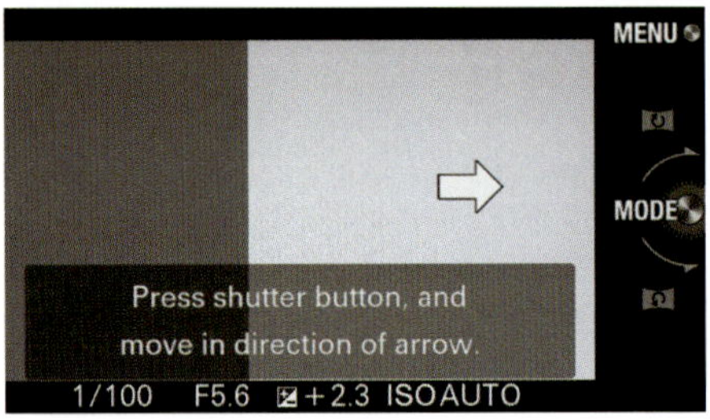


**Figure 8-6**: Sweep Panorama starting point, to the right of the grayed section

Make any needed adjustments to the WB and exposure. Add a Creative Style if you like. Keep in mind that the Navigation button and other button customization are disabled in this Shoot Mode. You will have to make WB and Creative Style changes through the menu. You will find it easier to make these changes before entering 3D Sweep Panorama mode since you won't have the panorama controls in your way when you view the commands. After you complete your adjustments, press the shutter button halfway again to make sure your focus is still intact.

You have one more step to complete before you can take your panoramic shot. Getting a realistic shot depends on a smooth, level, and constant sweep. It also depends on creating a very tight radius when you do the sweep. As you pan the camera, hold it as close to the center of the sweep as possible. The best way to accomplish this is either to hold the camera up to your eye and use the viewfinder as your sweeping guide, or mount your camera on a tripod and pan in a vertical or horizontal direction. These two methods are best because they keep the pan in a tight, short radius. Holding the camera away from your body and using the LCD screen as your sweeping guide makes the radius larger and can create some distortion.

Now you are ready to record. While holding your camera steady, press the shutter button down and start panning. As you pan, you will notice that the arrow moves across the screen along a simulated bar. The bar represents the full amount of time you need to hold the shutter button down and pan the camera. Continue to pan the camera until the arrow has traveled the full distance. If you take your finger off the shutter button while the camera is firing, the process will stop and will generate an error message. We have found it best to continue the pan until the camera actually stops shooting. That way we know we have not prematurely ended the process.

### Panorama Results

Each panorama has an element of mystery as to what exactly you will capture. This is what can make the feature so exciting and inviting to use. Yes, you can end up with a flawless panorama where everything is a true representation of the scene. Most of these are pictures of stationary landscapes. But even with these ordinary scenes, you can still end up with new and exciting results.

Keep in mind that although using a tripod with a pan head should result in best-quality images, sometimes creative images can be obtained when sweeping by handholding the camera.

Try moving the camera slightly up or down within the narrow range of allowable vertical movement. The resulting image may have a slightly wavy effect, or it may be narrower in height (or width, depending on the sweep direction) due to the camera's need to create a rectangular image and trim extremes that are out of bounds.

Another experiment is to take panoramic pictures of moving subjects. Depending on the subject's speed, panning in the direction the subject is moving may shorten or truncate it, and panning in the opposite direction may lengthen or elongate it. Even taking panoramic pictures of stationary objects can give you some interesting results. When panning, the camera takes images that overlap. Most of the time, the camera's stitching software eliminates the overlapping and creates a smooth panned image, but there will be times when the resulting panoramic picture will contain multiple images of the same object.

> **Viewing 3-D without a 3-D TV**
>
> Just because you don't have a 3-D TV doesn't mean you can't view your images in 3-D. You can produce anaglyph images with third-party software.
>
> Anaglyph images have been around for a long time. They are created when two images are taken of a subject—one is angled slightly differently from the other; one has a red color layer, and the other has a cyan color layer. These layers are superimposed to create a composite image. When they are viewed with 3-D glasses (cyan filter over one lens and red filter over the other), the offset of the images creates a combined image, which appears three-dimensional. This works best if the main subject is in the center and therefore appears to be in the foreground, and the remainder of the image appears to be in the background.
>
> We work with Anaglyph Workshop software for Mac OS X. (There is also a version for Windows XP, Vista, or higher.) For more information, visit *www.tabberer.com/sandyknoll/more/3dmaker/anaglyph-software.html*.

### Panning Problems

Taking a panoramic image can require some trial and error before you are successful. If the camera detects inconsistent panning—that is, too fast, too slow, or not level—or if you don't start the panning after the shutter button is pressed, the camera will stop recording and display an error message. Although there might be some frustration, we are sure you will ultimately enjoy the results.

The camera will display the following message if you pan the camera too slow or not in a straight line:

**Could not shoot 3D panorama. Move the camera straight in the direction of the arrow.**



The camera will display the following message if you pan the camera too fast or in the wrong direction:

**Could not shoot 3D panorama. Move the camera slowly.**

It can be difficult to pan at a consistent speed each time you record. Most likely you will notice some results with a section of gray at the end of the picture (figure 8-7). This means you panned too quickly, and the remaining portion of the allotted size did not have anything recorded to fill that space. Try retaking the picture while panning a bit slower.

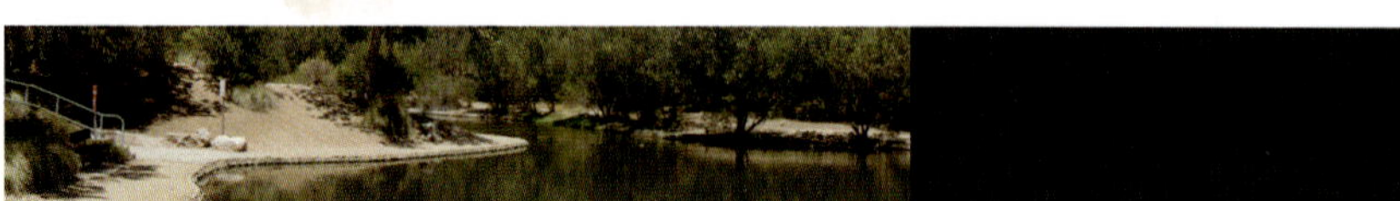

**Figure 8-7**: Panorama results with unrecorded space grayed out

## Anti Motion Blur Mode

One way the NEX-7 handles noise resulting from dim lighting is to fire multiple shots and average the images to reduce noise. This feature is available in SCN Hand-held Twilight mode. Unfortunately, this mode limits you: all of the exposure settings are automatically set for you. In essence, you have to trust the camera to make the settings for you. This prevents you from setting the camera to exposure values that create a uniquely personal image.

The Anti Motion Blur mode is very similar to the SCN Hand-held Twilight mode, but with some advantages. The Anti Motion Blur mode also fires multiple shots and averages the images to reduce the noise, but in addition, it provides you with more flexibility to control the camera's exposure. You can use the Exposure Compensation tool, change the WB, and apply a Creative Style to the image, all of which are unavailable in the SCN Hand-held Twilight mode.

The Anti Motion Blur mode can be found in the Shoot Mode menu (figure 8-8):

MENU>Shoot Mode>[Anti Motion Blur]

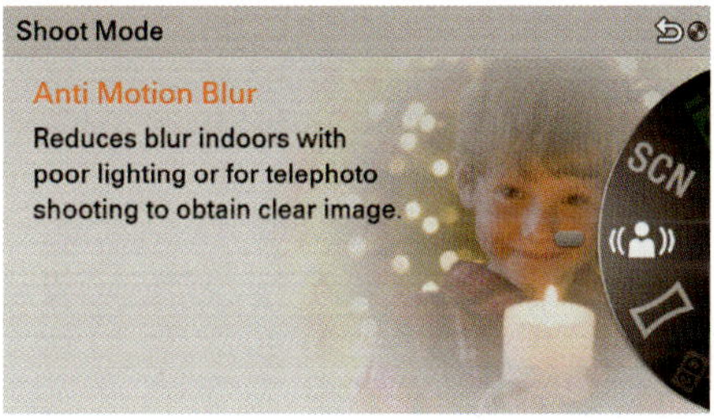


**Figure 8-8**: Shoot Mode positioned on Anti Motion Blur mode

When this mode is activated, the camera takes six shots at high sensitivity and merges them to form a single image with reduced noise. The resulting image can only be saved as a [Fine] or [Standard] JPEG.

Use Anti Motion Blur mode when there is low light or slight movement. The camera's software will reduce noise and slight blurs due to both of these scenarios.

8

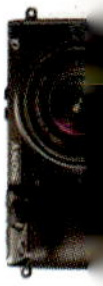

Generally low light causes noise to be recorded within the image. The Anti Motion Blur mode allows you to increase the ISO to 3200 or 6400 in low-light handheld situations, and obtain relatively noise-free image. But Anti Motion Blur is not effective in all situations. In order to align the six images into one, the camera will need to be able to determine the location of each object within the image. Therefore the image content must have sufficient color contrast so the camera can merge the six images together and match up the content of each image to build a final image.

This will be difficult if the subject's movement is too extreme or if the light source emits a discontinuous spectrum, like fluorescent lights, and causes differences in each of the six images. In addition, problems can occur when the color scheme in the image is monotone or has repeating patterns, which will confuse the camera when it is trying to merge the multiple images into one.

Figures 8-9a and 8-9b show the results when Anti Motion Blur and P modes were used in a low-light environment. Both images have been enlarged to show the amount of noise.

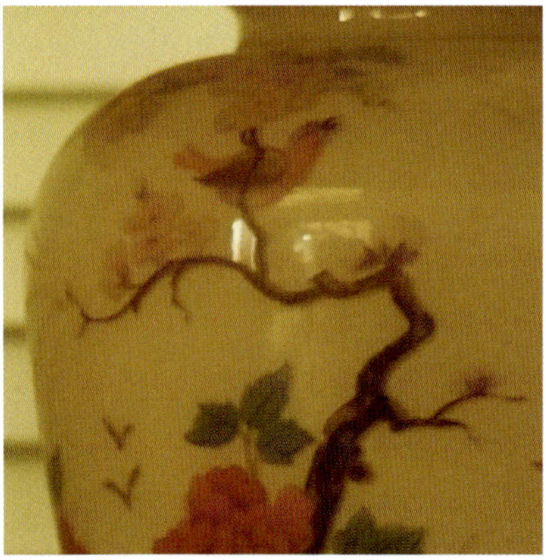

**Figure 8-9a**: Low-light Anti Motion Blur mode results

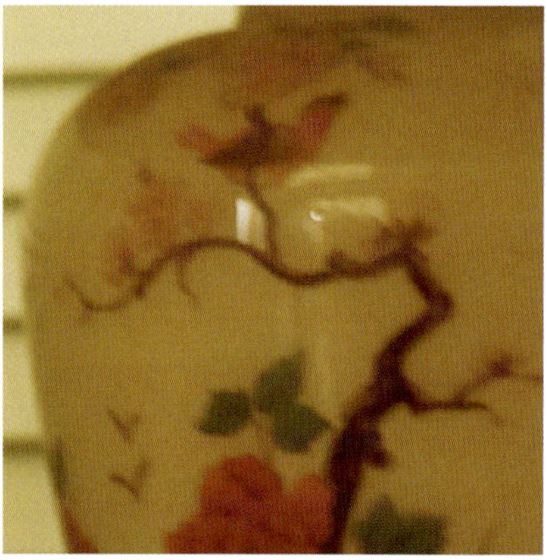

**Figure 8-9b**: Low-light P mode results

## DRO/Auto HDR Function

When photographing, you sometimes encounter a scene with overly bright regions that show little to no detail. Or you might encounter a subject with deep shadows that appear as a featureless black mass. Between these two extremes are regions with midtones that lack contrast. To an extent, downloading the image to a computer and post-processing the image with programs like Photoshop can remedy these deficiencies. But Sony has designed the NEX-7 so you can correct these deficiencies in the camera with two processes: Dynamic Range Optimization (DRO) (figures 8-10a and 8-10b) and Auto High Dynamic Range (Auto HDR) (figures 8-11a and 8-11b). When you select either of these operations, the camera will process the image automatically and then save it to your memory card.

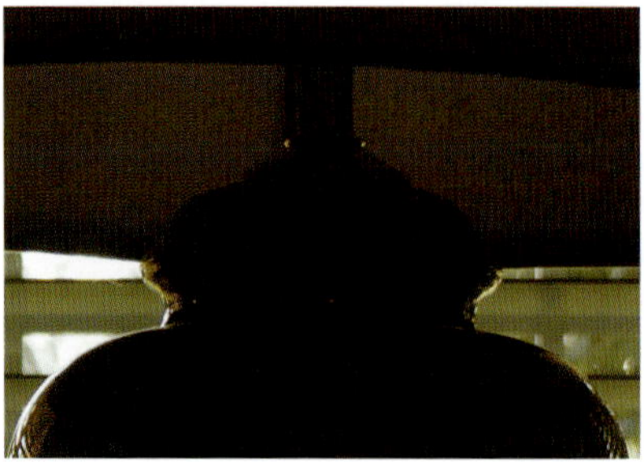

**Figure 8-10a**: Image without DRO Auto

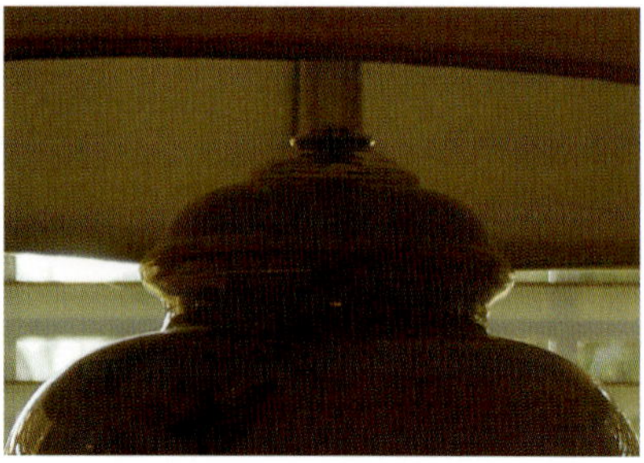

**Figure 8-10b**: Image with DRO Auto

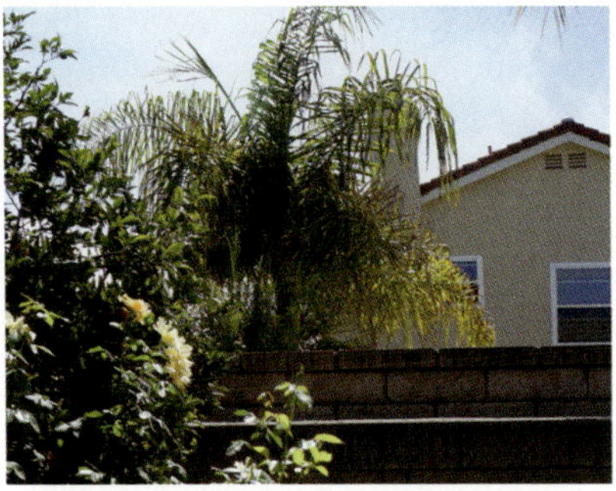

**Figure 8-11a**: Image without HDR Auto

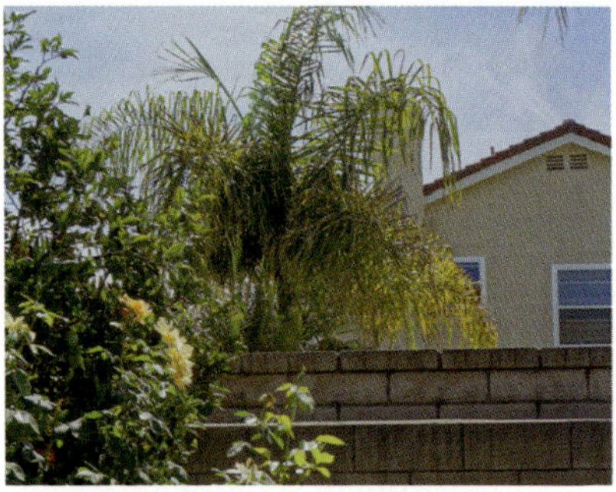

**Figure 8-11b**: Image with HDR Auto

Choose DRO when one exposure can record all of the intensity values for the scene. If the scene has too great a variation in intensity values and the extreme light levels overwhelm the sensor, use Auto HDR. This setting employs three exposures taken in rapid succession: one for recording highlights, one for recording midtones, and one for recording shadows. By using multiple exposures you can record a greater range of intensities than can be recorded in a single photograph. By combining these three images, it is possible to create a composite where shadows can be lightened, highlights can be darkened, and midtones can be maintained.

The DRO and Auto HDR functions are accessed through the menu, where you can turn both functions off or select one of them:

MENU>Brightness/Color>DRO/Auto HDR>[D-R Off], [DRO Auto], [HDR Auto]

You can also customize the Custom Key Settings' Right Key Setting and any of the Soft Key C Setting's five Custom options and assign DRO/Auto HDR:



MENU>Setup (Main Settings)>Custom Key Settings>Right Key Setting

MENU>Setup (Main Settings)>Custom Key Settings>Soft Key C Setting>Custom>[Custom 1], [Custom 2], [Custom 3], [Custom 4], [Custom 5]

## DRO Function

Access the [DRO] function with the following command:

> MENU>Brightness/Color>DRO/Auto HDR>DRO AUTO>[DRO AUTO], [Lv1], [Lv2], [Lv3], [Lv4], [Lv5]

The submenu options of the [DRO] function are shown in table 8-3. The DRO level options determine the extent to which shadows are lightened in an image—the maximum effect occurs at [Lv5], and the minimum effect occurs at [Lv1]. It is difficult to estimate what level you need for a given scene. We recommend trying multiple levels until you get to know how each looks. With practice, you should be able to implement this function to your liking. There is a DRO Auto option where the camera makes the decision, but this does not guarantee you will like the image that is recorded.

| DRO Function Icon | DRO Function Name | Description |
|---|---|---|
| D-R OFF | D-R Off | Disables DRO/Auto HDR function. |
| DRO | D-Range Optimizer | Brings out detail in shadows by lightening, and brings out bright, washed-out areas by darkening, so that fine details in both areas are more easily discerned. |
| Sub-Options | DRO AUTO | Executes DRO automatically when the image has deep shadows and bright highlights. The camera chooses what level to use to adjust the blacks and whites. |
| | DRO Lvl 1 | Level 1: The least amount of change to blacks and whites in the image. |
| | DRO Lvl 2 | Level 2: The second least amount of change to blacks and whites in the image. |
| | DRO Lvl 3 | Level 3: The middle amount of change to blacks and whites in the image. |
| | DRO Lvl 4 | Level 4: The second most amount of change to blacks and whites in the image. |
| | DRO Lvl 5 | Level 5: The most amount of change to blacks and whites in the image. |

**Table 8-3**: DRO options of the DRO/Auto HDR function

Even if you select a specific level, only the DRO AUTO icon will appear on the display screen, without any indication of the level you selected, regardless of the type of data display format you selected. To see which level you selected, you will have to revisit the command structure.

The DRO function is available in P, A, S, and M modes only. You can shoot in RAW or JPEG or both. When you photograph in [RAW & JPEG], you will find that the RAW files, when opened with most image processing software programs, may not show the effects of DRO, but JPEG files do. The one program where you can see a RAW file emulating the contrast changes with DRO is Sony Image Data Converter 4.0. You can add a Creative Style to affect the results, although picture effects are not enabled with the DRO function.

### Auto HDR Function

Traditionally, HDR photography involves downloading pictures taken with different exposures and combining them on a computer to form a composite image. Then an operation called tone mapping is performed to create an image that displays details in the brightest and darkest areas of the scene. Frequently, the resulting image displays oversaturated colors and a surreal appearance, which gives the image a unique appearance. For example, when you merge three different exposures with third-party software like Photomatix, the final composite image will have dramatically different colors than the original scene (figure 8-12).

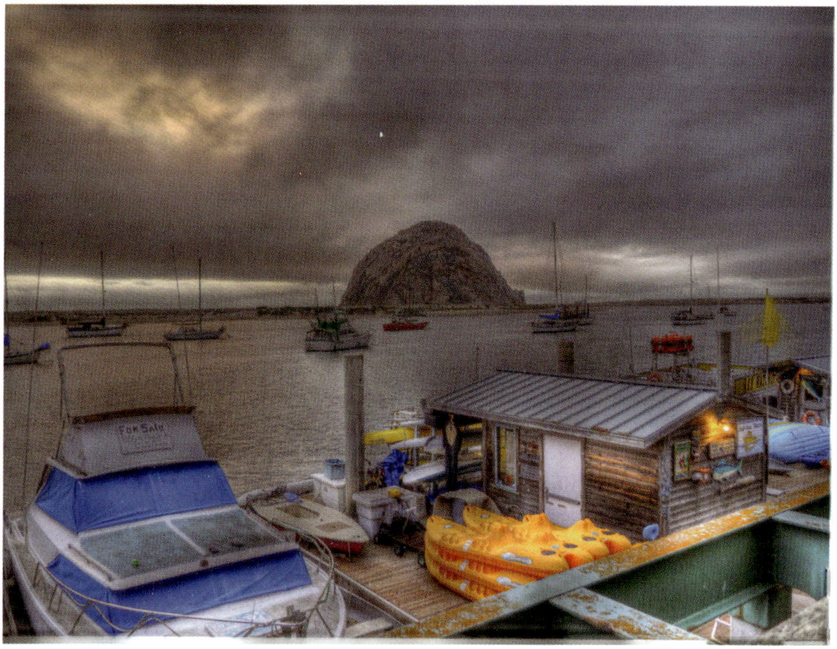

**Figure 8-12**: Image created by merging three exposures in Photomatix

8

When you use the Auto HDR function, you might be surprised to find that the final image does not have the supersaturated colors seen when the same images are processed with Photomatix. Instead, the color balance and saturation of Auto HDR are similar to a DRO image. It appears that Sony engineers have adjusted the Auto HDR output so the resulting image retains the color balance and tonality associated with a typical photograph. To mimic the surreal appearance characteristic of HDR images, you might want to try the Picture Effect HDR Painting option. When compared to Auto HDR, the HDR Painting option provides more saturated colors like a typical HDR process.

Even though Sony NEX-7 Auto HDR and DRO images resemble each other, there is an important difference. First, DRO images can be captured in RAW format, but the HDR function saves only JPEG files. Also, if you look in the deep shadows, the DRO image has higher noise levels than an image captured with Auto HDR. This is because a longer exposure is used in Auto HDR for capturing shadow detail thereby reducing the appearance of noise. In contrast, a single-exposure DRO image uses image processing to increase the brightness in the shadow areas, which makes the noise more evident. In addition, Auto HDR takes three exposures and merges them into one, making it ill suited for recording moving subjects. In contrast, DRO takes only one exposure; therefore, the impact of the subject moving on the resulting image is minimal.

The following command enables the Auto HDR process, and the options are described in table 8-4:

MENU>Brightness/Color>DRO/Auto HDR>Auto HDR>[HDR AUTO], [1.0EV], [2.0EV], [3.0EV], [4.0EV], [5.0EV], [6.0EV]



After Auto HDR is selected, you have the choice of letting the camera determine the best EV by setting [HDR AUTO]. Alternatively, you can take control and select a specific EV value ranging from 1.0 to 6.0. The selected value becomes the +/– range over which the three shots are distributed. Use a low EV value when the scene has a moderate range of light intensities; use a high EV value when the range of intensities is more extreme.

| HDR Function Icon | HDR Function Name | Description |
|---|---|---|
| HDR | Auto HDR: Exposure Diff. | The camera shoots three images and combines them to bring out detail, especially in the shadows and bright, washed-out areas. The process closely retains the subject's coloring. |
| Sub-Options | HDR AUTO | The camera determines the best EV value to use to bracket the three shots. |
| | HDR 1.0EV | The camera brackets the three shots within a total+/-1.0EV. |
| | HDR 2.0EV | The camera brackets the three shots within a total+/-2.0EV. |
| | HDR 3.0EV | The camera brackets the three shots within a total+/-3.0EV. |
| | HDR 4.0EV | The camera brackets the three shots within a total+/-4.0EV. |
| | HDR 5.0EV | The camera brackets the three shots within a total+/-5.0EV. |
| | HDR 6.0EV | The camera brackets the three shots within a total+/-6.0EV. |

**Table 8-4**: HDR option of the DRO/Auto HDR function

The Auto HDR function is available in P, A, S, and M modes only, and it is enabled for JPEG files only (Quality = [Fine] or [Standard]). If the camera is set to HDR AUTO and the Quality value is changed to include RAW, the DRO/Auto HDR command's value will automatically be changed to DRO AUTO. It will not automatically change back if you reset the Quality command to a JPEG-only value. As with DRO, Picture Effect command is not enabled, but you can add a Creative Style option to affect your results. Auto HDR is not available for Drive Mode options that generate multiple shots.

As with DRO, even if you select a specific EV increment, only the HDR AUTO icon will appear on the display screen, regardless of the type of data display format you selected. To determine which EV increment you selected, you will have to revisit the command structure.

### Using DRO and Auto HDR

We encourage you to try these imaging techniques and see if they help your photography. They can be a benefit. But as you gain more experience, you may decide to forego these processes.

We rarely use DRO for still photography. We prefer to post-process RAW images on our computer, where we can try various DRO levels to obtain the effect we want. Sony's PMB software allows you to approximate the DRO effect by working with RAW images. Although the effect is not identical, we prefer having greater control over the process rather than relying on an automated camera rendering.

Where we have found DRO to be a powerful benefit is in recording movies. Your ability to post-process these files may be limited, and DRO provides a simple means of taming extremes in contrast to make a pleasing movie.

Like DRO, Auto HDR can improve an image, but also like DRO, it is difficult to anticipate the appearance of the image. We prefer shooting in RAW, which is not available with Auto HDR. Then we post-process the images on our computer, which allows us to experiment with different interpretations of the composite image. To generate the image files for this task, we describe how to acquire various exposures with auto bracketing in chapter 6.

## Recommendations

At first we didn't see the value of setting the locking mechanism, until we bumped one of the control wheels at a crucial time and changed the camera settings by mistake. We have learned that when it matters, we should set the lock. It isn't often, but when we know the camera will be in a situation where having its settings changed will cause more of a problem than normal, we initiate the locking mechanism. We have also decided that if we are going to lock any controls, we will lock them all and set the Dial/Wheel Lock command set to its default, [All].

We love panoramic shots. They are fun to shoot, and the results are impressive. We have experimented with many different shots, varied the level and/or panning speed, and taken shots of moving and stationary subjects, which gives us a variety of results. We have also played around by applying Creative Styles to add some punch to the results. We are sure that you, too, will want to play with this feature.

We did not buy a 3-D television to see our 3-D panoramas. Instead, we ordered inexpensive glasses with red and cyan filters and generated anaglyphs from MPO files. Then we viewed our saved 3-D pictures on our computer screen. It was definitely impressive to see how the pictures popped with the glasses. We recommend that you experiment and see if taking 3-D pictures is something you enjoy. It isn't for everyone, but you won't know unless you try it.

Although we have used the SCN Hand-held Twilight mode when we wanted to reduce image noise, we have used the Anti Motion Blur mode more often. We like the flexibility of being able to adjust the camera's exposure and some other settings. This mode also covers more than just low-light scenarios. Both modes are very useful. We recommend you try both and see which suits you best and with what scenarios.

Quite often we leave DRO set to DRO Auto to give our images an edge over images with DRO turned off.

We have tested the Auto HDR function of the Sony NEX-7 and have achieved very good results. But we are still old-school camera users and prefer generating HDR images by bracketing and combining the multiple RAW images in our computer with third-party software. RAW format gives us the most recorded data for maximum post-processing capability. We also prefer HDR images from third-party software. We recommend that you run two tests to see which result you prefer: (1) generate an HDR image with the camera's Auto HDR function, and (2) generate an HDR image of the same subject with third-party software. Using the Auto HDR function is simple and quick, but it is not the same as capturing the images and generating the HDR image yourself.

# Chapter 9: Using Accessories

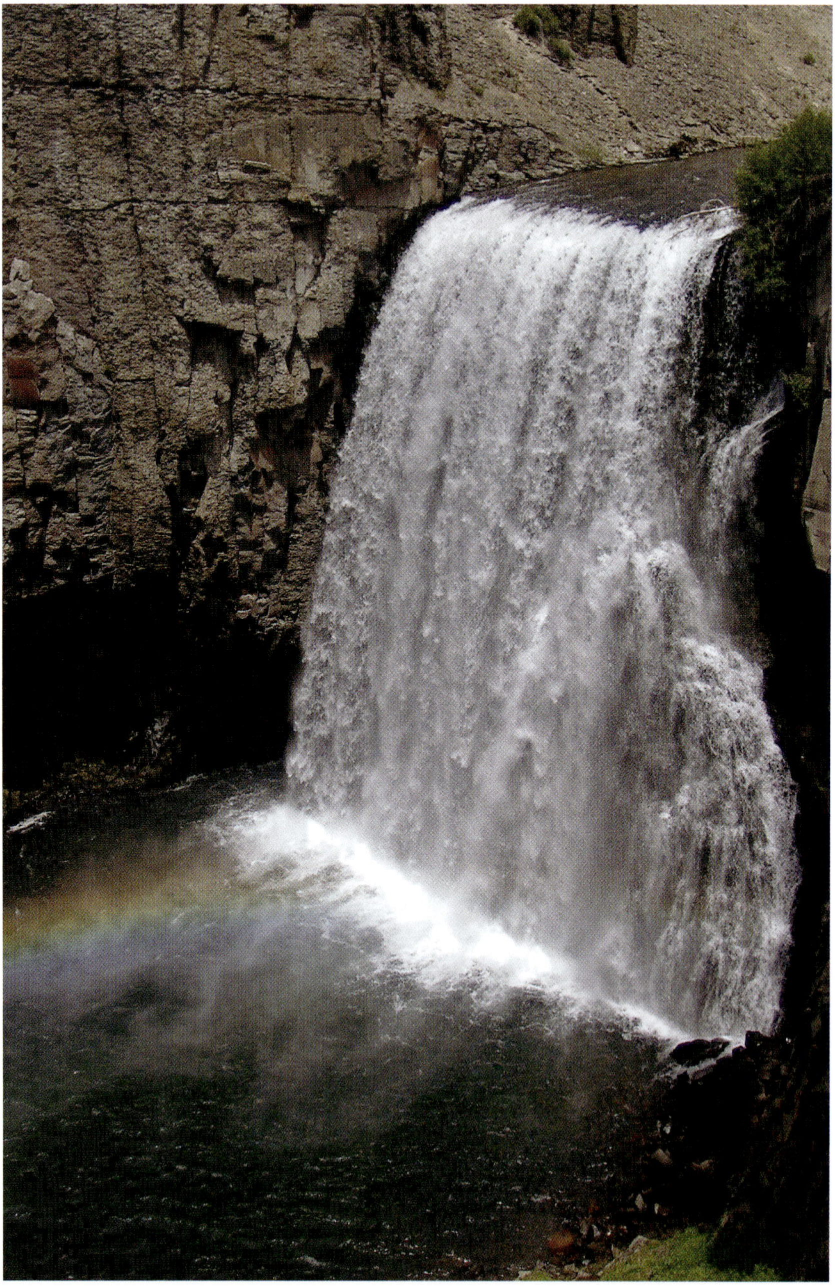

## Introduction

By itself, the Sony NEX-7 is a versatile instrument capable of recording a diverse variety of subjects; however, its potential for extending your view of everyday objects is elevated by its accessories. By adding to your camera, you increase the range of subjects you can photograph, and more importantly, it will help you develop new ways of creating a photograph that matches your inner vision.

The accessories include additional lenses that give you unique perspectives for recording scenes. A super wide-angle lens can encompass a greater area and create a dramatic perspective of enlarging close objects and making background objects appear smaller and farther away. A telephoto lens can bring you close so you can record portraits of animals, or it can flatten a scene and make foreground and background subjects appear close together. A macro lens can make an inch-long praying mantis appear to be a monstrous creature suitable for a science fiction movie.

You don't have to restrict yourself to Sony lenses. The NEX-7 camera body can be outfitted with adapters to take virtually any camera lens that has a helicoid focusing mount and an adjustable iris diaphragm. There are adapters for virtually any of the older lenses designed for film cameras. If you own Sony lenses for an SLT or SLR camera, you can buy an adapter so you can use them on your NEX-7. If you feel even more adventurous, there are adapters so you can take pictures through telescopes and microscopes, allowing you to take dramatic closeups of the Moon or explore the single-cell animals that live in a drop of pond water.

However, all accessories are not optical. One of the most important is a mechanical device for improving your photography: a tripod. There are situations when this becomes an indispensible tool for taking critical shots.

## The Kit Lens

At the time of writing, Sony made eight lenses specifically for the NEX series of cameras and the Sony camcorder. Their bayonet mount is defined as an E-mount and is designed to focus rapidly and reliably with the contrast detectors used by the NEX cameras. In addition, they have a built-in mechanism for dampening camera movement during handheld photography. These lenses were designed to be compact in size and lightweight to complement the light NEX bodies.

Sony also makes a larger and heavier series of lenses for their SLT and SLR camera bodies. They are descendants of the Minolta lens mount and are described as having an A-mount. They are designed to work optimally with the phase detection sensors on Sony's larger cameras, and they focus significantly faster than the E-mount lenses. In addition, they can be made to work well on the NEX-7 by using the Sony LA-EA2 adapter.

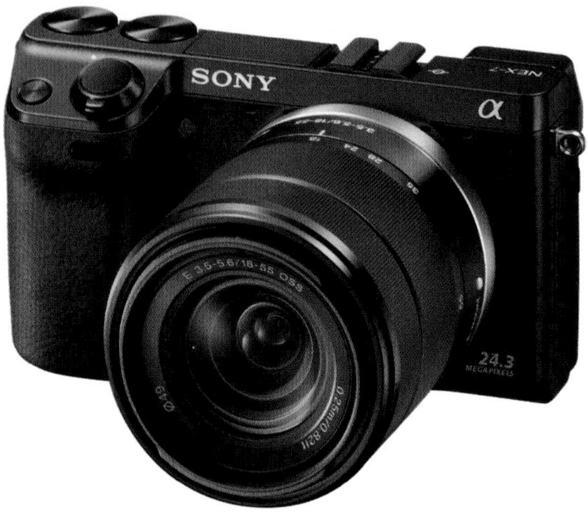


**Figure 9-1**: Sony camera with the 18–55mm f/3.5–5.6 kit lens

When you buy a Sony NEX-7, you need to decide whether to buy a camera with the supplied kit lens, or just the body and buy a lens separately. Typically, people who are new to the Sony system buy the camera with a compact 18–55mm kit lens (figure 9-1). This is the most convenient time to purchase the lens. It is very cost effective because the lens is sold at a deep discount. Essentially you pay $150 for the lens, which by itself sells for $300. If your budget and time allows, you may consider buying just the body and then buying an accessory lens that goes from 18–200mm. This will add substantially to the cost of the system because the lens costs $898, but it can be an attractive convenience when you're on the road and your goal is to be a tourist. It has a broader range and effectively takes the place of two lenses. Normally, if picture taking is your primary goal, the inconvenience of carrying two lenses is minor. However, for a tourist, constantly changing lenses is annoying when you are trying to enjoy the sights. So what are the disadvantages of having a single-lens outfit with the 18–200mm lens? Well, the camera and lens combination gains almost three-quarters of a pound. This weight increase can feel fairly substantial if you carry it all day. For us the weight increase is tolerable in exchange for the expanded picture-taking capabilities. Figures 9-2a through 9-2c show the difference between results taken at 18mm, 55mm, and 200mm.

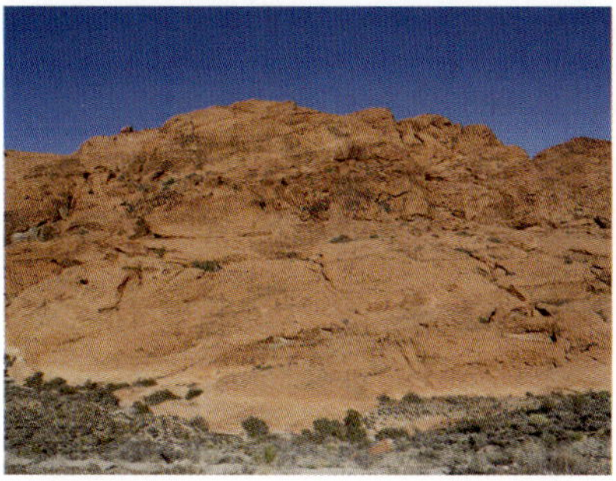

**Figure 9-2a**: The view obtained with a kit lens set to 18mm

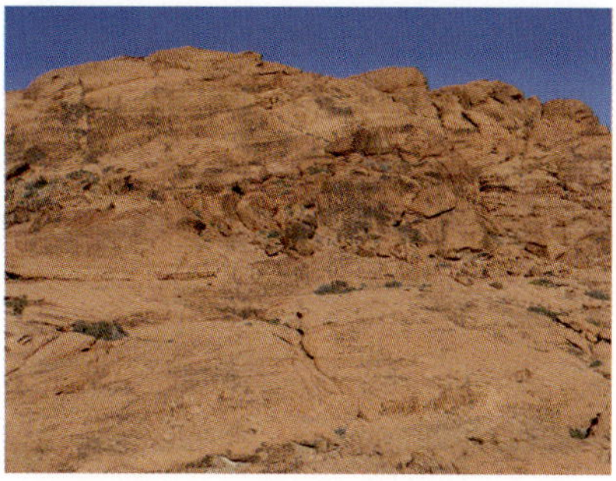

**Figure 9-2b**: The view obtained with a kit lens set to 55mm

Both the 18–200mm lens and the compact 18–55mm kit lens are capable of handling most photographic assignments. Which one should you chose? Consider the following:

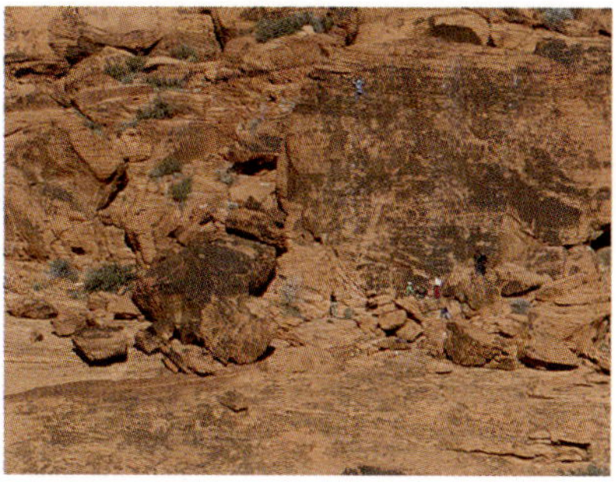

**Figure 9-2c**: The view obtained with a kit lens set to 200mm

- Price: The 18–200mm lens currently sells for about $900, and the 18–55mm lens costs $300. If you buy the 18–55mm kit lens with the body, it is only $150. Sadly, you don't get a price break with the 18–200mm lens.
- Optical characteristics: The 18–200mm lens has more reach than the 18–55mm lens. It will give you almost 4x greater magnification, which can be handy for shots that require a long range.
- Weight: The 18–200mm lens is much heavier, weighing about 18.5 ounces, compared to the 18–55mm at 7 ounces.
- Convenience: A single lens mounted on the camera body is easier to deal with than having to swap out lenses. Remember, when you remove the lens, it should always be stored with its rear and front lens covers attached. Taking an extra lens means you will have to remove these covers every time you change lenses and of course you will be attaching these covers onto the lens you just removed from your camera body.



So, which lens should you get? We have used the 18–55mm lens and find it to be a great lens when you need a compact and economical system. Its disadvantage is you may find the 55mm focal length constraining. If you want a universal lens that will allow you to photograph most subjects, you should consider getting the 18–200mm lens. Although it is heavier and more expensive, its versatility makes it a convenient lens to take on trips and family vacations.

## Sony E-mount and A-mount Lenses

The NEX-7 has an E-mount—a design made specifically for the NEX series of cameras and camcorders. It is designed for the contrast detection autofocus system. To minimize handheld-caused camera movement, a stabilization mechanism was built within the lens. There are many lenses available for this camera (table 9-1), the majority of which are made by Sony. Zeiss, in partnership with Sony, makes a high-quality 24mm f/1.8 lens that interfaces well with the camera body. The independent lens manufacturers Kenko, Sigma, and Tamron make alternatives to the Sony E-mount lenses. Generally, these lenses are less expensive, making them a cost-effective substitute for a Sony product.

<table>
<tr><th>Brand</th><th colspan="2">Lens Focal Length</th><th>Description</th><th>Ounces</th><th>Price</th></tr>
<tr><td>Rokinon</td><td colspan="2">8mm f/3.5 (fisheye)</td><td>Ultrawide angle</td><td>15.6</td><td>$299</td></tr>
<tr><td rowspan="3">Sony</td><td colspan="2">16mm f/2.8</td><td>Wide angle</td><td>2.5</td><td>$248</td></tr>
<tr><td rowspan="2">Attachments for 16mm f/2.8</td><td>Fisheye converter + 16mm = 10mm equivalent</td><td>Attachment</td><td>5.3</td><td>$150</td></tr>
<tr><td>Ultra-wide converter + 16mm = 12mm equivalent</td><td>Attachment</td><td>4.4</td><td>$130</td></tr>
<tr><td>Sony</td><td colspan="2">18–55mm f/3.5–5.6</td><td>Normal zoom</td><td>6.8</td><td>$300</td></tr>
<tr><td>Sony</td><td colspan="2">18–200mm f/3.5–5.6</td><td>Normal zoom</td><td>18.5</td><td>$900</td></tr>
<tr><td>Sony</td><td colspan="2">18–200mm f/3.5–6.3</td><td>Normal zoom</td><td>16.3</td><td>$850</td></tr>
<tr><td>Tamron</td><td colspan="2">18–200mm f/3.5–6.3</td><td>Telephoto zoom</td><td>16.2</td><td>$739</td></tr>
<tr><td>Sigma</td><td colspan="2">19mm f/2.8</td><td>Moderate wide angle</td><td>7.9</td><td>$199</td></tr>
<tr><td>Zeiss (Sony)</td><td colspan="2">24mm f/1.8</td><td>Wide angle</td><td>7.9</td><td>$1,100</td></tr>
<tr><td>Sigma</td><td colspan="2">30mm f/2.8</td><td>Normal</td><td>4.8</td><td>$199</td></tr>
<tr><td>Sony</td><td colspan="2">30mm f/3.5</td><td>Macro</td><td>4.9</td><td>$280</td></tr>
<tr><td>Sony</td><td colspan="2">50mm f/1.8</td><td>Moderate telephoto</td><td>7.3</td><td>$300</td></tr>
<tr><td>Sony</td><td colspan="2">55–210mm f/4.5–6.3</td><td>Telephoto zoom</td><td>12.1</td><td>$350</td></tr>
<tr><td>Kenko</td><td colspan="2">400mm f/8</td><td>Catadioptric mirror telephoto</td><td>12.0</td><td>$298</td></tr>
</table>

**Table 9-1**: Sony-compatible E-mount lenses (compiled July 1, 2012)

Sony makes another line of lenses for their SLT and SLR cameras. It is defined as the A-mount, which originated when Minolta started to make AF (autofocus) lenses. These lenses do not have a stabilization mechanism built into their barrels. Rather, the mechanism is built directly into the camera body.

Sony makes and sells two adapters for attaching A-mount lenses to the NEX-7. The least expensive adapter is model LA-EA1 ($199), which allows automatic exposure, diaphragm control, and limited autofocus capability. This adapter cannot be used with autofocus lenses that lack a built-in focusing motor. Because the adapter relies on the contrast detection sensors in the NEX camera body, its autofocusing speed is slow and you may prefer to use manual focusing.

In our opinion, the other Sony adapter model LA-EA2 ($299) is superior. This adapter is more expensive, but the increased price is offset by its greater capabilities. First, it can focus Sony lenses that do not have a built-in focusing motor. It has a focusing motor for driving some of the older Minolta and Konica Minolta AF lenses so that they can be used with automatic focus. This also includes Sigma and Tamron lenses that require the focusing motor to be contained in the camera body. Second, the focusing speed is dramatically increased. It focuses as rapidly as a Sony A77; in essence, it converts the NEX to an SLT camera (figure 9-3). When the adapter is used this way with an A-mount lens, it will focus more rapidly than E-mount lenses on the NEX cameras. It accomplishes this with a phase detection sensor, and a semitransparent mirror that splits the light between the focus detector and the imaging sensor.

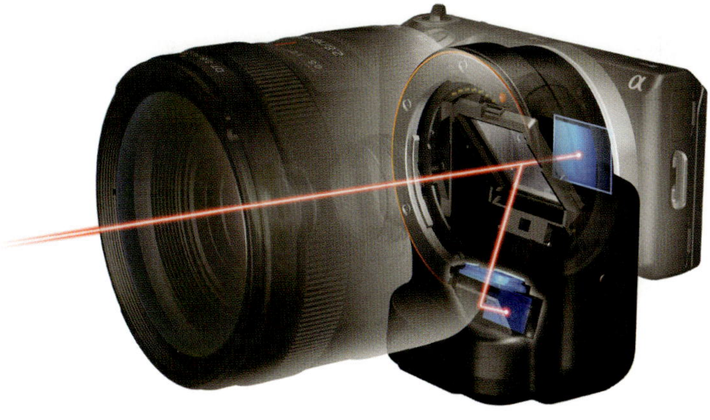

**Figure 9-3**: Light path through LA-EA2 adapter. Note the SLT mirror and how it splits the light between the sensor and the focus detector.

The LA-EA2 adapter's versatility is a major advantage because some of the older Minolta lenses can be used on the NEX-7. For example, we bought a 100–300mm apochromatic (APO) lens with outstanding optical quality and we use it on our NEX-7 for still photography. The following lists some of the Sony descriptions for their A-mount lenses:

- G: Premium optics and superior mechanical design.
- D: Distance Encoder. This allows the camera to use the distance of the subject from the camera to modify the flash output.
- DT: Digital Technology. These lenses can only be used on cameras with APS-C sized sensors. They vignette when used with full-frame camera sensors. Since the NEX uses an APS-C sized sensor, all of the Sony lenses can be used on the NEX body.
- HS: High Speed. HS is found on lenses that rely on a motor in the camera body. The gears for moving the lens are optimized for speed. This is relevant only when using the LA-EA2 adapter.
- SSM: Super Sonic Wave Motor. This motor resides in the lens body and provides fast and quiet operation. The lack of noise is important when taking movies since any extraneous noise disrupts audio recording. This is relevant when using the LA-EA2 and LA-EA1 adapters because these lenses can be autofocused.
- SAM: Smooth Autofocus Motor. This motor resides in the lens body. It tends to be noisier than lenses with SSM and is associated with lower-priced lenses. This is relevant to the LA-EA2 and LA-EA1 adapters because these lenses can be autofocused. However, the focusing speed is slow for the LA-EA1.

### Legacy and Used Lenses

A major advantage of the NEX-7 camera is that it can be fitted to older lenses that have a manual focusing ring and an external control for the diaphragm. All you need is an adapter. Many of them are simple tubes; one side has a mount to accept the lens, and the opposite side inserts into the NEX-7 body. These adapters work because of the short distance between the lens flange and the sensor. If the manufacturer makes the adapter the right length, the attached lens will reach infinity focus. The least expensive adapters can be purchased for about $20.



A glance at an online auction site or a visit to a camera store reveals an abundance of used manual focus lenses that fit this requirement. Usually they are on sale because they are discontinued models that were orphaned when the widespread manufacture of film cameras was abandoned. These lenses cannot take advantage of the latest advances in automatic focusing, image stabilization, or automatic exposure. However, if you can tolerate these absences, you may find an optically excellent lens that can project a sharp image onto the sensor at a bargain price. They can be excellent optical tools for your Sony NEX-7 at a very reasonable price.

We tested a variety of lenses. Table 9-2 contains a short list of lenses that we found to work with the NEX-7 camera body. This list is not extensive and is always changing as we acquire older lenses. Regardless, you should always evaluate a lens before you buy it. In some cases, we found the lenses to be subject to more flare than we expected. Because of this, we use a lens shade outdoors and are cautious about photographing toward the light.

| Focal Length and Aperture | Manufacturer | Lens Type |
|---|---|---|
| 18–35mm | Nikon | Wide-angle zoom |
| 20mm f/2.8 | Nikon | Fixed focal length wide angle |
| 28mm f/2.8 | Nikon | Fixed focal length wide angle |
| 50mm f/1.8 | Olympus | Fixed focal length |
| 55mm f/2.8 | Nikon | Macro fixed focal length |
| 55mm f/3.5 | Nikon | Macro fixed focal length |
| 75–150mm f/4.0 | Olympus | Telephoto zoom |
| 75–300mm f/4.5-5.6 | Nikon | Telephoto zoom |
| 80–400mm f/4.5–5.6 | Nikon | Telephoto zoom |
| 80–200mm f/2.8 | Nikon | Telephoto zoom |
| 90mm f/2.8 | Tamron | Macro fixed focal length |
| 90–180mm f/4.5 | Tokina | Macro zoom |
| 105mm f/2.8 | Nikon | Macro fixed focal length: MF version |
| 105mm f/2.8 | Nikon | Macro fixed focal length: AF version |
| 150–500mm f/5.6 | Tokina | Telephoto zoom |
| 180mm f/2.8 | Nikon | Telephoto fixed focal length |
| 300mm f/2.8 | Nikon | Telephoto fixed focal length |
| 300mm f/4.0 | Nikon | Telephoto fixed focal length |
| 400mm f/5.6 | Tokina | Telephoto fixed focal length |
| 400mm f/5.6 | Sigma | Telephoto fixed focal length |
| 500mm f/8 | Olympus | Telephoto fixed focal length (catadioptric) |
| 500mm f/8 | Tokina | Telephoto fixed focal length (catadioptric) |
| 500mm f/8 | Nikon | Telephoto fixed focal length (catadioptric) |

**Table 9-2**: Legacy lenses that we have used satisfactorily on the NEX-7 with an adapter

Nikon, Minolta, Canon, Leica, Leicaflex, and Pentax K mount or Pentax screw mount are among the manual focus lenses that can be used on the NEX-7. Before you buy a lens, we strongly urge you to learn about it by looking for online reviews. This is critical because some lenses were discontinued because of poor optical performance. For instance, many of the 500mm f/8 mirror lenses are disappointing because of poor quality control. The mirror lenses from well-known manufacturers, such as Nikon, Canon, Pentax, Tamron, and Minolta, are generally good, but they tend to have lower contrast than a lens with an iris diaphragm. These specific lenses work at only one aperture. In contrast, the macro lenses from the major camera manufacturers usually provide excellent sharpness.

When you use legacy lenses, you will have to focus manually, so you should take advantage of the NEX-7's Peaking function or the MF Assist command, both described in chapter 6. Since there is no electronic coupling, the diaphragm ring of the lens controls its aperture. This means that P and S modes are handicapped in their operation. P mode cannot work since it is unable to synchronize the adjustment between the shutter and the aperture. The S mode sort of works, but there is no exposure indicator at the bottom of the screen at M.M. (Manual Meter). The M.M. indicator is locked at 0. You will have to estimate the exposure by using the histogram as your measure of intensity and adjusting your shutter speed and the lens diaphragm manually. M mode works because the M.M. indicator is active, so you have an exposure meter that you can apply controlled adjustments of over- or underexposure.

Our preferred setting is A mode because the camera adjusts its shutter speed in response to the light level on the sensor. You can override the recommended exposure by using control dial R. When you use this mode, the benefits of having an electronic viewfinder are threefold. First, you have an automatic gain that keeps the display screen bright, even when you close down the diaphragm and deprive the sensor of light. Second, you can display a histogram to help you estimate your exposure. Third, you have a real-time depth of field preview capability. If you had an optical viewfinder, the screen would become dim, there would be no histogram, and the depth of field would be hard to estimate because of the lack of light. It is our experience that the A mode provides the fastest means of adjusting exposure with a legacy lens.



The disadvantage to using these legacy lenses is that you lose the Sony SteadyShot feature. For handheld shooting you have to constantly monitor your shutter speed, or else you can select a long shutter speed and risk introducing blur from handholding. Especially for long telephoto work, we recommend that you use a tripod or set your shutter speed faster than 1/focal length. For example, a 400mm lens should be handheld at 1/400 second or faster.

The results from our experiments are so gratifying that we do not hesitate to recommend the purchase of a legacy lens for your NEX-7. We have an unusually good sample of a Tokina 400mm f/5.6 lens that provides crystal-sharp images. Considering that there is no E-mount lens with this long of a focal length, this legacy lens can provide unique images that are not available to photographers who restrict themselves to using only the E-mount lenses. One intriguing aspect for considering legacy lenses is that the Leica screw mount and bayonet mount will fit the NEX-7 with the appropriate adapter. The optical quality of these lenses are superb, as might be expected by the high price they demand. But their compactness and lightness with precision focusing helicoid make them a premium addition to your lens collection.

| Mount | Fotodiox | Novoflex | Rayqual | Sony | Voigtländer |
|---|---|---|---|---|---|
| Pentax M42 | X | X | X | | |
| Canon EOS | X | X | | | |
| Canon FD | X | | X | | |
| Contax/Yashica | X | | X | | |
| Leica M | X | X | | | X |
| Leica M39 | X | | | | |
| Leica R | X | X | X | | |
| Sony Alpha | | | | X | |
| Minolta MD | X | X | | | |
| Nikon F | X | X | X | | X |
| Olympus OM | X | X | X | | |
| Pentax K | X | X | X | | X |
| Pentax M42 | X | X | X | | |

**Table 9-3**: Adapters available for the NEX-7

Table 9-3 contains a list of the lens adapters available for the NEX-7. You may wonder why some adapters are more expensive than the ones that are available on eBay. This is a relevant question, and our answer is that the listed adapters are of higher quality. We have used examples of each and have been satisfied with their fit and finish. More importantly, we have confidence in these vendors to sell us a product that we can rely on. However, for many people new to legacy lenses, the question remains whether the quality of the adapters is worth the increase in cost. We think this is a matter of personal preference and need. For our microscope work, our adapters have to hold the sensor perpendicular to the optical axis of the microscope and at a precise distance from the projection eyepiece. Some of the low-cost adapters don't meet these requirements. We have had a couple of low-cost adapters fall apart, and we have seen others with poor machining. You may or may not get a good unit; consequently, we do not recommend the low-cost adapters.

This is not to say that you should avoid them. Maybe you are unsure if using a legacy lens will fit your photographic style. If so, by all means get an inexpensive adapter to experiment with. If you find that using legacy optics suits your photographic style, you can buy a more expensive adapter later. You may be lucky and the inexpensive adapter will be perfectly satisfactory, in which case you will have saved yourself some money. One final note, adapters that have a tripod mount are preferable to those that don't have one. Especially with some of the heavier telephoto lenses, this is a welcome feature for balancing the lens on a tripod.

If you want to try legacy lenses, here is a list of camera settings and lens requirements:

- A legacy lens must have a smooth-focusing helicoid ring.
- A legacy lens must have a diaphragm ring that closes down the aperture, or else make sure the adapter has a way to manipulate the diaphragm.
- Set the camera for Peaking, medium.
- Set the Peaking color to red or yellow.
- Dedicate one soft key for MF Assist.
- Use the A mode.
- Set camera to fire without a lens as follows:

MENU>Setup (Shooting Settings)>Release w/o lens>[Enable]

## Telescopes

Long-distance photography fascinates many photographers. The thought of obtaining a closeup of the Moon makes some photographers long for a supertelephoto lens. The longest NEX-7 lens is 210mm, and the longest legacy lens is commonly a 500mm (figures 9-4a and 9-4b).

To get a "long view" at a reasonable cost, you may consider using an apochromatic spotting scope or a telescope (figure 9-4c). These can be expensive, but they are more economical than the long telephoto lenses sold by camera manufacturers. Sony sells a 500mm f/4.0 long telephoto for $13,000. Instead, try a Tele Vue apochromatic refractor telescope. A new 85mm Tele Vue costs about $2,500 and has a 480mm focal length. Though this is still expensive, it serves a dual function. Not only are such refractors good photographic accessories, but they can also be used in their intended role as visual instruments for long-distance viewing. The Tele Vue is a favorite among telescope aficionados for its clarity and its ability to provide high-contrast images of the night sky. With this telescope the Moon can be recorded in amazing detail (figure 9-5).

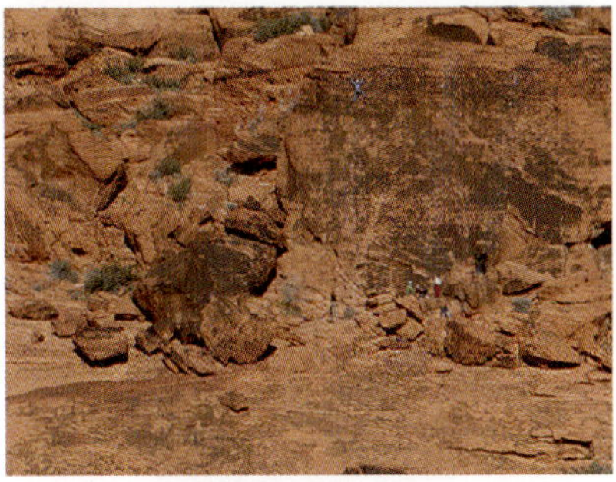

**Figure 9-4a**: View from the longest telephoto lens (200mm) in the NEX lineup

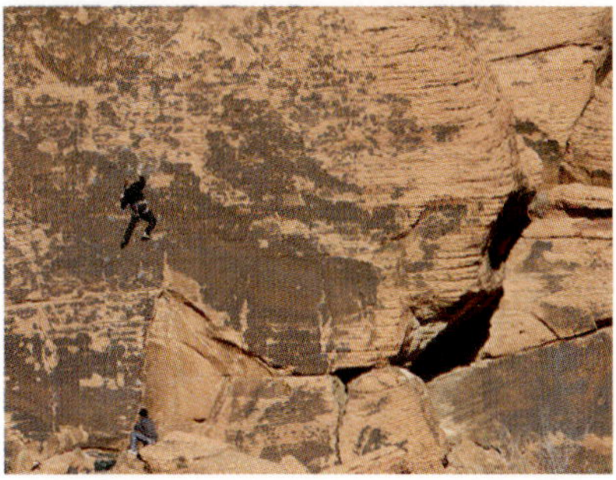

**Figure 9-4b**: View from the longest telephoto lens (500mm) in the Sony A-mount lineup

Another option is to purchase a catadioptric system, made popular by Meade and Celestron. These units tend to be less expensive and use a combination of lenses and mirrors to fold the optical path length into a relatively short tube. The classic 8-inch diameter telescopes can fold a 2,000mm (79 in) focal length into a tube only 432mm (17 in) long. Purchased new, today these telescopes range in cost from $600 to $2,500. If you have friends who are astronomy buffs, they can guide you on the selection of a telescope, and in most cases, telescopes can be adapted to fit an NEX-7.

Most of these telescopes are equipped with a focusing tube that takes either 1.25 in or 2 in diameter eyepieces, and we found that there are simple adapters that will fit in the eyepiece tube (figure 9-6). When you equip these adapters with a bayonet mount for the NEX-7, you are ready to take pictures. You may have heard of digiscoping, where a point-and-shoot camera is held over a telescope eyepiece. Results from this simple technique are quite impressive. But you can obtain even better results by using your NEX-7. Remove the lens from

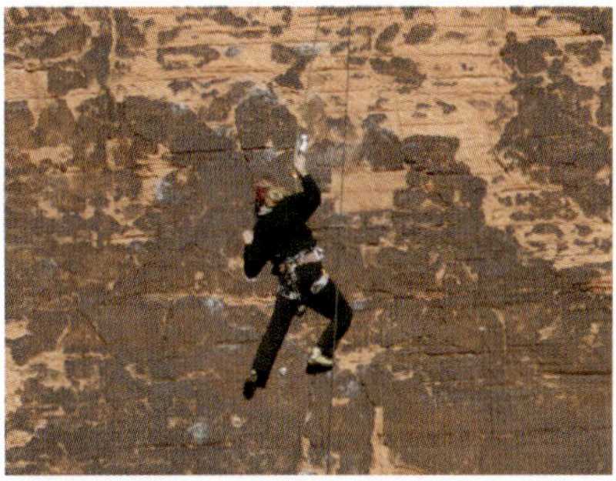

**Figure 9-4c**: View from a telescope with a camera adapter (1600mm)

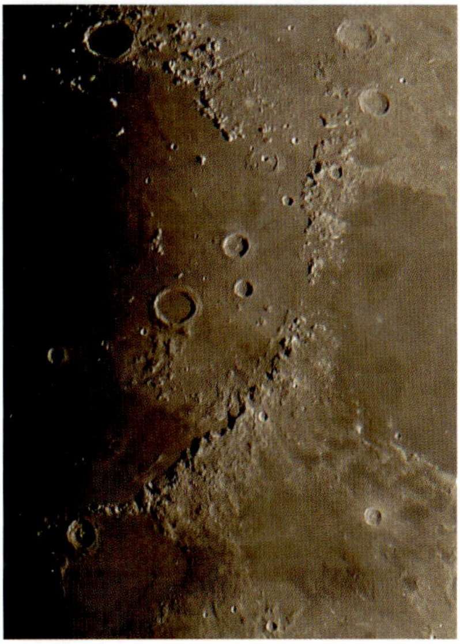

**Figure 9-5**: A closeup of a lunar mountain range recorded with NEX-7 and a Tele Vue 85

9

the NEX-7, attach the telescope adapter to the lens mount, and then insert the mount into the eyepiece. The telescope will project an image directly onto the camera's sensor, and you will not have any image degradation resulting from an extraneous lens (which was not designed for this use) in the optical path.

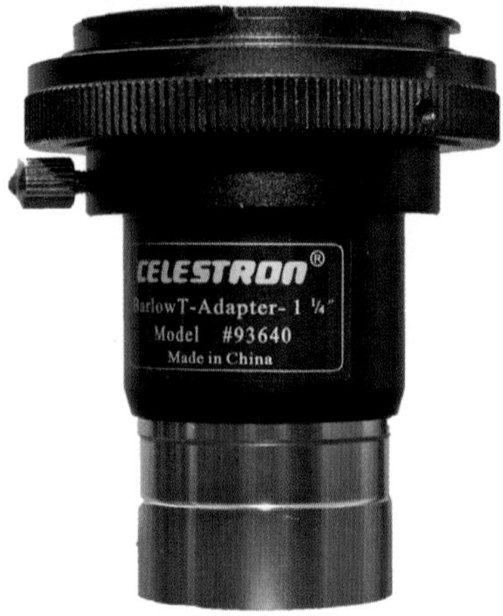


**Figure 9-6**: This adapter fits in a 1.25 in eyepiece holder and can carry an NEX-7 body

The first step is to find a telescope that can be used with your camera. Today there are a tremendous number of telescopes of varying sizes to choose from, so we will restrict our discussion to smaller telescopes that can double for terrestial fieldwork. These telescopes typically have lenses with a front element ranging in diameter from 50 to 100mm (2 to 4 inches). Telescopes smaller than this can be matched by the performance of a telephoto lens. Although they are usable, telescopes with an objective larger than 100mm are too cumbersome to carry and too difficult to handle for fieldwork. An excellent telescope in the 50–100mm range is expensive; however, its optical performance equals the best telephoto lenses. Also consider a heavy tripod to support a telescope.

One company that makes telescopes with resolving power suitable for photography is Tele Vue. We have used their 60mm, 76mm, and 85mm telescopes, which all provide exceptionally high resolving power. The 60mm telescope (360mm f/6) sells for less than $1,000; the 76mm telescope (480mm f/6.3) sells for $2,000; and the 85mm telescope (700mm f/7) sells for $2,495. Their optical performance rivals, and perhaps exceeds, that of the finest Nikon or Canon telephoto lenses whose 500mm optics cost $6,000 to $8,000. We have used teleconverters (in this case Nikon and Tokina) in the optical path to further increase the magnification from the telescope.

This is not to say that these telescopes can replace a professional telephoto lens. They cannot. For one thing they lack an iris diaphragm, so you need to shoot wide open. Also, they are not compact. Most professional telephoto lenses are physically shorter than their focal length, enabling them to be used in the field for handheld photography without a tripod. Remember, the modern interchangeable lens camera with an appopriately designed lens is equipped with an image stabilization feature to aid handheld exposure. Finally, focusing is done manually. But considering the dual role a telescope plays and its relatively economical cost, they may not seem so expensive.

We have tested the Sony NEX-7 extensively on a Tele Vue 85 and a Tele Vue 60. The Tele Vue 85 has a 2 inch eyepiece holder, and the Tele Vue 60 has a 1.25 inch eyepiece holder. Both telescopes can accept camera adapters that fit in the eyepiece tube, and they have T-mounts for attaching a Sony E-mount. Neither adapter caused vignetting. To use these telescopes with the Sony NEX-7 requires only that the eyepiece holder be removed and replaced with the adapter. The camera should be set to A mode and manual focusing. To ensure that the camera will fire, use the following command:

MENU>Setup (Shooting Settings)>Release w/o Lens>[Enable]

We typically use the viewfinder when aiming the telescope at terrestrial objects. Ambient daylight can obscure the LCD screen. Make sure Peaking is active to allow rapid identification of when the camera is in focus.

**A Telescope Caveat**

The previously mentioned telescopes work well for terrestrial and Moon shots, but if you hope to shoot the planets, nebulae, or galaxies, you will have to invest in far more expensive equipment. You will need to mount the telescope on an equatorial mount so you can compensate for the movement of the night sky as the Earth rotates. Furthermore, you will need to learn how to carefully align the equatorial mount and also how to take much longer exposures. The NEX-7 is unsuitable for this type of low-light astrophotography.

## Microscopes

For more than 50 years, SLRs have been used on microscopes to take high-magnification pictures of single-cell plants and animals, as well as slides of human tissue. Nikon and Olympus used to sell elaborate and expensive accessories for mounting film cameras onto microscopes. However, their SLRs (film and digital) were ill equipped for the task, and more complex accessories were designed to correct the disadvantages of using an SLR camera. For example, special viewfinders and viewing screens replaced the camera's optical viewfinder. In addition, to avoid the movement of the mirror and the camera's shutter, which generates vibrations and blurs the image during exposure, the camera body was treated as a simple film carrier. Its mirror was locked up and the focal plane shutter held open. Exposure was accomplished with a special low-vibration shutter contained in the adapter that joined the camera to the microscope.

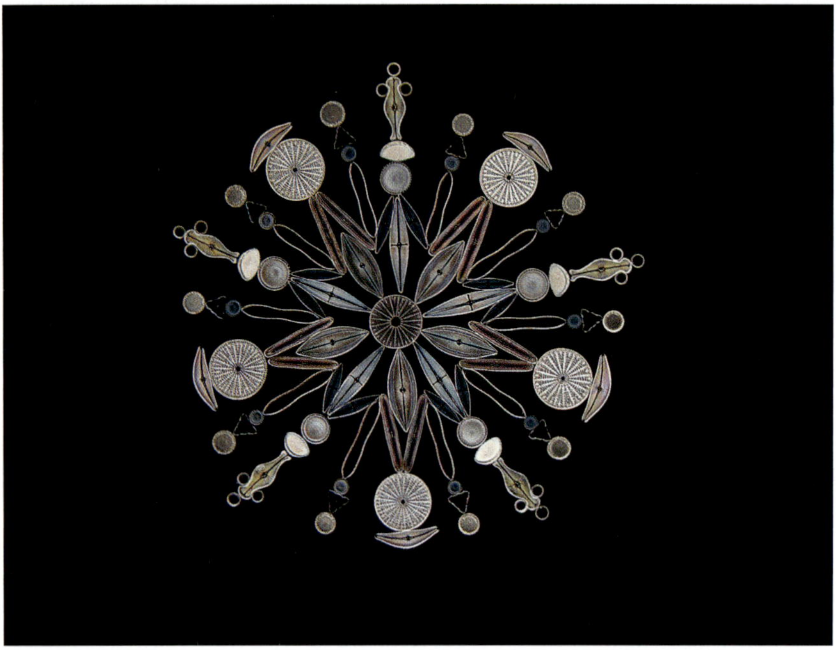

**Figure 9-7**: A diatom arrangement of 100 individuals; the whole array is 1/32 inch across

With the NEX-7 these deficiencies are remedied. The camera's Live View finders allow accurate focusing. Because there is no moving mirror or mechanical first curtain shutter, the NEX is practically vibration free when it records an image. Figure 9-7 is an example of what can be recorded with a microscope. This is a diatom slide prepared by Klaus Kemp, who arranged more than 100 diatoms in this star pattern. The whole pattern has a diameter of only 1/32 inch.

To aid focusing, the Live View screen can work at an increased magnification, thanks to MF Assist. An additional focusing aid is the Peaking function. When focus is achieved, a fringe of color highlights the borders of the in-focus structures. If there is any criticism of the Live View monitor or eyepiece, it is the small size of the image. But even this deficiency can be remedied by using the camera's HDMI output to drive an HDTV or large monitor so you can get a better view.



Microscopes designed for photography are equipped with a trinocular head, where two of the eypeieces are used for viewing the specimen and the third is used to mount the camera. This photographic port is usually a vertical tube. In the case of a modern research microsocope, it is 30–50mm with a bayonet or screw mount for attaching the camera. Older microscopes have a 25mm tube, and they need adapters that clamp onto the outside of this tube. The other end of the adapter has a bayonet mount for the camera. Research microscopes are expensive and are not usually available to hobbyists. Attaching the camera can be expensive as well. A company that makes adapters to fit research microscopes is Martin Microscope Company (www.martinmicroscope.com/MMSLR.htm). This company has an adapter for about $500 that can make it easy to mount the Sony NEX-7 onto your microscope.

If you are interested in obtaining a home microscope, you can find affordable used microscopes on eBay; however, we recommend finding a seller with a brick-and-mortar store. The cost will probably be higher, but you will have more assurance that the microscope has been checked and adjusted for proper operation. We have purchased used microscopes and cameras from Bunton Instrument Company (www.buntgrp.com/used_microscopes.htm) that have provided excellent photographic performance.

There are simple and inexpensive accessories for mounting the camera onto such stands. You can find simple tube adapters that clamp onto the vertical tube. At the oppositie end of the adapter is a male screw threaded to take a variety of bayonet mounts. This is usually a T-mount, and you can easily buy an adapter for this.

### Light and the Microscope

The key to getting good photographs with a microscope is using the correct lighting. At very low powers, say from 10x to 100x, you can generate credible images with little effort. But when you start working at higher powers, your images can appear fuzzy and ill defined. One cause of this is improper illumination. You need to learn how to manipulate the microscope light source to ensure that your lens is working under optimum conditions.

To familiarize yourself with using the microscope at higher powers, there is an excellent free reference at the following site: www.olympusmicro.com/primer/basicsandbeyond.pdf. The section describing Kohler illumination is particularly important, because it is necessary for getting the best out of a microscope.

Follow these steps when you use the Sony NEX-7 on a microscope:

1. Adjust the microscope with a slide to get a sharp image through the eyepiece.
2. Adjust the microscope's light source intensity so the view through the eyepiece is comfortable. If the light is controlled with a voltmeter, run it at the voltage recommended by the manufacturer. If it is too bright, reduce the light intensity with neutral density filters.
3. Set the camera's ISO to 100.
4. Set the camera for Peaking at the medium setting.
5. Set the Peaking color to red or yellow.
6. Dedicate one soft key to the MF Assist command.
7. Set the camera to A mode.
8. Set the camera to fire without a lens:

   Menu>Setup (Shooting Settings)>Release w/o lens>[Enable]

9. Set the WB to Incandescent, or set the color temperature scale to 3200 K. If this does not work, use Custom WB (described in chapter 6).
10. Focus the image using the microscope control while viewing it on the LCD screen.
11. Fire the camera with a remote release or set the camera's self-timer to a 2 second delay. This keeps any vibrations caused by manually pressing the shutter button from disturbing the picture.

## Remote Release

Sony does not sell a cable release for the NEX-7. Instead, they sell the RMT-DSLR1 infrared Remote Commander. This small accessory resembles a television remote and emits infrared light that is detected by a sensor located on the front of the camera. You can turn it on with the following command:



MENU>Camera>Drive Mode>[Remote Cdr.]

You can also turn on the command by using the Drive Mode button on the control wheel and selecting [Remote Cdr.].

Use the remote to fire the camera. At first, you might think that you have to aim the remote directly at the camera's sensor. This is not the case when you're indoors. The beam is sufficiently intense, and the sensor is sufficiently sensitive, that the infrared beam can be detected after it is reflected off the walls of the room. When you use the camera outdoors, you can employ this strategy by placing your hand in front of the camera (outside the view of the lens) and aiming the remote at your hand.

If you forget to pack your remote release, remember that you can eliminate vibration by setting the Drive Mode command to Self-timer, and set it for 2 seconds. The only disadvantage is that the 2 second delay may cause you to miss the shot.

## Tripods

You may already own a tripod, but if you don't, this section is for you. This accessory is often overlooked when you first start taking pictures and movies. For a lightweight, small camera like the NEX-7, using a tripod may seem counterproductive. However, a steady support for the camera is essential for taking pictures requiring long exposures, extreme telephoto work, and obtaining maximally sharp images. Nonetheless, many photographers object to using a tripod, arguing that it is bulky, reduces mobility, and hinders spontaneous photography. These arguments are all true, but it is also true that consistently using a tripod will improve the quality of your work. In fact, its inconvenience may be its strongest benefit because it forces you to work at a more deliberate pace—carefully framing the subject, evaluating depth of field, and ensuring that the horizon is not canted. This deliberate pace trains you to visualize the image before snapping the shutter and allows you to precisely adjust exposure.

Professional tripods are usually sold in two parts: the legs and the head. The legs provide the support, but they do not have a mechanism for aiming the camera. The head is attached to the legs and is the actual aiming mechanism. Although you can buy a tripod with legs and head, many, if not most, serious photographers buy the two components separately. In this way, you can have a custom unit that suits your personal photographic style.

A good tripod can easily cost $300, with more expensive units running over $1,000. Although it is initially expensive, a good tripod will outlast a typical camera and lens. One of our tripods is more than 30 years old and is still in use. It seems our tripod collection grows with our experience in photography. We have a heavy studio tripod for home use. Although its weight prevents us from taking it into the field, we appreciate its stability when we work with critical subjects in the laboratory. For fieldwork, we use more expensive tripods made of carbon fiber. They weigh only a few pounds so their light weight lets us take them wherever we go, but they can aim a 400 mm telephoto with precision. This is not a good time to skimp on equipment. Inexpensive tripods are not only flimsy, but they take longer

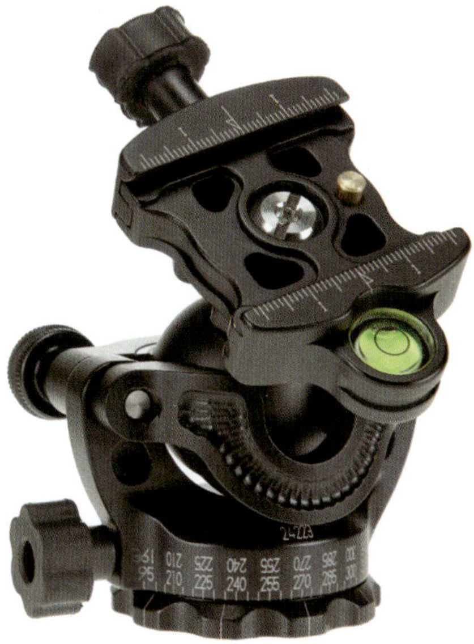

**Figure 9-8**: Acratech GP-SS ball head

to set up and sometimes are not able to hold their settings. After you mount and position your camera, an inexpensive tripod may drift slowly out of position or even topple over with your camera attached.

Plan to spend a minimum of around $400 for the tripod's two components: the legs for support and the head for aiming the camera. This last unit can be surprisingly expensive, especially if you tend to use long telephoto lenses.

There are two types of tripod heads: pan and tilt heads, and ball heads. Pan and tilt heads are heavier and less expensive (about $65 for the Manfrotto 804RC2 3). They allow you to pan across the scene (horizontal movement) and tilt the camera (vertical movement). To lock the tripod, there are usually two locking knobs: one for the pan and the other for the tilt. Ball heads (figure 9-8) are lighter and more expensive (about $350). They allow you to move the camera on the tripod any way you want in a smooth motion. Moreover, they are locked with a single knob: loosening it to aim the camera and tightening it to lock it into position. We started out more than 40 years ago with a Bogen 3047 pan and tilt head, but we replaced it when we found that we preferred the speed of working with an Acratech ball head.

We use an older Acratech GV2 ball head for our photography. This accessory has a nifty design; a gimbal slot can be engaged with a small key by rotating the ball 90 degrees to its side. This allows the head to swing along a vertical plane while the base rotates along a horizontal plane. In essence, the head works like a pan and tilt head, with increased stability when tilting the lens up and down along the vertical plane and when rotating the entire head on the horizontal plane. With a long telephoto lens attached, it places the center of balance of a large lens close to the swivel point for much better balance and control. This wonderful feature is carried over into newer Acratech models. When we use our 18–55mm lens, we do not need to use the gimbal feature. Instead, we use it as a ball head which has two tightening knobs. One is applied to provide just enough friction to keep the camera in place so that when you release the camera it will stay in position, rather than flopping over. This allows the camera to be quickly aimed and then the second kob is tightened to lock the head completely. By using the two knobs, you can have a very fast operating system. You only need release the second knob to allow rapid aiming of the camera. It can then be tightened to ensure the camera is locked into position.

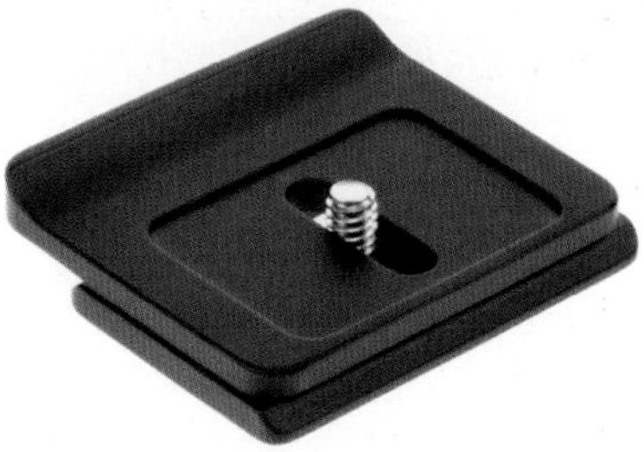

**Figure 9-9**: Quick-release clamp for attaching the tripod head to the camera

We recommend that you get a quick-release clamp for your tripod head. Typically, a basic head allows you to attach the camera to the tripod head with a 1/4-inch threaded screw. Attaching and detaching the camera can be time consuming and awkward. To speed up the operation, use a tripod head with a quick-release clamp (figure 9-9). This clamp engages a plate that is attached to the bottom of your camera. Attaching and detaching the camera from the tripod becomes a fast and simple operation. To attach the camera, simply place the plate into the head's quick-release clamp and secure it with a lever. To detach the camera, release the lever. The main disadvantage with a quick-release plate on the NEX-7 is that it extends beyond the camera body and makes it less pocketable.

The next thing to consider is the tripod legs. Fortunately, their connection to the tripod head is standard; a screw secures the head of your choice. The price of tripod legs ranges from $300 to more than $600. Premium models are made of light and durable carbon fiber. Typically, the legs collapse for convenient transport. Gitzo makes some of the best legs and they may cost over $500. The legs are built in sections and telescope into each other to shorten their length.

We use the less expensive legs by Manfrotto (about $300) and combine them with an Acratech ball head. Several of our colleagues have been satisfied with Velbon, Slik, and Hakuba carbon fiber tripod legs that cost about $200 to $300.

> **Buying Tripods**
>
> We have acquired several tripods over the years. Our low-cost favorite is a Tiltall tripod purchased 40 years ago. The basic design of this older tripod is impeccable. Its only fault is its 7 lb weight. We typically use this tripod indoors, so we do not have to walk far or set it up quickly. At one time, Leitz sold this high-quality tripod. Now you can buy them used online for under $100. Just beware of functional damage and wobbly legs on used tripods. The tripod does not come with a quick-release head mechanism. Instead, you have to screw the camera on and off the head.
>
> We also have carbon fiber tripod legs from Manfrotto and a tripod ball head from Acratech. Their combined weight is only 4 lb. For faster setup, the head is equipped with a quick-release clamp. Without this accessory, we would have to turn and tighten a screw to fasten the camera onto the tripod. With the aid of the quick-release clamp, we can quickly attach and detach the camera from the tripod.

## Recommendations

Thanks to Sony's technology—the mirrorless design, the electronic first curtain shutter, and the electronic viewfinder—the NEX-7 is remarkably versatile. It can be used effectively on specialized optical instruments such as telescopes and microscopes. The absence of vibration and the ability to precisely focus on the subject lends itself to macro photography. As your expertise increases along with your desire to explore new areas, you may find that the accessories cost more than the camera. Even something as mundane as a tripod may prove to be surprisingly expensive; however, these accessories expand the camera's full potential.

The Sony NEX-7 kit lens is an excellent photographic tool. We recommend you get to know the strengths and limitations of your kit lens before you acquire any additional lenses. If you decide to buy more lenses, consider the Sony lenses (including Zeiss lenses sold by Sony) first. Optically, these lenses are high quality, and you can be confident that they are fully functional with your camera. If the price is too high, you can purchase third-party lenses instead; Sigma and Tamron are reputable brands with good-quality optics. Many photographers think they provide the maximum return for the money. In some cases, the optical quality of these lenses is impeccable. The Tamron 90mm macro is reputed to be one of the best in its class. The risk of buying third-party lenses is that they may not function properly on the NEX-7 camera body. If you purchase a new lens from a reputable manufacturer, you can rest assured that the company will try to satisfy its customers. Manufacturers such as Tamron and Sigma are very conscientous and honor their warranties. However, if you buy used, you will not have the benefit of a warranty. Before purchasing a used lens, check online reviews to make sure that it has a good optical and mechanical reputation.

When you're taking pictures and movies, you will find that the appearance of the subject changes radically between a wide-angle focal setting and a moderate telephoto setting. Experiment with choosing a single focal length and then walking up close to the subject or walking away from it.

For example, fishermen prefer the use of wide-angle lenses that magnify the size of their catch. They proudly pose holding the fish in front of them and have the photographer move in close, framing the fish so it appears double to triple its actual size. If you use a moderate telephoto lens instead and then step back to photograph the fisherman holding the fish out in front, the fish will appear to have shrunk dramatically. This moderate telephoto provides a more accurate perspective and shows the fish properly, much to the chagrin of a proud fisherman.

# Chapter 10: Flash Photography

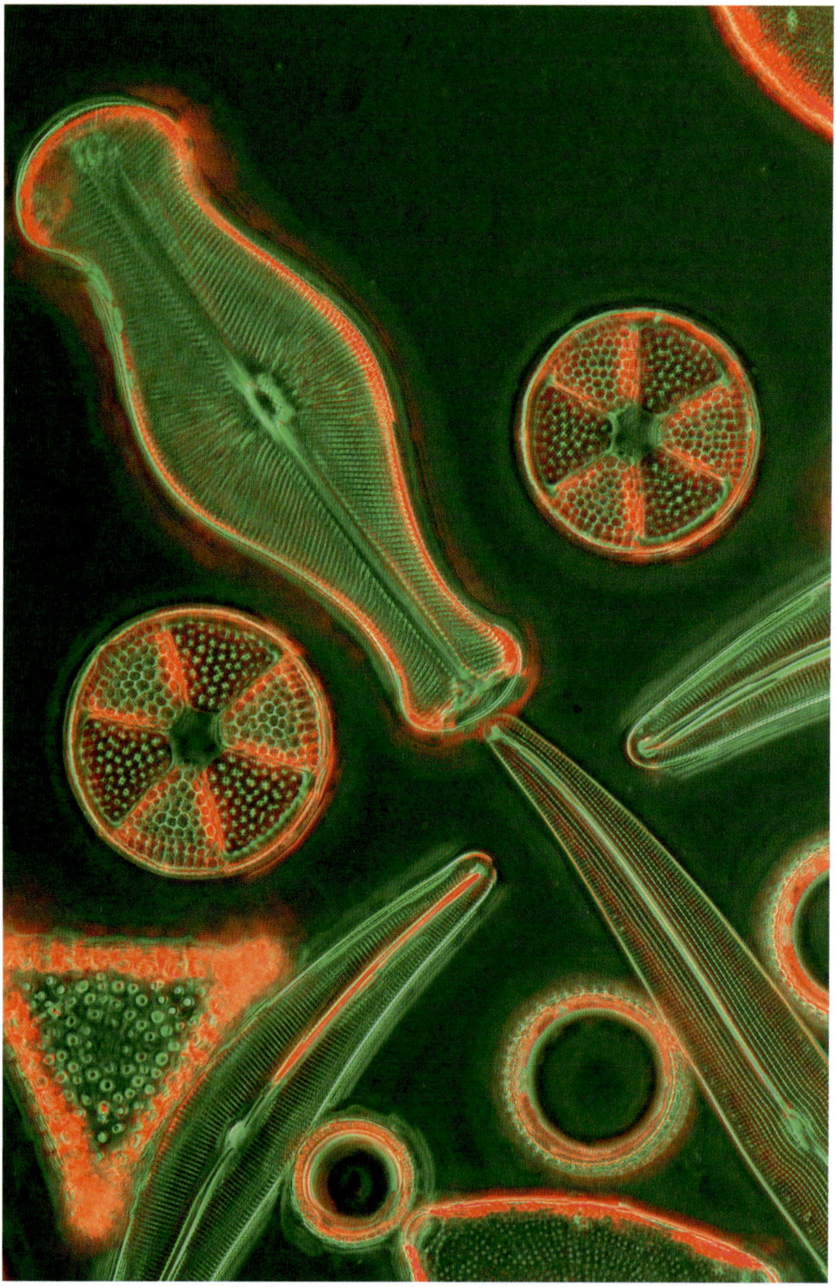

10

## Introduction

As sensitive as the Sony NEX-7 is to light, there are times when it requires a little help and additional lighting has to be supplied. This situation can arise when photographing indoors. Supplemental lighting can be easily and conveniently obtained with the camera's built-in flash. However, the flash is a low-powered unit that does not have sufficient output to illuminate a large room. It should be regarded as a supplemental light source rather than a primary light source. If you anticipate doing much interior work, you should consider getting an external flash unit that fits on the camera's hot shoe (figure 10-1). An external flash unit will at least double, or even quadruple your light output, depending on the size of the unit.

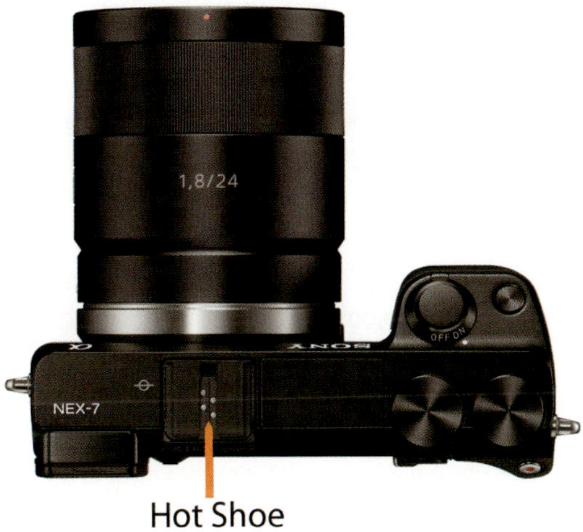


**Figure 10-1**: Top of the camera showing the hot shoe

Sony has several attachable external flash units that will provide the light you need to photograph a group of people. The larger accessory units have greater coverage, and you can control the direction of the light by tilting or rotating the flash head. This allows you to take advantage of what is known as bounce flash, where you aim the flash toward the ceiling rather than illuminating the subject straight on. These units have enough power so the reflection off the ceiling (i.e., the bounced light) will provide flattering, soft light to your subject.

## Principles of Electronic Flash

The Sony NEX-7 electronic flash uses a small tube filled with xenon gas. When the flash fires, it generates a short burst of light (1/1000 second or less). The light's WB approximates daylight; however, its color temperature is a bit cooler. So, if you use the preset daylight WB value, you will record an image with a slight bluish tinge. Using AWB or presetting WB to electronic flash will impart a warmer tone to the picture and will produce a more pleasing color image.

The flash duration is much shorter than the camera's shutter speed, so you need to use a shutter speed that is slow enough to fully expose the sensor to light. For the NEX-7, this occurs at 1/160 second (flash synchronization shutter speed) or longer. At shorter shutter speeds, the shutter is a moving slit with an opening that progressively decreases as you set higher shutter speeds. As a consequence, when the flash fires at shutter speeds shorter than 1/160 second, only a portion of the sensor can be exposed to the burst of light. When you manually control the shutter speed (using S or M mode), you can set it to 1/160 second and use the flash. In contrast, the fastest you can set the camera shutter for using the flash in Intelligent Auto or SCN modes is 1/60 second.

Flash exposure is governed by the duration of the light emitted by the flash. The maximum light output occurs when the burst of light lasts 1/1000 second, and it can be reduced to as little as 1/50,000 second. To determine how much light is needed, the camera fires a brief burst of known intensity. This light reflects off the subject and is collected by the camera lens for measurement. This is known as Pre-flash TTL (Through The Lens). By using this light, the meter measures what the sensor sees. So no matter what f-stop is used, or what filter is placed over the lens, the light meter sees what the sensor will record. This is especially advantageous when using zoom lenses. Not only does focal length vary, but so does the working aperture as the magnification is altered. This change in light transmission is compensated automatically when the measured light passes through the lens.

### Guide Number and Estimating Exposure: Caveats

With automated electronic flash, many of today's photographers are unfamiliar with the guide number (GN). The GN describes the power of a flash and can be used to calculate what lens opening should be set if you know the distance between the flash and the subject. For example, the flash's GN is divided by the distance between the subject and the flash, which gives the f-stop to obtain a correct exposure.

Two factors should be noted. The first is ISO. If unstated, it is assumed that the ISO is 100; a higher ISO will raise the GN. The second is the units used to measure the distance from the camera to the subject. Sony specifies that the built-in flash of the NEX-7 has a GN of 6, with ISO 100 and the distance measured in meters

The major problem with NEX-7's built-in flash is that it does not emit very much light, and if you want greater range, you will have to buy an attachable flash. Sony sells a small compact unit, the HVL-F20AM, which has a GN of 20—meaning it will cover three times the distance of the built-in camera flash. Sony has two other units that are larger and more expensive, the HVL-F43AM (figure 10-2) with a GN of 43, and the HVL-F58AM with a GN of 58. If you prefer to use flash units made by other companies, their GNs can provide a useful comparison.

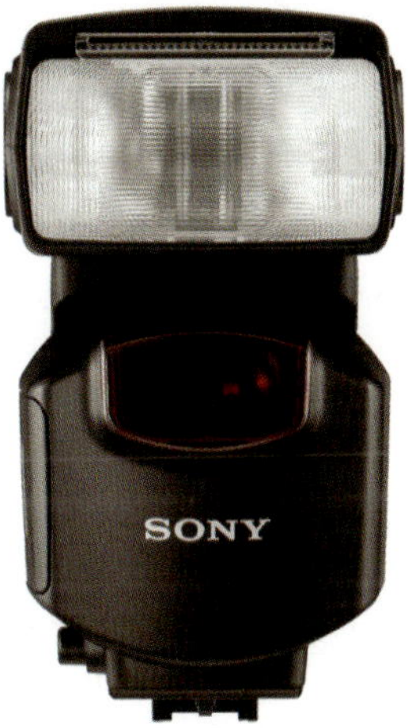


**Figure 10-2**: External flash that can be attached to the hot shoe

## Flash Artifact: Red Eye

When you use a flash to help illuminate a friend's face, you may record an unflattering portrait. The person may appear to be demonically possessed because the pupils are glowing a bright red. To reduce this red eye artifact, use the following command:

MENU>Setup (Shooting Settings)>Red Eye Reduction>[On]

This command needs a bit of background to explain how it works. The camera's flash unit sends out light, and if a person—or an animal—is looking directly at the lens, the light will enter the eye, pass through the retina, and be reflected back through the camera's lens onto the sensor. Since the human retina has a dense vascular network, the blood absorbs green light and the remaining light appears red. If the camera lens captures this light, the resulting photograph displays the pupils as red orbs. As an aside, cats and dogs have a reflective layer behind their retinas, causing their eyes to glow yellow rather than red. This is significant for pet photographers because automated software for red eye removal may fail to take the glow out of their pets' eyes.

When the Red Eye Reduction command is set to [On], the camera's flash sends out several flashes prior to the main flash. Theoretically, this makes the subject's pupils constrict, reducing the chance that light from the flash will enter the eyes and be reflected directly back to the camera.

This command has three flaws. First, it is not foolproof, and you can still have pictures with glowing red eyes. Second, the additional flashes can annoy subjects enough that they blink or squint, ruining the shot. Third, the delay imposed by using these flashes can cause you to miss the image you really wanted. For this reason, we recommend that you turn this command to [Off].

### Alternate Ways of Reducing Red Eye

If you want to avoid red eye, there are three strategies. The first is to position the flash away from the camera's lens, reducing the chance that light entering the subject's eye will be reflected back into the lens. You can't do this with the built-in flash. However, if you add an external flash unit to the hot shoe, the flash will be situated above the lens and help reduce red eye.



The second strategy is to constrict the subject's pupils by increasing the surrounding light—when you're indoors, turn up the light. The third strategy is to have the subject look slightly away at a point to the right or left of the camera, thus reducing the chance that reflected light from the eyes will enter the camera lens.

## Flash Command

You control the flash through the Flash Mode menu command. The command has six options (table 10-1) but not all of the options are available in each of the shooting or drive modes.

MENU>Camera>Flash Mode

| Icon | Name | Description |
|---|---|---|
|  | Flash Off | Prevents the flash unit from firing. Only works when the flash is manually raised.<br>This option is disabled in P, A, S, M, and the following SCN predefined modes: Night Scene, Hand-held Twilight, and Night Portrait. |
| AUTO | Autoflash | The camera decides when the flash is needed. You must first manually pop up the flash unit so the camera can fire it in low light.<br>This option is enabled only in Intelligent Auto and the following SCN predefined modes: Portrait and Macro. |
|  | Fill-flash | When this option is selected, the flash always fires and lights the subject. The flash unit must be manually raised.<br>This option is available only in P, A, S, M, and the following SCN predefined modes: Portrait, Sports Action, Macro, Landscape, and Sunset. |
| SLOW | Slow Sync. | Use this option with a slow shutter speed. The flash goes off and the camera's shutter speed is prolonged to capture the background that is not illuminated by the flash.<br>This option is available only in P, A, S, and M modes. |
| REAR | Rear Sync. | The flash goes off at the end of the exposure just before the second shutter curtain closes. If the subject moves during the exposure, it may be recorded as a blur. When the flash discharges, the subject will be frozen in position with a blur extending opposite its direction of movement.<br>This option is available only in P, A, S, and M modes. |
| WL | Wireless | This option requires a Sony external flash unit that is capable of wireless triggering. When such a flash is attached, it will send a pulse of light to trigger the firing of other external flash units.<br>This option is available only in P, A, S, and M modes. |

**Table 10-1**: Flash Mode options

To maintain the streamlined shape of the camera body, the built-in flash head is folded into the camera body, and must be raised to be used. Unlike many other cameras, the flash unit does not pop up automatically when it's needed. You have to decide whether you need to use it.

## Using Flash in Intelligent Auto

Only the first two Flash Mode options are available in Intelligent Auto: [Flash Off] and [Autoflash].

These commands are pretty straightforward. The [Flash Off] option turns the flash unit off, and [Autoflash] lets the camera decide whether it should use flash. You can expect the flash to fire when you take a picture inside where the light is dim. Both commands assume that the flash has been raised manually.

### What You Can Do with Flash in Intelligent Auto

The [Autoflash] option is for people who are interested in using the camera as a point-and-shoot recorder. You might expect that the camera will fire the flash only if the light is too dim, but this is not the case. The flash can fire during daylight if the camera determines that there is too much variation in the lighting between the subject and the background. For example, it may fire when you are trying to take a picture of a person sitting in front of a window that looks outdoors into bright light; in other words, it will fire under backlighting conditions where the subject is rendered as a silhouette (figure 10-3a). By doing so, it will illuminate the subject with enough light to balance the light coming through the window. Thus, you can record both the subject and the scene outside the window (figure 10-3b).

The [Flash Off] command is a safety command; it ensures the flash won't fire even if the flash unit has been raised. Since the flash won't fire when you fold it back into the camera body, this command seems redundant.

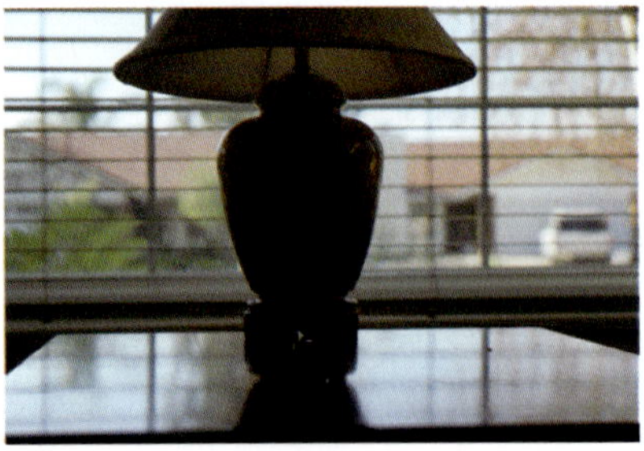

**Figure 10-3a**: An imbalance between foreground and background lighting renders a lamp as a silhouette

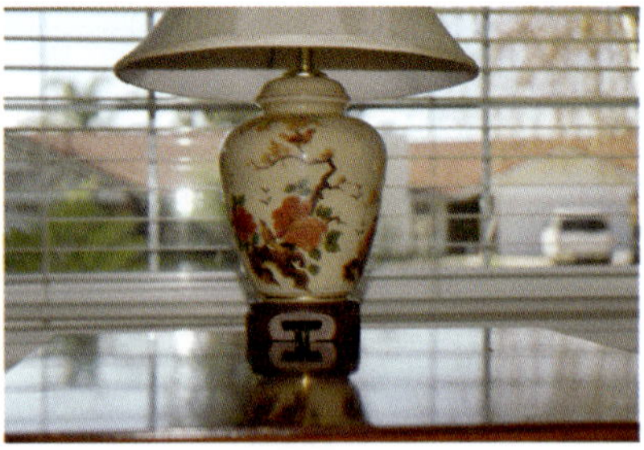

**Figure 10-3b**: The flash can illuminate shadows and reveals the surface of the lamp

### What You Can't Do with Flash in Intelligent Auto

As you take more pictures, you will realize that you are constrained by your lack of exposure control. First, when the flash is used for dim interior shots, the lens will be at its largest aperture. Therefore, you can't increase the depth of field. This reflects the automatic nature of the camera as it tries to capture the image with available light.

Under these conditions, the camera tries to brighten the recorded image by opening the lens aperture, raising the ISO, and setting the shutter speed to 1/60 second. This is a disadvantage if you want to capture a detailed view of people scattered throughout a room. Since the lens is wide open, the depth of field is narrow, causing many of the people to be recorded indistinctly. To record all the people sharply, you need to close down the lens aperture; however, this is not an option in Intelligent Auto.

Second, you may notice that when the flash fires in response to high-contrast lighting conditions (such as a subject in front of a window, described earlier), the foreground may not be exposed the way you like. The flash may cause the subject to be too light, and it would be more flattering if the flash illumination was reduced. You can't control the flash intensity in Intelligent Auto.

Under these situations, you will have to take greater control. Move away from Intelligent Auto and start using the camera in the P, A, S, or M modes.

## Flash Options in P, A, S, or M Modes

When you switch over to P, A, S, or M mode, your built-in flash is under your absolute control. The Flash Mode's [Autoflash] and [Flash Off] options are grayed out. If the flash is down, it will never fire. So this is the straightforward replacement for [Flash Off]. If you raise the flash, it will always fire. In this mode, the flash operates as a fill light. When it is fired under bright light conditions, its role becomes supplementary to the ambient illumination. That is to say, in harsh light that casts deep shadows, your flash is designed to fill in the dark areas with light.

To adjust the amount of light that the flash emits, use the following menu command:

MENU>Brightness/Color>Flash Comp.>[n]



You can dial in a flash exposure, [n], with an EV value ranging from -3.0 to +3.0, where the increments are graded in 0.3 EV units (one-third f-stops). No compensation is indicated by setting the command to 0.0 EV.

The flash output is variable, so if you decide that the fill-in light is too intense, you can reduce it with [Flash Comp.]. This command differs from Exposure Compensation in that it adjusts the exposure for just the flash. In contrast, Exposure Compensation keeps the ratio between flash output and daylight intensity constant so varying this will make the overall picture lighter or darker. Conversely, using [Flash Comp.] alters this ratio by varying the amount of flash intensity and making the flash-illuminated subject brighter or darker relative to the overall picture.

There are two additional Flash Mode options available in the semiautomatic and manual modes: [Rear Sync.] and [Wireless]. The former is used for special effects and coordinates the firing of the flash to the movement of the camera's internal shutter. Normally the flash is timed to fire at the beginning of the camera's internal shutter. However, you can synchronize the flash to fire at the end of the shutter movement. You use this feature to enhance the impression of motion. When Flash Mode is set to [Rear Sync.], it uses a slow shutter speed, so a forward-moving car is recorded as an elongated blur. When the flash fires at the end of the exposure, the flash exposure makes the car appear frozen. However, because the shutter was open while the car was moving forward, the car has a blurred trail behind. The viewer interprets the car as having moved at such a high velocity that it left a streak behind it. If you tried a long exposure with the flash firing at the beginning of the exposure, the car will appear with the streak in front of it.

The [Wireless] option allows you to fire an external flash unit that is not physically attached to the camera. It gives you access to all kinds of different lighting scenarios that would not be available to you if the flash unit had to be physically tethered to the camera. We will discuss this in more detail later in the chapter.

### Controlling Lens Aperture While Working with Flash

Switching to P, A, S, or M mode gives you greater control when you use either an external or internal flash. Specifically, you can close down the lens aperture and move away from its maximum aperture. Table 10-2 illustrates the active controls when you take the camera out of Intelligent Auto mode.

| Mode | Camera Shutter Speed | Aperture |
|---|---|---|
| P | 1/60 second | Maximum aperture |
| A | 1/60 second | User defined |
| S | User defined from 1/160 second or longer | Maximum aperture |
| M | User defined from 1/160 second or longer | User defined |

**Table 10-2**: Shutter speed and aperture in P, A, S, and M modes

As you can see, P mode does not differ much from Intelligent Auto. The camera sets the shutter speed to 1/60 second and attempts to use a large aperture for the lens. If you want to use a narrower aperture and increase the depth of field, the A mode is better; it allows you to increase the depth of field by closing down the lens aperture, though you are still forced to use a shutter speed of 1/60 second. The S mode allows you to select the shutter speed, anywhere from 1/160 second to several seconds. Sadly, this mode tends to use the maximum aperture of your lens.

The M mode is the prize. It allows you to control both the lens aperture and the shutter speed. Most importantly, it allows you to use a camera shutter speed faster than 1/60 second, and you can use smaller lens apertures. This is critical because it increases your ability to use the flash outdoors as a fill light.

Recall that the camera's normal ISO is 100. For a sunny day, the base exposure is 1/60 second at f/22. But suppose you want less depth of field and an aperture of f/16. You cannot do this in Intelligent Auto, P, or A modes because the shutter speed is locked at 1/60 second. Nor can you accomplish this in S mode; while you can get a minimum of 1/160 second shutter speed, you cannot change the aperture. The solution is to use M mode and switch the lens aperture to f/16 and the shutter speed to 1/160 second.

This higher flash synchronization speed gives you greater flexibility when you use your flash in daylight as a fill flash; it actually increases the potential range of your flash unit. As mentioned in the section on GN, the primary determinants for flash exposure are the distance from the camera to the subject and the lens opening for a given ISO. With a higher synchronization speed, you can open your lens aperture by 1 1/3 f-stops for ambient lighting. Using a larger aperture increases the range of your flash.

Another advantage of the higher synchronization speed becomes evident if your subject has some movement. To freeze movement, a shutter speed of 1/160 second is more effective than a shutter speed of 1/60 second.

When using the flash for fill work, we routinely use M mode. Remember, this does not prevent you from using slower shutter speeds. Indeed, not only can you still take flash exposures at 1/60 second, but you can also use longer shutter speeds, such as a full second!

### M Mode and Viewfinder Brightness: A Note for Studio Photographers

When we adjust the aperture and shutter speed in M mode for interior photography, we sometimes run into a problem. Our viewfinder and LCD screens become so dark that they are unusable. This is a complaint that studio photographers reported on earlier SLT camera models. It results from having a live preview that attempts to show how your image will be recorded before you press the shutter button. This works well when you use the camera in a semiautomatic exposure mode (P, A, or S) with ambient lighting because the camera is always adjusting its settings to ensure you have a recordable image. Unfortunately, the shutter speed and aperture are not adjusted for ambient lighting when you use a studio flash. Instead, they are set for the high-intensity light from the flash. The ambient light is usually so low that the Live View screen is black, making it unusable for framing the subject. This can be an annoying situation. Fortunately, Sony has heard the complaints from earlier adoptees of their SLT cameras and designed a menu command to help flash photographers.

To keep the viewfinder and LCD screen bright when doing flash photography, set the following menu command:

MENU>Setup (Shooting Settings)>Live View Display>[Setting Effect ON], [Setting Effect OFF]

The default for this command is [Setting Effect ON], which allows you to see the effects of Exposure Compensation. However, when you turn this to [Setting Effect OFF], the screen will not show the effects of Exposure Compensation. Instead, the screen will have a constant display brightness no matter what Exposure Compensation was applied; or in the case of M mode, it keeps the screen at a constant brightness no matter what you set your shutter speed or aperture to. The disadvantage in using this setting is that all the altered color recording modes and special enhancement effects of Creative Style and Picture Effect will not be shown. However, if you are using your camera only for flash photography, this is an incredibly useful command, one that studio photographers should have in their repertoire.

## Sony Accessory Flash Units

Sony sells accessory (external) flash units for the NEX-7. Table 10-3 summarizes the models and their pricing.

| Flash Model | GN | Zoom Head | Max Wide Angle with Diffuser | Weight in Ozs. | Bounce Capable | Power | Price (Sony Store) |
|---|---|---|---|---|---|---|---|
| HVL-F20AM | 20 | No zoom | 27mm | 3.2 | Yes | 2 AAA | $150 |
| HVL-F43AM | 43 | Yes: 24–105mm | 15mm | 12 | Yes | 4 AA | $350 |
| HVL-F58AM | 58 | Yes: 24–105mm | 16mm | 15.6 | Yes | 4 AA | $500 |

**Table 10-3**: Sony NEX-7 external flash units

As you can see, there is a flash for most everyone, ranging from the family photographer who needs a bit more power for interior shots to the professional who needs to work with a unit that provides considerably more light. All of the flashes have their own internal power source, either AA or AAA batteries, ensuring that you will not drain your camera batteries when doing flash photography.

### Focal Length and Variations in Flash Head Focal Length

Sony offers two flash units (HVL-F43AM and HVL-F58AM) with a zoom lens system for focusing light into a smaller area when you use a moderate telephoto setting. This elegant system tells the flash head what zoom is set on your lens. As you zoom in or out with your lens, you can hear a motor within the flash unit drive its lens system. This is all done automatically. Essentially, when you use a telephoto setting, it provides a more efficient use of the flash, matching its light distribution to the coverage of the lens.

A nice feature of the Sony accessory flash units is that they use inexpensive batteries that can be purchased at the corner drugstore. However, we would be remiss if we didn't talk about the charge cycle time of these units. Typically, when the flash is used in an automatic mode for relatively short distances, it fires a very brief burst of light that is much shorter than the maximum duration. This short burst doesn't use much battery power, and the capacitor recharges very rapidly. Rather than fire the flash at full power every time, the flash conserves the unused energy and uses it for the next flash. So instead of having to fully recharge, it needs to only partially recharge to reach full capacity.

But after you start using the flash in a large room and it fires at maximum duration, you will note that the charge cycle time increases. You can check this on the camera's display screen, where you will see an orange circle. If it is flashing, it means the flash is recharging and it cannot be fired. As you drain the batteries, the recharge time becomes progressively longer.

However, there are situations when you want the flash to fire more quickly. You might consider replacing the flash's normal disposable alkaline batteries with rechargeable nickel metal hydride batteries. These batteries have a lower internal resistance and reduce the recharge time between flashes. Since they can be recharged, they can be an economical choice if you do a lot of flash photography. If they have any disadvantage, it is that they do not hold as much energy as alkaline batteries. But this is of little concern as an extra set of batteries can be kept on hand.



Sony's smallest and least expensive external flash unit is the HVL-F20AM. It can be a handy little unit to keep in your camera bag. You can aim the flash directly at the subject or adjust the head so it fires a beam at a 75-degree angle toward the ceiling. This provides bounce lighting and reduces the harshness that results if the flash is aimed directly at a subject. Bounce flash tends to produce a more flattering portrait because the soft light hides wrinkles. The disadvantage of this unit is its low-intensity flash—about one-third to half the power of Sony's more expensive units. But remember, it more than doubles the output of the built-in flash. We like its compact size and light weight, which makes it balance nicely on the NEX-7 body.

Although they are huge and look oversized when they are mounted on the NEX-7, we prefer using the two larger, more expensive units: the HVL-F43AM and the HVL-F58AM. Their larger size is justified by their greater power, giving us more range and making them especially appropriate for bounce flash. Both of their heads can be aimed toward the ceiling to reflect their light down onto the subject, and they create a flattering rendition of your subjects. Both flashes have what Sony calls a Quick Shift Bounce. When you take a vertical shot with your camera, the head of the shoe-mounted flash swivels so it remains horizontal. Other manufacturers' flash heads shift and become vertically oriented. Sony's clever design ensures that their flash units provide the most efficient coverage for bounce lighting, whether you hold your camera in a vertical or horizontal position. Just be aware that depending on how you position the camera and the flash unit, there are a couple of problems. There are some configurations where you can get to the shutter button, but it is an uncomfortably tight fit for your fingers. In addition, the flash unit can completely block access to the Navigation button.

Both the HVL-F43AM and the HVL-F58AM have a motorized lens system to distribute their light so it matches the zoom setting of your lens. This provides efficient coverage of your subject when you aim the flash directly at it, and it also increases the maximum range of the flash. If we use the GN as a rough approximation of maximum distance, the HVL-F20AM provides a 3x range increase, the HVL-F43AM provides a 6x range increase, and the HVL-F58AM provides a 9x range increase.

Of the three flash units, we found that the HVL-F43AM is best suited for our needs. It provides sufficient power for our applications, and we think the additional cost of the HVL-F58AM is not justified.

### Bounce or Indirect Lighting: Flash Accessories

One of the benefits of an accessory flash with a tilting and rotating head is the ability to use bounce flash. When the flash is aimed directly at your subject, the light can be unflattering. The lighting is harsh (figure 10-4a), and it displays facial wrinkles and misplaced strands of hair with distressing clarity.

One simple strategy for reducing this effect is to swivel the flash head; instead of aiming it directly at the subject, aim it at a ceiling or an adjacent wall. The light will bounce from these areas onto the subject and therefore be diffused. As a result, the light is softer, so it masks wrinkles and deemphasizes individual strands of hair to produce a more pleasing image. In figure 10-4b, the diffused light softens the dog's appearance.

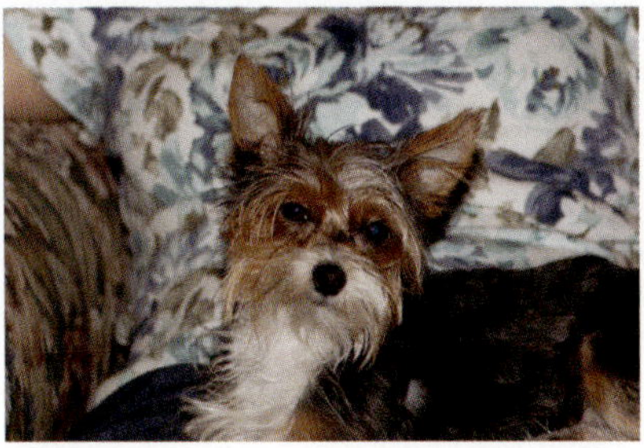

**Figure 10-4a**: Dog photographed with direct flash

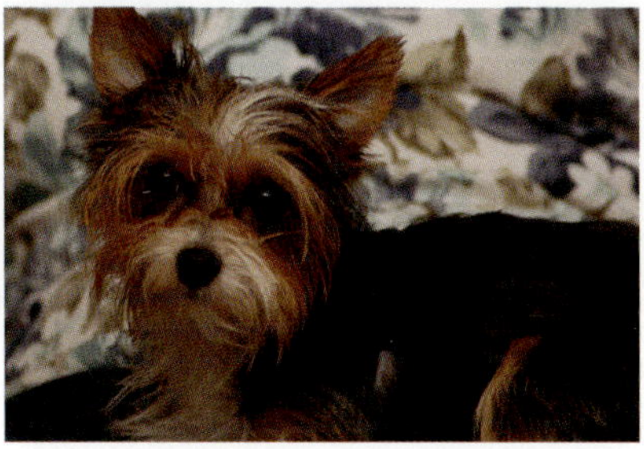

**Figure 10-4b**: Dog photographed with bounce flash

One reason we do not use the inexpensive Sony HVL-F20AM flash unit is its lower power output, which limits its functionality as a bounced light. Although the light can be tilted up at a fixed 75-degree angle, we cannot stop down the lens as much as we would like to. The higher output of the HVL-F43AM flash unit allows considerable flexibility in closing down the aperture if we so desire.

One caveat on using a bounce flash is that if you have the camera set for red eye reduction, the flash will emit small bursts of light prior to the main flash for exposure. This is not needed, so make sure you turn the Red Eye Reduction command to [Off]. Doing so will make your camera more responsive and the camera will record the picture without delay.

If you use external flashes for much of your photography, you will want additional ways of diffusing the light. Although we like to bounce the light, it is not always possible. For example, if the ceiling or walls are heavily colored, they will impart their color to the reflected light and destroy the WB.

One helpful accessory is a little plastic diffuser that attaches directly to the flash head. Sto-Fen makes the Omni-Bounce that attaches directly to the front of the Sony flash head. It is fitted by friction, which is advantageous since you don't need to tape it to the flash. The device is small enough that you can keep it in your camera bag, and although it does diffuse the light, it may not diffuse it enough.

There is no substitute for using large reflectors or diffusers, but they can be cumbersome and expensive accessories. If you wish to experiment with them, you can assemble your own for pennies. The following website has several tutorials for assembling your own flash accessories: *www.digital-photography-school.com/diy-flash-and-lighting-hacks-for-digital-photographers*.

Several books are also available. Check out *Low Budget Shooting: Do It Yourself Solutions to Professional Photo Gear* by Cyrill Harnischmacher.

On occasion, we tilt our flash head vertically and attach a white sheet of heavy paper to it with tape. By folding the top of the sheet over the flash head and arranging it so it directs the light forward onto the subject, it serves as an inexpensive reflector and diffuser that can be discarded as soon as the session is over.

## Sony Wireless Flash

To take advantage of the Flash Mode [Wireless] option, which can be accessed with the following command, you will need a Sony accessory flash capable of generating a wireless signal:

MENU>Camera>Flash Mode>[Wireless]

This option enables you to fire a flash remotely. It requires that you attach a flash with wireless capability (master) to wirelessly fire your external accessory flash (slave). A flash that serves well as a master is the small, lightweight HVL-F20AM. The first step involves pairing the two units so they can communicate with each other. You can do this with the following sequence of steps:

1. Set the Shoot Mode to P, A, S, or M.
2. Take the flash to be used as a slave and mount it on the camera's accessory shoe.
3. Turn both the external flash unit and the camera on.
4. Use the menu to get to the Flash Mode command and select [Wireless]. Press soft key C.
5. Remove the flash unit. You should see a red light slowly blinking on the unit, indicating that the flash is ready to use as a slave.
6. Attach the master flash to the hot shoe. Turn it on.
7. Use the following steps to test that the two flash units are communicating:
   a. Press the AEL button.
   b. The master flash will emit a small burst of light.
   c. In response, the slave flash will fire a burst of light to confirm that the two flash units are communicating.

After you complete this operation, you can position your accessory flash (slave) so it can see the light from the master flash . This light can be a reflection, so the slave unit need not be pointed at the camera. It takes surprisingly little light to activate the signal, and it can operate from light reflected off the subject or a wall. Once you have placed the slave flash unit, check again to see if the communication link is still active by pressing the AEL button.

The advantage of the [Wireless] option is that the external flash does not need to be connected to the camera body. You can position it in a variety of places. For example, you may notice that some photographers have brackets for holding the flash unit away from the camera body. You can use such devices to ensure that the light is flattering and reduce the chances of red eye. Or you can put your Sony flash on its pedestal, supplied with external flash unit, and position it well away from the camera body.

One trick we use at family gatherings is to mount the flash on the pedestal, place it on a strategically located table, and aim it at the ceiling. We then use the wireless option to fire the flash for our group shots. The lighting can be very flattering, and you can move about as you fire the camera. The most convenient flash setup would be to use the small, lightweight HVL-F20AM as the master flash positioned on your hot shoe. You can then use the heavier HVL-F43AM or HVL-F58AM as the slave flash so you gain the power of using these units without having to carry their weight on your camera.

### Slow Sync. Flash

When you are photographing someone against a scenic background at night, you may wish to record both the person and the background. If you use the standard synchronization speed of 1/60 second or shorter, this may be impossible. But you might be able to record the background with a longer exposure—perhaps an exposure of one or two seconds, or more. You can obtain a picture like this with the following command:

MENU>Camera>Flash Mode>[Slow Sync.]

Keep in mind that instead of using this menu command you may wish to simply try a longer shutter speed in M mode. Remember, you can use slow shutter speeds with a manual exposure.

## Recommendations

Although the built-in flash can be used in Intelligent Auto or SCN mode, we urge you to use it in P, A, S, or M mode. It is especially important to learn how to use the flash with the camera set to M mode. This allows you to adjust both the shutter speed and the aperture. You can dramatically increase the depth of field if you adopt this strategy. If you use the flash as a fill light outdoors, set the shutter speed to 1/160 second rather than 1/60 second to fill in the shadows.

If you do a lot of interior photography, you may wish to consider getting an external flash unit. In our opinion, the HVL-F43AM has an excellent feature set for its cost. If you wish to do wireless flash, a good combination is to use the HVL-F20AM for the master flash and the HVL-F43AM or HVL-F53AM for a slave.

# Chapter 11: Making Movies

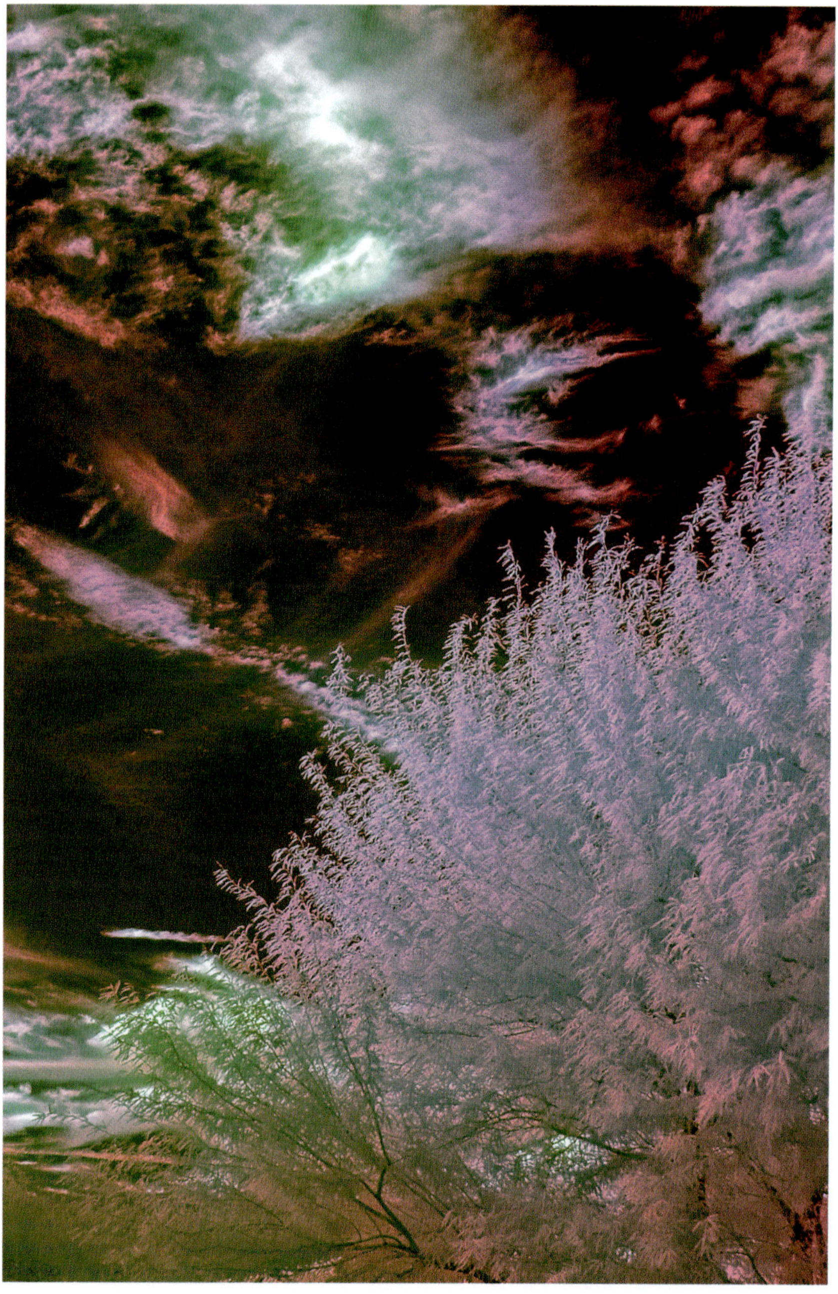

11

## Introduction

The Sony NEX-7 is a hybrid that is capable of taking excellent still pictures and movies. As such, it allows you to carry one camera to do two tasks. To switch from taking still shots to shooting movies is as easy as pressing the Movie button to begin recording (figure 11-1). Moreover, the movies are of excellent quality and can be played on HDTVs or recorded to DVD discs.

In this chapter, we introduce the movie operation of the Sony NEX-7 and approach the topic at a beginner's level for users who are more familiar with still photography. We also provide an explanation of file formats and the commands that are used to record movies.

The general rule to remember when taking movies is that the camera uses the settings that you last used for still photography. If you have set the Shoot Mode to Intelligent Auto, P, A, S, or M, those settings are used for shooting the movie.

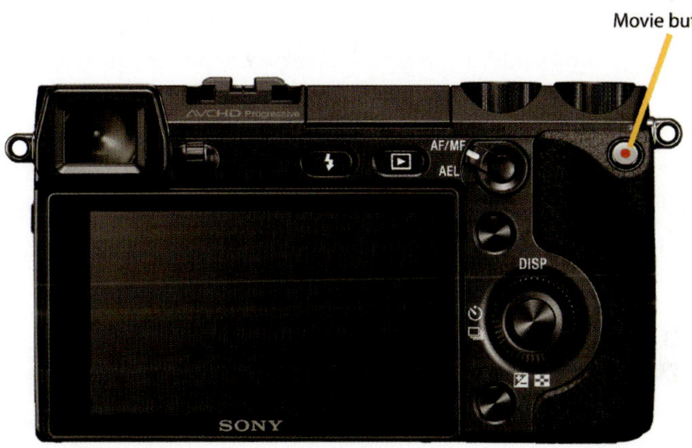


**Figure 11-1**: Movie button

When you set the camera to Intelligent Auto, your camera is a completely automatic camcorder and sets the ISO value, shutter speed, and WB. Fortunately, the automatic mode is so reliable that you will get great-looking movies. This may be all you need for recording family vacations.

Eventually, you may decide to take more control. By using the P, A, S, or M modes, you gain control of the shutter speed, aperture, ISO, and WB. In addition, you can modify the exposure—increasing it to brighten the image or dimming it to darken the image—to create the desired mood for your movie. You can also tame extremes in brightness by using DRO, or you can introduce unique coloration by using the Creative Style or Picture Effect options.

One thing that may surprise you is the amount of preparation that is needed to take a high-quality movie. It is necessary to preplan the scene and spend time to ensure camera stability and correct lighting.

As popularized in some professionally made movies, there is a technique of shooting handheld movies where the videographer rapidly shifts position to provide diverse vantage points. The subject appears to bounce about within the frame, providing a powerful effect of conveying fast, tension-filled action. However, this technique is not suitable for a documentary movie or recording a family birthday party. Such events require smooth panning so the subject does not appear to be jittering within the frame. You may be disappointed in your results if you handhold the camera, as hand tremors will make the object move about within the frame, distracting your audience.

Just as with still pictures, recording a good movie requires using a tripod and some careful planning. Pay attention to your light source. If your framed image has areas that are extremely bright or dark, you may need to sacrifice details in either the highlights or the shadows. This is when you might consider using the DRO command to bring out shadow detail. Consider whether you intend to create a certain mood. For example, dark shadows can add an ominous feeling to a clip. You may wish to underexpose the scene to attain this ambience.

Preplanning is important because there is little opportunity for correcting errors in the final movie. Unlike still photography, where you have some latitude in adjusting your pictures with RAW files, you do not have that flexibility when shooting movies.

## Frame Rate versus Shutter Speed

To introduce still photographers to movies, we compiled table 11-1 to define many of the terms we use. You can refer to this table while reading the chapter.

| Term | Description |
|---|---|
| Aspect ratio | Describes the dimension of the image, expressed as a ratio of width to height. For example, 16:9 represents a 1.78:1 width to height ratio, and 4:3 represents a 1.38:1 width to height ratio. |
| AVCHD | Advanced Video Coding High Definition. This is a file format for recording and saving high-definition videos. It provides a high degree of data compression and is typically not edited in its native format. Instead, the file is translated, or transcoded, before it is worked on. |
| Bit rate | The rate that data is being processed per unit of time. |
| Frame rate | Defines the number of still pictures (frames) recorded per unit of time. It is generally expressed as frames/second (or fps). |

| Term | Description |
|---|---|
| Interlaced scanning | A method for capturing or projecting images by creating two fields per frame. Together, the two fields contain the full number of lines for the frame; individually, the field captures only half the number of lines. To view the complete image, the two fields are integrated. At a rate of 30 frames per second (fps), interlaced scanning actually captures 60 fields per second. |
| Mbps | The rate of information being processed expressed as megabits per second. This is a measure of data content. Higher-quality videos will be recorded at higher Mbps values. |
| MP4 | A multimedia format based on the QuickTime file format for storing digital video files. |
| NTSC | National Television System Committee. This television and video standard is used in the United States and contains 525 vertical lines. For video it is associated with collecting the images at approximately 30 fps. |
| PAL | Phase Alternating Line. This television standard is used in Europe and Asia. It delivers 625 vertical lines of resolution. For video it is associated with collecting the images at 25 fps. |
| Progressive scanning | A frame that is captured in its entirety with a single scan. |

**Table 11-1**: Movie-related terms

Recording movies requires a new perspective. You must always be conscious that you are taking a sequence of images (frames) that, when played back, will give the viewer a prolonged interval to study the subject. Distractions that are of little importance in still images will distract and annoy an audience that is watching a movie. For example, it is annoying when the brightness of the scene changes while Exposure Compensation is applied, or when the scene transitions from blurred to sharp while the focus is adjusted.

**NTSC and PAL**

The number of frames per second depends on the camera's country of origin. The standard in the United States, NTSC, is 30 fps; and the standard in Europe, Asia, and other countries, PAL, is 25 fps. As a matter of convenience, we will use the NTSC standard. You don't have to be concerned with setting your camera to use either standard. The manufacturer does that for you automatically.

Because you are capturing at least 24 frames per second (fps), you will find limits to your shutter speed. For example, in low light you cannot use long exposures to let more light reach the sensor. With the NEX-7, you can record at a frame rate of either 25 fps (for the PAL standard) or 30 fps (for the NTSC standard); for high-quality work, you can shoot at the faster frame rates of 50 fps or 60 fps.

Since you are recording a sequence of shots, you will find that you cannot use long shutter speeds such as 1 second. When you use film to shoot a movie, it is obvious that the longest shutter speed you can use is 1/30 second for recording at 30 fps. But you can use a faster shutter speed. Occasionally, new videographers think that if they are shooting at a fast shutter speed then their frame rate goes up. This is not the case. You can set a shutter speed of 1/4000 second. You will still be taking 30 fps, but each frame is being exposed for only 1/4000 second.

The shutter speed you use for each frame can create different effects. When you shoot in modes where the camera sets the shutter speed, you will see that the camera attempts to keep the shutter speed at 1/30 second or 1/60 second (depending on the Shoot Mode), and it avoids shutter speeds shorter than 1/125 second. In part, this is done to provide the smoothest perception of motion. But when you take control of the shutter speed in M or S mode, you may be surprised that you can set the shutter speed to as long as 0.25 second. This not only gives you better low-light capability with very slow moving subjects, but it also provides a special effect. A rapidly moving subject will be seen as a blur and have a ghostly tail extending behind it. This longer shutter speed is one of the benefits of working with a digital sensor rather than film for recording movies. There is a bit of image processing invoked when using such longer shutter speeds.

At the opposite extreme is using a fast shutter speed of 1/1000 second. When you play the movie back at 30 fps, the movement appears strobe like. Instead of a smooth motion, the action appears to move in jumps. This comes from having sharply defined edges recorded within each individual frame. When you move from frame to frame, you can just perceive the detailed edges of the subject, and if the movement is sufficiently fast there is a distinct gap in the subject's movement. Since the movie is being displayed at 30 fps, a crisp edge exaggerates the fact that you are seeing a series of individual frames. While this crisp rendering is disconcerting during playback, it is desirable if you need to see all the details within a frame. For example, in surveillance work, it is advantageous for reading the numbers and letters off the license plate of a speeding car.

For most videographers, a good starting place for setting your shutter speed is about 1/60 second if you are shooting at 30 fps, or 1/120 second if you are shooting at 60 fps. This is a good compromise for providing a sense of sharpness and smooth movement.

## Choosing a Movie File Format

Because the frame rate is important for what you will record, you have to decide whether you want to record at 24, 30, or 60 fps. This is when you start thinking of the file format you would like to use. There are two file formats available: AVCHD and MP4 (table 11-2).

| File Format | Use |
|---|---|
| AVCHD | Provides the highest-quality movies. Can be viewed directly when the camera is coupled to a suitable HDTV. The PMB software program can translate the file so it can be burned to a disc and be played and viewed on an HDTV. |
| MP4 | A computer file type that works well on older, slower machines. This file type can easily be attached to emails or uploaded to websites. |

**Table 11-2**: Sony NEX-7 movie file formats

When you use AVCHD, you can record at 24 or 60 fps. If you are using MP4 you will record at 30 fps. If you are new to recording movies, we recommend choosing AVCHD if you wish to view the movie at its highest resolution on your HDTV. You can, with the aid of your Sony PMB software, create DVDs or Blu-ray Discs for playback on a suitable player. If you think you would like to use the movie for computer related activities, i.e. attaching to an email or viewing on the computer, you may record and save the file in MP4 format.

As you gain more experience, you may decide to use your computer to edit and work with AVCHD files. To get a feel for this, download your movies and work with them in the PMB software. You can shorten the movie by removing extraneous material and then merge the clips to make a coherent, succinct story. If you have an Apple computer, we recommend buying the iMovie program for working with your AVCHD files.

To select the movie's file format, use the following command:

MENU>Image Size (Movie)>File Format>[AVCHD 60i/60p], [MP4]

Keep in mind that if you purchased your camera outside of the United States, you will see [AVCHD 50i/50p] instead of [AVCHD 60i/60p].

At least two camera manufacturers recommend using AVCHD for directly viewing your movies on a TV or making playable DVDs for an HDTV. Their recommendation is very conservative, so you may wish to ignore it if you want to edit your movie files. After all, Sony does provide PMB, which can serve this purpose.

### AVCHD

AVCHD files provide the highest fidelity and smoothest perception of movement for your movie. However, they make greater demands on your computer and software. Although you can work with these files on older computers, newer computers with plenty of RAM and large, fast hard drives handle these files better.

If you decide to work with AVCHD files, you will eventually want to buy a more capable software package. We use Final Cut Pro X, which can read Sony's 60p 28 Mbps files directly. At the time of this writing, our less-capable software, iMovie '11, cannot do so, but it can read the lower-quality 60i 24 Mbps files. We can edit our AVCHD files with either iMovie or PMB. Both of these software packages are basic, inexpensive editors; PMB comes free with your camera, and Apple users can download iMovie '11 for $15. If you decide to work with a higher-end movie editor, such as Final Cut Pro X or Adobe After Effects for Windows, you will have to pay considerably more: $300 and $240 (for a 1-year subscription), respectively.

### MP4

The MP4 movie file format is the easiest one to work with, since it can generate data files that are easily read by other software programs. There are free programs available for opening and viewing MP4 files, such as Apple QuickTime. If you decide you want more power in your movie editing, you can buy QuickTime Pro from Apple for only $30 from the following website: http://store.apple.com/us/product/D3381Z/A.

The vertical number of pixels is the same for both MP4 and AVCHD, so if you choose MP4 format, you do not give up much in regards to resolution. What you do lose is some width in the image, which becomes a concern if you want to display the movie in a widescreen 16:9 format. Also, you have the option of saving MP4 files in a 640 x 480 pixel display, the smallest pixel array for saving your movies. This is an advantage if you intend to attach the movie file to an email.

## Record Settings (Quality)

Several things determine the clarity of the movie playback: fps, bit rate, and format type. We have talked about the format type already (AVCHD or MP4). The Record Setting command determines the quality retained in these file types. Selecting the option for this is more complex, simply because of the bewildering number of choices available. When you use the AVCHD file format, you have five possible settings to choose from, and which of them you select can be confusing (table 11-3).

Here are some general guidelines to simplify the selection task:

- For editing your AVCHD files on your computer, use the highest movie quality your software can read. Most likely this will either be 60p or 60i. If you are new to taking movies, make sure that your software can handle 60p before using this option.
- For burning a movie to a DVD, choose the lowest quality settings (24p).
- For burning a movie to a Blu-ray Disc, choose the medium to high quality settings (60i or 60p, respectively). PMB will allow you to burn these discs.
- For playing a movie back onto an HDTV, find out what standard your TV uses and select the Quality setting based on what the HDTV can accept.

| File Format = [AVCHD 60i/60p]/[AVCHD 50i/50p] | | |
|---|---|---|
| **Record Setting Value** | **Average Bit Rate** | **Movie Recording Size and fps** |
| 60i 24M(FX) / 50i 24M(FX) | 24 Mbps | Records high-quality videos at 1920 x 1080 pixels and 60i/50i fps |
| 60i 17M(FH) / 50i 17M(FH) | 17 Mbps | Records standard-quality videos at 1920 x 1080 pixels and 60i/50i fps |
| 60p 28M(PS) / 50p 28M(PS) | 28 Mbps | Records highest-quality videos at 1920 x 1080 pixels and 60p/50p fps |
| 24p 24M(FX) / 25p 24M(FX) | 24 Mbps | Records high-quality videos at 1920 x 1080 pixels and 24p/25p fps |
| 24p 17M(FH) 25p 17M(FH) | 17 Mbps | Records standard-quality videos at 1920 x 1080 pixels and 24p/25p fps |

**Table 11-3**: AVCHD file recording settings

The number of bits being processed determines how finely the details are rendered. If there are too few, the movie will have unsatisfactory definition and detail.

### Interlaced Scanning

Older analog cameras and displays for broadcast television relied on forming an image by interlaced scanning. This was due to technological limitations. To display enough images sequentially for a smooth perception of movement, a television camera would use two fields to make a single frame. This strategy would allow the viewer to see an object moving smoothly across the screen without flickering. The interlaced scanning method is an option on many cameras, including the Sony NEX-7.

With interlaced scanning, a recording device with a spatial resolution of 600 horizontal lines actually collects only 300 lines. It starts with the top line and then collects every other line to create an image with 300 horizontal lines (figure 11-2). If you define the top line as number one, the sensor collects every odd line for the first field. Then the sensor collects the remaining 300 lines for the second field, starting with the second line from the top. The two fields are combined to yield a single frame of 600 lines. In essence, to display a movie at 30 frames per second, a camera or television has to collect 60 fields per second—meaning two sets of 30 fields per second to be interlaced to form 30 frames per second.

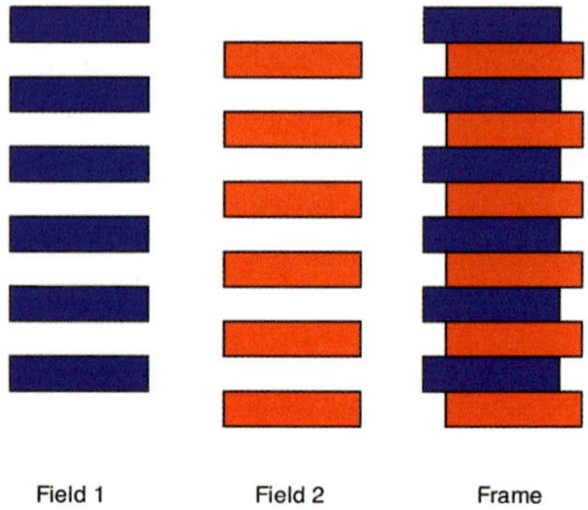


**Figure 11-2**: How an interlaced scan combines two fields to make one frame

If you see the letter "i" with an fps number in your viewfinder or on the LCD screen, it means interlaced scanning, indicating that two sets of fields were combined (interlaced) to form a single frame. If one field has a moving object, its edges will display an offset artifact because the first field collected the image before the second field. This blurs the edges of the moving object, but due to how the human eye works, the motion will be perceived as smoother.

### Progressive Scanning

Progressive scanning is the modern way of recording and playing back movies. All computers use this method to display images on their monitors. The newest cameras, such as the Sony NEX-7, also have the progressive scanning option. If you see the letter "p" with an fps number in your viewfinder or on the LCD screen, it stands for progressive scanning.

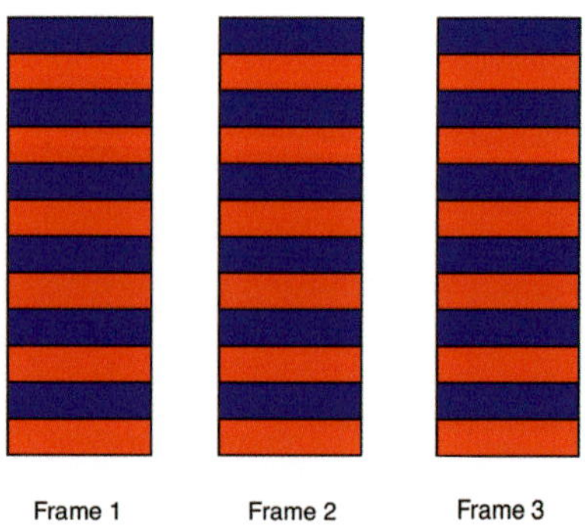


**Figure 11-3**: Progressive scanning format

This method is pretty straightforward. Basically, the movie camera and the display projector collect all the vertical lines of a frame in sequence and then display them all at once (figure 11-3). For a moving object, this provides a sharper display of its edges. If you had to deal with a single frame, that frame would provide the highest definition for regions that move from frame to frame. For image processing, this is the preferred image type.

Progressive scanning is considered the ultimate in image quality. However, it has one peculiarity. Because of the sharpness of the individual images, movement during playback may not be perceived to flow as smoothly as with interlaced scanning. This is most apparent when you record at 24 fps with a fast shutter speed. If you look at the shutter speeds used when you take movies in Intelligent Auto, you will see that the camera tries to keep the shutter speed duration longer than 1/125 second when shooting at 60 fps. This is to ensure a smooth movement from frame to frame during playback. If you select a shutter speed of 1/1000 second, the motion appears strobe like. However, a single frame of a movie captured with progressive scanning will show a subject with high definition in those parts that are moving.

So, should you use interlaced or progressive scanning? For video editing, it is tempting to simply use the highest quality mode. However, an argument against this is that the slight blurring of moving edges with interlaced scanning helps hide the transition from frame to frame. The overall perception of movement looks better. In contrast, at the level of an individual frame, an image obtained with progressive scanning is sharper. For video editing you will probably opt for progressive scanning. If you are just viewing the movies and are not interested in using the freeze frame to study fine details, then most people will be satisfied with interlaced scanning. Experiment with each and decide which you prefer.

### Bit Rate and Frame Rate

AVCHD and MP4 files are highly compressed. The amount of data that is preserved is determined by the amount of data being processed—the more data being processed, the more fine detail is being preserved. In computing, the measure of data being processed is called bit rate (bits/second). In the case of a movie, so much information is processed that you need to express the data in terms of millions of bits per second, or Mbps (megabits per second). The Sony NEX-7 processes movies from 28 Mbps (highest quality) to 3 Mbps (lowest quality).

These data rates reflect the fact that movies are a sequential series of images recorded at different frame rates. AVCHD files recorded at the highest frame rate, 60 fps, generate the greatest amount of data and have the highest Mbps value.

So, which file format should you chose? There is no clear answer to this question, simply because it depends on what you plan to do with your movies. If you intend to view the files directly on your TV or make them into playable DVDs, then select AVCHD and use the highest recording quality your playback device will support. If you like to use the freeze frame and carefully study the details in the individual frame, then you should use the highest Mbps data. Also, the highest values are useful for video editing.

Remember, if you decide to use PMB and burn your movies to a DVD, you must record at 24p 17 Mbps or 60i 17 Mbps. For recording to a Blu-ray Disc, you can take advantage of your camera's capabilities and record using the higher-quality record settings.

### AVCHD Record Setting Command

The AVCHD Record Setting is one of the more complicated commands. When you select the AVCHD file format, you will see an extensive range of options. The command for selecting the movie quality, for cameras sold in the United States, is as follows:

> MENU>Image Size (Movie)>Record Setting>[60i 24M(FX)], [60i 17M(FH)], [60p 28M(PS)], [24p 24M(FX)], [24p 17M(FH)]

Most of these options may appear cryptic to a still photographer, but the selections can be summarized by their bit rates (table 11-3). The maximum quality is 28 Mbps, which is described as [60p 28M (PS)]. Referring to the glossary in table 11-1, this translates into a format that is recording at 60 frames per second in progressive mode, with 28 megabits of data per second being recorded. You may wish to contrast [60p 28M (PS)] with the next highest resolution mode, [60i 24M (FX)]. The difference between these file formats can be subtle if your goal is to observe the movie stream on your television. The individual frames will have sharper edges on moving objects when they are taken in 60p instead of 60i (figure 11-4). Remember, "i" stands for interlaced scanning, where two fields are interlaced to form a single frame.

The 24p frame rate is referred to as cinematic because it is used in theatrical motion pictures. If your subjects are rapidly moving about—for example, at a sports event—we would not recommend this frame rate. You will get better results if you use 60p fps, which renders rapid motion more realistically by gathering more images. At 24p fps, you may find that the playback looks jittery. This may be even more apparent if you select a very short shutter speed, which freezes the subject's motion in the individual frame. However, for an artistic rendition of a scene and to present a movie that looks like a Hollywood director created it, feel free to use 24p.

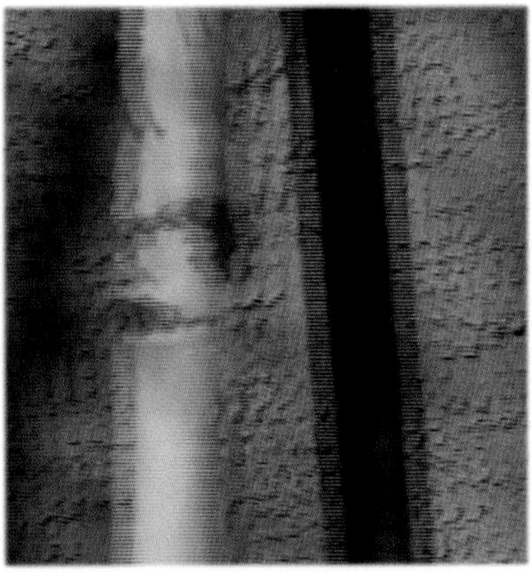

**Figure 11-4**: An artifact of interlaced scanning. The edges are blurred when the camera pans across a stationary object.

### MP4 Record Setting Command

When you select MP4 for your file format, you will have two Record Setting command options to choose from. The one you select depends on the number of pixels you wish to display (table 11-4).

MENU>Image Size (Movie)>Record Setting>[1440x1080 12M], [VGA 3M]

| File Format = [MP4] | | |
|---|---|---|
| **Record Setting Value** | **Average Bit Rate** | **Movie Recording Size** |
| 1440 x 1080 12M | 12 Mbps | 1440 x 1080 |
| VGA 3M | 3 Mbps | VGA (640 x 480) |

**Table 11-4**: MP4 Record setting values

The first option, [1440x1080 12M], is easy to understand; your pixel array will be 1440 x 1080 pixels. The second option, [VGA 3M], is a bit cryptic. The letters VGA refer to an old monitor resolution standard, Video Graphics Array, that had a 640 x 480 pixel array. VGA provides a much smaller movie frame and generates a small movie file that can be emailed.

## Additional Movie Controls

There are some additional controls available when you record movies. The first is whether you want to record sound with your movie. Normally the answer is yes. Since audio tracks can be removed later through editing, you can always capture the audio and then decide later whether to keep it. To select audio recording, use the following command:

MENU>Setup (Shooting Settings)>Movie Audio Rec>[On], [Off]

If you are recording on a windy day, the camera microphone can pick up the distracting sound of the wind. To reduce this annoyance, you can invoke a wind noise reduction feature. Use the following command:

MENU>Setup (Shooting Settings)>Wind Noise Reduct.>[On], [Off]

We recommend selecting [Off] for Wind Noise Reduct. when you are recording indoors. Set it to [On] only when you shoot outdoors and there is a noticeable wind noise. Otherwise you may cut down on the quality of your audio recording.

## Framing and Starting the Movie

The Sony NEX-7 Live View is set at a 3:2 aspect ratio for still photography. When you press the Movie button, you will find that your display screen changes appearance. Basically, the field of view becomes smaller, and your frame drops to a 16:9 aspect ratio. This can be disconcerting if you carefully framed your subject before starting recording. To ensure that you get accurate framing before you press the Movie button, change your screen so it shows grid lines as discussed in chapter 3. If you do this, you will see a set of four marks within the display that indicate the corners of your movie screen (figure 11-5). If you frame your subject within these marks, you can see what will be in your movie.

After you frame your scene, you can start recording with a single press of the Movie button. The maximum length of a single recording session is 30 minutes for AVCHD files.

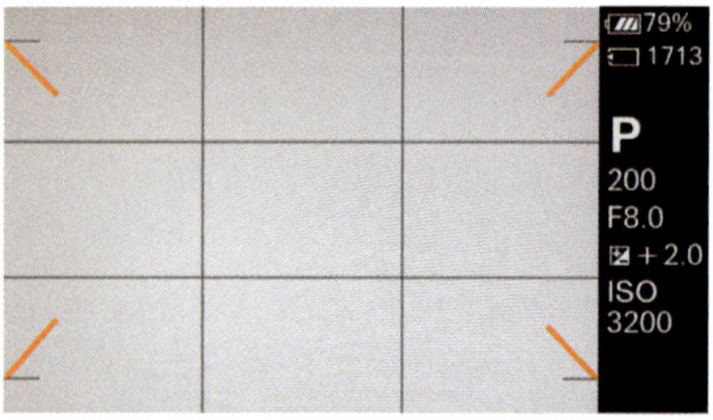


**Figure 11-5**: The arrows point to the edges of the movie frame

## P, A, S, or M for Controlling your Recording

When you shift from Intelligent Auto to P, A, S, or M mode, you gain control of your aperture, shutter speed, ISO, WB, and Exposure Compensation settings. You can also give your movie a unique appearance by using the Creative Style or Picture Effect options.

To use one of these shooting modes, execute the following command and select one of the options:

Menu>Shoot Mode>[P], [A], [S], [M]

Basically, P mode (Program Priority) is fully automated, and the camera selects both the aperture and the shutter speed. The A mode (Aperture Priority) is used for selecting the lens aperture and controlling the depth of field. The S mode (Shutter Priority) is used for selecting the shutter speed and determining how much you wish to freeze the motion in the movie frame. The M mode (Manual) is used to adjust both the aperture and the shutter speed.

Changing the shutter speed can be useful to avoid the flickering caused by recording under fluorescent lights. Fluorescent bulbs have a cyclic output with a frequency that can, at certain shutter speeds, cause a distracting brightening or fading in the movie. If this occurs, try selecting a shorter or longer shutter speed to remove this effect. You might find that adjusting the shutter speed to 1/100 or 1/125 second will record more uniform lighting. Also, by using M or S mode, you can select a very long shutter speed (up to 0.25 second). This can create an artistic effect where motion is recorded as a blur and moving objects have ghostly images trailing behind them.

## Adding Creative Style, Picture Effect, or DRO

Since PMB does not allow you to digitally enhance your recorded movies, you will find the Creative Style, Picture Effect, and DRO commands highly useful. You can create movies with modern, supersaturated color or old-fashioned sepia. If you wish to create a film noir effect, you can record in black and white. In order to use Picture Effect, make sure that you set Quality to [Fine] before starting to record a movie.

The Picture Effect command is not available if Quality is set to record RAW files. Creative Style is more forgiving because it can be set in either RAW or JPEG. Under extremely harsh lighting conditions that produce deep shadows, DRO can lighten the shadows and reveal details within them. Using this command effectively requires some practice, and there are no rules to guide you.

## Recommendations

We enjoy taking movies with the Sony NEX-7. In some cases, we have planned carefully prior to recording and meticulously executed the movie with the camera mounted on a tripod. In other cases, we have acted on an impromptu desire to record an event by handholding the camera. In both cases, the Sony NEX-7 has performed well.

For the most satisfying and professional-looking movies, you should mount the camera on a tripod. Although you can certainly create a pleasing movie without this accessory, failing to use a tripod may result in a movie where the subject appears to bounce up and down within the frame. The resulting movie may look unpolished and unprofessional, especially if you intend to distribute the results.

Do not be afraid to work with AVCHD. If you take short movie recordings, you should be able to easily edit these files on your computer. In the case of Mac computers, you will have to buy additional software; however, the cost is nominal. You can download iMovie '11 for $15; however, at the time of this writing, the program would not read the highest-quality (60p 28 Mbps) recording from the Sony NEX-7. If you own a PC, be sure to load Sony's supplied program, PMB, and use it to work with AVCHD files and create DVDs.

If you simply want to dive in and play and edit your movies on your computer, then use the MP4 file format. Using this format is straightforward and requires minimal software and hardware upgrades, in comparison to the AVCHD format.

# Appendix A: Menu and Function Commands

This appendix lists all of the Sony NEX-7 menu commands in order of the camera's six main menu groups, moving from top left to bottom right: Shoot Mode, Camera, Image Size, Brightness/Color, Playback, and Setup. Both the Image Size and Setup menus also have submenus, which appear on a separate line within a set of parentheses.

The list is broken into sections with the menu name—and if applicable, the submenu listed in parentheses—identified at the beginning of the associated commands. Each command is listed along with a description and useful information. The commands' available options and their descriptions are listed below the command. **Please note that the commands' default options are bolded**.

Example 1 shows the AEL command within the Setup's Shooting Settings submenu. The AEL command has two options: [Hold] and [Toggle], where [Hold] is the default.

### Example 1

| **Setup (Shooting Settings)** | | |
|---|---|---|
| **Command** | **Description** | |
| AEL. | Controls how the camera's recommended exposure will be retained when the AEL button is pressed.<br>Function is enabled only when AF/MF/AEL lever is switched to AEL, enabling the button to utilize the AEL command's setting. | |
| | **Hold** | The camera will retain the exposure for as long as the AEL button is depressed. Every recorded picture will use the set exposure as long as you continue to hold down the AEL button. |
| | Toggle | The camera will retain the exposure even when the AEL button is released. Each time the button is pressed, the camera will reevaluate the exposure, change it if necessary, and retain the new exposure until it has been pressed again. In other words, the button acts as a toggle between saved exposure settings. |

A few of the commands have subcommands. The subcommand options are listed and then further broken out with their individual options. Example 2 shows the first part of the Slide Show command, with Repeat and Interval subcommands displayed. Note that the Repeat subcommand has two options: [On] and [Off], where [Off] is the default. The Interval subcommand has five options, where [3 Sec] is the default.

## Example 2

<table>
<tr><th colspan="4">Playback</th></tr>
<tr><th>Command</th><th colspan="3">Description</th></tr>
<tr><td rowspan="10">Slide Show</td><td colspan="3">Displays still images stored on the memory card in sequence as a slide show. Press soft key B to initiate slide show using the [Repeat], [Interval], and [Image Type] values.<br>Command is disabled when the memory card does not contain still pictures.</td></tr>
<tr><td rowspan="3">Repeat</td><td colspan="2">Determines if the slide show runs through the images once or loops continuously.</td></tr>
<tr><td>On</td><td>Slide show loops continuously through the images.</td></tr>
<tr><td>Off</td><td>Plays the images once and stops.</td></tr>
<tr><td rowspan="6">Interval</td><td colspan="2">Controls the time each still picture is displayed.</td></tr>
<tr><td>1 Sec</td><td>Displays each picture for 1 second.</td></tr>
<tr><td>3 Sec</td><td>Displays each picture for 3 seconds.</td></tr>
<tr><td>5 Sec</td><td>Displays each picture for 5 seconds.</td></tr>
<tr><td>10 Sec</td><td>Displays each picture for 10 seconds.</td></tr>
<tr><td>30 Sec</td><td>Displays each picture for 30 seconds.</td></tr>
</table>

Use this list as a dictionary and quick reference of a command's function and location. Many of the commands are covered in detail in the chapters, so think of this as an index for reviewing the commands.

## Sony NEX-7 Menu Commands

<table>
<tr><th colspan="4">Shoot Mode</th></tr>
<tr><th>Command</th><th colspan="3">Description</th></tr>
<tr><td>Manual Exposure</td><td colspan="3">The camera allows you to set both the shutter speed and the aperture value manually.</td></tr>
<tr><td>Shutter Priority</td><td colspan="3">The camera automatically sets the aperture and allows you to set the shutter speed manually.</td></tr>
<tr><td>Aperture Priority</td><td colspan="3">The camera automatically sets the shutter speed and allows you to you adjust the aperture value manually.</td></tr>
<tr><td>Program Auto</td><td colspan="3">The camera automatically synchronizes the shutter speed and aperture setting for the exposure and allows you to select different combinations.</td></tr>
<tr><td>Intelligent Auto</td><td colspan="3">The camera evaluates the framed image and attempts to identify the scene type to find the best picture-taking mode and exposure.</td></tr>
<tr><td rowspan="5">SCN</td><td colspan="3">The camera allows you to select a specific predefined scene mode. The camera evaluates the shooting conditions based on the selected mode and applies the appropriate settings.</td></tr>
<tr><td></td><td>Portrait</td><td>Use when you want to focus on people's faces. This mode enables the Face Detection/Registration function. The detected face(s) acquires focus while the background is blurred with an open aperture to reduce the depth of field. The skin tones are softened.</td></tr>
<tr><td></td><td>Landscape</td><td>Use when photographing distant objects outdoors. The camera closes down the aperture to increase the depth of field.</td></tr>
<tr><td></td><td>Macro</td><td>Use when the subject is close to the camera. The definition of "close" depends on the lens. For the DT 18–55mm zoom lens, the minimum focusing distance is 25 cm (about 10 inches). Generally image is recorded at 1/10 life size or larger. Since any camera movement will affect the picture this close to the subject, use a tripod for the best results.</td></tr>
<tr><td></td><td>Sports Action</td><td>Use when taking pictures of a moving subject. Object Tracking is enabled. The camera is set to a fast shutter speed and a higher ISO to freeze the subject's motion. The camera is set to fire continuously when the shutter is fully depressed, and continuous focus is used to keep subject in focus as it moves.</td></tr>
</table>

| Shoot Mode – (con't) | | | |
|---|---|---|---|
| **Command** | **Description** | | |
| | | Sunset | Use when taking pictures of sunrises or sunsets. This mode enhances the image's red and orange tones. |
| | | Night Portrait | Use when shooting a portrait in a nighttime environment. Face Detection/Registration is enabled. The shutter speed is reduced to capture more light on the sensor; therefore, use a tripod for the best results. |
| | | Night Scene | Use when taking nighttime pictures . The camera's shutter speed is opened longer to capture more light on the sensor. Use a tripod for the best results. |
| | | Hand-held Twilight | Use this mode when shooting night scenes without a tripod. The camera takes a number of shots and uses built-in image processing software to combine them into a single image to reduce image noise and blur (due to low light and camera shake, respectively). This option only produces JPEG files. If you have the Quality command set to RAW or RAW & JPEG, the camera automatically changes the file to JPEG Fine.<br>Your results can be marred: if the subject has too little contrast, making it difficult for the software to merge multiple images; if the subject moves significantly during the capture sequence; or if the image has repeating patterns that create a moiré effect, much like you sometimes see with flickering light sources like TVs, computer screens, or fluorescent lighting. |
| Anti Motion Blur | Fires multiple shots to provide noise reduction for low-light shooting. You can adjust the image's exposure using the Exposure Compensation tool, unlike [Hand-held Twilight]. | | |
| Sweep Panorama | The camera builds a horizontal or vertical composite panoramic image. | | |
| 3D Sweep Panorama | The camera builds a horizontal 3-D composite panoramic image. | | |

<table>
<tr><th colspan="6">Camera</th></tr>
<tr><th>Command</th><th colspan="5">Description</th></tr>
<tr><td rowspan="11">Drive Mode</td><td colspan="5">Determines how the camera will fire to capture the picture(s).</td></tr>
<tr><td></td><td>Single Shoot-ing</td><td colspan="3">Camera fires one shot per press of the shutter button.</td></tr>
<tr><td></td><td>Cont. Shooting</td><td colspan="3">Camera shoots continuously at three shots /second as long as the shutter button is held down and the memory card has room to store the images. Camera maintains the selected fir-ing rate until the buffer is filled. Exposure and focus are updated during the series and takes place between shots.</td></tr>
<tr><td>S</td><td>Spd Priority Cont.</td><td colspan="3">Records continuously at 10 shots/second as long as the shutter button is held down and the memory card has room to store the images. Camera maintains the selected firing rate until the buffer is filled. Focus and expo-sure are set at the start of the series.</td></tr>
<tr><td rowspan="3"></td><td rowspan="3">Self-timer</td><td colspan="3">Delays firing the camera after the shutter but-ton is pressed.</td></tr>
<tr><td>10<br>(Default)</td><td colspan="2">Uses a 10-second delay. Use this option when you need to get into a group shot.</td></tr>
<tr><td>2</td><td colspan="2">Uses a 2-second delay. Use this option when you don't have a remote release and you want to ensure that the camera does not move when you press the shutter button.</td></tr>
<tr><td rowspan="3">C</td><td rowspan="3">Self-timer (Cont.)</td><td colspan="3">Delays firing the camera after the shutter but-ton is pressed, and then fires a continuous set of shots.</td></tr>
<tr><td>C3<br>(Default)</td><td colspan="2">Delays firing for 10 seconds and then fires three shots.</td></tr>
<tr><td>C5</td><td colspan="2">Delays firing for 10 seconds and then fires five shots.</td></tr>
</table>

**Camera – (con't)**

| Command | Description | | | |
|---|---|---|---|---|
| | BRK C | Bracket: Cont. | | To activate, press and hold down the shutter button. This function takes a series of three shots with the EV varied +/– by the selected amount. |
| | | | 0.3EV | Takes three shots, where the first shot is recorded with the base exposure, then -0.3EV then +0.3EV exposures. |
| | | | 0.7EV | Takes three shots where the first shot is recorded with the base exposure, then –0.7EV then +0.7EV exposures. |
| | | Remote Cdr. | | When this option is selected, the camera expects the shutter to be released with a Wireless Remote Control. Sony sells a remote control unit that works for the Sony NEX-7. This allows you to be away from the camera when initiating a shot. |
| Flash Mode | Determines how and when the flash unit will fire when capturing a picture. You must first raise the flash head manually for the flash unit to fire. | | | |
| | | Flash Off | | Prevents the flash unit from firing. This option is disabled in P, A, S, M, and the following SCN predefined modes: Night Scene, Hand-held Twilight, and Night Portrait. |
| | AUTO | Auto-flash | | The camera decides when the flash is needed. You must first manually pop up the flash unit so the camera can fire it in low-light levels. This option is enabled only in Intelligent Auto and the following SCN predefined modes: Portrait and Macro. |
| | | Fill-flash | | When this option is selected, the flash always fires, providing light to the subject. This option is available only in P, A, S, M, and the following SCN predefined modes: Portrait, Sports Action, Macro, Landscape, and Sunset. |
| | SLOW | Slow Sync. | | Use this option with a slow shutter speed. The flash goes off and the camera's shutter speed is prolonged to capture the background that is not illuminated by the flash. This option is only available in P, A, S, and M modes. |

A

| Camera – (con't) | | | |
|---|---|---|---|
| **Command** | **Description** | | |
| | ϟ REAR | Rear Sync. | The flash goes off at the end of the exposure just before the second shutter curtain closes. If the subject moves during the exposure, it can be recorded as a blur. When the flash discharges, the subject will be frozen in position with a blur extending opposite its direction of movement.<br>This option is only available in P, A, S, and M modes. |
| | ϟ WL | Wireless | This option requires a Sony external flash unit that is capable of wireless triggering. When such a flash is attached, it will send a pulse of light to trigger the firing of other external flash units.<br>This option is only available in P, A, S, and M modes. |
| AF/MF Select | Used to select the autofocusing method for the camera to use. | | |
| | **AF** | Autofocus | Sets the camera to autofocus capability. |
| | DMF | DMF | Direct Manual Focus works as a combination of autofocus and then manual focus. After the camera has locked focus on the subject, the focusing ring of the lens is engaged and you can manually adjust the focus. Autofocus Mode must be set to Single-shot AF. If the camera doesn't obtain autofocus, the focusing ring is not enabled. |
| | MF | Manual Focus | Sets the camera to use manual focus only. Note that the Peaking function is not activated when the camera is using Autofocus. |
| Autofocus Area | Used to set the area where autofocusing will occur within the framed image. | | |
| | | **Multi** | The camera determines which of the 25 autofocus areas will be used for focusing. When you frame a still image, press the shutter button halfway. A green bracket is displayed around the areas that are in focus.<br>The Face Detection command must use this option. |

**Camera – (con't)**

| Command | Description | | |
|---|---|---|---|
| | [ ] | Center | The camera uses the center of the framed image exclusively for the focusing area.<br>Note that the size of the center is slightly larger than the center spot in the Flexible Spot option.<br>Face Detection is disabled when the Autofocus Area is set to [Center]. |
| | [•] | Flexible Spot | Gives you the flexibility of selecting a specific spot for the camera to establish focus. Press the rims of the control wheel to access up to 187 (17 columns by 11 rows) spots within the framed image. You can rotate the control wheel or the left or right control dials to rapidly move through the various spots.<br>Press soft key B to return the focusing area back to the center of the screen.<br>Face Detection is disabled when Autofocus Area is set to [Flexible Spot]. |
| Autofocus Mode | Determines if the camera will focus once and lock focus or continuously refocus when needed while the shutter button is held down. | | |
| | AF-S | **Single-shot AF** | When focus is locked, the camera won't try to refocus as long as you keep the shutter button depressed. Best used on stationary subjects. |
| | AF-C | Continuous AF | The camera will continue to find focus as long as you hold down the shutter button. Use this option when the subject is moving. |
| Object Tracking | The camera locks onto a subject and tracks it as it moves within the framed image and continuously refocuses to keep the subject in focus. | | |
| | OFF | **Off** | Disables Object Tracking functionality. |
| | ON | On | Enables Object Tracking functionality. |
| Prec. Dig. Zoom | Digitally zooms into a recorded image. This takes the center of the screen and then interpolates the pixels to generate a 24 megapixel image. Starts generating a 1.1x image and can provide up to a 10x image. This option works only with JPEG files. It is disabled for modes in which multiple images are taken and merged into one image. | | |
| | From 1.1x to 10x times with 0.1 increments. Use the right or left control dials to increase or decrease the zoom. | | |

| Camera – (con't) | | | |
|---|---|---|---|
| **Command** | **Description** | | |
| Face Detection | Allows the camera to detect and focus on faces within a framed image. | | |
| | | **On (Regist. Faces)** | Activates Face Detection and prioritizes focus for registered faces.<br>Face Detection is automatically set to this value when Smile Shutter is on. |
| | | On | Activates Face Detection but does not use registered faces to establish focus prioritization. |
| | | Off | Deactivates Face Detection. The camera does not attempt to identify a face in the framed image unless you select it as an object for tracking.<br>Face Detection is unavailable in shooting modes that involve recording more than one image: Sweep Panorama, 3D Sweep Panorama, Anti Motion Blur, and the SCN Handheld Twilight shooting mode. |
| Face Registration | Allows you to register and maintain up to eight faces in the camera for autofocus preferences. | | |
| | New Registration | | Allows you to register new faces one at a time for up to eight total. |
| | Order Exchanging | | Allows you to change the registered faces' prioritization. |
| | Delete | | Allows you to delete a single registered face. |
| | Delete All | | Allows you to delete all registered faces at one time. |
| Smile Shutter | Triggers the shutter when a smile is detected on at least one face. The camera needs to detect only one smiling face, regardless of whether the person is registered.<br>The size of the smile is subjective. The camera seems to trigger the shutter when there is any change to a person's mouth-related facial expressions.<br>This command is disabled for continuous shooting modes and modes where multiple images are taken and merged into one image. | | |
| | | Off | Does not attempt to identify whether smile occurred. |
| | | On: Slight Smile | Triggers the shutter when a slight smile is detected. |

A

**Camera – (con't)**

| Command | Description | | |
|---|---|---|---|
| | | **On: Normal Smile** (Default when Smile Shutter is On) | Triggers the shutter when a normal smile is detected. |
| | | On: Big Smile | Triggers the shutter when a big, full smile is detected. |
| Soft Skin Effect | Softens details in areas of low contrast while retaining detail in the areas of high-contrast. Will remove small skin blemishes such as fine wrinkles.<br>This command is disabled in the Sweep Panorama, 3D Sweep Panorama Anti Motion Blur modes, RAW files, and Movie recordings. | | |
| | OFF | **Off** | Deactivates the Soft Skin Effect command. |
| | LO | On: Low | Sets the intensity to Low. |
| | MID | **On: Mid** (Default when Soft Skin Effect is On) | Sets the intensity to Medium. |
| | HI | On: High | Sets the intensity to High. |
| LCD Display (DISP) | Used to select one option from a list of display formats. The selected data display format is displayed on the LCD screen when you exit the menu. Note that the LCD Display(DISP) value will reflect automatically in the data display format currently displayed at the time you selected this command.<br>The available options mimic the selected options in the DISP Button(Monitor) command. | | |
| | Graphic Display | Displays full-size image, major shooting settings, and two scales (shutter speed and aperture), each with its current setting indicated as a vertical bar. | |
| | Display All Info. | Displays full-size image with the camera shooting settings superimposed around three of the image's borders. | |

| Camera – (con't) | | |
|---|---|---|
| **Command** | **Description** | |
| | Big Font Size Disp. | Displays full-size image and the minimal shooting settings displayed in a larger font than the other data display formats. The data is superimposed on the top and bottom of the image. |
| | No Disp. Info. | Displays full-size image, Shoot Mode, and exposure settings only. |
| | Live View Priority | Displays full-size image, Shoot Mode, and the exposure settings displayed in a vertical bar on the right side of the screen. The soft key button icons are not displayed. |
| | Level | Displays full-size image, Shoot Mode, exposure settings, plus the digital level gauge tool in the center of the screen. The digital level gauge's indicator turns green when the camera is level both horizontally and front to back. |
| | Histo-gram | Displays full-size image, Shoot Mode, exposure settings, plus the live white histogram in the lower right of the display screen. |
| | For view-finder | Displays only the camera shooting settings. |
| Finder Display (DISP) | Allows you to select from a list of three data display formats that can be applied to the viewfinder when previewing an image. | |
| | Disp. Basic Info. | Displays image with the camera exposure settings on the top and bottom outside of the image border. |
| | Level | Displays image plus the camera exposure settings on the top and bottom outside of the image border and the digital level gauge tool in the center of the screen. The digital level gauge indicator turns green when the camera is level both horizontally and front to back. |
| | Histo-gram | Displays image plus the camera exposure settings on the top and bottom outside of the image border, and the live white histogram in the lower right of the display screen. |

| Camera – (con't) | | |
|---|---|---|
| **Command** | **Description** | |
| DISP Button (Monitor) | Allows you to select from a list of eight data display formats that can be applied to the LCD screen to preview your images. Use the DISP button (top rim of the control wheel) to cycle through each selected data display format.<br>To apply your selections, back out of the command using soft key A. If you exit the command via another method, such as pressing the shutter button, your changes to the selected data display formats are not accepted.<br>Note that each time you press the DISP button and scroll to the next data display format, the LCD Display(DISP) command value will change to reflect the currently displayed format. | |
| | Graphic Display | Displays full-size image, major shooting settings, and two scales (shutter speed and aperture), each with its current setting indicated as a vertical bar. |
| | **Display All Info.** | Displays full-size image with the camera shooting settings superimposed around three of the image's borders. |
| | Big Font Size Disp. | Displays full-size image and the minimal shooting settings displayed in a large font superimposed on the top and bottom of the image. |
| | **No Disp. Info.** | Displays full-size image, Shoot Mode, and exposure settings only. |
| | Live View Priority | Displays full-size image, Shoot Mode, and the exposure settings displayed in a vertical bar on the right side of the screen. The soft key button icons are not displayed. |
| | **Level** | Displays full-size image, Shoot Mode, exposure settings, plus the digital level gauge tool in the center of the screen. The digital level gauge's indicator turns green when the camera is level both horizontally and front to back. |
| | **Histogram** | Displays full-size image, Shoot Mode, exposure settings, plus the live white histogram in the lower right of the display screen. |
| | For viewfinder | Displays only the camera shooting settings. |

| Image Size (Still) | | |
|---|---|---|
| **Command** | **Description** | |
| Image Size | Defines the image size in pixels. Different values are presented based on the selected Aspect Ratio value. Works only on JPEG files. RAW file sizes are constant at 6000 x 4000 pixels. | |
| | When Aspect Ratio = [3:2] | |
| | **L: 24M** | 6000 x 4000 equivalent pixels |
| | M: 12M | 4240 x 2832 equivalent pixels |
| | S: 6.0M | 3008 x 2000 equivalent pixels |
| | When Aspect Ratio = [16:9] | |
| | **L: 20M** | 6000 x 3376 equivalent pixels |
| | M: 10M | 4240 x 2400 equivalent pixels |
| | S: 5.1M | 3008 x 1688 equivalent pixels |
| Aspect Ratio | Specifies the image's width-to-height ratio. | |
| | **3:2** | Represents a width of 3 units to a height of 2 units. This is the default still picture ratio. |
| | 16:9 | Represents a width of 16 units to a height of 9 units. This is the default movie frame ratio. |
| Quality | Sets the still image's file format.<br>RAW files contain all of the image data with minimal to no changes. JPEG files are compressed, modified, or changed. Note that the Image Size command for individual image sizes and equivalent pixels applies only to JPEG files. | |
| | RAW | The data is stored with minimal digital processing. Contains more data than JPEG file types.<br>File extension is ARW. |
| | RAW & JPEG | Two files are created: RAW and JPEG Fine. The RAW file is stored with minimal digital processing. The JPEG file is more compressed than RAW, and its image reflects the results of the camera's digital processing.<br>File extensions are ARW and JPG. |
| | Fine | The JPEG default compression rate, with an intermediate degree of compression and retention of image detail.<br>File extension is JPG. |
| | Standard | The highest compression rate of the two JPEG file types. Can lose fine detail.<br>File extension is JPG. |

| **Image Size – (con't) (3D Panorama)** | | |
|---|---|---|
| **Command** | **Description** | |
| Image Size | Determines the size of a 3-D panoramic picture. Command is enabled only when shooting mode is set to 3D Sweep Panorama. | |
| | 16:9 | 3-D panorama picture size is 1920 x 1080 pixels. |
| | **Standard** | 3-D panorama picture size is 4912 x 1080 pixels. |
| | Wide | 3-D panorama picture size is 7152 x 1080 pixels. |
| Panorama Direction | Defines the direction to pan the camera when executing a 3D Sweep Panorama. Command is enabled only when Shoot Mode is set to 3D Sweep Panorama. | |
| | Right | Pan the camera from left to right. |
| | Left | Pan the camera from right to left. |
| **(Panorama)** | | |
| Image Size | Determines the size of a 3-D panoramic picture. Command is enabled only when shooting mode is set to 3D Sweep Panorama. | |
| | **Standard** | When Panorama Direction = [Right] or [Left]: |
| | | 2-D panorama picture size is 8192 x 1856 pixels. |
| | Wide | When Panorama Direction = [Up] or [Down]: |
| | | 2-D panorama picture size is 3872 x 2160 pixels. |
| Panorama Direction | Defines the direction to pan the camera when executing a Sweep Panorama. Command is enabled only when the Shoot Mode is set to Sweep Panorama. | |
| | **Right** | Pan camera from left to right. |
| | Left | Pan camera from right to left. |
| | Up | Pan camera upward from the bottom. |
| | Down | Pan camera downward from the top. |

A

| (Movie) | | |
|---|---|---|
| File Format | Defines the file format for storing movie files. Note: Your camera will either show [AVCHD 60i/60p] or [AVCHD 50i/50p] but not both, depending on the country where your camera was made. | |
| | **AVCHD 60i/60p or AVCHD 50i/50p** | US standard: Records movies in AVCHD using either interlaced or progressive scanning at either 60 frames/second (fps) or 24 fps. European standard: Records movies in AVCHD at either 50 fps using interlaced or progressive scanning (50i) or 25 fps using progressive scanning (25p). |
| | MP4 | Records movies in MPEG-4 format at 30 fps. These MP4 movies are suitable for attaching to e-mails and uploading to websites. |
| Record Setting | | |
| | When File Format = [AVCHD 60i/60p]/[AVCHD 50i/50p] | |
| | 60i 24(FX) or 50i 24(FX) | Average bit rate = 24 Mbps<br>Records high-quality movies, 1920 x 1080 pixels at 60i/50i fps. |
| | **60i 17M(FH) or 50i 17M(FH)** | Average bit rate = 17 Mbps<br>Records standard-quality movies, 1920 x 1080 pixels at 60i/50i fps. |
| | 60p 28M(PS) or 50p 28M(PS) | Average bit rate = 28 Mbps<br>Records highest-quality movies, 1920 x 1080 pixels at 60p/50p fps. |
| | 24p 24M(FX) or 25p 24M(FX) | Average bit rate = 24 Mbps<br>Records high-quality movies, 1920 x 1080 pixels at 24p/25p fps (cinema-like movies). |
| | 24p 17M(FH) or 25p 17M(FH) | Average bit rate = 17 Mbps<br>Records standard-quality movies, 1920 x 1080 pixels at 24p/25p fps (cinema-like movies). |
| | When File Format = [MP4] | |
| | 1440x1080 12M | Average bit rate = 12 Mbps<br>Records 1440 x 1080 pixel movies. |
| | VGA 3M | Average bit rate = 3 Mbps<br>Records 640 x 480 pixel movies. |

<table>
<tr><th colspan="4">Brightness/Color</th></tr>
<tr><th>Command</th><th colspan="3">Description</th></tr>
<tr><td rowspan="2">Exposure Comp.</td><td colspan="3">Allows you to adjust the exposure by one-third EV (Exposure Value) increments.</td></tr>
<tr><td colspan="3">When the command is selected, a curved vertical scale displays at the right side of the display screen with tick marks ranging from -5 EV to +5 EV. An orange circle is positioned at the current exposure compensation (default 0 EV). Rotate the control wheel counterclockwise to reduce exposure and clockwise to increase exposure. The orange circle will move 0.3 EV with each click of the control wheel.<br>The command is disabled in the Intelligent Auto, SCN, and manual focus modes.</td></tr>
<tr><td rowspan="3">ISO</td><td colspan="3">Specifies how sensitive the sensor is to light. The higher the ISO, the more sensitive the sensor is, allowing for a faster shutter speed to be set. The lower the ISO, the less noise recorded with the image.</td></tr>
<tr><td>ISO AUTO</td><td colspan="2">Allows the camera to determine its sensitivity to the light within the framed image. ISO ranges from 100-1600.</td></tr>
<tr><td>100, 200, 400, 800, 1600, 3200, 6400, 12800, and 16000</td><td colspan="2">Allows the user to specify the sensor's level of sensitivity to the light in the framed image.</td></tr>
<tr><td rowspan="7">White Balance</td><td colspan="3">Defines how the camera should interpret the available light and make adjustments due to the light source and surrounding environment.<br>Each option, except [Custom Set], has a submenu for you to assign blue, amber, green and magenta tints.</td></tr>
<tr><td>AWB</td><td>Auto WB</td><td>WB is set automatically by the camera.</td></tr>
<tr><td></td><td>Daylight</td><td>WB is set for the subject in direct sunlight.</td></tr>
<tr><td></td><td>Shade</td><td>WB is set for the subject positioned in the shade and not illuminated by direct sunlight.</td></tr>
<tr><td></td><td>Cloudy</td><td>WB is set for subject on a cloudy, overcast day where the Sun is hidden by the cloud cover.</td></tr>
<tr><td></td><td>Incandescent</td><td>WB is set for the subject illuminated by indoor light (assumes the light is tungsten filament).</td></tr>
<tr><td>-1</td><td>Fluor.: Warm White</td><td>WB is set for the subject illuminated by warm fluorescent light (3000 K).</td></tr>
</table>

**Brightness/Color – (con't)**

| Command | Description | | |
|---|---|---|---|
| | 0 | Fluor.: Cool White | WB is set for the subject illuminated by cool fluorescent light (4100 K). |
| | +1 | Fluor.: Day White | WB is set for the subject illuminated by day white fluorescent light (5000 K). |
| | +2 | Fluor.: Daylight | WB is set for the subject illuminated by daylight fluorescent light (6500 K). |
| | WB | Flash | WB is set for an electronic flash unit's light. Some yellow tints are added to enrich and warm up the picture. |
| | K | C.Temp. /Filter | Allows you to set the WB based on a specific color temperature value represented in K units (kelvin), so you can apply the effect of color compensation filters.<br>Your light bulbs should have a kelvin rating on the packaging.<br>Set the WB to that specific value with the following steps:<br>1. Navigate to the White Balance command.<br>2. Scroll through the option list by rotating control dial L. Select [C. Temp./Filter].<br>3. Press soft key B. The LCD screen will show the letter K opposite this button.<br>4. Scroll through the color temperature values by rotating control dial L.<br>5. Select the value matching the kelvin rating on the package. Press soft key C to select the value.<br>6. Exit out of the White Balance command. |
| | | Custom | Use this option for the custom WB setting. |
| | SET | Custom Setup | Use this option to set up the custom WB to be stored. |

| Brightness/Color – (con't) | | | |
|---|---|---|---|
| **Command** | **Description** | | |
| Metering Mode | Defines the method the camera will use to determine the available lighting and, therefore, the overall exposure. | | |
| | | Multi | The camera divides the framed image into multiple areas, measures the lighting in each, and determines an overall exposure.<br>Intelligent Auto, SCN, Movies, Face Detection and Smile Shutter can use only [Multi]. |
| | | Center | The camera biases its exposure on the central area and provides less emphasis on the periphery. |
| | | Spot | The camera uses only the center of the framed image to determine exposure. A faint circle displays on the screen indicating the area the camera will use. |
| Flash Comp. | Adjusts the light emitted from the flash to balance against the ambient light. Compensation is done in 0.3 EV increments in a range of -3.0 EV to +3.0 EV. The higher the EV, the more light generated by the flash. The lower the EV, the less light generated by the flash; therefore, the resulting image will be darker. | | |
| | Available EV changes are as follows: –3.0, –2.7, –2.3, –2.0, –1.7, –1.3, –1.0, –0.7, –0.3, 0.0, +0.3, +0.7, +1.0, +1.3, +1.7, +2.0, +2.3, +2.7, and +3.0. | | |
| DRO/Auto HDR | Allows you to reveal details in areas of shadows that would normally be rendered as black.<br>Dynamic Range Optimization (DRO) automatically optimizes the capture and recording of an image's brightness and contrast from one exposure.<br>High Dynamic Range (HDR) employs three exposures taken in rapid succession: one for recording highlights, one for recording midtones, and one for recording shadows. By combining the three images, it is possible to create a composite where shadows are lightened, highlights are darkened, while maintaining details in the midtones. | | |
| | D-R OFF | D-R Off | Disables DRO/Auto HDR function. |
| | DRO On | The DRO On icon (left) acts as a marker in this table and does not exist in the camera menu. The camera smoothes out the contrast between light and dark areas within the image, bringing out detail in shadows by lightening, and reducing bright, washed-out areas by darkening, so that fine details in both areas are more easily discerned. | |

| Brightness/Color – (con't) | | | |
|---|---|---|---|
| **Command** | **Description** | | |
| | | DRO AUTO (Default) | Executes DRO automatically when the image has deep shadows and bright highlights. The camera chooses what level to use to adjust the blacks and whites. |
| | | DRO Lvl 1 | Level 1: The least change to blacks and whites in the image. |
| | | DRO Lvl 2 | Level 2: The second least change to blacks and whites in the image. |
| | | DRO Lvl 3 | Level 3: The middle amount of change to blacks and whites in the image. |
| | | DRO Lvl 4 | Level 4: The second most change to blacks and whites in the image. |
| | | DRO Lvl 5 | Level 5: The most change to blacks and whites in the image. |
| | HDR On | The HDR On icon (left) acts as a marker in this table and does not exist in the camera menu. The camera shoots three images and saves two on the memory card: one with the proper exposure and another with a combined image consisting of three images, each with a different exposure (EV) to bring out detail, especially in the shadows and bright, washed-out areas. The process closely retains the subject's coloring.<br>HDR = High Dynamic Range | |
| | | HDR AUTO (Default) | The camera determines the best exposure (EV) value and automatically sets the EV for each of the three images based on the subject's contrast. |
| | | HDR 1.0EV | The camera brackets the three shots within a total ±1.0 EV range. |
| | | HDR 2.0EV | The camera brackets the three shots within a total ±2.0 EV range. |
| | | HDR 3.0EV | The camera brackets the three shots within a total ±3.0 EV range. |
| | | HDR 4.0EV | The camera brackets the three shots within a total ±4.0 EV range. |
| | | HDR 5.0EV | The camera brackets the three shots within a total ±5.0 EV range. |
| | | HDR 6.0EV | The camera brackets the three shots within a total ±6.0 EV range. |

A

**Brightness/Color – (con't)**

| Command | Description | | | |
|---|---|---|---|---|
| Picture Effect | Applies different effects involving color, intensity, and detail representation to only your JPEG images. Several of the options have suboptions, which allow you to further identify how the Picture Effect will be applied. | | | |
| | OFF | **Off** | Turns off Picture Effect. | |
| | Toy | Toy Camera | Creates an image appearing as if it were taken with a toy camera. Colors and shadowing are more pronounced with less smoothness and gradation. | |
| | | | Suboptions | Sets image color tone to one of the following options: [Normal], [Cool], [Warm], [Green], [Magenta]. |
| | Pop | Pop Color | Emphasizes color tones and makes them more vivid. | |
| | Pos | Posterization | Emphasizes primary colors; or, in the case of a black-and-white image, makes these two more pronounced. Creates a more contrasting, abstract look. | |
| | | | Suboptions | Select primary colors or black-and-white: [Color], [B&W]. |
| | Rtro | Retro Photo | Creates the image in an old-fashioned photo style using sepia and reduced contrast. | |
| | Sfth key | Soft High-key | Creates a softer and more ethereal image. | |
| | Part | Partial Color | Creates an image that retains one color and turns the rest of it black-and-white. Suboptions determine retained color. | |
| | | | Suboptions | Select retained color: [Red], [Green], [Blue], [Yellow]. |
| | HC BW | High Contrast Mono. | Creates a high-contrast black-and-white image. | |
| | Soft | Soft Focus | Creates a soft lighting effect. Suboptions set the effect intensity. | |
| | | | Suboptions | Set effect intensity: [Low], [Mid], [High]. |

<table>
<tr><th colspan="5">Brightness/Color – (con't)</th></tr>
<tr><th>Command</th><th colspan="4">Description</th></tr>
<tr><td rowspan="5"></td><td rowspan="2">Pntg</td><td rowspan="2">HDR Painting</td><td colspan="2">Takes three images and merges them to create an HDR image. The image colors and detail are heightened. Suboptions set the effect intensity.</td></tr>
<tr><td>Suboptions</td><td>Set effect intensity: [Low], [Mid], [High].</td></tr>
<tr><td>Rich BW</td><td>Rich-tone Mono.</td><td colspan="2">Takes three images and merges them to create an HDR image in black-and-white.</td></tr>
<tr><td rowspan="2">Mini</td><td rowspan="2">Miniature</td><td colspan="2">Creates an image with the main subject in focus and the background out of focus. Often used for miniature model images where the model is in focus and the background is not. Suboptions set focus area.</td></tr>
<tr><td>Suboptions</td><td>Set focus area: [Auto], [Top], [Middle(Horizontal)], [Bottom], [Right], [Middle(Vertical)], [Left].</td></tr>
<tr><td rowspan="8">Creative Style</td><td colspan="4">Applies different styles involving color to both RAW and JPEG images. Each of the Creative Style options, except B/W and Sepia, have three suboptions: Contrast, Saturation, and Sharpness. B/W and Sepia have only Contrast and Sharpness. Each of the suboptions can be adjusted within a -3 to +3 range.</td></tr>
<tr><td>Std.</td><td>Standard</td><td colspan="2">Default; captures image with natural coloration.</td></tr>
<tr><td>Vivid</td><td>Vivid</td><td colspan="2">Accentuates colors, making them stand out more.</td></tr>
<tr><td>Ntrl</td><td>Neutral</td><td colspan="2">Tones down colors, making them more subdued.</td></tr>
<tr><td>Clear</td><td>Clear</td><td colspan="2">Captures images in clear tones with fluid colors in highlighted areas. Good choice for radiant light.</td></tr>
<tr><td>Deep</td><td>Deep</td><td colspan="2">Enables intense coloration to stand out while maintaining color differentiation.</td></tr>
<tr><td>Light</td><td>Light</td><td colspan="2">Enables light color tones to brighten the scene, and increase contrast for better viewing.</td></tr>
<tr><td>Port.</td><td>Portrait</td><td colspan="2">Softens skin tones for a more pleasing effect.</td></tr>
</table>

| Brightness/Color – (con't) | | | |
|---|---|---|---|
| **Command** | **Description** | | |
| | Land. | Landscape | Heightens saturation, contrast, and sharpness to produce more vivid and crisp results. |
| | Sunset | Sunset | Accentuates existing tones and adds warm sunset/sunrise tones. |
| | Night | Night Scene | Accentuates contrast to capture an image closer to the actual night scene. |
| | Autm | Autumn leaves | Accentuates existing tones and adds warm red, orange, and yellow tones. |
| | B/W | Black & White | Transforms the image into black-and-white with gradations of gray. |
| | Sepia | Sepia | Transforms the image into old-fashioned sepia coloration. |
| | Icon | Fine Adjustment Option | Description |
| | | Contrast | Controls the intensity of highlights and shadows. Plus values increase highlight and shadow intensity, reduces white and black color variations, and gives the image a bolder, stronger look. A minus value reduces highlight and shadow intensity, increases white and black color variations, and gives the image a smoother overall look. |
| | | Saturation | Controls the richness of the colors. A plus value makes the colors bolder and accentuates them, giving the image more color. A minus value mutes and softens the colors, giving the image a more homogenous look. This adjustment option is not available for Black & White and Sepia options. |
| | | Sharpness | Controls edge definition. A +3 value heightens the edges, accentuating fine details and noise. A –3 value softens the edges, creating a more blended look and helps hide noise. |

| Playback | | |
|---|---|---|
| **Command** | **Description** | |
| Delete | Allows you to delete one, many, or all unprotected images within a selected folder. The selected folder is determined by the file type of the last viewed or recorded image. To change the selected folder, use the MENU>Playback>View Mode command.<br>The Delete command will be disabled when there are no files within the selected folder. | |
| | **Multiple Img.** | Default option display, regardless of the current file type, as long as there is at least one file within the current folder stored on the memory card.<br>Displays one image at a time with its associated delete check box. Scroll through individual images using the control wheel or either of the two control dials. Press soft key C to check or uncheck the delete box. When all files have been identified for deletion, press soft key B and then soft key C to confirm, or press soft key A to exit. |
| | All in Folder | Displays only in the still picture or MP4 view when there is at least one still picture or MP4 file stored on the memory card.<br>Displays a confirmation screen to delete all of the images in the folder. Select soft key B (OK) to delete; select soft key A (Exit) to exit the process. |
| | All AVCHD view files | Displays only in the AVCHD movie view when there is at least one AVCHD movie file stored on the memory card.<br>Displays a confirmation screen to delete all images in the folder. Select soft key B (OK) to delete; select soft key A (Exit) to exit the process. |

<table>
<tr><th colspan="4">Playback – (con't)</th></tr>
<tr><th>Command</th><th colspan="3">Description</th></tr>
<tr><td rowspan="13">Slide Show</td><td colspan="3">Displays still images stored on the memory card in sequence as a slide show. Press soft key B to initiate slide show using the [Repeat], [Interval], and [Image Type] values.<br>This command is disabled when the memory card does not contain still pictures.</td></tr>
<tr><td rowspan="3">Repeat</td><td colspan="2">Determines if the slide show runs through the images once or loops continuously.</td></tr>
<tr><td>On</td><td>Slide show loops continuously through the images.</td></tr>
<tr><td>Off</td><td>Plays the images once and stops.</td></tr>
<tr><td rowspan="6">Interval</td><td colspan="2">Controls the time each still picture is displayed.</td></tr>
<tr><td>1 Sec</td><td>Displays each picture for 1 second.</td></tr>
<tr><td>3 Sec</td><td>Displays each picture for 3 seconds.</td></tr>
<tr><td>5 Sec</td><td>Displays each picture for 5 seconds.</td></tr>
<tr><td>10 Sec</td><td>Displays each picture for 10 seconds.</td></tr>
<tr><td>30 Sec</td><td>Displays each picture for 30 seconds.</td></tr>
<tr><td rowspan="3">Image Type</td><td colspan="2">Controls the type of still pictures to be played back in the Slide Show. [Display 3D Only] is enabled only if there are 3-D images saved on the memory card.</td></tr>
<tr><td>All</td><td>Displays all types of still pictures.</td></tr>
<tr><td>Display 3D Only</td><td>3-D still pictures only. Option enabled when camera is connected to a 3-D compatible TV.</td></tr>
<tr><td rowspan="4">View Mode</td><td colspan="3">Enables you to select a specific type of image folder that will be displayed when executing the Image Index, Protect, Delete, Playback, and Specify Printing commands.</td></tr>
<tr><td>Folder View(Still)</td><td colspan="2">Selects the Still Picture folder.</td></tr>
<tr><td>Folder View(MP4)</td><td colspan="2">Selects the MP4 folder.</td></tr>
<tr><td>AVCHD View</td><td colspan="2">Selects the AVCHD Movie folder.</td></tr>
</table>

A

<table>
<tr><th colspan="3">Playback - (con't)</th></tr>
<tr><th>Command</th><th colspan="2">Description</th></tr>
<tr><td rowspan="3">Image Index</td><td colspan="2">Allows you to view multiple images at one time. Image Index screen contains up to 6 or 12 images at one time. Rotate or press the right or left rim of the control wheel to scroll through the images. A vertical bar on the right side shows how far the currently viewed images are within the total number of saved images. Select a specific image and press soft key C to display image on the screen by itself.</td></tr>
<tr><td>6 Images</td><td>Displays up to 6 images at a time.</td></tr>
<tr><td>12 Images</td><td>Displays up to 12 images at a time.</td></tr>
<tr><td>Rotate</td><td colspan="2">Allows you to rotate an image while reviewing it. Scroll through the saved still images. To rotate one, press soft key C. The image will be rotated 90 degrees with each press of the button.<br>The Rotate command is only enabled with non-3D Panorama still pictures that are saved on the memory card.</td></tr>
<tr><td rowspan="5">Protect</td><td colspan="2">Allows you to protect or unprotect saved images on the memory card. Protected images cannot be erased through the camera's Delete command or button but can be removed with the Format command. This command displays only images within the selected View Mode.<br>The Protect command will be disabled when the current folder is empty.</td></tr>
<tr><td>Multiple Img.</td><td>When the Protect command is enabled, this option displays regardless of the current view mode.<br>Displays one image at a time with its associated protect check box. Use the control wheel or either of the two control dials to scroll through the individual images. Press soft key C to check or uncheck the protect box. When all files have been identified for protection, press soft key B (OK) and then soft key C (OK) to confirm, or press soft key A (Exit) to exit.</td></tr>
<tr><td>Cancel All Images</td><td>Displays a confirmation screen to unprotect all protected Still Pictures images. Press soft key B (OK) to unprotect; press soft key A (Exit) to end the process.<br>Option displays only in the Still Picture view when there are still picture files on the memory card.</td></tr>
<tr><td>Cancel All Movies(MP4)</td><td>Displays a confirmation screen to unprotect all MP4 protected images. Press soft key B (OK) button to unprotect; press soft key A (Exit) to end the process.<br>Option displays only when in the MP4 movie view when there are MP4 files on the memory card.</td></tr>
<tr><td>Cancel All AVCHD view files</td><td>Displays a confirmation screen to unprotect all AVCHD movie files that are protected. Press soft key B (OK) to unprotect; press soft key A (Exit) to end the process.<br>Option displays only in the AVCHD movie view when there are AVCHD files on the memory card.</td></tr>
</table>

<table>
<tr><th colspan="4">Playback – (con't)</th></tr>
<tr><th>Command</th><th colspan="3">Description</th></tr>
<tr><td rowspan="3">3D Viewing</td><td colspan="3">Allows you to play back 3-D pictures recorded in 3D Sweep Panorama mode on a 3-D compatible TV or computer. Command is enabled only when the camera is connected to a 3-D compatible device.</td></tr>
<tr><td>Enter</td><td colspan="2">Initiates playback.</td></tr>
<tr><td>Cancel</td><td colspan="2">Exits the command process.</td></tr>
<tr><td rowspan="2">Enlarge Image</td><td colspan="3">Allows you to enlarge a saved still picture.<br>Command is enabled only when in Still Picture View Mode.</td></tr>
<tr><td colspan="3">Automatically puts the camera in playback mode and enlarges the last viewed or saved still picture image. Rotate the control wheel clockwise to enlarge the image further, rotate it counterclockwise to decrease the image size.</td></tr>
<tr><td rowspan="2">Volume Settings</td><td colspan="3">Allows you to set the volume level for playing back movies. This does not affect the volume at which movies are recorded.</td></tr>
<tr><td colspan="3">Available options range from [0] (mute) to [7] (loudest), with [2] as default.</td></tr>
<tr><td rowspan="6">Specify Printing</td><td colspan="3">Allows you to identify and check an image's print indicator. You can also specify whether you want the date of capture imprinted on the picture.<br>To print identified images, connect the memory card directly or through a computer to a Digital Print Order Format (DPOF) printer or send it to a photo printing service. Note: The print indicator/date imprint information is retained even after the pictures have been printed.<br>Command is enabled only in Still Picture View Mode.</td></tr>
<tr><td>OK</td><td colspan="2">Initiates the DPOF Setup value.</td></tr>
<tr><td>Exit</td><td colspan="2">Exits (soft key A) the Specify Printing command.</td></tr>
<tr><td rowspan="3">DPOF Setup</td><td colspan="2">Controls the selection and deletion of images for printing.</td></tr>
<tr><td>Multiple Img.</td><td>Displays one image at a time with its associated print check box. Scroll through individual images and press soft key C to check or uncheck each print box. When all files have been identified for printing, press soft key B (OK) and then soft key C (OK) to confirm.</td></tr>
<tr><td>Cancel All</td><td>Deletes all DPOF print indicators.</td></tr>
</table>

| Playback – (con't) | | | |
|---|---|---|---|
| **Command** | **Description** | | |
| | Date Imprint | Controls if recorded date will be included on printed images. | |
| | | **On** | Recorded date will be included on the print of the selected images. |
| | | Off | Recorded date will not be included on the print of the selected images. |
| Display Contents | Allows you to select one of the three playback data display formats to be used when you enter Playback mode or one of the Playback menu commands, such as Delete. After you enter Playback mode, you can still use the DISP button to cycle through the three formats and select another one as the format to view a saved image the next time you enter Playback mode or the Playback menu structure. | | |
| | Display Info. | Displays the image with the recorded settings superimposed on the top and bottom of the image. | |
| | Histogram | Displays the image in the upper left quadrant of the screen, setting data in the lower left quadrant, and intensity range of the luminosity and color channels (red, blue, and green) of the recorded picture on the right side of the screen. | |
| | No Disp. Info. | Displays only the image. | |

| Setup | | |
|---|---|---|
| **Command** | **Description** | |
| AEL | Controls how the camera's recommended exposure will be retained when the AEL button is pressed.<br>Function is enabled only when AF/MF/AEL lever is switched to AEL, enabling the button to utilize the AEL command's setting. | |
| | **Hold** | The camera will retain the set exposure for as long as the AEL button is depressed. Every recorded picture will use the set exposure as long as you continue to hold down the AEL button. |
| | Toggle | The camera will retain the exposure even when the AEL button is released. Each time the button is pressed, the camera will reevaluate the exposure, change it if necessary and retain the new exposure until the AEL button has been pressed again. In other words, the button acts as a toggle between saved exposure settings. |

**Setup – (con't)**

| Command | Description | |
|---|---|---|
| AF/MF control | Controls whether the camera will autofocus or require manual focus when the AF/MF button is pressed.<br>Function is enabled only when AF/MF/AEL lever is switched to AF/MF, enabling the button to utilize the AF/MF command's setting. | |
| | **Hold** | The camera will set the focusing mode for as long as the AF/MF button is pressed. Every recorded picture will use the focusing mode as long as you continue to hold down the AF/MF button. |
| | Toggle | The camera will retain the focusing mode even when the AF/MF button is released. But each time the button is pressed, the camera will switch between autofocus and manual focus and retain the focusing mode until either the command is changed or the AF/MF button has been pressed again. In other words, the button acts as a toggle between the two focusing modes. |
| Dial/Wheel Lock | Controls whether the control wheel and control dials are locked in preview mode. Locking occurs when the Navigation button is held down for several seconds. A "Locked" message is displayed on the screen and a small orange circle blinks when a locked control is rotated. Press the Navigation button for several seconds to unlock the controls. An "Unlocked" message is displayed on the screen. | |
| | **All** | Prevents anything from happening when either the control dials or the control wheel are rotated. |
| | Control Wheel | Prevents anything from happening when the control wheel is rotated. |
| | Off | Control wheel and control dials both have full functionality. |
| AF Illuminator | Controls the emission of a beam of red light from the AF Illuminator to aid autofocusing of dimly lit subjects. The light emanates either from the camera body or from an attached external flash unit.<br>The AF Illuminator does not work under the following conditions: when the Autofocus Mode is set to [Continuous AF]; when recording movies; in either of the Panorama modes; when the SCN [Landscape], [Night Scene], or [Sports Action] modes are selected; or when using an A-mount lens. In all of these cases, having the camera emit a beam of light would either disturb the recording process or, in the case of an A-mount lens, would not be recognized.<br>When the AF illuminator is used, the AF area is indicated with a dotted green line. | |
| | **Auto** | AF Illuminator turns on when in low-light environments. |
| | Off | AF Illuminator never turns on. |

A

| Setup – (con't) | | |
|---|---|---|
| **Command** | **Description** | |
| Red Eye Reduction | The camera's flash sends out several small flashes prior to the main flash to prevent or reduce red glowing eyes. | |
| | On | Red Eye Reduction process is in effect. |
| | **Off** | Red Eye Reduction process is not in effect. |
| FINDER/ LCD Setting | Both the viewfinder and the LCD display screen cannot be active at the same time. This command sets how the camera will switch between the two. | |
| | **Auto** | Allows the camera to automatically switch between displaying through the LCD monitor and the viewfinder. |
| | Viewfinder | When the camera senses something close to the viewfinder, it displays images only through the viewfinder. |
| | LCD Monitor | When the camera does not sense something close to the viewfinder, it displays images only on the LCD monitor. |
| Live View Display | Allows you to choose whether or not to show the effects of exposure compensation, etc., on the Live View screen display. | |
| | **Setting Effect ON** | Gives a real-time view of how your image will look. Live View displays the subject with the current lighting, exposure, WB, and other selected effects, such as Creative Style and Picture Effect. |
| | Setting Effect OFF | Live View does not take into account any changes to the camera's settings that affect the resulting image. This option keeps the Live View image at a constant brightness. Note: Picture Effects and Creative Styles are not displayed, but they are recorded.<br>This option is available in P, A, S, and M modes only. If you have this command set to [Setting Effect OFF] and then switch to a shooting mode other than P, A, S, or M modes, the command's value will be changed to [Setting Effect ON] for as long as you are in that mode. It will switch back to [Setting Effect OFF] when you return to P, A, S, or M mode. |
| Auto Review | Displays the recorded picture immediately after it is taken and before you take the next picture. Movies are not displayed after being recorded. | |
| | 10 Sec | Displays captured image for 10 seconds. |
| | 5 Sec | Displays captured image for 5 seconds. |
| | 2 Sec | Displays captured image for 2 seconds. |
| | **Off** | Does not display captured image. |

| **Setup – (con't)** | | |
|---|---|---|
| **Command** | **Description** | |
| Grid Line | Superimposes a grid pattern on the display screen in Live View as an aid for composition. | |
| | Rule of 3rds Grid | Pattern consists of a 3 x 3 array of rectangles. |
| | Square Grid | Pattern consists of a 6 x 4 array of squares. |
| | Diag. + Square Grid | Pattern consists of a 4 x 4 array of rectangles overlaid with diagonal lines radiating from the center to each corner. |
| | **Off** | No grid pattern is superimposed on the display screen. |
| Peaking Level | In Live View, adds a color fringe to borders that have high contrast and therefore are in focus. Available for previewing still pictures and when framing an image to take a movie. This command is enabled only when the camera's MENU>Camera>AF /MF Select command is set to [MF] or [DMF]. | |
| | High | Adds maximum size fringe to in-focus areas. |
| | Mid | Adds midsize fringe to in-focus areas. |
| | Low | Adds small size fringe to in-focus areas. |
| | **Off** | Turns off the Peaking function. |
| Peaking Color | Determines the color used to identify high-contrast areas. This command is only enabled when the Peaking Level command is not set to [Off]. | |
| | **White** | Color fringe for high-contrast areas displayed white. |
| | Red | Color fringe for high-contrast areas displayed red. |
| | Yellow | Color fringe for high-contrast areas displayed yellow. |

A

## Setup - (con't)

| Command | | Description |
|---|---|---|
| MF Assist | | Allows the Live View image to automatically magnify when focusing manually (MENU>Camera>AF/MF Select command is set to [MF] or [DMF]).<br>This command is disabled when AF/MF Select command does not equal [MF] or [DMF]. |
| | **On** | Magnifies the Live View image when AF/MF Select command is [MF] or [DMF]. When it is magnified, use the control wheel rim or control dials to move through the image.<br>In the case of AF/MF Select = [MF], just turning the focus ring will automatically magnify the preview image. When AF/MF Select = [DMF], the shutter button must first be pressed and held down halfway, then the Live View image will be magnified when the focus ring is rotated. Scrolling through the magnified image is difficult. |
| | Off | Magnification will not automatically occur. |
| MF Assist Time | | Sets the length of time the Live View image will be shown in its magnification form. Clock starts once you stop moving the lens focusing ring. |
| | No Limit | Magnification will be retained until a camera button is pressed. |
| | 5 Sec | Magnification will be retained for 5 seconds. |
| | **2 Sec** | Magnification will be retained for 2 seconds. |
| Color Space | | Allows you to select one of two preset color spaces for reproducible colors. |
| | **sRGB** | Common standard for most electronic display and recording units. |
| | AdobeRGB | Common standard for CMYK four-color professional printing. |
| SteadyShot | | Enables internal camera stabilization. Allows you to obtain sharp still pictures at slower shutter speeds when handholding the camera. The camera will compensate for small movements caused by hand tremors. Do not use if your camera is mounted on a tripod; the camera's SteadyShot software will attempt to compensate, which can make a sharp image blurry. |
| | **On** | Enables SteadyShot. |
| | Off | Disables SteadyShot. |

<table>
<tr><th colspan="3">Setup – (con't)</th></tr>
<tr><th>Command</th><th colspan="2">Description</th></tr>
<tr><td rowspan="3">Release w/o Lens</td><td colspan="2">Allows you to shoot pictures and movies when a Sony or Minolta AF lens is not attached to the camera. Set this command to [Enable] when the camera is attached to a telescope, microscope, or legacy lens with an adapter.</td></tr>
<tr><td>Enable</td><td>Enables the camera to shoot without a Sony A mount lens attached.</td></tr>
<tr><td>Disable</td><td>Prevents camera from shooting without a lens attached.</td></tr>
<tr><td rowspan="3">Eye-Start AF</td><td colspan="2">This command is enabled only when an A-mount lens is attached to the camera body using a LA-EA2 Mount Adaptor (sold separately). Sets whether or not to automatically initiate autofocus when you look through the viewfinder. Setting this command to [On] can use a lot of battery power due to continuous autofocusing. The camera will not autofocus when set to [On] when the camera is in sleep mode.</td></tr>
<tr><td>On</td><td>Initiates autofocusing when the camera senses an object, such as the user's eye, approaching the viewfinder.</td></tr>
<tr><td>Off</td><td>Prevents autofocusing from occurring when the camera senses an object approaching the viewfinder.</td></tr>
<tr><td rowspan="3">Front Curtain Shutter</td><td colspan="2">Determines whether the shutter opens using the electronic first curtain shutter or whether the shutter opens mechanically.<br>Using the electronic first curtain shutter speeds up the shutter release time and eliminates camera vibrations due to the movement of the mechanical shutter during exposure.</td></tr>
<tr><td>On</td><td>Initiates use of the electronic first curtain shutter.</td></tr>
<tr><td>Off</td><td>Initiates use of the mechanical shutter.</td></tr>
<tr><td rowspan="3">Long Exposure NR</td><td colspan="2">Controls noise reduction for pictures taken with exposures of one second or more. The camera uses dark frame subtraction to reduce noise. The time needed to accomplish this is more than twice the exposure time. Camera should be mounted on a tripod.<br>This command is enabled only in P, A, S, and M modes when Drive Mode is not set to multiple-shot option. Long Exposure NR command automatically set to [Off] when Drive Mode is set to a multiple-shot option.<br>The command is automatically set to [On] in Intelligent Auto and SCN predefined scene modes, excluding [Sports Action] and [Hand-held Twilight].</td></tr>
<tr><td>On</td><td>Enables the noise reduction process.</td></tr>
<tr><td>Off</td><td>Disables the process.</td></tr>
</table>

A

| Setup – (con't) | | |
|---|---|---|
| **Command** | **Description** | |
| High ISO NR | Assigns noise reduction processing for high-sensitivity JPEG still images shot at high ISO. Although noise can occur at lower ISOs, we have noticed that noise starts showing up consistently at ISO 1600.<br>Noise reduction processing occurs after taking the image. Processing must be complete before the camera is available to take another picture. The [High] and [Normal] options reduce image sharpness. This command is not available for RAW images or in Intelligent Auto, Sweep Panorama, 3D Sweep Panorama, and SCN modes. | |
| | High | Reduces the greatest amount of noise and takes the longest time to complete the process. |
| | **Normal** | Reduces an average amount of noise. |
| | Low | Reduces the least amount of noise and takes the shortest time to complete the process. |
| Lens Comp.: Shading | Enables automatic adjustment to eliminate vignetting. The results are applied only to JPEG files. | |
| | **Auto** | Automatically adjusts JPEG images to hide lens-induced vignetting. |
| | Off | Disables function. Any vignetting from the lens is retained in saved JPEG images. |
| Lens Comp.: Chro. Aber. | Enables automatic adjustment to eliminate chromatic aberration. The results are applied only to JPEG files. | |
| | **Auto** | Automatically adjusts the JPEG images to hide chromatic aberration. |
| | Off | Disables function. Any chromatic aberration is recorded in saved JPEG images. |
| Lens Comp.: Distortion | Enables automatic correction of lens distortion. The results are applied only to the JPEG files. | |
| | Auto | Automatically corrects any lens distortion in JPEG images. |
| | **Off** | Disables function. Lens distortion is uncorrected in saved JPEG images. |

<table>
<tr><th colspan="4">Setup – (con't)</th></tr>
<tr><th>Command</th><th colspan="3">Description</th></tr>
<tr><td rowspan="3">Movie Audio Rec</td><td colspan="3">Determines whether audio is included when recording a movie.</td></tr>
<tr><td>On</td><td colspan="2">Audio records with the movie.</td></tr>
<tr><td>Off</td><td colspan="2">No audio records with the movie.</td></tr>
<tr><td rowspan="3">Wind Noise Reduct.</td><td colspan="3">Reduces the effects of wind noise on captured audio.</td></tr>
<tr><td>On</td><td colspan="2">Reduces wind noise on captured audio.</td></tr>
<tr><td>Off</td><td colspan="2">Does not reduce wind noise on captured audio.</td></tr>
<tr><td rowspan="7">AF Micro Adj.</td><td colspan="3">Allows you to finely adjust the autofocused position when using an A-mount lens with the Sony LA-EA2 Mount Adaptor (sold separately).<br>Allows you to obtain optimum focus if the lens is either back or front focusing. The camera registers up to 30 lenses and allows you to save a fine adjustment setting for each registered lens, which will be automatically applied when the camera senses the lens has been mounted to the camera body and AF Adjustment Setting is set to [On].</td></tr>
<tr><td rowspan="3">AF Adjustment Setting</td><td colspan="2">Controls the adjustment process activation.</td></tr>
<tr><td>On</td><td>Enables the adjustment process.</td></tr>
<tr><td>Off</td><td>Disables the adjustment process.</td></tr>
<tr><td>Amount</td><td colspan="2">This option is enabled only when an A-mount lens is attached to the camera using Sony's LA-EA2 Mount Adaptor. Displays a scale ranging from –20 to +20 in increments of 1, with 0 as default. This option is enabled only when AF Adjustment Setting is [On].</td></tr>
<tr><td rowspan="2">Clear</td><td>OK</td><td>Clears all of the saved adjustment with the lens name.<br>There is a second confirmation step to complete the clearing process: [Enter], [Cancel], with [Cancel] as default where [Enter] completes the clearing process and [Cancel] exits the process without clearing anything.</td></tr>
<tr><td>Exit</td><td>Exits the process without clearing anything.</td></tr>
<tr><th colspan="4">(Main Settings)</th></tr>
<tr><td rowspan="3">Menu start</td><td colspan="3">Displays the menu starting at either the first command or from the last command displayed.</td></tr>
<tr><td>Top</td><td colspan="2">Displays the menu beginning at MENU>Shoot Mode. When you select one of the six Menu icons, the menu structure will display on the first command.</td></tr>
<tr><td>Previous</td><td colspan="2">Displays the menu beginning at the last displayed Menu icon. When you press soft key C, the menu structure will display on the last displayed command.</td></tr>
</table>

<table>
<tr><th colspan="4">Setup – (con't)</th></tr>
<tr><th>Command</th><th colspan="3">Description</th></tr>
<tr><td rowspan="8">Function Settings</td><td colspan="3">Sets the functions (commands), which will be displayed when cycling through the Navigation button. Each function will utilize Sony's Triple-dial-control process to review and set a command's settings.</td></tr>
<tr><td>Function Settings 1</td><td colspan="2" rowspan="4">Options are always enabled. Each Function Settings can be assigned one of the following values:<br>Focus Settings (Function Settings 1 default)<br>White Balance Settings (Function Settings 2 default)<br>D-Range Settings (Function Settings 3 default)<br>Creative Style Settings (Function Settings 4 default)<br>Picture Effect Settings<br>Custom Settings<br>Not set<br>If one of the options is set to [Custom Settings], the Custom Settings 1 through 3 commands become enabled.</td></tr>
<tr><td>Function Settings 2</td></tr>
<tr><td>Function Settings 3</td></tr>
<tr><td>Function Settings 4</td></tr>
<tr><td>Custom Settings 1</td><td colspan="2" rowspan="3">Enabled only when one of the Function Settings 1 through 4 is set to the [Custom Settings] option. Each Custom Settings can be assigned one of the following values:<br>Exposure Comp.<br>Autofocus Mode<br>ISO<br>Metering Mode<br>White Balance (Custom Settings 1 default)<br>DRO/Auto HDR (Custom Settings 2 default)<br>Creative Style (Custom Settings 3 default)<br>Picture Effect<br>Quality<br>Not set</td></tr>
<tr><td>Custom Settings 2</td></tr>
<tr><td>Custom Settings 3</td></tr>
<tr><td rowspan="2"></td><td rowspan="2">Function Settings Start</td><td>Top</td><td>Causes the Function Settings 1 option to be displayed first when the Navigation button is first pressed, and then continue to cycle through the Function Settings as the Navigation button continues to be pressed.</td></tr>
<tr><td>Previous</td><td>Start the cycling of the Function Settings at the previously displayed setting when Navigation button is pressed.</td></tr>
</table>

**Setup – (con't)**

<table>
<tr><th>Command</th><th colspan="2">Description</th></tr>
<tr><td rowspan="4">Custom Key Settings</td><td colspan="2">Allows the user to further customize the camera and have direct access to several camera functions without going through the camera menu structure. Assigns functions to the following buttons: AF/MF, right key, soft key B, and soft key C. Customization can be further expanded if soft key C is assigned the [Custom] option. This will open up an additional five custom slots (Custom 1–5). Note: You do not have to assign all five Custom fields.<br><br>Custom Key Settings command is available in P, A, S, and M modes, when [MF Assist] is available and when [AF/MF Select] is set to [Manual Focus].<br><br>Custom setting for soft key B is invalid when Object Tracking is [On].</td></tr>
<tr><td>AF/MF button</td><td>Available options:<br>AF/MF control<br>MF Assist<br>Focus Settings</td></tr>
<tr><td>Right Key Setting</td><td rowspan="2">Available options:<br>Shoot Mode<br>AF/MF Series<br>Autofocus Mode<br>Autofocus Area<br>Prec. Dig Zoom<br>Face Detection<br>Smile Shutter<br>Soft Skin Effect<br>Quality<br>ISO<br>White Balance<br>Metering Mode<br>DRO/Auto HDR<br>Picture Effect<br>Creative Style<br>Flash Mode<br>Flash Comp<br>MF Assist<br>Focus Settings (Soft key B Setting default)<br>Not set (Right Key Setting default)<br>When Object Tracking command is set to [On], the custom setting of soft key B is invalid.</td></tr>
<tr><td>Soft key B Setting</td></tr>
</table>

| Setup – (con't) | | |
|---|---|---|
| **Command** | **Description** | |
| | Soft key C Setting | Available options:<br>**Shoot Mode**<br>Custom<br>When Soft key C Setting = [Custom], Custom 1–5 commands become enabled.<br>Note that the control wheel is superimposed with CUSTOM on the navigation vertical bar on the right side of the Live View display screen.<br>To activate the custom settings for the control wheel, press it while in Live View and use control dial R or press the control wheel on the left or right side to navigate through the custom settings. Use the control wheel or control dial L to navigate through the function's options. |
| | Custom 1<br>Custom 2<br>Custom 3<br>Custom 4<br>Custom 5 | Available Options:<br>AF/MF Series<br>Autofocus Mode<br>Autofocus Area<br>Face Detection<br>Smile Shutter<br>Soft Skin Effect<br>Quality<br>**ISO (Custom 1 default)**<br>**White Balance (Custom 2 default)**<br>Metering Mode<br>**DRO/Auto HDR (Custom 3 default)**<br>Picture Effect<br>Creative Style<br>Flash Mode<br>**Not set (Custom 4 and Custom 5 default)** |

| Setup – (con't) | | |
|---|---|---|
| **Command** | **Description** | |
| Beep | Creates audio beeps when rotating the control wheel and the control dials, when focus is achieved, or during self-timer operations. | |
| | **On** | Allows audio beeps. |
| | Off | Does not allow audio beeps. |
| Language | Displays a list of available languages based on the camera's country of origin. The language is used in the menu commands, values, help information, and error and warning messages. | |
| Date/Time Setup | Sets the camera's date, time, and location. Use the control wheel to move through the following fields and their available values. | |
| | Daylight Svg | Daylight saving indicator. [ON] indicates Daylight Saving is currently in effect. [OFF] indicates Daylight Saving is not currently in effect. |
| | Date | Contains the current date. Order of month, day, and year is determined by the selected Date Format option. |
| | Time | Contains current time in hours and minutes. |
| | Date Format | Select the format the date should be displayed in: [Y-M-D], [D-M-Y], or [M-D-Y]. |
| Area Setting | Lets the camera know what time zone you're in based on the selected location on the world map. | |
| | World map is broken into time zones | The current selected time zone is highlighted on the map. Use the control wheel or control dial L to move through the map. Press soft key C to select a location. Control dial R toggles the daylight saving indicator. Because its location on the map changes, so does the date and time in the lower left corner. It conforms to the highlighted location. |

A

| Setup – (con't) | | |
|---|---|---|
| **Command** | **Description** | |
| Help Guide Display | Controls the display of an additional screen with help information when any Menu option is selected. | |
| | **On** | Displays the help information screen when a Menu option is selected. Press the right or left rim of the control wheel to close the informational screen. |
| | Off | Does not display the help information screen; camera goes directly to the selected Menu option. |
| Power Save | Determines the amount of time before an inactive camera is placed into sleep mode. | |
| | 30 Min | Camera enters sleep mode after 30 minutes of inactivity. |
| | 5 Min | Camera enters sleep mode after 5 minutes of inactivity. |
| | **1 Min** | Camera enters sleep mode after 1 minute of inactivity. |
| | 20 Sec | Camera enters sleep mode after 20 seconds of inactivity. |
| | 10 Sec | Camera enters sleep mode after 10 seconds of inactivity. |
| LCD Brightness | Controls the LCD screen's brightness either automatically or manually. The LCD screen must be active when setting this command. | |
| | **Auto** | Camera adjusts the LCD monitor's brightness on the basis of ambient lighting. Make sure you do not cover the light sensor in the lower left of the LCD screen. |
| | Manual | Allows you to set the LCD monitor's brightness between –2 and +2 at ± 1 increments, where –2 is less bright and +2 is the brightest setting. |
| | Sunny Weather | Camera maximizes the LCD monitor's brightness. |

**Setup – (con't)**

| Command | Description | |
|---|---|---|
| Viewfinder Bright. | Controls the viewfinder's brightness automatically or allows you to set it manually. The viewfinder must be active when setting this command. | |
| | **Auto** | Relies on the camera to determine the viewfinder's brightness. |
| | Manual | Allows you to set the viewfinder's brightness between –1 and +1, at ± 1 increments, where –1 is the dimmest and +1 is the brightest setting. |
| Display Color | Assigns the menu screen's color scheme. | |
| | Black | Menu background is black with commands displayed in white lettering, and command options are displayed in orange lettering. |
| | **White** | Menu background is white with commands displayed in black lettering, and command options are displayed in orange lettering. |
| Playback Display | Determines whether vertical recorded images are displayed in landscape or portrait orientation during playback. | |
| | **Auto Rotate** | Vertically-oriented recorded images are played back vertically on the display screen. The vertical images are displayed smaller than landscape formatted images, but you don't have to turn the camera to view them properly. |
| | Manual Rotate | Displays vertically-oriented images in landscape format, filling the screen during playback. When you play back the image on a TV or a computer, the portrait-oriented image will display vertically regardless of this command's setting. |
| HDMI Resolution | Controls how the camera determines whether to use progressive or interlaced video scan for HDMI resolution when connected to a compatible TV. | |
| | **Auto** | Leaves it up to the camera to choose between 1080p and 1080i resolution. |
| | 1080p | Selects 1080p resolution. |
| | 1080i | Selects 1080i resolution. |

A

**Setup – (con't)**

| Command | Description | |
|---|---|---|
| CTRL FOR HDMI | Determines if you can use a remote control when playing back your stored images from your camera on a Bravia Sync-supported TV.<br>When the camera is connected to a compatible TV and the command is set to [On], use the TV's remote to control the playback. You can play slide shows, display images one at a time, view 3-D images, switch View Modes, and delete images through your TV. | |
| | **On** | Plays camera-stored images on a compatible TV using a remote control unit. |
| | Off | Does not play camera-stored images on a compatible TV using a remote control. |
| USB Connection | Determines the type of connection your camera establishes with your computer or with a USB device when using a USB cable. | |
| | **Auto** | Leaves it up to the camera to choose between Mass Storage and MTP. |
| | Mass Storage | Selects USB Mass Storage Class, which is useful for drag-and-drop file transfers. Supported by Apple operating systems and utilized by Windows. |
| | MTP | Selects Media Transfer Protocol used by Windows and PICT Bridge-compatible printers. |
| Cleaning Mode | Executes the sensor cleaning process by applying ultrasonic vibration to the sensor to loosen dirt and dust particles.<br>This command will turn off the camera at the end of cleaning. Since the sensor cleaning process is executed whenever you turn off the camera, this command appears to be superfluous. | |
| | OK | Initiates cleaning process. |
| | **Exit** | Exits the process and returns you to Live View. |
| Version | Displays the camera body name and current version of firmware. | |

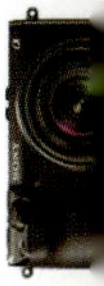

| **Setup – (con't)** | | |
|---|---|---|
| **Command** | **Description** | |
| Demo Mode | Enables the camera to play a recorded movie from the memory card after a period of inactivity, such as in a retail store.<br>Per Sony Tech Support, the Demo Mode command becomes enabled when the camera is powered by an AC-PW20 AC Adaptor. | |
| | On | Enables the demo mode. |
| | **Off** | Disables the demo mode. |
| Reset Default | Allows you to reset the camera's command values back to the manufacturer's defaults  Excludes registered faces, camera date and time data, Area Setting, AF Micro Adj., Protect and Specify Printing information. | |
| **(Memory Card Tool)** | | |
| Format | Quickly erases all images from the card, including protected still pictures and movies, by reformatting the memory card. Does not erase stored registered faces. A confirmation screen is displayed.<br>Do not turn off the camera or remove the memory card while reformatting. Do not reformat the memory card outside the camera. | |
| | OK | Reformats the memory card. |
| | Exit | Exits the process. |
| File Number | Determines how file numbers are assigned to images and maintained. | |
| | **Series** | Assigns file numbers in sequence from 0001 to 9999. Does not reset file numbers even if the folder is changed, images are deleted, the memory card is reformatted, or a new memory card is inserted. |
| | Reset | Assigns file numbers in sequence from 0001 to 9999, but starts over at 0001 if the folder is changed, all the files within a folder are deleted, the memory card is reformatted, or a new memory card is inserted. Does not reuse file numbers when individual files within a folder are deleted until all of the individual files are deleted, at which time the numbering starts over at 0001. |

| Setup – (con't) | | |
|---|---|---|
| **Command** | **Description** | |
| Folder Name | Allows you to choose between two folder name structures for storing your still picture images. | |
| | **Standard Form** | Folder number + MSDCF (example: 100MSDCF). MSDCF is a file naming convention created by JEITIA (Japan Electronics and Information Technology Industries Association). |
| | Date Form | Folder number + last digit of the year + two-digit month + two-digit day (Example: 10020210 where folder number = 100, last digit of the year = 2, month = 02 and day = 10). |
| Select Shoot. Folder | Enabled only when at least one still picture image folder exists on the memory card and the Folder Name command is set to [Standard Form].<br>Allows you to choose from a displayed list containing both Standard Form and Date Form folders used to hold still images on the memory card. Use the control wheel to scroll through the list and press soft key C to select one.<br>Note: Folders with AVCHD and MP4 files cannot be selected. | |
| New Folder | Allows you to create a new folder on the memory card in the Standard Form naming convention to hold new still pictures. The newly created folder becomes the default for any new still pictures. Press soft key C to create a new folder. | |
| | **OK** | Creates a new still picture folder on the memory card. |
| Recover Image DB | Attempts to recover a corrupted movie image database on the memory card. Execute this command if you receive the error message "Check Image Database File?" Make sure you have a fully charged battery when executing this command. | |
| | **OK** | Initiates recovery. |
| | Exit | Exits the process. |
| Display Card Space | Displays an estimate of how many available images and how much movie time remains on the memory card. The calculations are only for the current Still and Movie Image Size and Quality command values. | |
| | **OK** | Exits and returns you back one level to the Display Card Space command. |

| Setup – (con't) | | | |
|---|---|---|---|
| **Command** | **Description** | | |
| Upload Settings | Sets the upload function of the camera when an Eye-Fi card is used. This command appears in the menu structure only if an Eye-Fi card is inserted into the SD slot on the camera. | | |
| | On | Enables the upload function so you can send images to outside devices and websites, including your cell phone, computer, or photo storing or printing web-sites. The camera will display an upload status icon in the display screen according to the communication status of the camera. | |
| | | 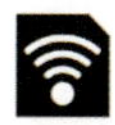 | Standby. No images available to be sent. |
| | |  | Connecting to Wi-Fi. |
| | |  | Upload standby. Waiting for images to be sent. |
| | | 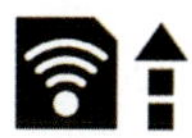 | Uploading images. |
| | | 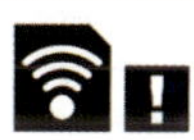 | Error occurred. |
| | Off |  | Disables the upload function. Set the command to this value when not in use or while traveling, for example on an air-plane, to prevent the camera from con-stantly trying to find Wi-Fi hot spots. |

# Appendix B: Common Error or Warning Messages and Resolutions

The Sony NEX-7 displays error or warning messages and icons as you utilize the camera's functions. The following tables contain common messages and icons whose meaning may not be obvious. Note that many error or warning messages are displayed when you try to select a command or function that is not available in the current mode. Such messages are very explicit and are not included in this appendix.

| Message | Description | ... |
|---|---|---|
| **Camera Error** | This is a nonspecific error message. | |
| **Camera overheating. Allow it to cool.** | The camera generates heat when in use. Excessive heat can build up when recording long movies or when rapidly recording still pictures, such as in Drive Mode = Cont. Shooting or Spd Priority Cont. mode. In addition, the camera temperature can increase when it is used in high-temperature environments. | |
| **Cannot create more folders** | You cannot create a new folder because the maximum number of folders has already been reached. This occurs when you try to create a new folder on the inserted memory card and the camera finds that a folder name beginning with 999 already exists, indicating it has reached the maximum number of folders on the card. | |
| **Cannot recognize lens. Attach it properly.** | The camera does not recognize that an E-mount lens is attached. | |
| **Could not shoot 3D panorama. Move the camera slowly.** | The camera was panned too fast or in the wrong direction. | |
| **Could not shoot 3D panorama. Move the camera straight in the direction of the arrow.** | The camera was panned too slowly or not all the way, or the camera was not level either horizontally or vertically. | |

| ... | Resolution |
|---|---|
| | Turn the camera off. Remove the battery pack and reinsert it. Turn the camera back on. If the message persists or over time appears more frequently, contact a Sony dealer or authorized Sony service facility. |
| | Stop recording and turn the camera off to allow it to cool. |
| | Download the memory card's files to a computer and reformat the card in the camera. |
| | If a lens is currently attached, check to see if it is attached properly. If not, remove it and ensure that the contacts on both the lens and the camera body are clean. Reattach the lens. If the error message persists, validate that the lens is appropriate for the camera.<br>If the lens is attached properly and it is not an E-mount Sony lens, set MENU>Setup (Shooting Menu)>Release w/o Lens>[Enable]. This command must be used when working with legacy lens, telescopes, or microscopes.<br>Reboot the camera by turning it off and back on to see if the camera can then recognize the lens. |
| | Resolutions:<br>1. Reshoot the picture and pan a bit slower.<br>2. Reshoot the picture and pan the camera in the direction of the arrow on the display screen. |
| | Resolutions:<br>1. Reshoot the picture and pan a bit faster.<br>2. Reshoot the picture and make sure you pan completely to the end.<br>3. Reshoot the picture and hold the camera both horizontally and vertically level. Use a tripod if you are having problems. |

B

| Message | Description |
|---|---|
| **Custom WB Error** | When setting a custom WB value, the calculated value is beyond an acceptable range. The camera will still store the WB value in the custom repository, and it is usable; however, when you select it, the Custom WB icon will display yellow in the preview screen. |
| **Image Database File error** | An error has been encountered in the Image Database File, usually due to an inconsistency created between what the camera needs to read on the memory card and what was saved when the memory card was used outside of the camera, such as when files were downloaded to a computer. |
| **Image Database File error. Recover?** | The memory card's Image Database File is damaged. This message appears when you try to record or play back an AVCHD movie and the Image Database File has been corrupted. Processing saved images on the computer and then saving them onto the memory card can damage the Image Database File. In addition, playing AVCHD movies on a computer directly from the camera can cause damage to the file. |
| **Image protected** | You tried to delete an image that is protected. |
| **Incompatible battery. Use correct model** | The inserted battery pack is not authorized by Sony for the NEX-7 camera. |
| **Memory Card Error** | The inserted memory card is incompatible with the camera. |
| **Memory card locked** | The memory card's write-protect switch is set to LOCK. |
| **No images** | The memory card does not contain any stored images for the currently selected file type. |
| **No images changed** | You have executed a multiple image DPOF printing function but did not select any images for printing. |
| **No images selected** | You have executed a multiple image delete function but did not select any images for deletion. |
| **Power insufficient** | The cleaning mode, MENU>Setup (Main Settings)>[Cleaning Mode], was executed when the battery level was too low. |

| ... | Resolution |
|---|---|
| | Choose a different light source that emits white light and reset the Custom WB. Light that is heavily colored by passing through a filter will generate this error message. |
| | Execute the database recovery command: MENU>Setup (Memory Card Tool)>Recover Image DB command. Ensure that the camera's battery is sufficiently charged prior to executing the command.<br>If the error message persists, use a different memory card. |
| | The camera will prompt you with instructions to recover the data. Ensure that the camera's battery is sufficiently charged. Executing these instructions with an insufficiently charged battery can cause further damage to the files. |
| | Unprotect the image by executing MENU>Playback>Protect, then select the image and unprotect it.<br>If you want to delete all of the memory card's images, execute the MENU>Setup (Memory Card Tool)>Format command to reformat the card. All files, including protected files, will be deleted. |
| | Replace the battery pack with a rechargeable InfoLithium (NP-FW50) battery. |
| | Use a compatible memory card. Make sure it was formatted using the Sony NEX-7. |
| | Set the write-protect switch to UNLOCK. |
| | Resolutions:<br>1. If you use multiple memory cards, make sure you have the correct one with the files you expected to view inserted into the camera.<br>2. Change the current file type by either changing the View Mode command value or recording a movie or snapping a still picture.<br>3. The memory card might be completely empty, so the message will not be resolved until you have recorded images on the card. |
| | If your intent was to specify images for DPOF printing, execute the command again and select at least one still picture image to be printed. If your intent was to exit the Specify Printing process without selecting any images, exit out of the error message and the process. |
| | If your intent was to delete images, execute the command again and select at least one image to be deleted. If your intent was to exit the delete process without deleting any images, exit out of error message and the process. |
| | Charge the battery fully or connect the camera to a wall outlet with the AC adapter, then execute the cleaning mode command. |

B

| Message | Description |
|---|---|
| **Processing . . .** | Indicates the camera is completing an executed command. This message appears when the camera is executing a long exposure or High ISO noise reduction process. |
| **Recording is unavailable in this movie format** | The camera cannot record an AVCHD movie. |
| **Reinsert memory card** | The camera cannot recognize the memory card due to incorrect insertion, damage, or dirty terminal connectors. |
| **Set Area/Date/Time** | The camera's area, date, and time are not set. There are two explanations:<br>1. The camera's area, date, and time information have never been set.<br>2. The camera's internal battery is drained and can no longer maintain the information. |
| **This memory card may not be capable of recording and playing normally** | The memory card is incompatible with the NEX-7 camera. |
| **Unable to display** | Only Sony NEX-7 recorded and maintained images can be displayed on the camera. This message indicates that the inserted memory card has images recorded and/or modified from another medium or camera. |
| **Unable to magnify** | This message indicates that the currently displayed image was recorded by another camera and therefore cannot be magnified. |
| **Unable to rotate image** | This message indicates that the currently displayed image was either recorded using the 3D Sweep Panorama mode or was recorded by another camera and therefore cannot be rotated. |
| **Unable to print** | The selected image's RAW format is not compatible with a DPOF mark. |
| **Unable to use memory card. Format?** | The memory card was not formatted with the Sony NEX-7, or the memory card's file format was modified outside the camera. |

| ... | Resolution |
|---|---|
| | Wait until the process is completed. |
| | Switch the File Format command to [MP4]. |
| | Resolutions:<br>1. Reinsert the memory card. Ensure that the card is solidly inserted.<br>2. Replace the memory card (the memory card is damaged).<br>3. Clean the memory card's terminal connectors then reinsert it. If the message persists, replace the memory card. |
| | Resolutions:<br>1. Set the camera's area, date, and time information using MENU>Setup (Main Settings)>[Date/Time Setup] and MENU>Setup (Main Settings)>[Area Setting].<br>2. Recharge the camera's internal battery by inserting a charged battery pack or by connecting the camera to a wall outlet with the AC adapter for 24 hours. |
| | Replace the memory card with a compatible card for the Sony NEX-7. |
| | Resolutions:<br>1. Delete all of the memory card images by reformatting the memory card. Note: You may want to save the files onto your computer prior to reformatting the card.<br>2. Delete only the memory card images that cannot be displayed. First download the affected files to your computer then delete them on the card. Once done then reuse the memory card in your camera. |
| | Chose another image to display. To magnify the image, download the affected file to your computer and use third-party software. |
| | Chose another image to display. To rotate the image, download the affected file to your computer and use third-party software. |
| | Ensure that only JPEG images are marked within the camera for printing. If you wish to print a RAW file, download the image to third-party software, save it to a printable format, and then print it from outside the camera's memory card. |
| | Reformat the memory card with the Sony NEX-7. Note: If the memory card contains files you wish to save, transfer them to your computer first. If the message persists, use a different memory card. |

| Message | Description |
|---|---|
| 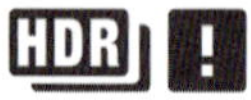 | Auto HDR Warning: There is insufficient contrast within the image, or the HDR function cannot determine how to rebuild the image from the series of three shots. Insufficient contrast can occur in low light, very bright light, or monotone light. The inability to rebuild the image can also be caused by camera movement, making it impossible for the camera's software to align the subject. |
|  | Camera Shake Warning: Occurs when the camera senses movement and the shutter speed is too long to obtain a sharp image. |
| 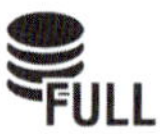  | Database Error: The maximum number of images has been reached in the database. |
| 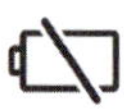 | Drained Battery Warning: The camera's battery is drained. |
|  | Eye-Fi Status Error: An Eye-Fi communications error has occurred. |
| 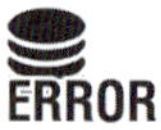  | File Registration Error: Unable to register the still image file in the database. |
| 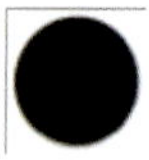 | Focus Error: Cannot obtain focus. Occurs in autofocus mode. |
| 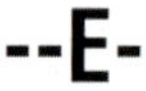  | Memory Card Error: A memory card error has occurred. |
| 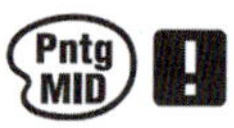  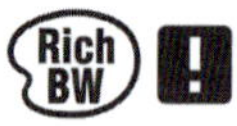  | Picture Effect Error: Selected [HDR Painting] or [Rich-tone Mono.]. Picture Effect does not work with the current scenario.<br>This occurs when there is insufficient contrast within the image or when the selected Picture Effect cannot determine how to rebuild the image from the series of three shots. Insufficient contrast can occur in low light, very bright light, or monotone light. The inability to rebuild the image can also be caused by camera movement, making it impossible for the camera's software to align the subject. |
| 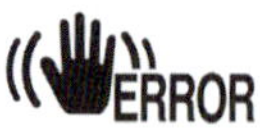  | SteadyShot Error: The SteadyShot function does not work. |
| 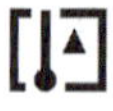 | Temperature Error: The internal camera temperature is too high. |

| Resolution |
|---|
| Adjust the lighting, reframe the image, or reduce camera movement. Reshoot the image. |
| Mount the camera on a tripod, brace the camera to reduce shaking, or turn on the SteadyShot command. |
| Download all of the images to a computer and reformat the memory card. |
| Recharge the battery. |
| Resolutions:<br>1. Remove the memory card and reinsert it.<br>2. Turn the camera's power off and back on.<br>If the error persists, the Eye-Fi card may be damaged. |
| Download all of the images to a computer and reformat the memory card. |
| Resolutions:<br>1. Change one or more of the camera settings to obtain focus.<br>2. Change the metering mode and target a specific part of the image.<br>3. Switch to manual focus. |
| Remove the memory card and insert it again. Make sure the contacts are clean. If the problem persists, reformat the memory card. Note: If the memory card has files you wish to save, try to save them on your computer first. If the memory card error continues after reformatting, use a different memory card. |
| Adjust the lighting, reframe the image, or reduce camera movement. Reshoot the image. |
| Turn the camera off and back on. If the SteadyShot error continues to appear, contact Sony technical support. |
| Stop recording and turn off the camera. Allow the camera to cool down prior to using it again. |

# Index

## O



## P



## R



## S



## T



## V



## W



## Z